# CHRISTIAN
# PERFECTION
## AND
# CONTEMPLATION

# Books by the Author Translated into English

God, His Existence and His Nature: A Thomistic Solution of Certain
Agnostic Antinomies (1914)

Christian Perfection and Contemplation, according to St. Thomas
Aquinas and St. John of the Cross (1923)

The Love of God and the Cross of Jesus (1929)

Providence (1932)

Our Savior and His Love for Us (1933)

Predestination (1936)

★The One God (1938)

The Three Ages of the Interior Life: Prelude of Eternal Life (1938)

The Three Ways of the Spiritual Life (1938)

★The Trinity and God the Creator (1943)

★Christ the Savior (1945)

The Priesthood and Perfection (1946)

Reality: A Synthesis of Thomistic Thought (1946)

Life Everlasting (1947)

★Grace (1947)

The Priest in Union with Christ (1948)

The Mother of the Saviour and Our Interior Life (1948)

★The Theological Virtues—Vol. 1: Faith (1948)

★Beatitude (moral theology, 1951)

Last Writings (spiritual retreats, 1969)

# Books by the Author Not Translated into English

Le sens commun: la philosophie de l'être et les formules dogmatiques (1909)

Saint Thomas et le neomolinisme (booklet, 1917)

De Revelatione per ecclesiam catholicam proposita (1918)

De methodo sancti Thomae speciatim de structura articulorum summae
theologicae (booklet, 1928)

Le réalisme du principe de finalité (1932)

Le sens du mystère et le clair-obscur intellectuel: nature et
surnaturel (1934)

Essenza e attualità del Tomismo

Dieu accessible à tous (booklet, 1941)

★De Eucharistia: Accedunt de Paenitentia quaestiones dogmaticae (1942)

Les XXIV Theses Thomistes pour le 30e Anniversaire de leur
Approbation (booklet, 1944)

Verite et immutabilite du dogme (booklet, 1947)

★De virtutibus theologicis (1948)

---

★*Commentaries on St. Thomas Aquinas'* Summa Theologica.

# CHRISTIAN
# PERFECTION
## AND
# CONTEMPLATION

## ACCORDING TO ST. THOMAS AQUINAS
## AND ST. JOHN OF THE CROSS

## Fr. Reginald Garrigou-Lagrange, O.P.

*Translated by*

Sister M. Timothea Doyle, O.P.
Rosary College, River Forest, Illinois

TAN BOOKS AND PUBLISHERS, INC.
Rockford, Illinois 61105

Nihil Obstat:       F. J. Holweck
                    *Censor Librorum*
                    St. Louis, Missouri
                    November 13, 1937

Imprimatur:        ✝ John J. Glennon
                    Archbishop of St. Louis
                    St. Louis, Missouri
                    November 14, 1937

ISBN 0-89555-758-4

TAN BOOKS AND PUBLISHERS, INC.
P.O. Box 424
Rockford, Illinois 61105
2003

To the Blessed Virgin Mary, Mother of God and mediatrix, who leads the humble to the intimacy of Christ, as He Himself leads them to the Father, I offer this very imperfect homage of profound gratitude and filial obedience

# PREFACE

WE are happy to have an English translation of this book in which our purpose was to establish, according to the principles formulated by St. Thomas Aquinas and St. John of the Cross, that Christian perfection consists especially in charity according to the plenitude of the two great precepts: "Thou shall love the Lord thy God with thy whole heart, and with thy whole soul, and with all thy strength, and with all thy mind: and thy neighbor as thyself" (Luke 10 · 27). We also show that infused contemplation of the mysteries of faith, the mysteries of the Blessed Trinity present in us, of the redeeming incarnation, of the cross, of the Eucharist, sacrament and sacrifice, is in the normal way of sanctity. This contemplation proceeds from faith illumined by the gifts of understanding and wisdom, which are in all the just; that is, from living faith, which has become penetrating and sweet.

This view of perfection is by no means something novel. The number of theologians who of late consider it as traditional has increased notably. This doctrine seems to us the theological commentary of our Savior's words: "If any man thirst, let him come to Me, and drink. . . . Out of his belly shall flow rivers of living water" (John 5 : 37 f.). All are invited to drink from the fountain of living water, as St. Catherine of Siena says in her *Dialogue* (chap. 53); the only condition laid down for reaching the fountain is a true thirst for virtue, the honor of God, and the salvation of souls.

FR. REGINALD GARRIGOU-LAGRANGE, O.P.

# TRANSLATOR'S PREFACE

THE works and reputation of the great Dominican theologian, Father Reginald Garrigou-Lagrange, are already well known to American readers. Two of his outstanding contributions to theological literature have been translated and published within the last two years.

It is the earnest wish of the translator of this volume on mystical theology to make accessible to souls eager for instruction the treasures of light so marvelously organized and synthesized by Father Garrigou-Lagrange, and also to offer them his encouragement to "seek the things that are above."

The translator is deeply indebted to the Very Reverend Peter O'Brien, O.P., and to the Very Reverend Norbert Georges, O.P., prior and subprior respectively of the Dominican House of Studies in River Forest, Illinois, who kindly read the manuscript and gave invaluable assistance. She wishes also to acknowledge the help of the Reverend H. J. Schroeder, O.P., and of the members of the Department of English of Rosary College.

For the courtesy of permission to use quotations from their publications, she is indebted to the Benedictines of Stanbrook, to Thomas Baker of London, and to Houghton Mifflin Company. She acknowledges the permission of Burns, Oates and Washbourne to use quotations from their publications, especially from the *Summa theologica* of St. Thomas Aquinas, and of The Macmillan Company for quotations from *The Imitation of Christ.*

The translator will feel amply repaid if this volume opens up a new perspective and a wider spiritual horizon to even one soul.

SISTER M. TIMOTHEA DOYLE, O.P.

Rosary College
Feast of St. Catherine of Siena, 1937

## ARCHBISHOP'S HOUSE

### 5418 Moeller Avenue

#### norwood, ohio

THE learned author of *Perfection chrétienne et contemplation,* Father Garrigou-Lagrange, needs no introduction. His works in philosophy and theology have given him wide renown. Sister Timothea's translation, *Christian Perfection and Contemplation,* makes available to English readers a valuable treatise on ascetical and mystical theology which is clearly expounded and is solid in doctrine. The author gives reasonable attention to the historical and traditional aspects of the questions treated. He wisely chooses as his guides the great teachers of ascetical and mystical theology, St. Augustine, St. Thomas Aquinas, St. John of the Cross, St. Francis de Sales, and St. Teresa of Avila.

Sister Timothea, while faithfully adhering to the French text, has given us a smooth, idiomatic translation in which little, if any, of the clarity and charm of the original is lost.

Everyone is called to advance in the way of perfection according to his state of life. Ascetical and mystical theology, as Father Garrigou-Lagrange remarks, is the application of moral theology, as expounded by St. Thomas, in directing souls to an ever closer union with God. Too many imagine that ascetical and mystical theology is for the select few. They therefore wrongly think that it is confined to priests, religious, and a few chosen souls in the world.

The appearance of Father Garrigou-Lagrange's work in English should not only aid greatly in dispelling this false idea but should, we trust, lead many souls to a higher state of perfection and to a closer union with God. It should find a place in the library of every priest and seminarian, in the libraries of sisters' convents, and in homes where there is Catholic reading. May *Christian Perfection and Contemplation* awaken in many an appreciation of the higher things of the spiritual life.

JOHN T. McNICHOLAS
Archbishop of Cincinnati

# CONTENTS

# CONTENTS

# CONTENTS xvii

# CONTENTS

# CHRISTIAN
# PERFECTION
### AND
# CONTEMPLATION

# CHAPTER I

## Introduction

THIS work is based on the teaching of St. Thomas Aquinas and of St. John of the Cross. St. Thomas, "Doctor Communis" as he is called in Pius XI's encyclical *Studiorum ducem,* is preeminent among theologians because he attained to the heights of acquired and infused wisdom. To explain the secrets of this twofold wisdom, he received in a very high degree the special grace which St. Paul calls *sermo sapientiae.* By acquired wisdom he marvelously synthesized the knowledge of the philosopher and that of the theologian, and the gift of wisdom raised him to the highest degree of infused contemplation. Often accompanied by ecstasy and the gift of tears, it taught him what human language could not express. It was this infused contemplation which prevented him from dictating the end of the *Summa theologica;* what he could put in words seemed to him only straw in comparison with what he beheld.[1]

The encyclical *Studiorum ducem,* by presenting St. Thomas to us as the undisputed master of dogmatic and moral theology, and also of ascetical and mystical theology, draws particular attention to a beautiful doctrine, which we have developed at length in this book (chaps. 4–6), namely, that the precept of the love of God has no limit and that the perfection of charity falls under this precept, not, of course, as something to be realized immediately, but as the end toward which every Christian must tend according to his condition.[2]

---

1 See his *Life* by Guillaume de Tocco; also the Bollandists, March 7. Cf. the recent work of Father Petitot, O.P.: *Saint Thomas d'Aquin, la vocation, l'œuvre, la vie spirituelle,* 1923.

2 Encyclical *Studiorum ducem,* June 29, 1923: "Haec igitur a Deo delapsa seu infusa sapientia, ceteris comitata donis Sancti Spiritus, perpetuum in

1

St. Francis de Sales taught the same doctrine, which has often been misunderstood, although it was clearly formulated by the fathers of the Church, in particular by St Augustine.[3]

St. Thomas, in his treatise on the infused virtues and the gifts of the Holy Ghost, sets forth particularly their nature and properties. St. John of the Cross explains the various phases of their progress, up to their perfect development. Among spiritual authors, we have taken him as our guide: (1) He is certainly one of the greatest Catholic mystics. (2) He is canonized, and his doctrine, which underwent the test of criticism and was examined by the Church, is perfectly sound. (3) Coming as he did in the sixteenth century, he benefited by all the earlier tradition, especially by the works of St. Teresa, which

---

Thoma accepit incrementum, aeque ac caritas, omnium domina et regina virtutum. Etenim illa huic erat certissima doctrina, amorem Dei numquam non oportere crescere 'ex ipsa forma praecepti: Diliges Dominum tuum ex toto corde tuo; totum enim et perfectum idem sunt. . . . *Finis praecepti caritas est,* ut Apostolus dicit, I Tim. 1: 5; in fine autem non adhibetur aliqua mensura, sed solum in his quae sunt ad finem' (IIa IIae, q. 184, a.3). Quae ipsa est causa quare sub praeceptum perfectio caritatis cadet tanquam illud quo omnes pro sua quisque conditione niti debent. . . . Itaque praeceptum de amore Dei quam late pateat, caritas eique adjuncta dona Sancti Spiritus quomodo crescant, multiplices vitae status, ut perfectionis, ut religiosorum, ut apostolatus, quid inter se differant et quae cujusque natura visque sit, haec et talia asceticae mysticaeque theologiae capita si quis pernosse volet, is Angelicum in primis Doctorem adeat oportebit."

[3] The encyclical written by Pope Pius XI for the third centenary of St. Francis de Sales, January 26, 1923, calls attention to this doctrine in the following terms: "Christ constituted the Church holy and the source of holiness, and all those who take her for guide and teacher must, according to the divine will, aim at holiness of life: 'This is the will of God,' says St. Paul, 'your sanctification.' What type of sanctity is meant? Our Lord Himself explains it in the following manner: 'Be ye perfect as your heavenly Father is perfect.' Let no one think that this invitation is addressed to a small, very select number and that all others are permitted to remain in a lower degree of virtue. As is evident, this law obliges absolutely everybody without exception. Moreover, all who reach the summit of Christian perfection, and their name is legion, of every age and class, according to the testimony of history, all have experienced the same weaknesses of nature and have known the same dangers. St. Augustine puts the matter clearly when he says: 'God does not command the impossible, but in giving the commandment, He admonishes us to accomplish what we can according to our strength, and to ask aid to accomplish whatever exceeds our strength.' " Concerning this doctrine, see St. Francis de Sales, *Treatise on the Love of God,* Bk. III, chap. 1.

he knew thoroughly and explained by connecting the mystical states she experienced and described with the supernatural principles from which they proceeded; especially with the theological virtues and with the gifts of the Holy Ghost, which had attained their full development in her. Thus he goes beyond even St. Teresa and as a theologian treats very lofty problems on which she wrote but little. In so doing, he unites the data of descriptive mysticism and the speculative theology of the virtues and gifts. (4) St. John of the Cross, like all Carmelite theologians, is fully in accord with St. Thomas on the great questions of predestination and grace.[4]

The doctrine of these teachers is the safe expression of tradition, as we shall see by comparing it with that of the doctors who preceded them and of those who followed them.

Our aim is to explain the unitive way, that we may lead souls to aspire to it, and may encourage them to make generous efforts to attain it.

Some persons talk about mysticism, but misunderstand it and abuse it. These persons must be enlightened by the sound teaching of theology. Others, far greater in number, are altogether ignorant of mysticism and apparently wish to remain so. They rely only on their own efforts, aided by ordinary grace; consequently they aim only at common virtues, and do not tend to perfection which they consider too lofty. Hence religious and priestly lives, which might be very fruitful, do not pass beyond a certain mediocrity that is often due, at least in part, to their early imperfect training and to inexact ideas about the union with God to which every Christian can and must aspire.

Some, who should be well acquainted with the writings of the great saints, rarely consult them, under the pretext that their teaching on mysticism is beyond reach, that it leads to divergent interpretations, and that according to several theo-

---

[4] Following the example of St. Thomas, he distinguishes infused contemplation from the extraordinary phenomena that sometimes accompany it.

logians it is not possible as yet to determine in what their teaching consists, even along broad lines, and in particular on this fundamental question: Is the contemplation, which they speak of, in the normal way of sanctity or not?

Consequently in the matter of mystical theology a certain agnosticism exists, just as there is an agnosticism which maintains that true miracles cannot be discerned because not all the laws of nature are known, and that one cannot rely on the Scriptures because certain obscure passages of the Old and New Testaments have not been fully elucidated. We believe that this agnosticism about mystical theology is false, that it can do no good, and that it ends disastrously.

The teaching of St. Thomas and of St. John of the Cross on this problem seems very clear to us. If these great masters had left this important problem unsolved, the very elements of mystical theology would still have to be constituted.

Pope Benedict XV congratulated the editor of *La vie spirituelle* for making this doctrine known, and wrote to him as follows (September 15, 1921) : "In our day many neglect the supernatural life and cultivate in its place an inconsistent and vague sentimentalism. Hence it is absolutely necessary to recall more often what the fathers of the Church, together with Holy Scripture, have taught us on the subject, and to do so by taking St. Thomas Aquinas especially as our guide, because he has so clearly set forth their doctrine on the elevation of the supernatural life. We must also earnestly draw the attention of souls to the conditions required for the progress of the grace of the virtues and of the gifts of the Holy Ghost, the perfect development of which is found in the mystical life. This is exactly what you and your collaborators have undertaken in your review, in a manner at once learned and solid."

In the delicate questions that we have had to consider, in combating an error, it is not always easy to avoid alining oneself with the contrary error, and to formulate the doctrine which rises above these opposing deviations and which is a just mean only because it is a summit. If we have inadvertently employed any inexact expressions in this study, we retract them here and now, and declare that we reject all spirituality that deviates ever so little from that of the saints, which has been approved by Holy Church. That is why, as a rule, we have quoted only canonized mystics whose teaching is commonly received.

Our conclusions may be summed up in the table on the following page.[5]

This table gives some idea of the progress of doctrine on this subject from St. Augustine to St. Teresa, passing as it does from the general to the particular. St. Augustine made a distinction between the beginners, the proficients, and the perfect, a classification which, according to the terminology of Dionysius, corresponds to the purgative, illuminative, and unitive ways. St. Thomas several times in his writings noted the corresponding progress of the virtues and the gifts, which are the principle of supernatural acts, in particular the degrees of humility.[6] The passive purifications of the senses and of the spirit indicated by St. Gregory the Great were described by Tauler and especially by St. John of the Cross. The latter tells us [7] that in the passive purification of the senses "God begins to communicate Himself no longer by the senses as formerly, by means of reasoning . . . but in a manner purely spiritual, in an act of simple contemplation." Evidently we are here considering infused contemplation, as the saint already declared.[8] We can understand why St. John says: "The proficients are in the illuminative way. It is therein God nourishes and fortifies the soul by infused contemplation." [9]

---

[5] This table differs slightly from that published by Father Gerest, O.P., in his excellent little *Memento de la vie spirituelle*, 1922, in which he expresses the ideas which we hold in common, and according to which he revised the work of Father Meynard, O.P., *Traité de la vie intérieure.*

[6] See IIa IIae, q.161, a.6.

[7] *The Dark Night of the Soul*, Bk. I, chap. 9, 3d sign.

[8] *The Ascent of Mount Carmel*, Bk. II, chap. 13.

[9] *The Dark Night of the Soul*, Bk. I, chap. 14.

| Degrees of Charity | BEGINNERS<br><br>(purgative way)<br>Ascetical life | PROFICIENTS<br><br>(illuminative way)<br>Threshold of the mystical life | PERFECT<br><br>(unitive way)<br>Mystical life |
|---|---|---|---|
| Virtues | *Initial virtues*, first degree of charity, temperance, chastity, patience, first degrees of humility. | *Solid virtues*, second degree of charity, obedience, more profound humility; spirit of the counsels. | *Eminent and heroic virtues*, third degree of charity, perfect humility, great spirit of faith, abandonment, almost unalterable patience. |
| Gifts | *Gifts of the Holy Ghost rather latent*, inspirations at rare intervals, slight aptitude as yet to profit by them, feeble docility. The soul is above all conscious of its activity. | *The gifts of the Holy Ghost begin to manifest themselves*, especially the three inferior gifts of fear, knowledge, and piety. The soul, more docile now, profits more from inspirations and interior illuminations. | *The superior gifts manifest themselves more notably* and in a frequent manner. The soul is, as it were, dominated by the Holy Ghost. Great passivity, which does not exclude the activity of the virtues. |
| Purifications | *Active purification of the senses* and of the spirit, or exterior and interior mortification. | *Passive purification of the senses*, under the influence especially of the gifts of fear and knowledge. Concomitant trials. | *Purification of the spirit* under the influence especially of the gift of understanding. Concomitant trials in which are manifested the gifts of fortitude and of counsel. |
| Prayers | *Acquired prayer:* vocal prayer, discursive prayer, affective prayer, which becomes more and more simple, called the acquired prayer of recollection. | *Initial infused prayer*, isolated acts of infused contemplation in the course of the acquired prayer of recollection; then, prayer of supernatural recollection and of quiet; manifest influence of the gift of piety. | *Infused prayers* of simple union, of complete union (sometimes ecstatic), of transforming union, under the more and more marked influence of the gift of wisdom. Concomitant favors. |
| Mansions of St. Teresa | First and second mansions. | Third and fourth mansions. | Fifth, sixth, and seventh mansions. |

In another place he says: "The passive purification of the senses is common. It takes place in the greater number of beginners." [10] It is indeed the threshold of the mystical life, like the prayer of supernatural recollection described by St. Teresa.[11] This prayer is often preceded by isolated acts of infused contemplation in the course of the acquired prayer of recollection described by the saint.[12] In the illuminative way, the gifts of fear and of knowledge are clearly manifested (passive purification of the senses in which one recognizes the emptiness of created things) and also the gift of piety (quiet of the will in which this gift is found).

In this approximate table, we consider the ideal soul in an abstract manner. The illuminative and unitive ways are therein considered, not only in their imperfect form but in their plenitude, in the same way as they are considered by St. John of the Cross, who is a faithful echo of tradition.

This lofty perfection is that described by St. Augustine and St. Gregory; the perfection to which the twelve degrees of humility enumerated by St. Benedict or the seven degrees counseled by St. Anselm lead: (1) to acknowledge ourselves contemptible; (2) to grieve on account of this; (3) to admit that we are so; (4) to wish our neighbor to believe it; (5) patiently to endure people saying it; (6) willingly to be treated as a person worthy of contempt; (7) to love to be treated in this fashion.[13]

This great conception of Christian perfection and of the illuminative and unitive ways is the only one which seems to us to preserve all the grandeur of the Gospel and of the Epistles of St. John and St. Paul.

As we have just said, the precept of love knows no limit. "Thou shalt love the Lord thy God with thy whole heart and with thy whole soul and with all thy strength and with all thy

---

[10] *Ibid.,* chap. 8.
[11] *The Interior Castle,* fourth mansion, chap. 3.
[12] *The Way of Perfection,* chap. 28.
[13] See the explanation of these degrees of humility in St. Thomas, IIa IIae, q.161, a.6.

mind; and thy neighbor as thyself." [14] Christ adds for all of us: "Be ye perfect as your heavenly Father is perfect"; [15] and the whole Sermon on the Mount, which begins with the beatitudes, is a sort of commentary on this exhortation. To raise us to this perfection, "the Word was made flesh and dwelt among us, . . . and of His fulness we all have received." [16] The life of grace, which has been given to us, is the seed of the life of heaven, and is the same life in its essence. "Amen, amen I say unto you: He that believeth in Me, hath everlasting life." [17] The contemplation of the mysteries of Christ's life will be given to those who follow Him faithfully. "He that hath My commandments, and keepeth them, he it is that loveth Me. And he that loveth Me, shall be loved of My Father. And I will love him, and I will manifest Myself to him." [18] "I will ask the Father, and He shall give you another Paraclete, that He may abide with you forever. . . . The Paraclete, the Holy Ghost, whom the Father will send in My name, He will teach you all things, and bring all things to your mind, whatsoever I shall have said to you." [19]

Love of neighbor, too, must go far. "A new commandment I give unto you: that you love one another, as I have loved you." [20] "Greater love than this no man hath, that a man lay down his life for his friends." [21]

Our Savior, to make us understand in what the perfection of charity consists, prayed for us thus: "Holy Father, keep them in Thy name, whom Thou hast given Me; that they may be one, as We also are. . . . And the glory which Thou hast given Me, I have given to them; that they may be one, as We also are one." [22]

[14] Luke 10: 27.
[15] Matt. 5: 48.
[16] John 1: 14, 16.
[17] John 6: 47; 8: 51.
[18] John 14: 21.
[19] John 14: 16, 26.
[20] John 13: 34.
[21] John 15: 13.
[22] John 17: 11, 22.

St. Matthew's Gospel is not less sublime when it recalls these words of Christ: "I confess to Thee, O Father, Lord of heaven and earth, because Thou hast hid these things from the wise and prudent, and hast revealed them to little ones." [23]

Lastly, St. Paul shows us all that the mystical body of Christ is and should be; how the Christian must be incorporated into Christ by a progressive sanctification, which gives a very broad idea of the three phases distinguished later on.

*The purgative way.* Incorporated in Christ, the faithful must orient their lives toward heaven and die more and more to sin. "Mortify therefore your members which are upon earth . . . stripping yourselves of the old man with his deeds." [24] "For we are buried together with Him by baptism unto death. . . . For if we have been planted together in the likeness of His death, we shall be also in the likeness of His resurrection. Knowing this, that our old man is crucified with Him, that the body of sin may be destroyed to the end that we may serve sin no longer." [25] "And they that are Christ's have crucified their flesh with the vices and concupiscences." [26] Moreover, the Apostles bore in their bodies "the mortification of Jesus, that the life also of Jesus may be made manifest in their bodies." [27] He who sacrifices his life, finds it again transfigured. "Unless the grain of wheat falling into the ground die, itself remaineth alone. But if it die, it bringeth forth much fruit." [28]

*The illuminative way* is also indicated by St. Paul, when he tells us that the Christian, by the light of faith and under the inspiration of the Holy Ghost, must put "on the new, him who is renewed unto knowledge, according to the image of Him that created him. . . . Put ye on therefore, as the elect of

[23] Matt. 11: 25.
[24] Col. 3: 5, 10.
[25] Rom. 6: 4–6; 12: 2.
[26] Gal. 5: 24.
[27] See II Cor. 4: 10.
[28] John 12: 24.

God, holy and beloved, the bowels of mercy, benignity, humility, modesty, patience. . . . But above all these things have charity, which is the bond of perfection." [29] We must imitate Jesus Christ and those who resemble Him; [30] we must have His sentiments, catch the spirit of His mysteries, of His passion,[31] crucifixion,[32] death, burial,[33] resurrection,[34] and ascension.[35] St. Paul, moreover, suffers the pains of labor until Christ be formed in the souls of the faithful,[36] until they be perfectly illuminated by the light of life. "Furthermore, I count all things to be but loss for the excellent knowledge of Jesus Christ, my Lord: for whom I have suffered the loss of all things, and count them but as dung, that I may gain Christ." [37]

*The unitive way* is that followed by the supernaturally enlightened Christian who lives in a union that is, so to speak, continual with Christ. "Therefore, if you be risen with Christ, seek the things that are above; where Christ is sitting at the right hand of God. Mind the things that are above, not the things that are upon the earth. For you are dead (to the world); and your life is hid with Christ in God." [38] "And let the peace of Christ rejoice in your hearts, wherein also you are called in one body; and be ye thankful. Let the word of Christ dwell in you abundantly, in all wisdom, teaching and admonishing one another in psalms, hymns, and spiritual canticles, singing in grace in your hearts to God. All whatsoever you do in word or in work, do all in the name of the Lord Jesus Christ, giving thanks to God and the Father by Him." [39] Under the inspiration of the Holy Ghost, such is

[29] Col. 3: 10, 12, 14; cf. Eph. 4: 1–6; Gal. 2: 9.
[30] Phil. 2: 5; I Cor. 11: 1.
[31] Rom. 8: 7.
[32] Rom. 6: 5.
[33] Rom. 6: 4–11.
[34] Col. 3: 1.
[35] Ephes. 2: 6.
[36] Gal. 4: 19.
[37] Phil. 3: 8.
[38] Col. 3: 1–4.
[39] Col. 3: 15–17.

indeed union with God, through Christ and the loving and delightful contemplation of the great mysteries of faith.[40] It is the normal prelude to the beatific vision. "When Christ shall appear, who is your life, then you also shall appear with Him in glory." [41]

[40] See *infra*, pp. 311 f., what St. Paul says about the spirit of wisdom.
[41] Col. 3: 4.

# CHAPTER II

## The Actual Mystical Problem

### ARTICLE I

#### Object and Method of Ascetical and Mystical Theology

WHAT is to be understood by ascetical and mystical theology? Is it a special science or a part of theology? What is its particular object? Under what light does it proceed? What are its principles? What is its method? These questions must be settled before we seek the distinction between asceticism and mysticism, and before we take up the chief problems they must solve.

##### I. THE MEANING OF ASCETICAL AND MYSTICAL THEOLOGY; ITS OBJECT

Theology is the science of God. We distinguish between natural theology or theodicy, which knows God by the sole light of reason, and supernatural theology, which proceeds from divine revelation, examines its contents, and deduces the consequences of the truths of faith.

Supernatural theology is usually divided into two parts, dogmatic and moral. Dogmatic theology has to do with revealed mysteries, principally the Blessed Trinity, the incarnation, the redemption, the Holy Eucharist and the other sacraments, and the future life. Moral theology treats of human acts, of revealed precepts and counsels, of grace, of the Christian virtues, both theological and moral, and of the gifts of the Holy Ghost, which are principles of action ordained to the supernatural end made known by revelation.

Modern theologians have often exaggerated the distinction between moral and dogmatic theology, giving to the latter the great treatises on grace and on the infused virtues and gifts, and reducing the former to casuistry, which is the least lofty of its applications. Moral theology has thus become, in several theological works, the science of sins to be avoided rather than the science of virtues to be practiced and to be developed under the constant action of God in us. In this way it has lost some of its pre-eminence and is manifestly insufficient for the direction of souls aspiring to intimate union with God.

On the contrary, moral theology, as expounded in the second part of the *Summa theologica* of St. Thomas, keeps all its grandeur and its efficacy for the direction of souls called to the highest perfection. St. Thomas does not, in fact, consider dogmatic and moral theology as two distinct sciences; sacred doctrine, in his opinion, is absolutely one and is of such high perfection that it contains the perfections of both dogmatic and moral theology. In other words, it is eminently speculative and practical, as the science of God from which it springs.[1] That is why he treats in detail in the moral part of his *Summa* not only human acts, precepts, and counsels, but also habitual and actual grace, the infused virtues in general and in particular, the gifts of the Holy Ghost, their fruits, the beatitudes, the active and contemplative life, the degrees of contemplation, graces gratuitously bestowed, such as the gift of miracles, the gift of tongues, prophecy, and rapture, and likewise the religious life and its various forms.

Moral theology thus understood evidently contains the principles necessary for leading souls to the highest sanctity. Ascetical and mystical theology is nothing but the application of this broad moral theology to the direction of souls toward ever closer union with God. It presupposes what sacred doctrine teaches about the nature and the properties of the Christian virtues and of the gifts of the Holy Ghost, and it

[1] *Summa theol.*, Ia, q.1, a.2, 8.

studies the laws and conditions of their progress from the point of view of perfection.

To teach the practice of the highest virtues and perfect docility to the Holy Ghost and to lead to the life of union with God, ascetical and mystical theology assembles all the lights of dogmatic and moral theology, of which it is the most elevated application and the crown.

The cycle formed by the different parts of theology, with its evident unity, is thus completed. Sacred science proceeds from revelation contained in Scripture and tradition, preserved and explained by the teaching authority of the Church. It arranges in order all revealed truths and their consequences in a single doctrinal body, in which the precepts and counsels are set forth as founded on the supernatural mystery of the divine life, of which grace is a participation. Lastly, it shows how, by the practice of the virtues and by docility to the Holy Ghost, the soul not only arrives at belief in the revealed mysteries, but also at the enjoyment of them and at a grasp of the profound meaning of the word of God, source of all supernatural knowledge, and at a life of continual union with the Blessed Trinity who dwells in us. Doctrinal mysticism thus appears as the final crown of all acquired theological knowledge, and it can direct souls in the ways of experimental mysticism. This latter is an entirely supernatural and infused loving knowledge, full of sweetness, which only the Holy Ghost, by His unction, can give us and which is, as it were, the prelude of the beatific vision. Such is manifestly the conception of ascetical and mystical theology which has been formulated by the great masters of sacred science, especially by St. Thomas Aquinas.

This conception corresponds perfectly to the current meaning and etymology of the words "ascetical" and "mystical." The term "asceticism," as its Greek origin indicates, means the exercise of the virtues. Among the first Christians those were called ascetics who devoted themselves to the practice of mortification, exercises of piety, and other Christian virtues. Therefore asceticism is that part of theology which directs souls in the struggle against sin and in the progress of virtue.

Mystical theology, as its name indicates, treats of more hidden and mysterious things: of the intimate union of the soul with God; of the transitory phenomena that accompany certain degrees of union, as ecstasy; and of essentially extraordinary graces, such as visions and private revelations. In fact, it was under the title of "Mystical Theology" that Dionysius and many after him dealt with supernatural contemplation and the intimate union of the soul with God. By so doing, they pointed out the principal subject of this teaching.[2] All this is equivalent to saying that ascetical and mystical theology, or spiritual doctrine, is not a special science but a division of theology. The great body of theologians has always so understood it.

This does not in any way hinder a psychologist, even though an unbeliever, from studying the outward aspects of ascetical and mystical phenomena in Christianity or in other religions. But this study would be only psychological and would in no way deserve the name of ascetical and mystical theology. It would be mostly descriptive. If it should try to explain all these facts by the merely natural powers of the soul, it would be declared false by all Catholics, because we would see in it a materialistic explanation of the higher by the lower, similar to that which the mechanists propose for vital phenomena.

Having stated these considerations, we may easily answer the question proposed as to what is the object of ascetical and

[2] With certain modern authors, we may say that "mystical theology is based on dogmatic theology, as ascetical theology is based on moral theology," to use the expression of an anonymous authority quoted by Sauvé in his excellent treatise *Les états mystiques,* 6th ed., p. 1. We believe, however, that this manner of speaking gives rise to a less lofty conception of moral theology than that formulated by St. Thomas Aquinas, and that it would perhaps lead to an exaggerated distinction between ascetical and mystical theology, and to a lack of perception of the continuity of spiritual progress. We shall return to this question, on which Sauvé often expresses himself in a precise and traditional manner in the same treatise.

mystical theology, without as yet making a distinction between these two branches of spiritual doctrine. It is Christian perfection, union with God, the contemplation which this presupposes, the ordinary means leading to it, and the extraordinary helps favoring it.

We might now ask what distinguishes ascetical from mystical theology. But as this delicate problem is solved in a somewhat different way according to the method of treating these matters, it is better to propose at once the question of method.


## II. THE PRINCIPLES AND METHOD OF ASCETICAL AND MYSTICAL THEOLOGY

After what has just been said about the object of this branch of theology, it is easy to see what principles it must follow to attain this object.

The light of revelation contained in Scripture and tradition is explained by the teaching authority of the Church and commented upon by dogmatic and moral theology. From the principles of faith theology deduces the conclusions that they implicitly contain. By the light of these principles the facts of the ascetical and mystical life must be examined if we wish to go beyond simple psychology, and by this light the rules of direction must be formulated that they may be something more than unmotivated, practical prescriptions.

This much is clear and is admitted by all Catholic writers. But if we attempt a more exact statement of the question of method, we find among authors certain divergencies, which are not without influence on their theories. Some writers, especially in mystical theology, use almost exclusively the descriptive and inductive method, which proceeds from facts; others, on the contrary, follow principally the deductive method, which proceeds from principles.

*A. Descriptive or inductive method.* The descriptive school, without scorning the doctrine of the great theologians on the life of grace and on the ordinary or extraordinary helps of God, undertakes to describe the different spiritual states and particularly the mystical states by their signs, rather than to determine their nature theologically and to examine whether they proceed from the Christian virtues, from the gifts of the Holy Ghost, or from graces gratuitously bestowed, such as prophecy and the charisms connected with it.

Recently several works have been written that are instructive in certain respects. They are especially collections of descriptions of mystical states, followed by practical rules of direction and by some supplementary material on theoretical questions, such as the nature of the mystical union.[3] These treatises are analogous, as their authors declare, to manuals of practical medicine which teach how to make a diagnosis quickly and how to prescribe suitable remedies without an extensive examination into the nature of the ailment or into its relations with the whole organism.

These works, which are very useful from one point of view, contain only part of the science: the inductive bases or the facts, and practical conclusions. The light of theological principles and doctrinal co-ordination, however, are lacking. Therefore, the rules of direction contained in these books are generally, in the opinion of theologians, too empirical and insufficiently classified and justified. Science is the knowledge of things, not only from their appearances and their signs, but from their very nature and their causes. And, as action springs from the nature of things, no one can in a practical manner tell the interior soul what it must do, if he has not determined the very nature of the interior life. How can anyone say whether the soul may and ought without presumption to desire the mystical union, before determining the nature of this union and before recognizing whether it is an essentially

---

[3] An example of this type of book is *Les grâces d'oraison* by the learned and regretted Father A. Poulain, S.J. This book should be read attentively by all who wish to treat of these problems.

extraordinary gift or an eminent grace generally accorded to the perfect, a grace necessary, at least morally, for high perfection? If this question is treated merely as an appendix, as a purely speculative and quasi-insoluble problem, the rules of direction previously formulated will not have sufficient doctrinal foundation.

Certain partisans of the descriptive school, although admitting the truth of the theological doctrine of the gifts of the Holy Ghost, which are the principles of mystical contemplation, declare that it "has only historical interest," [4] because, they say, it does not throw light on the facts or on the practical questions of direction. Many theologians think, on the contrary, that it makes possible the solution of the important question we have just been speaking of, and also permits a distinction between what in the spiritual life belongs to the order of sanctifying grace in its eminent forms, and what pertains to gratuitous graces (*gratis datae*) which are essentially extraordinary. Perhaps this doctrine alone enables us to determine the culminating point of the normal development of the life of grace in an interior soul which is perfectly docile to the Holy Ghost. This problem is, in fact, one of the most important in the realm of spirituality.

To supply this doctrinal lacuna and absence of directing principles, authors who adhere too exclusively to the descriptive method sometimes give, at the outset of their treatise on mysticism, and as it were a priori, a so-called nominal definition of the mystical state (quiet or union), which declares it as extraordinary, or almost so, as visions or private revelations. Such a definition presupposes a whole theory. These partisans of the method of observation, struck by certain signs of the mystical state, which are perhaps only accidental signs, precipitately determine its nature, before asking theology what it thinks about the matter. But this supreme science alone, enlightened as it is by revelation, can say whether the state in

---

[4] Father Poulain, *Les grâces d'oraison*, 9th ed., pp. 132, 164.

question is the full, normal blossoming of the supernatural life of union with God, or whether it is an extraordinary gift in no way necessary for the highest sanctity.

The exclusive use of this descriptive method would lead one to forget that ascetical and mystical theology is a part of theology, and to consider it as a part of experimental psychology. In other words, whoever neglects to have recourse to the light of theological principles, will have to be content with the principles furnished by psychology, as do so many psychologists who treat of mystical phenomena in the different religions. This procedure, however, does not take faith into consideration at all; it permits a supernatural cause to be assigned only to facts which are essentially and manifestly miraculous. Other mystical facts, which are deeper and hence less apparently supernatural, it declares inexplicable, or it tries to explain them by placing undue stress on the merely natural powers of the soul. The same remark applies to biographies of the saints, and to the history of religious orders and even of the Church.

The descriptive method, useful and necessary as it may be, cannot be exclusive. It is inclined not to appreciate the value of a fundamental theological distinction which can throw light on all mystical theology: the distinction between the intrinsically supernatural (*supernaturale quoad substantiam*), characteristic of the intimate life of God, of which sanctifying grace, or "the grace of the virtues and the gifts," is a participation, and the extrinsically supernatural or preternatural (*supernaturale quoad modum tantum*), which is the character of the signs or extraordinary phenomena that the devil can imitate. St. Thomas [5] and also St. John of the Cross [6] have often stated that an abyss exists between these two forms of the supernatural. We have it, for example, between the essentially supernatural life of invisible grace (which even an angel

---

[5] "Sanctifying grace is nobler than gratuitous grace" (Ia IIae, q.3, a.5).
[6] *The Ascent of Mount Carmel*, Bk. II, chaps. 10, 19, 20, 25.

cannot know naturally) and the visible resurrection of a dead person, which is supernatural only by the mode according to which natural life is restored to the corpse; or again, between infused faith in the mystery of the Blessed Trinity and the supernatural knowledge of a future event in the natural order, such as the end of a war.[7] This is the difference between Christian doctrine and life on the one hand and, on the other, the miracles and prophecies which confirm its divine origin and which are merely concomitant signs.

This notable distinction between the two forms of the supernatural dominates all theology, and is quite indispensable in mystical theology. But the purely descriptive method pays scarcely any attention to this distinction; it is impressed especially by the more or less sensible signs of the mystical states, and not by the fundamental law of the progress of grace. The essentially supernatural character of the latter is too profound and too elevated to fall within the scope of observation. Yet this supernatural element is what most interests faith and theology.

Moreover, the works of purely descriptive mysticism, useful as they may be, contain hardly anything but the material of mystical theology. That is why we fully agree with the following words of an excellent Thomist who wrote to us, saying: "Mystical theology as a special science does not exist; there is only theology, along with certain applications of it that concern the mystical life. To treat mystical theology as a science with principles of its own is to impoverish and diminish it all, and to lose its directing light. The mystical life must be set forth by the great principles of theology. Then all is illuminated, and we have a science, not a mere collection of phenomena."

*B. Deductive method.* We must not, however, fall into the other extreme and employ simply the deductive theological

[7] Cf. *infra,* p. 59.

method. Some, with a tendency to simplify everything, would be led to deduce the solution of the most difficult problems of spirituality by proceeding from St. Thomas' doctrine about the infused virtues and the gifts of the Holy Ghost (clearly distinct from the graces *gratis datae*) without sufficiently considering the admirable descriptions of the various degrees of the spiritual life, notably of the mystical union, given by St. Teresa, St. John of the Cross, St. Francis de Sales, and other great saints. And since, according to St. Thomas and tradition, the gifts of the Holy Ghost are in every soul in the state of grace, some persons might suppose that the mystical state or infused contemplation is very frequent, and might confound with them what is only their prelude, as, for example, the prayer of simplicity, so well described by Bossuet.[8] Hence the inclination not to take sufficient account of the concomitant or auxiliary phenomena of certain degrees of the mystical union, such as the suspension of the faculties and ecstasy, and hence the danger of falling into an extreme opposed to that of the partisans of the solely descriptive method.

These two extremes should be avoided. They recall the opposition in philosophy between those who consider only miracles and prophecies (concomitant signs of revelation) and those who speak only of the harmony and sublimity of Christian life and doctrine.

As a result of these two excesses, there are two other extremes to be avoided in spiritual direction: advising souls to leave the ascetical way either too soon or too late. We will return to this point.

*Union of the two methods.* Evidently these two methods, the inductive and the deductive, or the analytical and the synthetical, must be combined.

[8] Bossuet, *Manière courte et facile de faire l'oraison en foi et de simple présence de Dieu* (a short work addressed to the Visitation Sisters of Meaux). This prayer may be called contemplation, but if it is compared with even the inferior passive states described by St. Teresa, evidently it does not deserve the name of essentially mystical contemplation, except perhaps for short moments, and in its second phase.

In the light of the principles of theology we must determine what Christian perfection should be, without in any way diminishing it; what is the nature of the contemplation it supposes, the ordinary means leading to it, and the extraordinary helps favoring it. To do this, we must analyze the concepts of Christian life, perfection, and holiness furnished by the Gospel; and we must also describe the facts of the ascetical and mystical life by studying the testimony of the saints who have best experienced them and revealed them. In this description of facts, accompanied by the analysis of the corresponding theological concepts, we must seek to determine the nature of these facts or interior states, and to distinguish them from the concomitant and auxiliary phenomena. The authors most helpful in this study are those who were both great theologians and great mystics, as St. Thomas, St. Bonaventure, Richard of St. Victor, St. John of the Cross, and St. Francis de Sales.

After analyzing these concepts and facts, we must synthesize them in the light of the evangelical conception of perfection or sanctity. We must show: (1) what is essential or conformable to Christian perfection, and what is contrary to it; (2) what is necessary or very useful and desirable to reach it, and what is essentially extraordinary and not required for the highest sanctity.

In all this study, a supremely important distinction is that between the intrinsically extraordinary (the miraculous) and the extrinsically extraordinary, which is the ordinary or the normal in the lives of the saints, being at the same time as rare as sanctity itself. The omission of this distinction is the source of frequent ambiguities in several modern works, which do not sufficiently appreciate the great divisions of the supernatural. Thus, in the light of theological ideas and principles, we shall be able to discern the facts and to formulate rules of direction by motivating them. In our opinion, this is the true method of ascetical and mystical theology. No other method will serve, since mystical theology is the application of theology to the direction of souls toward an ever closer union with God.

We must now examine the distinction between ascetical and mystical theology, their relations, and the unity of spiritual doctrine. This is a delicate question. In its consideration we must not forget that God calls all interior souls to drink from the fountain of living water, where they will find life in abundance, even beyond their desires, "that they may have life, and may have it more abundantly." According to the saints, the soul which, for the love of God, labors to strip itself of all that is not God, is soon penetrated with light and so united to God that it becomes like Him and enters into the possession of all His goods.

## ARTICLE II

*The Distinction Between Ascetical Theology and Mystical Theology and the Unity of Spiritual Doctrine*

Ascetical and mystical theology is the application of theology in the direction of souls toward an ever more intimate union with God. It must use the inductive and deductive methods, studying the facts of the spiritual life in the light of revealed principles and of the theological doctrines deduced from these principles. We must now see what distinguishes ascetical from mystical theology; and whether this distinction is such as to exclude continuity in the passage from one to the other, or unity in the spiritual doctrine. Earlier writers and a number of modern authors are not in agreement on this point.

### I. TRADITIONAL THESIS: THE UNITY OF SPIRITUAL DOCTRINE

Until the seventeenth and eighteenth centuries, it was generally held that mystical theology included not only the mystical union, infused contemplation, its degrees and the extraordinary graces that sometimes accompany it (visions and private revelations), but also Christian perfection in general, and the first phases of the spiritual life, the normal progress of which thus seemed directed toward the mystical union as its culminating point. All these together formed a whole that was truly one: a spiritual doctrine dominated by a very high idea of perfection, drawn from the Gospel and the saints, and unified by the commonly accepted principle that infused or mystical contemplation [1] is ordinarily granted to the perfect and proceeds especially from the gift of wisdom, the progress of which is proportionate to that of charity. In other words, they agreed in recognizing that an eminent degree of charity, which is the principle of a very intimate union with God, is normally accompanied by eminent, confused contemplation, which is at the same time very penetrating and delightful. This charity is likewise accompanied by a quasi-experimental knowledge of the mystery of God who is closer to the soul than it is to itself, of God who makes Himself felt by it and who acts constantly on it, in trial as well as in consolation, as much to destroy what should die as to renovate and build up.

These assertions may be verified by consulting the mystical theologies of Vallgornera (Dominican), of Thomas of Jesus, Dominic of the Blessed Trinity, Anthony of the Holy Ghost, Philip of the Blessed Trinity (Carmelites),[2] and, farther in the past, the works of St. John of the Cross, St. Teresa, Venerable Louis de Blois,[3] Venerable Dionysius the Carthu-

---

[1] This is quite distinct from visions and private revelations.

[2] For example, Philip of the Blessed Trinity, *Summa theolog. mysticae* (1874 ed.), says: "Debent omnes ad supernaturalem contemplationem aspirare: nihil honestius, utilius, delectabilius" (II, 299). "Debent omnes et maxime Deo specialiter consecratae animae, ad actualem fruitivam unionem cum Deo aspirare et tendere" (III, 43). "Contemplationis supernaturalis gratia aliquando conceditur imperfectis, aliquando denegatur perfectis" (II, 310). "Aliquando" indicates the exception rather than the rule. Cf. also Thomas of Jesus, *De contemplatione divina*, Bk. I, chap. 9.

[3] Louis de Blois sums up the traditional teaching on this point in his *Institutio spiritualis*, chap. 1: "All men should aspire to union with God"; chap.

sian, Tauler, Blessed Henry Suso, Blessed Bartholomew of the Martyrs, St. Thomas Aquinas, St. Bonaventure, St. Albert the Great, Dionysius the Mystic, and St. Augustine.

St. Thomas especially showed the relation between what are today called ascetical theology and mystical theology, by treating of the mutual relations of action and contemplation. With St. Augustine and St. Gregory, this is what he teaches: The active life, to which is attached the exercise of the moral virtues of prudence, justice, fortitude, and temperance,[4] and the outward works of charity, prepares for the contemplative life, in so far as it regulates the passions that disturb contemplation, and in so far as it makes us grow in the love of God and of our neighbor.[5] Then the contemplation of God, which is proper to the perfect, leads to action, directs it, and renders it much more supernatural and fruitful.[6] Thus in the natural order the image precedes the idea and then serves to express it; the emotion precedes the will and then serves to execute with greater ardor the thing willed; and so again, says St. Thomas, our acts engender a habit, then this habit makes us act more promptly and easily.[7] In this way asceticism does not cease when the contemplative life begins; on the contrary, the exercise of the different virtues becomes truly superior when the soul receives the mystical grace of almost continual union with God.

Some souls, remarks St. Thomas, by reason of their impetuosity are more fitted for the active life; others have by nature the purity of spirit and the calm which prepare them more for contemplation;[8] but all can prepare themselves for

---

12: "How the mystical union with God is brought about in the soul which has reached perfection: (1) He who perseveres ordinarily obtains the mystical union; . . . (3) Some opinions on this union; (4) Its effects."

[4] *Summa,* IIa IIae, q.181, a.1, 2.

[5] *Ibid.,* q.182, a.3.

[6] *Ibid.,* a.4.

[7] *Ibid.,* ad 2um.

[8] *Ibid.,* ad 3um.

the contemplative life,[9] which is the most perfect and in itself the most meritorious.[10] "Love of God is in fact more meritorious than love of our neighbor." [11] It is love which leads us, says St. Augustine, to seek the holy repose of divine contemplation.[12] "And if one of the signs of charity is the external labor that we impose on ourselves for Christ's sake, a far more expressive sign is to put aside all that pertains to the present life and to find our happiness in giving ourselves up exclusively to the contemplation of God." [13] "The more closely a man unites his own or another's soul to God, the more acceptable is his sacrifice to God." [14]

St. John of the Cross insists on this point: supernatural contemplation, which he speaks of in *The Ascent of Mount Carmel* and in *The Dark Night,* appears there as the full development of "the life of faith" and of the spirit of wisdom. "Faith alone," he says, "is the proximate and proportionate means which can unite the soul to God." [15] "Pure faith, in the denudation and abnegation of all, inclines far more to divine love than spiritual visions." [16]

This is true if we do not diminish, as several modern authors do, the essentially supernatural character of faith, and if we remember that even when this virtue is obscure and imperfect or separated from charity, it is, by reason of its first object and its motive, infinitely superior to the loftiest natural knowledge of the angels, or even to the supernatural prevision of natural, contingent futures. It is of the same essentially divine order as the beatific vision. St. Paul says that infused faith, the gift of God, is "the substance of things to be hoped for." Especially when accompanied by the gifts of wis-

9 *Ibid.*
10 *Ibid.,* a.2.
11 *Ibid.*
12 *City of God,* Bk. XIX, sec. 19.
13 *Summa,* IIa IIae, q.182, a.2 ad 1um.
14 *Ibid.,* ad 3um.
15 *The Ascent of Mount Carmel,* Bk. II, chaps. 2, 3, 8.
16 *Ibid.,* pp. 202 f.

dom and understanding in an eminent degree, it is, so to speak, the beginning of eternal life, *inchoatio vitae aeternae,* as St. Thomas says in *De veritate,* q. 14, a. 2.

If we wish to understand all the grandeur of the life of faith in which every Christian should make progress, we must read the masters of traditional mysticism. Once we have grasped their point of view, we will not be surprised that the perfect mystical life is the culminating point of the normal development of the life of grace. Thus the unity of doctrine and of the spiritual life is maintained in spite of the diversity of interior states.

## II. THESIS OF SEVERAL MODERN AUTHORS: SEPARATION OF ASCETICAL FROM MYSTICAL THEOLOGY

Since the seventeenth and eighteenth centuries, several authors have thought that it was necessary to separate ascetical from mystical theology, which since then have often become the subjects of special treatises called "Ascetical Directory" and "Mystical Directory."

This division followed upon lively discussions that were occasioned by abuses springing from a premature and erroneous teaching of the mystical ways. From the time of St. Teresa, these ways seemed to many theologians so suspect that the writings of St. John of the Cross had to be defended against the charge of illuminism, and superiors were roused to the point of forbidding their religious to read the works of Venerable John Tauler, Ruysbroeck, Blessed Henry Suso, St. Gertrude, and St. Mechtildis. After the condemnation of the errors of Molinos, the mystical ways were even more suspect.

Since then a rather large number of authors, who are excellent in many respects, have agreed on making an absolute distinction between ascetical and mystical theology. Excessively eager to systematize things and to establish a doctrine to remedy abuses, and consequently led to classify things materially and objectively, without a sufficiently lofty and profound knowledge of them, they declared that ascetical theology should treat of the "ordinary" Christian life according to the three ways, the purgative, the illuminative, and the unitive. As for mystical theology, it should treat only of extraordinary graces, among which they included not only visions and private revelations, but also supernatural, confused contemplation, the passive purifications, and the mystical union.

Therefore the mystical union no longer appears in their arrangement as the culminating point of the normal development of sanctifying grace, of the virtues, and of the gifts. According to their view, infused contemplation is not the life of faith and the spirit of wisdom carried to their perfection, to their full efflorescence; but it seems rather to be attached to graces *gratis datae,* such as prophecy, or at least to an entirely extraordinary or miraculous mode of the gifts of the Holy Ghost. Because they place the mystical union and infused contemplation among the graces *gratis datae,* these authors counsel already fervent souls against seeking not only visions and private revelations, but also the mystical union and infused contemplation, if they would avoid all presumption and would advance in humility: *altiora te ne quaesieris.* This seems quite like the mistake made by those spiritual directors who refused daily communion to these same souls, alleging that humility does not permit one to aim so high.

These authors thus distinguish a unitive life called "ordinary," the only one necessary, they say, to perfection, from a unitive life called "extraordinary," which, according to them, is not even required for great sanctity. From this point of view, asceticism does not lead to mysticism, and the perfection, or "ordinary" union, to which it leads, is normally an end and not a disposition to a more intimate and more elevated union. Hence mystical theology is of importance only to some very rare, privileged souls; we may just as well, then, almost ignore it in order to avoid presumption and delusion.

In their desire to remedy one abuse, are they not falling into another which is clearly and repeatedly pointed out in *The Ascent of Mount Carmel* [17] and in *The Spiritual Canticle?* Father Lallemant, one of the best spiritual writers of the Society of Jesus, complains rather bitterly of this conception of the mystical life as quasi-inaccessible. In his opinion, this conception bars the way to high perfection and intimate union with God.[18] As a result of this teaching, many souls have been diverted from reading St. John of the Cross, although he is the master who best fortifies against illusion and the desire for graces which are essentially extraordinary.[19]

### III. RETURN TO THE TRADITIONAL THESIS: UNITY OF SPIRITUAL DOCTRINE

The question may arise as to whether this absolute distinction and lack of continuity between ascetical and mystical theology does not notably diminish the elevation of Christian perfection which is the end of the normal progress of sanctifying grace and of charity in this life; whether it does not lose sight of the fact that the progress of the gifts of the Holy Ghost is proportionate to that of charity, which ought always to grow; and whether it does not confound strictly extraordinary graces with eminent and rather uncommon graces granted ordinarily to lofty perfection, a state that is rather uncommon by reason of the very great abnegation which it supposes. In

[17] "There is no more disturbing or more painful state for the soul than that of not seeing clearly into itself and of not finding anyone who understands it. Led by God to the heights of obscure contemplation and of aridity, it will seem to it that it is going astray; and in the midst of darkness, sufferings, anguish, and temptations, its director will say to it, as Job's consolers did to him: 'That is all melancholy and weakness. Perhaps you are guilty of hidden malice, as a result of which God leaves you in this abandoned condition'" (Prologue, p. 5).

[18] *La doctrine spirituelle,* 7th principle, chap. 6, a.3, sec. 11; 4th principle, "Docility to the Inspiration of the Holy Ghost," chap. 1, a.3; chap. 11, a.2. Among later Jesuit authors, consult also the works of Father de Caussade and Father Grou.

[19] *The Ascent of Mount Carmel,* Bk. II, chaps. 10, 11, 16, 17, 20, 28.

short, does not this distinction confound the extrinsically extraordinary, which is the very elevated ordinary of the life of
union with God in the saints in this life, and the intrinsically
extraordinary or the miraculous, which, more often than not,
is only a sign or a transitory help inferior in order to the life
of grace?

We may ask whether this teaching does not misunderstand
and lessen the traditional doctrine of the great theologians and
mystics on the essentially supernatural quality [20] of the life
of grace, of faith, of charity, of the gifts of the Holy Ghost.
That life is incomparably above the phenomenon of ecstasy,
which in a certain sense is external, above miracles and
prophecies, since in its perfection it is, as it were, the prelude
to the beatific vision, which a holy soul, already perfectly
purified, normally obtains without passing through purgatory.

During the past few years these questions have led several
writers, such as Father Saudreau, Father Lamballe, and Father Arintero, O.P., to reject such an absolute distinction
between ascetical and mystical theology and to note the continuity existing between them. They appealed to the testimony of St. John of the Cross, who says: "Those, who in the
spiritual life still exercise themselves in meditation, belong
to the state of beginners. When it pleases God to make them
leave it, it is for the purpose of introducing them into the way
of progress, which is that of contemplatives, and of making
them arrive safely and surely by this means at the state of the
perfect, that is to say, divine union." [21] This last, in the language of the author of *The Dark Night of the Soul,* is manifestly in the mystical order. As Father Lamballe [22] shows in
various texts taken from St. John of the Cross, it follows that
mystical contemplation is ordinarily granted to the perfect,

---

[20] Supernatural *quoad substantiam,* says sound theology in contradistinction
to supernatural *quoad modum* of sensible miracles or of prophetic knowledge of future events.
[21] *The Dark Night of the Soul,* Bk. I, chap. 1.
[22] *La Contemplation* (1912), pp. 61–71.

although certain perfect souls have it only in an imperfect manner and for short periods of time.[23]

St. Teresa expresses the same opinion, when she says: "His mercy is so great that He hinders no one from drinking of the fountain of life [infused contemplation]. . . . Indeed, He calls us loudly and publicly to do so. He is so good that He will not force us to drink of it." [24] The saint always teaches her daughters that they must direct all their efforts toward preparing themselves to receive this precious grace, even though certain souls, in spite of their good will, do not experience its joys in this life. Contemplation may, in fact, be arid for a long time, during which one may be a contemplative without knowing it.[25] Pius X, in his letter (March 7, 1914) on the

[23] St. John of the Cross (*The Dark Night of the Soul*, Bk. I, chap. 9) certainly says: "Let it be well understood that God does not lead to perfect contemplation all who give themselves resolutely to the interior life. Why is that? God alone knows. Whence it comes that there are souls from whom God never completely withdraws the power to consider and reason except for a time." The words "God alone knows," show that that is not the fundamental law of spiritual progress; quite the contrary. These words are an allusion to predestination, which St. John of the Cross understands as St. Thomas does, for he says, in *The Ascent of Mount Carmel*, Bk. II, chap. 5: "It is true that souls, whatever their capacity may be, may have attained union, but all do not possess it in the same degree. God disposes freely of this degree of union, as He disposes freely of the degree of the beatific vision." This is what St. Thomas says in Ia, q.23, a.5. The predestination of one soul rather than another does not directly concern the question proposed in this article: Is the mystical union in this life the summit of the normal development of the sanctifying grace of the virtues and of the gifts? The proof of this lies in the fact that, in all the just, grace is essentially ordained to glory, and yet all are not predestined to glory; some, in fact, lose grace and die in the state of mortal sin. "Many are called, but few are chosen."

[24] *The Way of Perfection*, chap. 20.

[25] Certain restrictions, expressed by St. Teresa in the *Way of Perfection* (chap. 17) and in *The Interior Castle* (fifth mansion, chap. 3), when they are compared with the general principle which she formulates and develops in *The Way of Perfection* (chaps. 18, 20, 25, 29), must be understood in this way. Consult the harmonizing of the different texts of St. Teresa by Father Arintero, O.P., *Evolución mística*, p. 639 note 2, and *Cuestiones místicas*, pp. 305 ff., as well as the excellent work of Father Garate, *Razón y Fe*, July, 1908, p. 325. It is certain that the joys of the mystical union are not necessary to perfection, and that supernatural contemplation is often very arid and painful. In *The Interior Castle* (fifth mansion, chap. 1), St. Teresa, speaking of the religious of her monasteries, says: "There are very few who do not enter this fifth man-

teaching of St. Teresa, says that the degrees of prayer enumerated by the saint are so many steps up toward the summit of Christian perfection: "Docet enim gradus orationis quot numerantur, veluti totidem superiores in christiana perfectione ascensus esse."

Moreover, according to several contemporary theologians, whose number is growing daily and who are eager to preserve the traditional teaching as it is formulated in the great classics of mystical theology, it is laudable for every interior soul to desire the grace of mystical contemplation and to prepare for it with the help of God by increasing fidelity to His holy inspirations.[26]

According to these theologians, especially Father Arintero, O.P., the mystical life is characterized by the predominance of the gifts of the Holy Ghost.[27] Ascetical theology, they say, treats of the Christian life of beginners, and of those who ad-

---

sion. As there are some who enter more and some less, I say the majority enter. Certain graces which are found therein, are, I believe, the portion of the few; but if the others merely reach the door, even that is an immense mercy on the part of God, for 'Many are called, but few are chosen.' "

[26] St. John of the Cross, *The Ascent of Mount Carmel*, Prologue: "In order to attain the divine light and the perfect union of the love of God, I speak of what can be realized in this life, the soul must pass through the dark night. Without a doubt, to explain this night and to make it understood, one should have deeper learning and greater experience than mine. . . . I hope that the Lord will help me to express useful truths, in order that I may in this way assist so many souls who are in urgent need of help. After the first steps in the path of virtue, when the Lord desires to make these souls enter the dark night, to lead them to the divine union, there are some who do not go any farther. Sometimes the desire to do so is lacking, or they are not willing to be led therein; sometimes it is because of ignorance, or because they seek in vain a guide capable of leading them to the summit. It is truly heartrending to see how many souls, favored by the Lord with gifts and exceptional graces (at times they would need only a little courage to attain high perfection), are content with inferior relations with God." The aim of this entire prologue is to correct many errors in the matter of direction. We know that, in the judgment of St. John of the Cross, the dark night is a period of mystical contemplation. In this same prologue he says so: "Led by God to the heights of obscure contemplation and of aridity, it will seem to the soul that it is going astray."

[27] These gifts are specifically distinct from the infused virtues (Ia IIae, q.68, a.1).

vance with the help of grace in the exercise of the Christian virtues, the mode of which remains a human mode adapted to that of our faculties. On the other hand, mystical theology treats especially of the unitive life of the perfect, in which there is clearly manifest the divine mode of the gifts of the Holy Ghost, in the exercise of which the soul is more passive than active, and in which it obtains a "quasi-experimental" knowledge of God present in it, as St. Thomas explains.[28] "These gifts," the great doctor tells us, "exist in all souls in the state of grace"; but normally they do not predominate, nor do they act in a manner both frequent and manifest except in very humble, mortified souls that are habitually docile to the Holy Ghost. Some souls excel in the gifts relating to the active life, such as the gift of fortitude; others in those of the contemplative life, as understanding and wisdom. The latter especially enter the "passive ways," because they no longer direct themselves, but are habitually directed immediately by God. He gives to their acts that mode which He alone can communicate to them, as, for example, when a master directs his pupil by holding his hand. These acts are thus doubly supernatural (reduplicative, as the Scholastics say): by their essence, as acts of the Christian virtues of the ascetical life; and by this superior mode, which surpasses the simple exercise of the Christian virtues aided by actual grace. This is what makes it possible for St. Teresa to speak of "supernatural prayer" when the passive ways begin.[29] But this divine mode of the supernatural acts, which spring immediately from the inspirations of the Holy Ghost, is not essentially extraordinary, like a miracle, a vision, a prophecy, but something eminent and ordinary in the perfect, who live habitually recollected

[28] See Ia IIae, q.68, and Bk. I of the *Sentences*, d.14, q.2, a.2 ad 3um.

[29] On this point, consult the following Dominican authors: Suso, *Mystical Works;* Tauler, *Sermons;* Piny, *L'abandon à la volonté de Dieu.* The following Jesuit authors should be read: Father Lallemant, *La doctrine spirituelle;* Father Grou, *Maximes spirituelles* (2d maxim); Father de Caussade, *L'abandon à la Providence.* See also St. John of the Cross, *The Dark Night of the Soul,* Part I.

in adoration of the mystery of the Blessed Trinity present in them.[30]

Such, in fact, is the principal subject treated by all the great mystical theologians from Dionysius to Tauler and St. John of the Cross, who often uses the single word "faith" to indicate this virtue and the gift of wisdom in a superior degree.

These masters discuss secondarily the so-called exterior phenomena, which accompany certain degrees of the mystical union—for example, ecstasy, which disappears with the transforming union. They always make a sharp distinction between this very intimate union with God, which is the goal of their desires and of their entire life, and the extraordinary graces of inferior order, such as visions, or the prophetic knowledge of the future; graces which, in their opinion, we ought not to desire.

From this point of view, interpreters of St. John of the Cross, such as Father Lamballe and Father Arintero, O.P.,[31] consider that the transforming union or spiritual marriage is in this life the summit of the normal development of the life of grace in souls which are entirely faithful to the Holy Ghost, especially in those consecrated to God and called to the contemplative life. Some theologians have thought that this normal goal of spiritual progress does not pass beyond the prayer of quiet, after which the extraordinary, properly so called, would begin with union and ecstasy.[32] According to

[30] A miraculous, sensible effect, such as life restored to a dead body, is not supernatural in its essence, but only in the mode of its production; while the exercise of the gifts of the Holy Ghost is supernatural both in its essence and in its mode, *quoad substantiam et quoad modum.*

[31] Lamballe, *La Contemplation*, p. 195. Arintero, *Evolución mística*, pp. 460–80; *Cuestiones místicas*, pp. 60, 571 note: "Explanation of the graces necessary for the transforming union." Sauvé seems favorably inclined to this thesis in *États mystiques*, pp. 85, 90–96, 100–05, 139–41, 162.

[32] Saudreau, in the first editions of his books, did not clearly affirm that the transforming union is the summit of the normal development of the life of grace on earth. It even seemed to us that, in his opinion, this summit did not reach beyond the prayer of quiet, a thesis which we could not admit. It is clear, from what he says in the second edition of *L'état mystique* (pp. 51, 192) and in the third edition of the *Vie d'union à Dieu* (p. 259), that we agree

what St. Teresa says of souls which do not progress beyond the prayer of quiet, it seems clear, however, that they failed in fidelity to the Holy Ghost, and that normally they should have arrived at a closer union with God, which she calls a "higher degree of perfection." [33] St. John of the Cross teaches the same doctrine.[34]

It may well be that ecstasy does not (at least necessarily) imply anything extraordinary in the real sense of the word. It seems often to come from the weakness of the organism which swoons under the divine action. It may be only the reaction of a profound interior grace, which absorbs all the attention and all the strength of the soul in God, who is intimately present to the soul and who makes Himself felt by it. From this point of view, continuity would exist between all the degrees of the mystical union, from the prayer of quiet to the transforming union, in which the soul no longer experiences "the weakness of ecstasy," to use the expression of St. Hildegarde.

---

completely. In this last reference he says clearly: "With these ordinary supernatural prayers, the soul may attain even the transforming union, the summit of the spiritual life, without ever having had an ecstasy or a vision."

[33] St. Teresa, *Life*, chap. 15: "Many are the souls who attain to this state (the prayer of quiet), and few are they who go farther." In *The Interior Castle*, fourth mansion, chap. 3, and fifth mansion, chap. 1, with regard to entrance into the fifth mansion (superior to the prayer of quiet), she says: "Even though all of us . . . are called to contemplation . . . there are few who prepare themselves so that the Lord may reveal to them this precious pearl of which we are speaking. For although in what concerns the exterior there is nothing reprehensible in our conduct, this does not suffice to reach so high a degree of perfection. How necessary it is to banish all negligence."

[34] Particularly when he describes (*The Dark Night of the Soul*, Bk. II, chaps. 18–20) the ten degrees of charity enumerated by St. Bernard, it is evident he believes that the inferior degrees should normally lead to the higher degrees, and to the highest of all. Besides, he adds that the progress of contemplation is proportionate to that of charity. The entire work of St. John of the Cross seems to manifest clearly the continuity of the degrees of the mystical union up to the transforming union. Some writers, it is true, have thought that St. John of the Cross writes only for a few rare contemplatives. He himself says, however, at the end of the Prologue of *The Ascent of Mount Carmel*, that he proposes "a solid and substantial doctrine which is addressed to all, on condition that they decide to pass through nudity of the spirit."

This is the opinion of Father Lamballe, of Father Arintero, O.P., and of several other contemporary theologians whom we have consulted. They hold, moreover, that simplified affective prayer, which precedes essentially mystical or passive prayer, is normally a disposition to receive the latter. Thus continuity would exist between the ascetical and the mystical life; the first would be characterized by the human mode of the Christian virtues, the second by the divine mode of the gifts of the Holy Ghost, intervening no longer in a latent or transitory way, but in a manner both manifest and frequent. Before the mystical or passive state, in a period of transition (the prayer of simplicity described by Bossuet) there would be transient mystical acts, which by their nature would dispose the soul for the true life of union. This would be the adult or perfect age of the spiritual life, or the life of grace aware of itself.

If the above is true—as we shall see, the authors cited adduce weighty reasons for their view—the soul which as yet possesses nothing of the mystical life has not passed beyond infancy or the adolescence of spiritual life. Such a soul should recall St. Paul's words: "Brethren, do not become children in sense: but in malice be children, and in sense be perfect." [35] This soul has not reached spiritual maturity, the perfect age attainable in this life. It may have great learning even in theology, may know how to live, may possess prudence, faith, charity, zeal, enthusiasm, and a great apostolic activity; but, in spite of its solid Christian virtues and zeal, it is not sufficiently spiritualized. Its manner of living remains too human, too exterior, and still too dependent on temperament. It does not give evidence of the entirely supernatural, divine mode of thinking, of loving God, and of acting, which characterizes those who are truly dead to themselves and perfectly docile to the Holy Ghost. Ordinarily the latter alone have, in all circumstances

[35] See I Cor. 14: 20.

whether agreeable or painful, "the mind of Christ," which enables them to judge soundly of spiritual things and to reconcile habitually in their lives virtues apparently contradictory in nature: the simplicity of the dove and the prudence of the serpent; heroic fortitude and gentle sweetness; humility of heart and magnanimity; a faith absolutely unyielding when principles are at stake and a great mercy for the misguided; an intense interior life, continual recollection, and a fruitful apostolate.

This last conception of the connection between ascetical and mystical theology deserves consideration. Those who have often read and meditated on the great masters of traditional mystical theology will be inclined to acquiesce, we believe, in this interpretation, when they recall the following principles, which are the certain expression of the teaching of St. Thomas.

1) Christian perfection consists in union with God, which supposes in us the full development of charity, of the other virtues, and of the gifts of the Holy Ghost, which supply for the imperfection of these virtues and are in us the immediate principle of supernatural contemplation.

2) The three theological virtues are supernatural in their essence (*quoad substantiam*) because of their formal motive and their proper object, both of which are unattainable by reason alone or even by the highest natural knowledge of the angels. Several theologians, following the inferior teaching of nominalism, have thought, on the contrary, that acts of faith and of the other Christian virtues are essentially natural acts, clothed with a supernatural modality (supernatural in manner only, not by reason of their formal object). They would thus more closely resemble a supernaturalized natural affection than an affection supernatural in its essence and by its formal motive. An immense difference exists between these two conceptions of faith and of the other theological virtues.

Only the former is true,[36] and shows clearly why faith in the mystery of the Blessed Trinity is infinitely superior to the natural intuitions of genius, and superior in general to graces *gratis datae,* even, for example, to the supernatural prevision of a future event, such as the end of a plague.[37]

3) The gifts of the Holy Ghost are doubly supernatural, not only in their essence (as the theological virtues and the other infused virtues), but in their mode of action. By them the soul no longer directs itself with the assistance of grace, but is directed and moved immediately by divine inspiration; and when, by perfect fidelity to the Holy Ghost, it lives habitually under the régime of the gifts, it is in a passive state.

4) These gifts, rendering us docile to the breath of God, grow with charity like the infused virtues. Now, charity ought always to increase in this life by our merits and by holy communion. Whoever does not advance, falls back, because, according to the observation of St. Augustine and of St. Thomas,[38] the first precept has no limit and only the saints fulfil it perfectly. "Thou shalt love the Lord thy God with thy whole heart, and with thy whole soul, and with all thy strength, and with all thy mind." [39]

5) If we consider, not what actually is, but rather what ought to be, not the weakness of our nature and the fickleness of our free will, but rather the very essence of the grace received at baptism and of charity, we must admit that normally, or according to its fundamental law, grace ought never to be lost (although many Christians fall into mortal sin). Similarly

---

[36] We have proved this at length elsewhere: *De revelatione,* I, 202–17, 458–515. Cf. St. Thomas, IIa IIae, q.5, a.1: "In the object of faith, there is something formal, as it were, namely, the First Truth surpassing all the natural knowledge of a creature, and something material, namely, the thing to which we assent while adhering to the First Truth."

[37] "Whether gratuitous grace is nobler than sanctifying grace" (Ia IIae, q.111, a.5).

[38] *Summa,* IIa IIae, q.184, a.3.

[39] Luke 10: 27.

this life of grace, the germ of glory, the beginning of eternal life, should normally develop to such an extent that the fire of charity would purify us of all stains before death and permit us to enter heaven without passing through purgatory. Through their own fault souls are detained in purgatory, where they no longer have any opportunity to merit. To see God face to face immediately after death would be in the radical order; that is why the souls in purgatory suffer so greatly at being deprived of this vision. Therefore, according to the fundamental law of the life of grace, the painful purifications that cleanse the soul of its impurities should be meritorious and should precede death, as they do in the saints; they should not follow death. Since all this is true, why should not the mystical union, accompanied by these passive purifications, be the normal flowering of the life of grace, although few souls actually reach it, just as few preserve baptismal innocence? If the mystical union, as a matter of fact, is not ordinary, why should it not at least be expected at the end of a very generous interior life? The extraordinary would then still consist in the bestowal of these eminent graces from infancy on, as has happened in the lives of several saints.

Everyone agrees that practically two excesses must be avoided in the direction of souls: urging souls to leave the ascetical way too soon or too late. If they leave too soon, they are exposed to the danger of falling into the idleness of quietism or a practical semi-quietism; if too late, they are in danger of abandoning prayer because they no longer find any profit in discursive meditation, where the director wishes to keep them, or in danger of not understanding anything about the obscure, but much more spiritual, way along which the Lord is beginning to lead them. On this point St. John of the Cross, in *The Ascent of Mount Carmel* [40] and in *The Dark Night,* has

40 Bk. II, chaps. 12, 13.

left us valuable teaching. Among recent works on this subject, one of the soundest is *Les voies de l'oraison mentale,* by Dom Vital Lehodey.[41]

What does experience teach? Does it not say that the actual condition and the normal ideal (that which should be expected) finally harmonize, at least at the end of a holy life? All the canonized saints seem to have had the mystical union often, except some martyrs who may have had it only at the moment of their torture.[42] St. Teresa declares that in her monasteries are many souls that reach the essentially mystical prayer of quiet; that some, more advanced, habitually enjoy the prayer of union; and that a number of others enjoy it at intervals.[43]

Especially in contemplative religious orders, at times souls are found that have certainly passed beyond discursive meditation or the prayer of simplicity. These souls experience great distress when they are obliged to cease their thanksgiving after holy communion; they are wholly caught up by God, as it were absorbed in Him, and live by the mysteries of the Blessed Trinity, the incarnation, and the redemption, in an incomparably deeper manner than the most learned theologian, if the latter is not truly a man of prayer. These lives, although acquainted with rather uncommon interior joys and sufferings, are not really extraordinary in the true sense of this word. They alone, on the contrary, are entirely in order. They even avoid the extraordinary as much as possible, according to the advice of St. John of the Cross,[44] which is their daily sustenance. This great doctor directs them more and more toward

---

[41] Fifth ed., pp. 227–36, 409.

[42] Father Poulain, S.J., concedes this: "Almost all canonized saints have had the mystical union, and as a rule abundantly" (*Les grâces d'oraison,* 9th ed., p. 554). Father Poulain also recognizes the existence of a period of transition between the ascetical way and the mystical, a period which denotes a certain continuity between the two. Cf. *Les grâces d'oraison,* pp. 13, 122.

[43] *Life,* chap. 15; *Foundations,* chap. 4; *The Interior Castle,* fifth mansion, chap. 1.

[44] *The Ascent of Mount Carmel,* Bk. II, chaps. 10, 19, 20, 25.

the Blessed Trinity dwelling in us; they experience great joy in reading the beautiful pages of St. Augustine and St. Thomas on this mystery; and they express themselves even on the Fatherhood of God, on the infinite value of the merits of Christ, on the fruit of a fervent communion, with a spontaneity and freshness quite different from that produced by scholarly learning obtained from books. To the end that we may live in this way, these supernatural mysteries have been revealed to us. Such is Christian life in its full development, the profound reign of God in our hearts.

Grace superabounds in these souls after they have passed through the painful purifications, which are the veritable dark night. They have, so to speak, caught a glimpse of the most pure, holy, and fathomless abyss of God. They overflow with love and, in their great desire to love God, they long to do so immeasurably, with the heart of the Word made flesh. The Spirit of love has penetrated them and, in trial as in joy, they rest in the charity of the heavenly Father like a child in the arms of its mother. They see the fulfilment of Christ's prayer: "That they all may be one, as Thou, Father, in Me, and I in Thee." [45] This is the unitive life, but without anything extraordinary, in the sense of the miraculous. And this is truly the mystical, contemplative life. This is also the apostolic life; in their profound faith in the superabundance of the redemption, these souls make an offering of themselves that the chalice may overflow on sinners. Moreover, they earnestly desire to leave this land of exile for heaven. This is the perfection described by St. Thomas when, after speaking of those who start and of those who advance in the spiritual life, he says of the perfect: "They tend principally to unite themselves with God, to enjoy Him, and they desire to die in order to be with Christ." [46]

---

[45] John 27: 21.

[46] "Man's third pursuit is to aim chiefly at union with and enjoyment of God: this belongs to the perfect who desire to be dissolved and to be with Christ" (IIa IIae, q.24, a.9).

Therefore we find not only a continuity between ascetical and mystical theology, but also a certain compenetration. They are not two distinct divisions of theology, but two parts or two aspects of the same branch, which shows us spiritual life in its infancy, adolescence, and maturity. Ascetical and mystical theology or, more simply, spiritual doctrine, is one. It must begin by setting before us the end attainable in this life, that is, spiritual perfection toward which spiritual progress should tend. It ought to show this perfection in all its elevation and grandeur, according to the testimony of the Gospel and of the saints. Then it should point out the means to this end: the struggle against sin, the practice of the virtues, perfect docility to the Holy Ghost. But the end proposed, such as we find it, for example, in the eight beatitudes when their full meaning is accepted, reaches beyond the domain of simple asceticism.[47] Ascetical life, however, does not cease when the soul enters the mystical union. The practice of the virtues becomes, on the contrary, much more perfect, as is shown by the great austerities of the saints, their patience, and their zeal. Even to the end the soul must remember our Lord's words: "If anyone will come after Me, let him deny himself, and take up his cross daily."[48]

This brings us back to the statement, based on the teaching of St. Thomas, which we made at the beginning of this article: Asceticism prepares the soul for the mystical union, which then renders the exercise of the virtues and our apostolate much more supernatural and fruitful. The practice of the virtues prepares for contemplation and is then directed by it.

When ascetical and mystical theology are separated from each other, the ascetical lacks vitality, depth, and elevation; the mystical loses its importance, its gravity, and its depth, and

[47] St. Thomas, *In Matthaeum* (5: 2), speaking of the eight beatitudes, says: "These merits are either acts of the gifts or acts of the virtues according as they are perfected by the gifts"; "in a superhuman manner," as he said a few lines previously in the same passage.

[48] Luke 9: 23.

seems to be solely a luxury in the spirituality of some privileged souls.

Such seems to us the conception of ascetical and mystical theology, or of the spiritual doctrine, which conforms most closely to traditional teaching. This is the conception that we will attempt to formulate in this work.

## ARTICLE III

### *Meaning of the Terms of the Problem*

The question of vocabulary presents one of the main difficulties encountered by those who study mystical problems. Many controversies arise on account of the lack of a previous agreement as to the meaning of the words used. For instance, in the question as to whether the mystical life is the normal crown of the interior life, the word "mystical" is understood by some in so broad a sense that the mystical life seems almost identified with a barely fervent Christian life, or with mere perseverance in the state of grace. Other authors use the word "mystical" in so limited a sense that there seems to be no mystical life without ecstasy, visions, and prophetic revelations. Likewise the word "contemplation" has for some a very broad sense, while for others it can be used only with the exact meaning of infused and passive contemplation. The same thing is true of the word "normal." If used by speculative theologians, it is applicable only to a general and superior law of the life of grace, a law which in very diverse ways applies sooner or later, perfectly or imperfectly, to the development of generous souls that are called to the contemplative or even to the active life. And this law exacts many conditions that may be lacking; it will have difficulty in functioning in the person who receives the grace, for instance, in an unfavorable environment, in too absorbing a life of study, or where proper direction is lacking, or in the case of a person who has an ungrateful temperament and certain imperfections, even though they are involuntary. Despite all these obstacles, this law governs the growth of the divine seed, a fact which the theologian considers and which experience proves. If, on the contrary, the word "normal" is used by a non-mystical director, seeing hardly anything but the particular phenomena and those from without, he gives the term "normal" a more concrete and material meaning, which seems to be contrary to fact when exceptions are noted. These exceptions he does not scrutinize from within that he may ascertain whether they proceed from grace itself or from the defects of the person receiving the grace, from the nature of the seed itself or from the effects of the barren soil which requires extraordinary labor for its transformation.

The same difficulty arises if we express the problem by asking whether all interior souls are called to the mystical life. Some who reply in the negative use the word "called" almost in the sense of "raised," "led," "predestined," or "chosen"; and then it is clear that all interior souls are not called to the mystical life. This view ignores the statement of Scripture, "Many are called, but few are chosen." These two words, "called" and "chosen," differ greatly. On the other hand, some authors admit the general call of souls to the mystical life, but seem to forget the common teaching about the special signs of the individual call, signs that are not present in every pious soul. They are three in number and are enumerated by St. John of the Cross, and before him by Tauler. We will refer to them later on.[1] The many consequent problems require a statement of the exact meaning of the word "call," which may designate a remote or an immediate call. The same difficulty occurs in connection with the word "merit" in the question: Can a soul merit mystical contemplation?

We must try to establish precise meanings for the terms we are using. Although we would meet with difficulties in com-

---

[1] Cf. *infra*, pp. 338 f.

ing to an immediate agreement as to the real definitions, which express the basis of things and are the fruit of long research, yet we ought at least to have an understanding about nominal definitions, about the meaning of the principal terms of mystical theology in use today. Since mystical terminology was given precision by St. Teresa, St. John of the Cross, and St. Francis de Sales, we should take into account this established precision which rests on their authority and is a real progress. If, for example, since the days of these great masters, the expression "essentially mystical prayer" means manifestly passive prayer, we ought henceforth to use the expression only with this precise meaning, which includes many degrees of prayer.

With a view to fixing the vocabulary, we wish to propose some definitions, at least nominal ones,[2] which are quite generally accepted by mystical theologians who follow simultaneously the doctrine of St. Thomas and that of St. John of the Cross, of St. Teresa, and of St. Francis de Sales.[3] In the course of this work, we will show the basic soundness of these definitions, or their real value.

St. Thomas defines contemplation as a simple intellectual view of the truth, superior to reasoning and accompanied by admiration.[4] It may be purely natural, as, for example, in an artist, a scholar, or a philosopher. Christian contemplation dwells on revealed truths and presupposes faith. Several theologians admit the existence of an acquired contemplation which follows upon meditation. They generally define this acquired contemplation as the loving knowledge of God which is the fruit of our personal activity aided by grace. On the contrary, infused contemplation, that which the mystics speak

---

[2] A nominal definition contains confusedly the real definition, and it may be more or less precise according as it is taken, for example, from an ordinary vocabulary or from a philosophcial or theological dictionary.

[3] We mean especially the Carmelites Philip of the Blessed Trinity, Anthony of the Holy Ghost, and Joseph of the Holy Ghost, the Dominican Vallgornera, several Jesuit theologians, some Franciscans, and some members of other orders.

[4] *Summa*, IIa IIae, q.180, a.1, 6.

of, is a loving knowledge of God, which is not the fruit of human activity aided by grace, but of a special inspiration of the Holy Ghost; so that it is not producible at will, as is an act of faith.[5]

In the supernatural life, we understand by the word "ordinary" every grace, every act, every state, which is in the normal way of sanctity; all that is morally necessary in the majority of cases for attaining sanctity. And by "sanctity" we must, at the very least, understand that which is generally required to enter heaven immediately after death, because a soul suffers in purgatory only through its own fault. The "ordinary" thus defined comprises eminent graces that may be called extraordinary in point of fact because they are rather uncommon, but that are ordinary according to the normal law if they are truly necessary for the attainment of sanctity, for the full perfection of Christian life, or for the complete purity of soul which merits immediate entrance into heaven.

Every favor, on the contrary, which is out of the normal way of sanctity and which is not at all necessary for its attainment, is extraordinary. We classify as such especially the graces called *gratis datae*, as miracles, prophecies, visions, and other phenomena of the same kind.[6]

As regards the word "call" or "vocation," we will attempt to distinguish in this work the different meanings it may have, according as it concerns a general and remote call of all just souls to mystical contemplation or, on the contrary, an individual and proximate call. As we shall see, this last may be merely sufficient and remain sterile; or it may be efficacious. In the latter case it may be an efficacious call either to lower degrees, or to higher degrees, of the mystical life.

In all these questions we must consider the full, normal development of the life of grace as such, and then see what it is in more or less well disposed souls which have received this

---

[5] Cf. *infra*, pp. 221–35.
[6] Cf. *infra*, pp. 235–38.

germ of eternal life. To do this, we need to recall first of all the traditional doctrine of grace, such as it has been conceived, following St. Paul and St. Augustine, by the prince of theologians, St. Thomas Aquinas, and by the great Catholic mystics.

# CHAPTER III

## MYSTICAL THEOLOGY AND THE FUNDAMENTAL DOCTRINES OF ST. THOMAS

### ARTICLE I

### *Natural Intellectual Life and Supernatural Life*

SEVERAL authors, struck by the difference which they find between the writings of the great mystical theologians (such as Dionysius, Richard of St. Victor, St. Bonaventure, Tauler, St. John of the Cross) and the writings of St. Thomas Aquinas, are surprised that we should expect to find in St. Thomas' writings the principles of mystical theology. Some even consider St. Thomas, not a great theologian who from a supernatural point of view used Aristotle for the defense and explanation of the divine truths of faith, but rather a philosopher of genius who gave us an interpretation of the Gospel, a Christian Aristotle, as later on Malebranche was a Christian Plato.

Anyone who accepts this view must lack an intimate knowledge of the writings of St. Thomas, especially his treatises on the Trinity, the incarnation, the Holy Eucharist, grace, the theological virtues, and the gifts of the Holy Ghost. Certainly such a person never read St. Thomas' commentaries on St. Paul, St. John, the Psalms, and the Canticle of Canticles. He must be ignorant of St. Thomas' short treatises on piety, his prayers, his office of the Blessed Sacrament; and he must be unacquainted with the saint's life, his nights spent before the tabernacle, his ecstasies, the eminent gift of contemplation which made him refer to his *Summa* as being only straw in comparison with what he beheld.

In this article we wish to show that this judgment of the great doctor springs from an entirely material manner of reading his works. We have a tendency to give a materialistic interpretation to everything—doctrine, piety, rules of conduct, action. This is the inclination of our fallen and wounded nature unless it is profoundly regenerated and completely vivified by grace which heals and elevates, and unless we are free from domination by our temperament; or if, despite the state of grace, we preserve a host of purely natural judgments, quite unconformable to the spirit of faith.

Influenced by these dispositions, we are unintentionally prone to interpret the loftiest doctrines materialistically; that is, we are inclined to note only their material elements which adapt themselves better to our tastes, and to lose sight of the spirit which determines their nature and is the soul of the doctrinal body. Once more St. Paul's expression is verified: "For the letter killeth, but the spirit quickeneth." [1] Following this way, under pretext of reliance on what is tangible, mechanically exact, and incontestably certain even for the incredulous, we would end by explaining the higher by the lower, by reducing the first to the second, which is the very essence of materialism in all its forms. We would be inclined to explain the soul by the body, much more than the body by the soul; in the same way, to explain the life of grace by nature, theological doctrines by the philosophical elements which they have assimilated, the life of religious orders by the social conditions in which they had their origin, without thinking sufficiently of the incessant but invisible work of God, who alone can raise up great doctors and saints. From this point of view, we would rapidly dwarf everything and, instead of living supernaturally according to the true sense of this word, we might, despite certain appearances, flounder about in what is mediocre and mean.

This disposition to explain the higher by the lower is found

[1] See II Cor. 3: 6.

in varying degrees, from the gross materialism which explains spirit by matter up to that which places a materialistic interpretation on spiritual philosophy, theology, exegesis, the history of the Church, asceticism, and the liturgy, the letter of which is kept, and not the spirit.

Even with a true desire to learn, we may read St. Thomas from this point of view. In his theological doctrine numerous material or philosophical elements are found, which he intends to subordinate to the idea of God, the Author of grace. If we unduly emphasize these lower elements, which are within the reach of reason, instead of rising to the summit of the synthesis, we will find a real opposition between this doctrine and that of the great mystical theologians, who have treated especially of union with God. The trees will prevent our seeing the forest. Absorbed in the details at the base of the structure, we shall fail to see the keystone of the arch. At least we shall be considering only from below the supernatural principle of this masterpiece of the mind; seeing it only by its reflection on the lower realities which it regulates, instead of judging these matters from above, as ought to be done by the "higher reason," so greatly prized by St. Augustine, and by theological wisdom, not to speak of the gift of wisdom, which is even more elevated. Thus the reading of St. Thomas' *Summa* and commenting on it may be only slightly supernatural and even anti-mystical. This manner of reading it directs the mind away from the view of the great commentators (Capreolus, Cajetan, Bannes, John of St. Thomas, the Carmelites of Salamanca), all of them inferior to the master. But they understood him better than we do, and lead us after him toward the same heights.

A delicate instrument of precision is easily injured so that it is no longer accurate; likewise the doctrine of St. Thomas is easily distorted. This results if we misplace the emphasis on what is secondary and material, thus explaining in a banal manner and without due proportion what is formal and principal in it. By so doing, we fail to see the glowing summits that should illumine all the rest.

We note here the chief confusions that would render this doctrine essentially anti-mystical. They have been made especially by nominalist theologians, who finally perceived nothing but words in the loftiest spiritual realities, when they did not see as materially evident that these realities had been revealed by God.[2] Nominalist theology is a considerable diminution of the science of God. We point out these confusions to show that the teaching of St. Thomas is, on the contrary, the same as that which St. John of the Cross and his disciples developed. We make this point evident by insisting on what constitutes the grandeur of his teaching, and by manifesting the supernatural wealth it contains. For one who has read the Salamanca theologians, evidently the Carmelite doctrine and that of the Angelic Doctor agree throughout, particularly with regard to the loftiest questions in the treatise on grace.

Let us consider briefly, in the Thomistic synthesis, the fundamental doctrines which are most closely allied to the spiritual life; especially those bearing on our natural, intellectual knowledge; then those bearing on the supernatural life, on the infused virtues, on the gifts of the Holy Ghost, on the efficacy of grace, and lastly on the very nature of God.

---

[2] These confusions have also been made, in a certain measure, by theologians who have undergone the sad influence of nominalism, which is a tendency that must end in seeing only words in everything which exceeds the immediate object of experience, sensible phenomena. For the nominalist there is no longer any human nature essentially distinguished from grace, but only an aggregation of human individuals. With greater reason, according to them, spiritual realities are naturally unknowable. For example, we cannot be certain of the spirituality and immortality of the soul unless God reveals them to us, and our intelligence cannot comprehend revealed formulas, because of the insufficiency of its ideas. This doctrine leads finally to a negation of theology and philosophy, to actual positivism. Occasionally, as a reaction, it has led certain souls to a mysticism, but a mysticism without doctrinal foundation, often composed of sentimentality proceeding from the powerlessness of diminished reason and from the necessity of finding something to cling to, rather than from the idea of the infinite grandeur of God. One can be a nominalist by tendency without knowing it; indeed, this happens frequently.

In the Thomistic synthesis our intellectual knowledge in the natural order is based on the first principles of reason: the principle of contradiction—no being, created or uncreated, can at the same time and under the same aspect be and not be; the principle of causality—all that has potential non-existence, whether spirit or matter, has a cause; the principle of finality—every agent, whether material or spiritual, acts for an end; the first principle of morality—one must do good and avoid evil. St. Thomas declares that the intellectual knowledge of these primordial truths springs in a certain way from the senses, because our intelligence abstracts its ideas from sensible things. Understanding this doctrine materially, some people have thought that the intellectual certitude of the first principles resolves itself essentially or formally into sensation, and that it relies on sensation as on its formal motive.[3] This point of view would reduce the higher to the lower, intelligence to sense; it would forget that rational principles are absolutely universal and necessary and that they reach even the loftiest realities, God Himself, whereas sensation reaches only sensible, singular, and contingent objects. Were this done, the absolute universality and necessity of rational first truths would no longer be explainable; reason would remain the prisoner of phenomena, like the senses of an animal, and our liberty, which follows from our intelligence, would disappear. We would not be able to resist the attraction of sensible goods, because we would not dominate them. Our nature, like that of animals, would be incapable of receiving grace and of being raised to the vision of God.

According to St. Thomas, on the other hand, intellectual

[3] Sensation has two elements: one material, the action of the nervous system carrying a stimulus from an exterior object to the brain, an action that follows laws governing similar actions in the lower order of nature; and one formal and specific, the rôle of which is to produce a representation of what disturbs the sense. It is almost always in this latter sense that St. Thomas uses the word "sensation." To restrict his use of the term to the material element is to materialize his doctrine still further. On the real sense of sentient being, cf. St. Thomas, Ia, q.14, a.1; q.78, a.3

certitude of rational first principles resolves itself only materially into the prerequisite sensation; [4] it resolves itself formally into purely intellectual evidence of the absolute truth of its principles, which appear as the fundamental laws not only of phenomena but of being or of all intelligible reality, whether corporal or spiritual. This evidence presupposes in us a constantly increasing intellectual light of an order infinitely superior to sensation or to the most subtle imagination; an intellectual light which is a distant image of the divine light and which can illumine nothing without the constant concurrence of God, Sun of spirits, Master of intelligences. [5] Although St. Thomas here treats of subjects in the natural order, he already speaks almost as a mystic: "As any human doctrine exteriorly proposed instructs us because of the intellectual light which we have received from God, it follows that God alone teaches us interiorly and as principal Cause." [6]

Malebranche and the ontologists exaggerated these words of St. Thomas and seemed to have a still higher idea of our natural intelligence by claiming that our intelligence sees first principles in God Himself. The apparent elevation of this Christian Platonism is not, however, that of true mystical theology because it tends to confound the natural order and that of grace, instead of maintaining the absolute superiority of the latter.

According to the ontologists, our intellect is capable of knowing being, because it is capable of knowing God; accord-

[4] "It cannot be said that sensible knowledge is the total and perfect cause of intellectual knowledge, but rather that it is in a way the material cause" (Ia, q.84, a.6).

[5] "For the intellectual light itself which is in us, is nothing else than a participated likeness of the uncreated light, in which are contained the eternal types" (Ia, q.84, a.5). "Therefore there must needs be some higher intellect, by which the soul is helped to understand" (Ia, q.79, a.4). Cf. Ia, q.105, a.3. Some Scholastics seem to consider in this intellectual light only its abstractive function and not its illuminating function which continues after the abstraction. Cf. De veritate, q.10, a.6.

[6] De veritate, q.11, a.1.

ing to St. Thomas, our intellect is capable of knowing God by grace, because it is first of all capable of knowing being by nature.[7] This teaching places it infinitely above the senses.

In respect to the supernatural life, we know the principle of St. Thomas: "Grace perfects nature and does not destroy it." [8] A great spirit of faith is necessary, however, if we are always to interpret this principle correctly without inclining practically toward naturalism. Some persons will understand this principle materially, or will be more attentive to nature which must be perfected than to grace which should produce this transformation in us. Furthermore, considering nature as it actually is since original sin, they will not sufficiently distinguish in nature what is essential and good, what ought to be perfected, from what ought to be mortified, egoism under all its forms gross or subtle. By failing to make this distinction, they find a real opposition between the doctrine of St. Thomas thus materialistically interpreted and the famous chapter of the *Imitation* (Bk. III, chap. 54), "On the Divers Movements of Nature and Grace." They forget what the holy doctor teaches about the wounds consequent upon original sin which remain in the baptized soul.[9]

They will forget even more completely what he says about the infinite distance which separates the most perfect nature, even that of the most exalted angel, from the slightest degree of sanctifying grace, which St. Thomas declares "superior to the natural good of the entire universe" [10] of matter and spirit.

[7] "Since the created intellect is naturally capable of apprehending the concrete form, and the concrete being abstractedly, by way of a kind of resolution of parts; it can by grace be raised up to know separate subsisting substance, and separate subsisting existence" (Ia, q.12, a.4 ad 3um). "The soul is naturally capable of grace; since from its having been made to the likeness of God, it is fit to receive God by grace, as Augustine says" (Ia IIae. q.113, a.10).

[8] See Ia, q.1, a.8 ad 2um; q.2 ad 1um. q.60, a.5.

[9] See Ia IIae, q.85, a.3; IIIa, q.69, a.3, 4 ad 3um; *Contra Gentiles*, Bk. IV, chap. 52.

[10] See Ia IIae, q.113, a.9 ad 2um.

All angelic natures taken together are not equal to the slightest movement of charity.

Nominalists have diminished this doctrine to the point of thinking that grace is not a supernatural reality by its essence, but that it has only a moral value which gives us a right to eternal life, as a bank note gives us the right to claim a certain sum of gold.[11] Likewise for them the baptismal and sacerdotal characters are only extrinsic titles, relations established by reason without a basis in reality (for example, an adopted son). Luther, a disciple of the nominalists, went so far as to say that sanctifying grace is not a reality in us, is not a new life, but only the pardon of our faults exteriorly granted by God.

Without going to such extremes, some theologians have thought that God could create an intelligence for which the beatific vision would be natural.[12] They failed to see the infinite distance which necessarily separates the nature of all created and creatable intelligence from grace, which is a "participation in the divine nature."[13]

To grasp what this distance is, we must bear in mind that grace is really and formally a participation in the divine nature precisely in so far as it is divine, a participation in the Deity, in that which makes God God, in His intimate life. As rationality is what makes man a man, the Deity is the constituent essence of God, such as He is Himself. Grace is a mysterious participation in this essence, which surpasses all natu-

[11] The nominalists (such as Occam, Gabriel Biel, and Pierre d'Ailly) judged everything by the facts of experience and not by the formal reasons of things which alone, however, can render facts intelligible. Unable to discern in human individuals that which constitutes human nature, they no longer saw what distinguishes human nature from the gift of grace. In their view this gift was supernatural only by a contingent institution by God, as metal or paper has money value only in virtue of a law promulgated by civil authority. Grace thus conceived is no longer really and formally the seed of glory.

[12] They lost sight of the abyss which separates the natural object of the divine intelligence from that of created intelligence.

[13] See Ia IIae, q.110, a.3.

ral knowledge. Even stones, by the fact of their existence, have a remote likeness to God in so far as He is being; plants also distantly resemble Him in so far as he is living; human souls and angels are by nature made to the image of God and resemble Him by analogy in so far as He is intelligent; but no created or creatable nature can resemble God exactly in so far as He is God. Grace alone can make us participate really and formally in the Deity, in the intimate life of Him whose children we are by grace. The Deity, which remains inaccessible to all natural created knowledge, is superior to all the divine perfections naturally knowable, superior to being, to life, to wisdom, to love. All these divine attributes, diverse as they appear to be, are one and the same thing in God and with God. They are in the Deity formally and eminently as so many notes of a superior harmony, the simplicity of which is beyond our comprehension.[14]

Grace makes us participate really and formally in this Deity, in this eminent and intimate life of God, because grace is in us the radical principle of essentially divine operations, that will ultimately consist in seeing God immediately, as He sees Himself, and in loving Him as He loves Himself. Grace is the seed of glory. In order to know its essence intimately, we must first have seen the divine essence of which grace is the participation. By grace we are veritably "born of God," as St. John says. This is what makes Pascal say: "All bodies together and all spirits together and all their productions are not equal to the slightest movement of charity, which is of another and infinitely more elevated order."

If we clearly understand this doctrine, we know that grace not only vivifies and spiritualizes us, but also deifies us. "As

---

[14] "All perfections existing in creatures divided and multiplied, pre-exist in God simply and united" (Ia, q.13, a.5). "As regards the object intended by the name, this name God is more proper than the name 'He who is,' as it is imposed to signify the *divine nature*" (Ia, q.13, a.11 ad 1um). "The formal reason of the Deity is before all in its being and in all its attributes, for it is above being and above unity, etc." (Catejan on Ia, q.39, a.1, nos. 7, 8).

only fire can render a body incandescent," says St. Thomas, "God alone can deify souls." [15]

Hence the slightest degree of sanctifying grace is infinitely superior to a sensible miracle, which is supernatural only by reason of its cause, by its mode of production (*quoad modum*), not by its intimate reality: the life restored to a corpse is only the natural life, low, indeed, in comparison with that of grace. The paralytic, when his sins are forgiven him, receives infinitely more than his cure. At Lourdes the greatest blessings are not those which heal the body, but those which revivify souls. The "modal" supernatural, or the preternatural, does not count, so to speak, in comparison with the essentially supernatural.

The slightest degree of sanctifying grace is, as a result, infinitely superior to the phenomenon of ecstasy, to the prophetic vision of future events, or to the natural knowledge of the loftiest angel.

The natural knowledge of the highest angel could in its natural order grow indefinitely in intensity, yet it would never reach the dignity of the supernatural knowledge of infused faith or of the gift of wisdom. It would never even obscurely attain the intimate life of God, just as the indefinite progress of the imagination would never equal the intelligence; as the indefinite multiplication of the sides of a polygon inscribed within a circle never equal the latter, for the side, no matter how small it may be, never becomes a point. While in the state of probation, the angels, and likewise man, possessed, over and above the natural knowledge of God, the knowledge which proceeded from infused faith and from the gifts.

From all this we see the distance separating the essentially supernatural character of sanctifying grace from the supernatural character of sensible miracles or even of prophecy.

---

[15] "For it is as necessary that God alone should deify, bestowing a partaking of the divine nature by a participated likeness, as it is impossible that anything save fire should enkindle" (Ia IIae, q.112, a.1).

We have elsewhere [16] examined at length the value of this division of the supernatural, which is generally admitted, and of its subdivisions. This is an important point in theology, and a particularly important one in mystical theology. This fact can be noted in the tabulation on page 59, where the supernatural *quoad substantiam* (by its essence) is clearly distinct from the miraculous *quoad substantiam* (miracles of the first order). In the first we consider the formal cause; in the second, an extrinsic cause, the efficient cause. Thus sanctifying grace is supernatural by its essence, or formal cause; miracles, even of the first order, are supernatural only because no created force can produce them. By the resurrection of a dead person, natural life is supernaturally restored to him.

The problem to be discussed in the present work can be reduced to the following terms: Does the mystical life belong to the category of sanctifying grace, the virtues, and the gifts, or to the relatively inferior category of miracles and prophecy?

For the solution of the actual mystical problem, the greatest consideration must be given to the supernatural elevation of sanctifying grace as it was conceived by St. Thomas.[17] No theologian, as we have shown,[18] has been able to make as clear a distinction as he did between the natural order and the essentially supernatural order. No one has better affirmed the absolute gratuity of the life of grace, and its elevation infinitely surpassing, as it does, every claim and innate desire of human and angelic nature. Yet no one has better shown how this gift, gratuitous though it is, is wonderfully suited to our loftiest aspirations. Nothing is more gratuitous and desirable than the beatific vision, and in this life nothing is more so than holy communion.[19]

[16] *De revelatione*, I, 197–217.
[17] See IIa IIae, q.110, a.3, 4; q.112, a.1.
[18] *De revelatione*, I, 206, 337–403, and especially pp. 395–403: Why there cannot be in our nature or in that of the angels an innate desire of the supernatural life or an active obediential power, but only a faint desire and the passive capacity of being raised to this infinitely superior order.
[19] See IIIa, q.79, a.1 ad 2um.

SUPERNATURAL

*quoad substantiam*
(in essence)

   Uncreated    God in His intimate life, mystery of the Blessed Trinity.
Uncreated Person of the Word made flesh.

   Created    Light of glory.
Habitual grace of the virtues and the gifts, and actual grace.

*quoad modum*
(in mode)

   By reason of final causality    The natural act of an acquired virtue, supernaturally related by charity toward a supernatural end.

   By reason of efficient causality    Miracle *quoad substantiam* (e. g., glorious resurrection) and prophecy.
Miracle *quoad subjectum* (e. g., resurrection without glory) and knowledge of the secrets of hearts.
Miracle *quoad modum* (e. g., sudden cure of an illness curable in time); gift of tongues and similar graces.

When we consider the conformity of Christianity with our natural aspirations, very often we cease to note the absolute gratuity of the divine gift and thus we incline toward practical naturalism. On the other hand, whoever fails to see this admirable conformity is led to conceive a rigid supernaturalness which is contrary to nature and lacking in simplicity. This conception would lead to exaltation and the follies of false mysticism.

St. Thomas maintains the infinite elevation of grace above our nature and also the harmony between the two. But he adds that this harmony really appears only after a profound purification of nature by mortification and the cross, as the lives of the saints show. He repeatedly tells us that this harmony has been fully realized in this world only in our Lord Jesus Christ. Bossuet says the same thing in speaking of Jesus: "Who would not admire the condescension with which He tempers the loftiness of His doctrine? It is milk for children and, at the same time, bread for the strong. It is full of the secrets of God, but it is evident that Jesus is not astonished at this, as other mortals to whom God communicates Himself. Our Lord speaks naturally of these matters, as one born in this secret and in this glory; and what He has without measure (John 3: 34) He bestows with measure that our weakness may be able to bear it." [20]

By this marvelous conciliation of qualities so diverse, that is, of the absolute gratuity and supreme fitness of grace, St. Thomas directs us toward the loftiest orthodox mystical theology, which is in reality a commentary on our Lord's expression: "If thou didst but know the gift of God."

We shall see this better when we speak of the supernaturalness of the infused virtues, both moral and theological, and of the gifts of the Holy Ghost.

[20] *Discours sur l'histoire universelle,* Part II, chap. 19.

## ARTICLE II

*Mystical Theology and the Essentially Supernatural Character of Infused Faith*

The doctrine of St. Thomas about our natural intellectual knowledge and the essence of sanctifying grace directs us toward the loftiest orthodox mystical theology. The same is true of his teaching about the supernatural character of the infused virtues and of the gifts of the Holy Ghost. In this article we will treat especially the supernatural character of faith. But first we must say a few words about the supernatural character of the Christian moral virtues.

These moral virtues are the four cardinal virtues (prudence, justice, fortitude, and temperance) and the virtues joined with them, particularly those of religion (or justice in regard to God), of magnanimity, patience, perseverance (all related to fortitude), of chastity, gentleness, modesty, and humility.

While reading the part of St. Thomas' *Summa* dealing with these Christian moral virtues, especially prudence, justice, fortitude, and temperance, many think these are only the natural virtues described by Aristotle and that they are clothed with a simple adventitious supernatural modality, springing from the influence of charity, which should direct all our acts to God. Some theologians have not gone beyond this conception.

The thought of St. Thomas is far loftier. According to his teaching, the Christian moral virtues are infused and, because of their formal object, essentially distinct from the highest acquired moral virtues described by the greatest philosophers. These acquired moral virtues, useful as they may be, could be continually developed without ever attaining the formal object of the Christian virtues. An infinite difference exists between Aristotelian temperance, governed solely by right reason, and Christian temperance, ruled by divine faith and supernatural prudence. St. Thomas says: "Evidently the measure to be imposed on our passions differs essentially according as it springs from the human rule of reason or from the divine rule. For example, in the use of food the measure prescribed by reason has for its end the avoidance of what is harmful to health and to the exercise of reason itself, while according to the divine law, as St. Paul says, man must chastise his body and bring it into subjection by abstinence and other similar austerities." [1] This measure, which belongs to the supernatural order, is in fact animated by that which unaided reason is ignorant of, but which faith teaches us about the results of original sin and of our personal sins, about the infinite elevation of our supernatural end, about the obligation of loving God, the Author of grace, more than ourselves and above all, and of renouncing self in order to follow our Lord Jesus Christ.[2]

St. Thomas is equally insistent on the necessity of a progressive purification in order that the Christian moral virtues, aided by the acquired virtues, may reach their perfection. He shows us what they should become in those who really strive for divine union. "Then," he says, "prudence scorns the things of the world for the contemplation of divine things; it directs all the thoughts of the soul toward God. Temperance abandons, so far as nature can bear it, what the body demands; fortitude prevents the soul from becoming frightened in the face of death and when confronted with the unknown supernatural. Justice leads the soul finally to enter fully on this entirely divine way." [3] Loftier still, he says, are the virtues of the soul that is already purified, those of the blessed and of the great saints on earth.

---

[1] See Ia IIae, q.63, a.4.

[2] Cf. B. Froget, *De l'habitation du Saint-Esprit dans les âmes justes*, Part IV, chap. 5, no. 3: "The infused moral virtues specifically distinct from the acquired moral virtues."

[3] See Ia IIae, q.61, a.5.

This teaching is not less elevated than that offered by Tauler in his *Sermons,* or by St. John of the Cross (*The Ascent of Mount Carmel* and *The Dark Night of the Soul*) in the chapters which he devotes to the active and passive purification of the soul.

In regard to the theological virtues, some, who read the *Summa theologica* in an entirely material manner, reach the conclusion that our act of faith is a substantially natural act clothed with a supernatural modality: substantially natural, because it reposes formally on the natural, historical knowledge of Christ's preaching and of the miracles which confirmed it; clothed with a supernatural modality, so that it may be useful to salvation. This modality is often said to resemble a layer of gold applied to copper in order to make plated metal. We would thus have "plated supernatural" life and not a new, essentially supernatural life.[4]

According to this conception, the certitude of our supernatural faith in the Blessed Trinity, the incarnation, and other mysteries, would rest formally in the last analysis on the inferior though morally certain knowledge which our unaided reason can have of the signs of revelation and of the marks of the Church. The act of faith would be a sort of reasoning, formally based on a certitude of inferior order. Often this certitude rests merely on the human testimony of our parents and of our pastors, for very few of the faithful can make a critical study of the origins of Christianity. The act of theological faith thus conceived is no longer infallibly certain, and preserves almost nothing that is supernatural and mysterious. It is no longer evident why interior grace is absolutely necessary not only to confirm it but to produce it. This last point was definitely defined by the Church against the Pelagians and the semi-Pelagians.

This material conception is simply another case of the reduction of the higher to the lower. It is an error analogous to

4 See Ia IIae, q. 63, a. 4; IIa IIae, q. 6, a. 1.

that discussed above in relation to rational first principles.

St. Thomas teaches that, just as sensation is only an inferior knowledge prerequisite to that of principles, a knowledge which is founded on intellectual evidence, so also the rational knowledge of the signs of revelation plays only the part of a preamble to prepare our intellect to receive the influence of grace, which alone can make us adhere infallibly to the formal motive of faith, to the authority of God revealing, in an order infinitely superior to the reasoning that went before.

St. Thomas saw the entire meaning and range of our Lord's words: "No man can come to Me, except the Father, who hath sent Me, draw him. . . . Everyone that hath heard of the Father, and hath learned, cometh to Me. . . . Amen, amen I say unto you: He that believeth in Me, hath everlasting life." [5] "My sheep hear My voice." [6] "Everyone that is of the truth, heareth My voice." [7] St. Paul says the same thing: "Faith is a gift of God. . . . Faith is the substance of things to be hoped for," [8] or the seed, the beginning of eternal life.

And the Council of Trent [9] defined as follows: "In justification man receives, with the remission of sins, the three virtues of faith, hope, and charity, infused at the same time into his soul by Jesus Christ, on whom he is grafted."

Thus, as St. Thomas teaches, faith is substantially supernatural, specified by a formal motive of the same entirely supernatural order, a motive that faith attains in an absolutely infallible manner. This is why, rather than call it in question, we must undergo the worst torments, as the martyrs did.

This absolutely infallible and essentially supernatural certitude resolves itself only materially into our morally certain knowledge (critical or non-critical) of the signs which confirmed Christ's preaching and also such knowledge of the

[5] John 6: 44, 45, 47.
[6] John 10: 27.
[7] John 18: 37.
[8] Heb. 11: 1.
[9] Sess. VI, chap. 7.

marks of the Church. It is based formally on the authority of God revealing, on the first revealing uncreated Truth which reveals itself with the mysteries that it manifests, which is believed with the mysteries in an order infinitely superior to rational evidence, just as physical light appears and is seen at the same time as it makes us see colors.[10] As the Thomists usually say, "The first revealing Truth is at once that which is believed and that by which one believes, as light is that which is seen and that by which one sees." [11] St. Augustine expressed this idea in his commentary on St. John.[12]

The question concerns not only belief in God, the Author of nature and of sensible miracles which reason can know by its own power; it concerns also belief in God, the Author of grace, in God considered in His intimate life, in God who leads us to a supernatural end by giving rise in us to essentially supernatural acts.[13]

If God had supernaturally revealed only the natural truths of religion, as, for example, His natural providence, without

---

10 Cf. St. Thomas, *De veritate*, q.14, a.8 ad 4um.

11 Cf. Cajetan, In IIa IIae, q.1, a.1; and on the same subject, John of St. Thomas, Bannes, the Salamanca theologians, Billuart, etc. Capreolus expresses himself in the same manner in his *Commentary on the Sentences, III Sent.*, d.24, q.1, a.3, 4.

12 St. Augustine, *In Joan.*, 8: 14, tr. 35. Migne, XXXV, 1658: "Light gives testimony of itself . . . and is a witness to itself that the light may be known. . . . Likewise Wisdom, the Word of God."

13 "Accordingly if we consider, in faith, the formal aspect of the object, it is nothing else than the First Truth. For the faith we are speaking of does not assent to anything, except for the reason that it is revealed by God. Hence the mean on which faith is based is the divine Truth" (IIa IIae, q.1, a.1). "Now it has been already stated that the object of faith is the First Truth. as unseen, and whatever we hold on account thereof" (q.4, a.1). "Nevertheless, we must observe that in the object of faith, there is something formal, as it were, namely, the First Truth surpassing all the natural knowledge of a creature, and something material, namely, the thing to which we assent while adhering to the First Truth" (q.5, a.1).

*De veritate*, q.14, a.8, corp.: "All created truth is defectible. . . . Therefore faith, which is set down as a virtue, must make the intellect of man adhere to the truth which consists in divine knowledge, by transcending the truth of his own intellect. And so the faithful soul through simple and unchanging truth is free from the fickleness of unstable error, as Dionysius says: *De div. nom. c. VII.*" Cf. *Ibid.*, ad 2um, ad 3um, ad 9um, ad 16um.

telling us anything about supernatural mysteries (e. g., the Blessed Trinity), our faith would have been supernatural only by reason of its origin, by its mode of production, but not at all by its formal object or by its essence. It would have been specifically inferior to Christian faith, whatever the semi-rationalists, who wished to prove the mysteries of Christianity, may have said about it. On the contrary, our infused faith is not specifically inferior to that which the angels had before enjoying the beatific vision, even though our faith expresses itself in acquired ideas and theirs in infused ideas.

In reality, it is the supernatural mystery of His intimate life which God has revealed to us. Consequently our faith is based on the very truth of God, the Author of grace, on the uncreated knowledge of His intimate life which He possesses: an entirely supernatural first Truth, to which the infused light of faith raises us, and to which it makes us adhere infallibly.[14] It is eternal first Truth, which is still obscure for us because transluminous, says Dionysius, and is infinitely superior not only to the evidence of rational principles which enable us to recognize a miracle, but even to the evidence which the angels naturally enjoy, and which the demons preserve;[15] "the First Truth which interiorly illuminates and teaches man."[16]

Therefore without the infused light of faith man remains in the presence of the Gospel like a hearer deprived of musical

[14] "A heretic does not hold the other articles of faith about which he does not err in the same way as one of the faithful does, namely, by adhering simply to the divine truth, because in order to do so, a man needs the help of the habit of faith; but he holds the things that are of faith by his own will and judgment" (IIa IIae, q.5, a.3 ad 1um). "For, since man by assenting to matters of faith, is raised above his nature, this must needs accrue to him from some supernatural principle moving him inwardly; and this is God" (q.6, a.1). *In Boetium de Trinit.*, q.3, a.1 ad 4um: "The things which are proposed exteriorly relate to the knowledge of faith, as though received through the senses for the recognition of principles."

[15] *De veritate*, q.14, a.9 ad 4um: "To believe is used equivocally of the faithful and of demons."

[16] *Quodlibet II*, a.6 ad 3um.

sense who listens to a symphony without really perceiving its beauty. "But," says St. Paul, "the sensual man perceiveth not these things that are of the Spirit of God; for it is foolishness to him, and he cannot understand, because it is spiritually examined." [17]

The faithful, on the contrary, understand "the deep things of God" spoken of by the revelation which is proposed by the Church. "This school, where God teaches and is understood, is far removed from the senses," says St. Augustine. "We see many men come to the Son of God, since we see many who believe in Christ; but where and how they have heard and learned this truth of the Father, that we do not see. This grace is entirely too intimate and too secret for us to see it." [18]

St. Thomas says: "Three things lead us to believe in Christ: "first, natural reason; . . . secondly, the testimony of the law and the prophets; . . . thirdly, the preaching of the Apostles; but when thus led we have reached belief; then we can say that we believe, not for any of the preceding motives, but solely because of the very truth of God . . . to which we adhere firmly under the influence of an infused light; because faith has certitude from light divinely infused." [19] Elsewhere St. Thomas says: "God dwells in us by living faith, according to the expression of St. Paul: [20] 'Christ dwells in your hearts by faith.' " [21]

This lofty doctrine has often been given a materialistic in-

[17] See I Cor. 2: 14. See the commentary of St. Thomas on this text. In the encyclical *Providentissimus*, Leo XIII says: "The sense of Holy Scripture can nowhere be found incorrupt outside the Church, and cannot be expected to be found in writers who, being without the true faith, only gnaw the bark of the Sacred Scripture, and never attain its pith." To discover the literal meaning of Scripture, it is not always sufficient to have grammar, a dictionary, and the rules of rational exegesis, but one must also follow positively those of Christian and Catholic exegesis which proceeds under the divine light of faith, as is stated in all good treatises on interpretation of Scripture.

[18] *De praedestinatione sanctorum, PL*, XLIV, 970. Also *PL*, XLV, 1019.

[19] St. Thomas, *In Joann.*, chap. 4, lect. 5, no. 2.

[20] Eph. 3: 17.

[21] *In Ep. ad Gal.*, 3: 11.

terpretation and has been considerably diminished. The great commentators of St. Thomas for the last seven centuries have always defended it and cherished it. To be convinced of this, we need only read what they have written about the articles of the *Summa* relative to the supernatural character of the theological virtues and especially of faith.[22] One should read particularly the fine writings of the Carmelites of Salamanca on this point, which they regard as the foundation of the mystical doctrine of their father, St. John of the Cross.[23] Both St. Fran-

[22] On this important point, Capreolus, Cajetan, Cano, Lemos, John of St. Thomas, and the Carmelites of Salamanca have always energetically opposed the nominalist conceptions or any that have sprung from nominalism, which disregard the essential supernaturalness of infused faith and of the motive which specifies it. Suarez agrees with St. Thomas on this point.

[23] Salmanticenses, *De gratia*, tr. XIV, disp. III, dub. 3, no. 40: "The formal motive of infused faith is the testimony of God, the Author of grace, which establishes a supernatural certitude. Man by his natural powers can rely on the testimony of God, the Author of nature (and of naturally knowable miracles), but he cannot without grace rely on the testimony of God, the Author of grace, on the voice of the heavenly Father, which is the principle of an essentially supernatural certitude, relative to an object and to an end of the same order." Cf. *Ibid.*, nos. 28, 40, 42, 45, 60. Salmant., *De fide*, disp. I, dub. 5, nos. 163, 193. Divine revelation is that by which we believe mysteries, and revelation itself is believed by the same act; we adhere to it supernaturally by faith. Thus we have said with St. Thomas (*De veritate*, q.14, a.18 ad 4um), light is seen and makes us see colors. These last formulas, as we have noted, are current among all the great commentators of St. Thomas (Dominicans or Carmelites), and are also used by Suarez.

Lastly, the same doctrine is well defended by Father G. Mattiussi, S.J., *Rivista di filosofia neo-scolastica*, December, 1918, pp. 416–19, "L'atto di fede," and by Father M. de la Taille, S.J., *Recherches de science religieuse*, September, 1919, p. 275, "L'oraison contemplative." Likewise several years ago Father G. Petazzi, S. J., in an interesting study, *Credibilità e fede*, rightly contrasted the faith of the devils, springing from the natural perspicacity by which they discern miracles (IIa IIae, q.5, a.2 ad 2um) with the infused faith of the faithful. "The acquired faith of the devils," he rightly says, "is neither essentially supernatural nor meritorious. It is not supernatural; although the formal motive of their belief is the authority of God, yet this is not the authority of God as the author of the supernatural order and in relation to a supernatural end. Consequently it is neither meritorious nor laudable, for the devils, while admitting the mysteries of faith, do not seek the good of God, but only their own (it would be stupid for them to deny the divine origin of a word confirmed by such striking signs). And since the authority of God as the author of the supernatural order, in relation to a supernatural end, constitutes a formal motive different from the authority of God considered simply as First Truth naturally knowable, it follows that the faith of the

cis de Sales and Bossuet likewise express the same opinion.[24] Among modern theologians, Scheeben, who clearly understood this teaching, wrote as follows: "The formal motive of faith is purely and immediately divine and therefore absolutely one and simple, firm and subsistent, identical with the first and immutable source of all truth (First Truth). On the other hand, faith itself appears as a direct commerce, an intimate union with the interior word of God, and consequently with His interior life. As this interior word not only existed at the time of the manifestation of the exterior word, but also subsists in its quality as eternal word of God, in an eternal present, it elevates our mind to participation in His truth and immortal life, and makes it rest therein.

"The contrary opinion, according to which the exterior act of revelation would be a partial motive of faith, rests on a mechanical conception, in which faith appears as a deductive process helping us to discover the truth of its contents. It lessens the transcendental character of faith, which is essentially an impulse toward God." [25]

This is what prompted Lacordaire to say: "What takes place in us when we believe is a phenomenon of intimate and superhuman light. I do not say that exterior things do not act on

---

devils differs specifically from that of the faithful, as St. Thomas says in *De veritate*, q.14, a.9 ad 4um: 'Belief is equivocally postulated of the faithful and of devils; in the latter there is no faith from any infused light of grace, as there is in the faithful.'

[24] St. Francis de Sales, *Treatise on the Love of God*, Bk. II, chap. 14: "The Almighty, to impart to us the gift of faith, penetrates the soul and speaks to it; not by reasoning, but by inspiration. He proposes to the understanding the objects of its belief in so gentle and persuasive a manner, that the will is powerfully inclined to exert its freedom and authority over the understanding, and thereby reduce it to acquiesce unhesitatingly and fully in the truths revealed." Bossuet (*Elévations sur les mystères*, 18th week, 17th elevation) says: "Above all, you must believe that those who believe owe all to God; that they are, as our Savior says, taught by God (John 6: 45): that it is necessary that He speak within, and that He search out the hearts of those He wishes especially to make hear Him. Therefore reason no longer: humble yourself. He who has ears to hear, let him hear (Matt. 11: 15): but let him know that it is God who gives these ears which hear."

[25] Scheeben, *Dogmatik*, I, sec. 40, no. 681.

us as rational motives of certitude; but the very act of this supreme certitude, which I speak of, affects us directly like a luminous phenomenon (infused light of faith), like a transluminous phenomenon. . . . We are affected by a transluminous light. . . . Otherwise where would be the proportion between our adherence, which would be natural and rational, and an object surpassing nature and reason? . . . It is somewhat like a sympathetic intuition that in a single moment establishes between two men what logic could not do in many years. Just so a sudden illumination at times enlightens the intelligence." [26] Bishop Gay holds the same opinion.[27]

To make us thus adhere to the supreme, essentially supernatural Truth, infused faith should therefore also be supernatural in its essence and not merely by an accidental modality. It is thus infinitely superior to the light of reason, as the latter is to the senses.[28]

[26] Lacordaire, *Conférences de Notre Dame de Paris,* 17th conference.

[27] *Les vertus chrétiennes,* I, 159 f., in the chapter on faith: "The senses and reason can indeed give us a physical or historical knowledge of supernatural, divine facts. This is their loftiest employment and in this their concurrence is indispensable. Without them the act of faith would be radically impossible; they are the soil in which this act germinates and which serves it as a support. But in regard to the real, commanded, meritorious perception of revealed supernatural truths, the most exquisite senses and the most highly cultivated reason remain utterly incapable of it. Faith alone can give us this perception. Faith is necessary to make us adhere to the content of revelation, that is, to the divine reality expressed in human language; and without grace, which inaugurates it in us, we could not surrender to the proofs on which it rests. Without faith the most intelligent and most learned person remains the purely natural man that St. Paul calls sensual; and the Apostle says that such a one 'perceiveth not these things that are of the Spirit of God . . . and he cannot understand' (I Cor. 2: 14). Even were the human mind capable of this adherence, there would still be the heart, which of necessity has its part here, and truly a very large part."

[28] If this doctrine is expounded to those who see things in the other way, some reply: "Those are mere words." Thus, without wishing to do so, they confess their unconscious nominalism. This nominalism is bound to lead them to see only meaningless words in the intimate life of God, inasmuch as that life underlies the order of the supernatural mysteries, essentially superior to the order of natural divine mysteries, which reason by itself can know. For the nominalists this distinction between the two orders was only a contingent distinction depending on the free will of God and not on the infinite elevation of His intimate life. Cf. *De revelatione,* I, 340.

When this great doctrine of St. Thomas is not lessened by a materialistic interpretation, it is, by reason of its loftiness, evidently the foundation of mystical theology, and is in no way inferior to the most beautiful pages on the life of faith in the writings of Dionysius,[29] Tauler,[30] Blessed Henry Suso,[31] or St. John of the Cross. We shall see that the passive purifications of the spirit especially, which are described in *The Dark Night of the Soul*, can be understood only by what we have just said about the absolute supernaturalness of the formal motive of the theological virtues. These painful passive purifications, in which the gifts of the Holy Ghost have a great share, bring out strikingly this pure, supernatural motive by freeing it more and more from every inferior motive accessible to reason.

To show that mystical contemplation is only the plenitude of the life of faith, the essence of which we have just determined, we need only quote some characteristic passages from the writings of St. John of the Cross. In *The Ascent of Mount Carmel* [32] he writes: "To be prepared for the divine union, the

---

Others say: "What you are speaking of presupposes an extraordinary mystical illumination," whereas we are speaking only of Christian faith, such as that possessed by a believer even in the state of mortal sin; faith with a value and grandeur often unknown.

[29] Dionysius, *De nom. div.*, chap. 7, no. 4: "The Logos [divine intelligence] is the simple and really existing truth, around which, as a pure and unerring knowledge of the whole, the divine Faith, the enduring foundation of the believers, is that which establishes them in the truth, and the truth in them, by an unchangeable identity, they having the pure knowledge of the truth of the things believed." The contemplative becomes more and more convinced that God is superior to every conception. "Then," says Dionysius, "the soul being freed from the sensible and from the intellectual world enters the transluminous obscurity of a holy ignorance and, renouncing every scientific fact, is lost in Him who can neither be seen nor understood" (*Theol. mystic.*, chap. 1). See also chap. 2.

[30] Tauler in his *Sermons* often speaks of entirely pure, naked faith, stripped of images and rational knowledge. He declares this type of faith very superior to consolations and revelations. This pure faith is certainly accompanied by the gifts of understanding and of wisdom in an eminent degree. Tauler's teaching on this point has been summed up in the *Institutions*, chapters 8 and 35. This work seems not to have been written by him, but to have been drawn from his writings.

[31] *Œuvres mystiques* (Thiriot ed.), II, 357.

[32] Bk. II, chap. 9.

understanding must be purified, emptied of all that comes from the senses, of all that may present itself clearly. It must be intimately at peace, recollected, and abandoned in faith. This faith alone is the proximate and proportionate means which can unite the soul to God, for faith is in such intimate connection with God that what we believe by faith and what we see by the beatific vision are one and the same thing. God is infinite; faith proposes the infinite to us. God is one and triune; faith proposes Him to us as one and triune. In the same way that God is darkness for our mind, faith enlightens our understanding by blinding it. By this means only does God manifest Himself to the soul in a divine light which exceeds all understanding; whence it results that the greater faith is, the more profound is the union. . . . For under the darkness of faith, the understanding is united to God; under cover of this mysterious darkness, God is found hidden."

Farther on in the same work,[33] St. John of the Cross says of spiritual visions in which creatures are seen: "I do not deny that the memory of them may give rise to some love of God and contemplation; but pure faith and detachment in darkness from all this stimulates and raises the soul much more thereto, without the soul's knowing how or whence it comes. If it happens that the soul experiences an anguish of very pure love of God, and is ignorant of its cause and motive, it is the effect of faith, which has developed in the night, in nudity and spiritual poverty, and which is accompanied by a more profound, infused love of God. Whence it follows that the more eager the soul is for obscurity, for annihilation in regard to every exterior and interior object which it is capable of possessing, the more it increases its faith, and also hope and charity, inasmuch as the three theological virtues form a unity. Often the person favored does not understand this love and has no feeling of it, since it is not established in the senses by

[33] *Ibid.*, Bk. II, chap. 24.

tenderness, but in the soul by a fortitude, courage, and daring hitherto unknown."

Previously St. John of the Cross had written: [34] "In order to be supernaturally transformed, the soul must enter the darkness (not only in regard to creatures, but in regard to what reason can know of God). It must remain in the darkness, like a blind person, relying on obscure faith, taking it as light and guide. The soul cannot help itself with any of the things which it understands, tastes, feels, or imagines. . . . Faith dominates all these ideas, tastes, sentiments, and images. If the soul does not wish to extinguish its lights by preferring total obscurity to them, it will not reach what is superior, that is, what faith teaches. . . . The soul creates great obstacles for itself in its ascent toward this lofty state of union with God when it relies on reasoning or is attached to its own judgment or will." Elsewhere the saint states that by so doing the soul mingles with its supernatural acts an act of coarse quality which does not attain the end. [35]

And again St. John of the Cross says: [36] "To busy oneself with things which are clear to the mind and of little value is to forbid onself access to the abyss of faith where God in secret supernaturally instructs the soul, and without its knowledge enriches it with virtues and gifts. . . . The Holy Ghost enlightens the recollected intellect according to the measure

[34] *Ibid.*, Bk. II, chap. 4.

[35] *Ibid.* St. John of the Cross speaks in like manner in *The Living Flame of Love*, 3d str., verse 3: "Spiritual directors, who do not know the spiritual ways and their characteristics, turn souls away from the delicate unctions by which the Holy Ghost prepares them for divine union. . . . They persist in not allowing souls—even if the desire of God formally manifests itself—to pass beyond their principles and methods which are limited to the discursive and the imaginary. They forbid souls to pass beyond the limits of a natural capacity. How poor is the fruit which they draw from it." Does not he who conceives faith itself as a discursive process, particularly merit these reproaches? If, on the contrary, we consider the act of faith as a simple act without any reasoning, we prepare ourselves by this very consideration to follow the way pointed out by St. John of the Cross.

[36] *The Ascent of Mount Carmel*, Bk. II, chap. 29.

of its recollection. But the most perfect recollection is that which takes place in faith, and for this reason the Holy Ghost does not communicate His lights outside of faith." In all these texts the saint is concerned with living faith enlightened by a gift of the Holy Ghost.[37]

We find the same teaching for more advanced souls in *The Dark Night of the Soul:* "The soul ought then to enter the second night in order to strip itself perfectly of all perceptions and savors, whether of sense or of spirit, in order to walk in the purity of obscure faith. There only can it find the fitting means by which the soul is united to God, as He Himself declares by the prophet Osee (2: 20); 'I will espouse thee to Me in faith.' "[38]

In *The Spiritual Canticle,* St. John beautifully sums up this doctrine and shows its loftiness. He insists on the absolute supernaturalness of the object which faith attains by the articles of the Credo:

> "O crystal well!
> Oh, that on Thy silvered surface
> Thou wouldest mirror forth at once
> Those eyes desired [39]
> Which are outlined in my heart!"

"By 'silvery surfaces' the soul means the propositions or articles of faith. To understand these verses and those which follow, we must observe that the articles of faith are represented by silver as compared to gold, which is the substance of faith or the truths which it contains considered in themselves. During our lives we adhere to this substance of faith, although it is hidden in a silvered envelope. It will appear unveiled in heaven, and we shall contemplate this pure gold with de-

---

[37] Father Poulain, in our opinion, correctly interprets St. John of the Cross on this point. Cf. *Les grâces d'oraison,* 9th ed., p. 227.

[38] Bk. II, Part II, chap. 2; also *The Living Flame,* 3d str., vers. 3, no. 9.

[39] That is, as explained farther on, the sight of God of which infused faith is a faint impression, since this faith is the prelude of the beatific vision.

light. . . . Thus faith gives us God even in this life, although under a veil of silver. This does not hinder us from truly receiving Him." [40]

St. Thomas holds the same opinion. In correcting Hugh of St. Victor, he observes that the only contemplation that surpasses faith is the beatific vision. According to his opinion, the contemplation of the angels and that of Adam before the fall was not superior to faith, but, he says, they received the light of the gift of wisdom in greater abundance than we do. [41] And he shows that uniform or circular contemplation, of which Dionysius speaks, presupposes the sacrifice of the senses and of reasoning, or the multiplicity in which they tarry. [42]

St. Thomas is not speaking here merely of the contemplation called "ordinary," and not at all of mystical contemplation. If we should thus misunderstand him, we would confound the latter with its concomitant phenomena and would forget that the holy doctor recognizes that the superior degree of uniform or circular contemplation is that called by Dionysius the great darkness, or the plenitude of faith. St. Thomas says: "Then we know God through ignorance, by a union which surpasses the nature of our soul and in which we are enlightened by the depths of divine wisdom, which we cannot scrutinize." [43] St. Albert the Great teaches the same doctrine. [44]

[40] *The Spiritual Canticle,* Part I, str. 12. Likewise in *Maxims and Spiritual Counsels,* maxim 24 (p. 557): "No perception or supernatural knowledge can aid us as much to love God as the slightest act of living faith and of hope freed from all intellectual support." Likewise maxim 27. See also *The Living Flame of Love,* str. 3, vers. 2: The overshadowings of the soul, the shadow of the divine perfections.

[41] See IIa IIae, q.5, a.1 ad 1um.

[42] "But on the part of the soul, before it arrives at this uniformity, its twofold lack of uniformity needs to be removed. First, that which arises from the variety of external things . . . and secondly, that which arises from the discoursing of reason" (IIa IIae, q.180, a.6 ad 2um).

[43] St. Thomas, *In libr. de divinis nomin.,* chap. 7, lect. 4. Likewise, *I Sent.,* d.8, q.1, a.1 ad 5um.

[44] *Comment. in Mysticam theologiam Dionysii,* chap. 1. See also *De adhaerendo Deo,* chap. 3, a work which for a long time was attributed to St. Albert.

This teaching is confirmed by the testimony of souls experienced in the mystical ways. "One day," says Blessed Angela of Foligno, "I saw God in a darkness and necessarily in a darkness, because He is situated too far above the mind, and no proportion exists between Him and anything that can become the object of a thought. It is an ineffable delectation in the good which contains all. Nothing therein can become the object either of a word or a concept. I see nothing, I see all. Certitude is obtained in the darkness. The more profound the darkness, so much the more does the good exceed all. This is the reserved mystery. . . . Pay attention. The divine power, wisdom, and will of which I have had marvelous visions at other times, seem less than this which I saw. This is a whole; one would say that the others were parts." [45] It is the Deity superior to being, to wisdom, to love, which are identical with each other in its infinity.

Such is manifestly the full development of infused faith, of which St. Thomas has so well determined the essential supernaturalness; it is faith based on a formal motive, inaccessible to reason and to the natural knowledge of the angels. Contemplative souls have found great light in learning the true thought of the holy doctor on this fundamental point.[46]

[45] *Le livre des visions et instructions de la B. Angèle de Foligno,* chap. 26.

[46] One of them writes on this subject: "This First Truth gives the soul great independence toward everything created, as though the soul had received shelter in the immutable. It can no longer suffer, as before, from exterior happenings, yet it endures continual suffering. This world, where it must continue to live, has its material, passing realities from which it cannot escape, and it sees itself subjected to deception. Everything but the contemplation of this First Truth is a heavy burden to it, which it bears without impatience. It performs all its external occupations with courage, although without any taste for them, because during the time of trial such is the will of God. And the will of God is truth. The soul loves it passionately no matter what suffering it may find therein. Thus the things of heaven and those of earth, immense happiness and continual suffering, harmonize in peace under this ray of Truth, which now illumines my life. I say 'O Truth,' as others say, 'O Love, O Mercy.' This is my ejaculatory prayer, my spiritual communion which gives me all my God. This First Truth, this subsistent truth, is God; it is His Being. This First Truth it is which gives me life and, by inclining toward me, nothingness and sin, it assumes the name of love and mercy.

In fact, if we are truly convinced of the essential supernaturalness of faith, we understand that mystical contemplation is the normal blossoming of this theological virtue united to charity and to the gifts of the Holy Ghost. Only the contemplative rises to the heights of his faith.

The certitude of his contemplation is based formally on a secret illumination of the Holy Ghost, while the concomitant phenomena of suspension of the faculties and of ecstasy are only effects and signs of a state with a supernatural quality beyond the grasp of observation. Here, as also for the natural knowledge of first principles and for the certitude of faith, we must distinguish clearly between the entirely spiritual, formal motive of our adherence and the sensible signs accompanying it.

If, on the other hand, the teaching of St. Thomas on the supernatural character of faith is interpreted materialistically, mystical contemplation will be materialized. Too much attention will be paid to the phenomena that sometimes accompany it, and it will be declared absolutely extraordinary because the fundamental law of the continual development "of the grace of the virtues and of the gifts" will be lost sight of.

What the holy doctor teaches about hope and charity will also be materialistically interpreted. If anyone should imagine that reason alone, studying historically the Gospel confirmed

---

"I well know that I have not seen this Truth, since it is not given to us to see God while we are in the prison of our body; but my faith possesses this Truth in this dark light.

"During one of these prayers of great darkness which I sometimes have, I was permitted to contemplate this essential glory of the Blessed Trinity, in comparison with which the most magnificent works of His wisdom, even that of the incarnation, do not count. And it seemed to me that the contemplative act of faith corresponded to this intimate life of God. I understood then the truth of that saying of St. John of the Cross, that the smallest act of pure love is of greater value in the eyes of God and more profitable to the Church than the greatest works. The desire to give contemplative souls to God and to His Church was greatly strengthened as a result. And I understood that the doctrine of St. Thomas on the supernaturalness of faith is intimately bound up with the contemplative and mystical life, which is none other than the life of faith par excellence."

by miracles, can without grace attain the formal motive which specifies infused faith, he would be led to think that reason can in the same way know the formal motive of hope and of charity. Were this the case, the acts of these virtues would be substantially natural, and would require only a supernatural modality in order to be useful to salvation. Our act of charity would thus resemble a natural and reasonable affection which had been supernaturalized in order to become meritorious. In this case we no longer see the infinite distance which separates, in their very essence and in their essential vitality, the natural desire to be happy from the act of infused hope, or again that distance which separates the natural love of the sovereign Good, which Plato speaks of in *The Banquet,* from the divine charity which is mentioned so repeatedly in the Gospel.

Some theologians, following the nominalists, have seriously diminished the supernatural character of the Christian virtues, even of the theological virtues; but such diminution is certainly not found in St. Thomas. In his opinion, these virtues are supernatural in their very essence, which raises infinitely the vitality of our intelligence and of our will. They are specified by a formal object, or a formal motive, which infinitely surpasses the natural powers of the human soul and those of the highest angels.

This doctrine of the essentially supernatural, formal motive of the three theological virtues places the teaching of St. Thomas on the same level as that of the greatest orthodox mystics.[47]

Finally, we are confronted with the question of the gifts of the Holy Ghost and of the supernatural inspiration to which they render us docile, as sails render a ship responsive to the breath of the wind. Some theologians, who did not see the necessity of the infused moral virtues, which are superior to

---

[47] "The species of every habit depends on the formal aspect of the object, without which the species of the habit cannot remain" (IIa IIae, q.5, a.3).

acquired moral virtues, were surprised to learn that in every soul in the state of grace there are, in addition, gifts of the Holy Ghost, superior by their divine mode to the infused moral virtues. They denied this essential superiority because they failed to recognize the supernatural riches which the mystical life especially manifests to us. Understanding St. Thomas materially, they confused the inspiration of the Holy Ghost with the actual grace necessary for the exercise of the virtues as soon as some special difficulty presents itself.

St. Thomas, on the contrary, teaches explicitly the essential distinction between the virtues and the gifts, and consequently he distinguishes exactly the inspiration of the Holy Ghost, which surpasses the human mode, from the simple actual grace which is adapted to this mode.[48] On this point also, by declaring the gifts necessary to salvation, St. Thomas agrees with the greatest mystics. He adds, as they do, that the gifts, although subordinated to the theological virtues, greatly assist in their development. The Holy Ghost communicates His lights to us in the recollection of faith. Thus the difference is very great between that supernatural faith which subsists without charity in a soul in the state of mortal sin, and living faith which is aided by the gifts and profound touches of the Holy Ghost.

We shall find the same loftiness in the doctrine of St. Thomas on actual grace, on the mode of God's presence in the just soul, and on the eminent and absolute simplicity of the divine essence.

The humble Thomas Aquinas, who was always inclined to silence and always recollected, lived this supernatural doctrine. His whole heart was given up to the love of God while he was pondering and solving the most difficult questions. How could it be otherwise in a great saint destined to remain throughout the centuries the light of theology? The

---

48 *Summa,* Ia IIae, q.68. See *infra,* chap. 5, art. 5. "The rôle of the gifts of the Holy Ghost; their predominance in infused contemplation."

heavenly gift of wisdom illumined his research, directed his intelligence and will toward an ever deeper possession of divine truth and life, and this it did although he was engaged in the most diverse studies. Questions seemingly remote from this supreme end are so only for a soul that has not yet reached that height where all is lost in God, the beginning and end of all things. Undoubtedly St. Thomas was raised to the highest degrees of mystical contemplation, and certainly his teaching will not hinder souls in their ascent.

## ARTICLE III

*Mystical Theology and the Doctrine of St. Thomas on the Efficacy of Grace*

Those who are surprised that we seek the principles of mystical theology in the writings of St. Thomas should consider especially his teaching on the efficacy of grace.

This doctrine, precisely because it is very lofty, is not generally well understood except by speculative theologians and souls that have entered the passive ways. The reason for this is found in the fact that speculative theologians are accustomed to consider everything in relation to God, the universal first cause and Author of salvation. Souls in the passive ways know from experience that in the work of salvation everything comes from God, even our co-operation— in this sense, that we can distinguish therein no part that is exclusively ours and that does not come from the Author of all good.

The expression "no part exclusively ours" occurs frequently in the works of the fathers and in those of St. Thomas. As we shall see, it clearly expresses his thought; but to grasp all its loftiness and profundity, we shall, first of all, state the less lofty conceptions proposed by certain theologians. It will be to our advantage to understand the efficacy of actual grace which we need for our conversion, then to resist temptation which at times is violent, so as to merit, to grow in the love of God, to pass through the crucible of the purifications, and to persevere in good until death.

Some theologians [1] thought that the grace which is profitable to salvation is called efficacious, not at all because of itself it leads us gently and mightily to consent to good, but because it is given to us at the moment when God has foreseen that by ourselves alone we would choose to accept it rather than to resist it. The divine prevision of man's response is what distinguishes efficacious grace from grace that is not efficacious. In other words, this efficacy does not come from the divine will, but from the human will; the grace is efficacious, not at all because God wills it so, but because man accepts it. According to this idea, it may happen that of two sinners under the same circumstances receiving equal actual graces, one will be converted and the other will remain in his sin. Hence this difference of determination between these two men springs solely from the human will, and not at all from the difference in the divine help which they received. The same grace, which was only sufficient and which remained sterile in one, was efficacious in the other because he himself made it efficacious. If this is the case, evidently the salutary act is called forth by the divine attraction, but the initial distinction separating the just from the sinner does

---

[1] St. Thomas did not, as a rule, otherwise designate the theologians whose opinion he did not share; but he set forth their thought very exactly in their own words. Charity gained thereby, and the discussion was more serene. We will follow his example so far as we can. At this point we merely recall the principal assertions of these theologians of whom we are speaking: "Whether a sufficient help is efficacious or inefficacious depends on the will of him to whom it is given. With equal grace one sinner may be converted and another not. One person may arise from sin and that with a lesser help of grace, when another with greater help will not arise and will remain hardened. Not that he who accepts a grace accepts it by his liberty alone, but this distinction arises from liberty alone, and not from a difference of antecedent grace (*auxilium praeveniens*)."

not come from God; it is exclusively ours. And this conception of the efficacy of grace is applied not only to the salutary
acts preceding justification, but also to all meritorious acts,
even to the last which crowns the work of salvation.[2]

Does such a very human explanation of this divine mystery
preserve the grandeur of the mystery? The School of St.
Thomas has never thought so.[3] Is not free determination the
most important part of the work of salvation? This determination is what distinguishes the just from the sinner in the
production of every salutary act; every time he avoids sin in
the course of his life, every time he triumphs over temptation, or merits and perseveres in good. According to St.
Thomas, we cannot admit that this important distinction
comes exclusively from us and not at all from God, the Author of salvation. St. Paul says: "For who distinguisheth
thee? Or what hast thou that thou hast not received? And if
thou hast received, why dost thou glory as if thou hadst not
received it?"[4] "Without Me," says our Lord, "you can do
nothing."[5] In these words the fathers, especially St. Augustine and following him St. Thomas, have seen the affirmation that in the work of our salvation all comes from God,
even our co-operation, even the distinction between the just
and sinners, so that we cannot find therein a part which is

[2] In this conception, what depends on the divine good pleasure is that Peter
be placed in circumstances where, according to God's prevision, he will infallibly be saved, and Judas in another order of circumstances where he will
infallibly be lost. The divine good pleasure might have made the inverse
choice. Setting aside this choice of circumstances, we see that in this theory
such a one is saved without being aided by grace more than another who
is lost. Furthermore, certain elect souls have been less aided by grace than
certain reprobate souls, not only in the course of their life but also at the
last moment.

[3] Cf. Salmanticenses, *De gratia,* tr. XIV, disp. VII, "De gratia efficaci": a comparison of the aforesaid doctrine with that of St. Thomas. The latter is set
forth in this treatise according to the texts in a much more correct manner
than in the article "Grâce" in the *Dictionnaire de théologie catholique.*

[4] See I Cor. 4: 7.

[5] John 15: 5. St. Thomas says (*In Matth.* 25: 15): "He who attempts more,
has more grace in fact; but to attempt more, he needs a higher cause." See also
*In Ep. ad Ephes.* 4: 7.

exclusively ours.[6] Moreover, if God were in no way the cause of our choice, He would not have been able to foresee it infallibly from all eternity; for He alone is eternal, and our free acts are future from all eternity [7] only because He decided to produce them in us and with us, or at least to permit them if they are bad.[8]

Other modern theologians have sought to correct the doctrine which we are examining, by saying that grace, followed by consent to good, is called efficacious because it is more adapted (congrua), than simply sufficient grace, to the temperament of the subject who receives it and to the circumstances of time and place in which he is. Grace thus urges us to give our consent, but the free determination of the latter remains exclusively our work. God's action inviting us to good, is analogous to that of a mother who, when she wishes to do so, can find the best means to persuade her child and to lead him to conduct himself well.

In spite of this slight modification, we can truly say that in this second doctrine as in the preceding the efficacy of grace does not come from the divine will, but from the hu-

---

[6] St. Cyprian, *Ad Quirin.*, Bk. III, chap. 4 (*PL*, IV, 734): "We should glory in nothing, because of ourselves we have nothing." St. Basil, *Hom.* 22, "De humilitate": "Nothing is left to thee, O man, in which thou canst glory." St. Chrysostom, *Sermones*, 2, *In Ep. ad Colos.* (*PG*, LXII, 312): "In the business of salvation all is the gift of God." St. Augustine, *De praedest. sanct.*, chap. 5. St. Thomas, Ia, q.23, a.5: "There is no distinction between what flows from free will, and what is of predestination; as there is no distinction between what flows from a secondary cause and a first cause." The first cause and the second cause are not, in fact, two partial co-ordinated causes, as two men tugging a ship, but two total subordinated causes, in such a way that the first applies or moves the second to act. Cf. Ia, q.105, a.5; *De pot.*, q.3, a.4, 7 ad 7um and ad 13um; *Contra Gent.*, III, chaps. 66, 149; *De malo*, q.3, a.2 ad 4um; *Contra errores Graecorum*, chap. 23.

[7] They are absolutely future or future under certain conditions only by virtue of a divine decree, because, being of themselves free, future events are not determined. If they were, they would impose themselves on God Himself as a fatality that would be superior to Him. Cf. IIa IIae, q.171, a.3: "Things remote from the knowledge of all men, through being in themselves unknowable: such are future contingencies, the truth of which is indeterminate." Cf. also Ia, q.14, a.5, 8, 13; q.19, a.8; q.22, a.4; q.23, a.4, 5.

[8] Cf. Ia, q.16, a.7 ad 3um; q.19, a.4; q.14, a.8; Ia IIae, q.79, a.1, 2.

man will and also from our temperament and circumstances. In other words, grace, in this doctrine also, solicits our good consent, but the determination of the latter is exclusively ours. If this were the case, the most important part of the work of salvation would not come from the Author of salvation; it would only have been foreseen by Him.[9]

In reality, according to St. Thomas, the action of God on the will of a converted sinner is infinitely deeper than that of a mother on the heart of her child. The mother's action could grow forever without ever attaining the action of God. Of God alone, Holy Scripture says: "For it is God who worketh in you, both to will and to accomplish, according to His good will." [10] He Himself says by the mouth of Ezechiel: "And I will give you a new heart, and put a new spirit within you; and I will take away the stony heart out of your flesh, and will give you a heart of flesh. And I will put My spirit in the midst of you; and I will cause you to walk in My commandments, and to keep My judgments, and do them." [11] "As the division of waters, so the heart of the king is in the hand of the Lord: whithersoever He will He shall turn it."[12] And St. Paul asks: "Or who hath first given to him, and recompense shall be made him?" [13] "So then it is not of him that willeth, nor of him that runneth, but of God that showeth mercy" [14] . . . "but the same God, who worketh all in all."[15] "For in Him we live and move and

---

[9] Cf. Del Prado, O.P., *De gratia et libero arbitrio*, III, 364 ff. (1907 ed.). As this learned author shows, it is inconceivable that God can infallibly foresee from all eternity a determination which would in no way come from Him. He alone is eternal; and no act of ours is future (absolutely or conditionally) from all eternity without being founded on a positive or permissive eternal decree of God. This is what St. Thomas establishes in the celebrated articles already cited: Ia, q.14, a.5, 8, 13; q.19, a.8; q.23, a.5, which we have explained elsewhere (*God, His Existence and His Nature*, II, 71–93).

[10] Phil. 2: 13.
[11] Ezech. 36: 26.
[12] Prov. 21: 1.
[13] Rom. 11: 35.
[14] Rom. 9: 16.
[15] See I Cor. 12: 6

are." [16] "For of Him and by Him and in Him are all things." [17]

After quoting two of these texts from Scripture,[18] St. Thomas remarks: "Some, who do not understand how God can cause in us the movement of our will without prejudice to liberty, have done their best to wrest a different interpretation from these divine words. For them, they mean that God causes in us the will and the act, in as far as He gives us the faculty to will, but not in as far as He makes us will this or that. Origen has understood it thus (*Peri Archon*, Bk. III). . . . To hold this opinion is manifestly to resist the authority of Holy Scripture. It is said in Isaias (26: 12): Thou hast wrought all our works for us. It is not, therefore, only the faculty of will that we have from God, but the very operation." [19]

The Council of Orange explains these words of Scripture by saying: "God effects in man several blessings without man's co-operation, but man can do no good without the help of God, who enables him to accomplish all his good works.[20] No one has anything of himself except his deceitfulness and sin. Whatever truth and justice we have in us, we have received from that source whence we should all drink in this life, if we do not wish to faint on the way." [21]

Following in this the doctrine of St. Augustine, expressed in the Council of Orange, St. Thomas teaches that grace is efficacious of itself and not by reason of the consent following

[16] Acts 17: 28.

[17] Rom. 11: 36.

[18] Prov. 21: 1; Phil. 2: 13.

[19] *Contra Gentiles*, Bk. III, chap. 89. See also *De veritate*, q.22, a.8; "Every act of the will, in so far as it is an act, is not only from the will as from an immediate agent, but from God as from a first agent that impresses it more vehemently; wherefore, just as the will can change its act into another, so much the more can God." *Ibid.*, q.22, a.9: "God alone can transfer the inclination of the will, which He gave to it, from one thing to another according as He wills."

[20] No supernatural good without a supernatural aid; no natural good without the natural aid of God.

[21] Denzinger, *Enchiridion*, pp. 193, 195.

it. Let us consider what occurs in the innermost depths of the will of a converted sinner. If God wishes efficaciously that a certain sinner should be converted at a given moment, "this divine will," says St. Thomas, "cannot fail to be accomplished"; as St. Augustine observes: "It is by the grace of God that all who are saved are very surely saved." "If then," continues St. Thomas, "it is in the intention of God, who moves wills, to convert or to justify a certain sinner, this sinner will be infallibly justified according to the expression of Jesus: Everyone that hath heard of the Father and hath learned cometh to Me." [22]

According to St. Thomas, divine grace, which efficaciously inclines us to salutary good, is not, therefore, indifferent or changeable. It is not made efficacious by our foreseen consent; but it moves us surely, powerfully, and gently to follow the way of good rather than that of evil.[23]

Thus in the work of salvation man can do nothing without the help of God, but unfortunately he is sufficient unto himself to fall or to sin. And precisely because sin as such is a deficiency or the privation of a good, it demands for its production only a defectible and deficient cause according to Scripture: "Destruction is thy own, O Israel: thy help is only in Me." [24] God permits this failure to occur, or rather does

[22] *Summa*, Ia IIae, q.112, a.3: "Man's preparation for grace is from God, as Mover, and from the free will, as moved. Hence the preparation may be looked at in two ways: first as it is from free will, and thus there is no necessity that it should obtain grace, since the gift of grace exceeds every preparation of human power. But it may be considered, secondly, as it is from God the Mover, and thus it has a necessity—not indeed of coercion, but of infallibility—as regards what it is ordained to by God, since God's intention cannot fail, according to the saying of Augustine in his book on the predestination of the saints (*De dono persev.*, XIV) that by God's good gifts whoever is liberated, is most certainly liberated. Hence if God intends, while moving, that the one whose heart He moves should attain to grace, he will infallibly attain to it, according to John 6: 45: Everyone that hath heard of the Father and hath learned cometh to Me."

[23] Cf. Ia, q.105, a.4; Ia IIae, q.10, a.4 c ad 3um; q.111, a.2 ad 2um; q.113 *passim;* IIa IIae, q.24, a.11; *De malo,* q.6, a.1 ad 3um; *De caritate,* a.12; *Rom.*, 9, lect. 3; *Eph.*, 3, lect. 2; *Heb.*, 12, lect. 3; 13, lect. 3.

[24] Osee 13: 9.

not prevent it, only because He is sufficiently powerful and good to draw a greater good from it—the manifestation of His mercy or justice.[25]

Accordingly no one who has attained the use of reason is deprived of the efficacious grace necessary for salvation, except for having freely resisted a sufficient grace, a good inspiration which recalled the duty to be accomplished. The sinner thus placed an obstacle in the way of efficacious grace which had been offered in the sufficient help. For example, fruit is offered in the flower, but if hail falls on a tree in blossom, we will never see its fruit. St. Thomas observes: "Only those are deprived of grace, who place in themselves an obstacle to grace. Thus when the sun is shining, if someone closes his eyes and falls over a precipice it is his own fault, even though sunlight is necessary for him to see. . . . On the subject of certain sinners, we read in Job (21: 14): Who have said to God: Depart from us, we desire not the knowledge of Thy ways. . . . They were enemies of the light." [26]

God is not obliged to remedy our voluntary faults, especially when they are repeated. The truth of the matter is that He often does remedy them, but not always. Therein lies a mystery.[27]

In this sense we understand the profound meaning of the words of the Council of Trent (Sess. VI, chap. 13): "If men do not resist His grace, as God has begun in them the work of salvation, He will pursue its accomplishment by working in them both to will and to accomplish.[28] But he that thinketh himself to stand, let him take heed lest he fall,[29] and let him with fear and trembling work out his salvation." [30] In the same chapter, the Council reminds us that "the grace of final

25 Cf. Ia IIae, q.79, a.1, 2; Ia, q.2, a.3 ad 1um; q.49, a.2.
26 *Contra Gentes*, Bk. III, chaps. 160, 161; IIa IIae, q.2, a.5 ad 1um.
27 Cf. Ia, q.23, a.3–5. Of this mystery it is said: "He that is a searcher of majesty, shall be overwhelmed by glory" (Prov. 25: 27).
28 Phil. 2: 13.
29 See I Cor. 10: 12.
30 Phil. 2: 12.

perseverance can come only from Him who has the power to sustain those who stand,[31] that they may persevere, and to lift up those who have fallen. No one can be absolutely certain of obtaining this final grace, although all should constantly place firm hope in the help of God."

The Church speaks as follows in her liturgy: "Forestall, we beseech Thee, O Lord, all our thoughts, words, and actions by Thy holy inspirations and carry them on by the assistance of Thy grace, so that every prayer and work of ours may begin always from Thee and by Thee be happily ended."

As St. Augustine says, "Free will is of itself sufficient for evil but, so far as good is concerned, it does nothing unless aided by all-powerful goodness." [32] Although our resistance to sufficient grace is of ourselves alone, we freely give our co-operation, our consent, to good only in virtue of intrinsically efficacious grace, a new gift of God which produces in us the will and the act. "Without Me you can do nothing," says our Lord; and, on the other hand, the soul united to God says with St. Paul: "I can do all things in Him who strengtheneth me"; [33] that is, co-operate in His sanctifying work, labor for eternity.

Some have thought that this doctrine of intrinsically efficacious grace destroys human liberty and contains an absurdity. Far from being absurd, in the opinion of St. Thomas it expresses a sublime mystery: the mystery of God more intimately present to our free will than our free will is to itself.

Grace does not destroy our liberty by its certain efficacy; rather by that very efficacy divine grace moves the free will without doing violence to it. This is the inspired idea of St. Thomas Aquinas when he interprets revelation. "When a cause," he says,[34] "is efficacious to act, the effect follows upon

[31] Rom. 14: 4.
[32] *De correptione et gratia,* chap. 11.
[33] Phil. 4: 13.
[34] Cf. Ia, q. 19, a.8, fundamental article of the *Summa theologica* on this great problem. Cf. Del Prado, O.P., *De gratia et libero arbitrio,* Vol. II, chap. 9.

the cause, not only as to the substance of the effect, but also as to its manner of being and of being made; when a cause is feeble, on the contrary, it does not succeed in giving to its effect the manner which is in it." It is not capable of leaving its imprint on the effect. The property of powerful agents in the physical, intellectual, and moral order is to imprint by the very force of their action their likeness on their works, on their children, on their disciples. Artistic geniuses are aware of it in themselves, great military leaders experience it. St. Thomas says: "Since the divine will is perfectly efficacious, it not only follows that things happen that God wills to happen, but happen also in the way that He wills from all eternity. God wills some things to happen necessarily, some contingently and freely." [35] With this end in view He has given us free will. And why should He be unable to produce in us and through us even the free manner of our acts? As Sophocles, Dante, and Corneille have their way of touching us and of stirring up our emotions, just so God has His way when He moves our will. St. Thomas states: "Free will is the cause of its own movement, because by his free will man moves himself to act. But it does not of necessity belong to liberty that what is free should be the first cause of itself, as neither for one thing to be cause of another need it be the first cause. God, therefore, is the first cause, who moves both natural and voluntary causes. And just as by moving natural causes He does not prevent their acts being natural, so by moving voluntary causes He does not deprive their actions of being voluntary: but rather is He the cause of this very thing in them; for He operates in each thing according to its own nature." [36] Thus a great master communicates to his disciples not only his knowledge, but his spirit and his manner. Leo XIII says the same thing in the encyclical *Libertas*. "God," adds St. Thomas, "immutably moves our will because

[35] Cf. Ia, q.83, a.1 ad 3um.
[36] Cf. *ibid.*

of the perfect efficacy of His power, which cannot fail; but liberty remains because of the nature (and of the unlimited amplitude) of our will (which is ordered to universal good, and which is as a result) indifferent in regard to the particular good which it chooses. Thus in all things Providence works infallibly, and yet contingent causes produce their effects in a contingent manner, for God moves all things proportionately to the very manner of the nature of each being." [37]

Under the impulse of intrinsically efficacious grace, the will moves itself freely, for it is moved by God in a manner befitting its nature. By nature it has for its object universal, limitless good, conceived by the intellect, which is infinitely superior to the senses; only the attraction of God seen face to face could invincibly captivate this faculty to will and to love. [38] It enjoys a dominating indifference in regard to every particular good, judged good under one aspect, but insufficient under another. The relation of our will to this object is not necessary; rather our will dominates the attraction of this good. The act is free because it proceeds, under the indifference of judgment, from a will, the universal amplitude of which projects beyond the particular good toward which it is inclined. [39] By His efficacious motion God does not change, and even cannot change, this contingent relation of our voluntary act with this object, since the act is specified by this

[37] *De malo*, q.6, a.1 ad 3um: "Deus movet quidem voluntatem immutabiliter propter efficaciam virtutis moventis, quae deficere non potest" (St. Thomas does not say because of the prevision of our consent). The dominating indifference which constitutes liberty is potential in the faculty and it becomes actual in the choice itself. The divine motion, far from destroying, actualizes it: at the moment when the divine motion desires it, our will, which is directed toward the universal good, actually dominates the attraction of the particular good which it chooses.

[38] Cf. Ia IIae, q.2, a.8: "Now the object of the will, i. e., of man's appetite, is the universal good: just as the object of the intellect, is the universal truth. Hence it is evident that naught can lull man's will, save the universal good. This is to be found, not in any creature, but in God alone: because every creature has goodness by participation."

[39] Cf. Ia IIae, q.10. a.2; q.2, a.8; q.5, a.3, 8.

object itself. The divine motion does not do violence to our will, since it exercises itself interiorly according to the natural inclination of our will toward the universal good, an inclination which comes from God and of which He is the master.[40] To say that liberty remains, is not contradictory; but in all of this we have an infinitely profound mystery analogous to that of the creative act: the mystery of God nearer to His creatures, whose existence He preserves, than they are to themselves.[41]

God moves our liberty *fortiter et suaviter.* Power and gentleness are so intimately united in efficacious grace that failure to recognize the first is a suppression of the second; it is a failure to see the infinite abyss separating the divine influence from the created influences that exert themselves on our free choice. The beings dearest to us exercise a great persuasive influence on us. Let us suppose it is continually on the increase. Then let us consider the influence which the greatest of the angels can exercise; and let us remember that God can always create more perfect angels who would exert over us a still greater influence. But all this will never attain the efficacy of divine grace.

Does it follow that efforts and willing are useless? Quite the contrary. Precisely because good will and holy effort are most important in the work of salvation, they cannot be exclusively our work. Grace is what causes us to make this choice, what makes us struggle against temptation and overcome it. As St. Augustine frequently says, God moves us, not that we should do nothing, but precisely that we should act. And often, if we demand too little of ourselves, this is because we do not count sufficiently on grace, because we do not sufficiently ask for it. If our spiritual life declines to a lower level, and if we are satisfied with an entirely natural life, this

---

[40] Cf. Ia, q.105, a.4 ad 1um.
[41] See Ia, q.8, a.1; Ia IIae, q.10, a.4; q.113, a.3; *Contra Gentes,* Bk. III, chap. 89.

is a consequence of our believing we are alone in acting, forgetting that God is in us and with us, nearer to us than we are to ourselves.

We now come to the foundation of the loftiest mystical theology, that of St. Paul, St. Augustine, Dionysius, St. Bernard,[42] St. Thomas, Tauler, Ruysbroeck, the author of the *Imitation,* and St. John of the Cross. In the work of salvation, all comes from God, even our co-operation. We cannot glory in contributing a single part, however small, that would be exclusively ours. Man of himself is sufficient for evil; but for good, he can do absolutely nothing without the natural or supernatural help of God. On the other hand, with God and through Him he can achieve the greatest actions: he can co-operate in the salvation of souls, each of which is of more value than the entire material universe; he can make acts of charity, the least of which has greater value than all angelic natures taken together.[43] "But they that hope in the Lord shall renew their strength, they shall take wings as eagles, they shall run and not be weary, they shall walk and not faint." [44]

In conclusion, we simply quote the masterly passage where Bossuet, in the eighth chapter of his treatise on free will, sums up this doctrine of St. Thomas. "To reconcile God's decree and His omnipotent action with our free will, we need not attribute to Him a concurrence (in our action) which is equally ready for anything, and which will become whatever we choose to make of it. Still less is it necessary for Him to await the decision of our will, that He might thereupon form His decree in accordance with our resolutions. Aside from this weak device, which deforms the whole idea of first cause, we need merely consider that the divine will, with its infinite power reaching not only into the essence of

[42] St. Bernard, *De gratia et libero arbitrio,* chap. 14. Cf. *Dict. théol.,* art. "Saint Bernard," col. 776.
[43] Cf. Ia IIae, q.113, a.9 ad 2um.
[44] Is. 40: 31.

all things but into their every mode of being, is of itself in accord with the whole and entire effect, producing in it whatever we conceive to be in it, because His will ordains that it shall come into being endowed with every property that belongs to it."

The same chapter continues: "In the creature there is nothing that has being, no matter how little of it, but what has, for that very reason, received from God everything it possesses. And no one may object that the special property of the exercise of free will is that it comes solely from free will itself. This would be true if man's liberty were a primary and independent liberty and not a liberty which flows from a higher source. God, who, as first being, is the cause of all being, as first mover must be the cause of all action so that He produces in us the action itself, just as He placed in us the power to act. And the created action does not cease to be an action because it was produced by God. On the contrary, it is action all the more because God has invested it with being. . . .

"If the power to produce our action in us were attributed to any other but our Maker, it might well be believed that He would do violence to our liberty and by moving it would break so delicate a spring which He had not made. But God does not have to guard against His action taking anything out of His work, because He produces everything in it down to the last detail. Consequently He produces not only our choice, but also the very freedom that is in our choice. . . . To put freedom in our action is to cause us to act freely; and to accomplish this, is to will that the action should exist; for with God, to accomplish is to will. . . . Thus in order to understand that God creates our free will in us, we must understand only that He wills us to be free. But He wills not only that we should be free in power, but that we should be free in its exercise. And He wills not only in general that we should exercise our liberty, but that we should exercise it in such and such an act. For He, whose knowledge and will extend to the uttermost detail of things, is not satisfied to will that they exist in general, but descends to what is called such and such, that is, to what is most particular; and all of this is comprised in His decree.

"Thus God from all eternity wills every future exercise of human liberty in so far as it is good and real. What could be more absurd than to say that it is not, because God wills it to be? On the contrary, we must say that it is, because God wills it; and since it happens that we are free in virtue of the decree which wills that we should be free, the result is that we act freely in such and such an act in virtue of the decree which reaches into all this detail."

Therefore absolutely everything in the world of material bodies and of spirits, in their being and their actions, comes from God, with the single exception of evil, which is a privation and a disorder. Evil is permitted by the supreme goodness only because God is powerful enough to draw an even greater good out of it: the striking manifestation of His mercy or justice.[45]

This doctrine praises the glory of God. Often it is not understood, because it is at one and the same time too lofty and too simple. Those who do not attain its loftiness disdain its simplicity. "But the humble of heart enter the depths of God without being disturbed and, remote from the world and its thoughts, they find life in the loftiness of the works of God." [46] They do not feel their liberty oppressed by the divine force of grace; rather they find in this power deliverance and salvation.

St. Thomas and the greatest mystics who have come after him tell us that this doctrine should lead us to great depths of humility, continual prayer, practical and sublime faith, abandonment in hope, thanksgiving, and intimacy of love.

[45] St. Thomas, *In Epist. ad Rom.*, chap. 9, lect. 4; Ia, q.23, a.5 ad 3um.
[46] Bossuet, *Élévations sur les mystères,* 18th week, 12th elevation.

## ARTICLE IV

*The Practical Consequences of the Doctrine of St. Thomas on Grace*

St. Thomas, following St. Augustine and opposing Pelagian or semi-Pelagian naturalism, grasped the depth and the height of our Lord's words: "Without Me you can do nothing," [1] and of St. Paul's words: "For it is God who worketh in you, both to will and to accomplish, according to His good will." [2] "For who distinguisheth thee? Or what hast thou that thou hast not received?" [3] In the work of salvation we cannot distinguish any part that is exclusively ours; all comes from God, even our free co-operation, which efficacious grace gently and mightily stirs up in us and confirms.

This grace, which is always followed by its effect, is refused to us, as we said, only if we resist the divine, *auxilium praeveniens*, sufficient grace, in which the efficacious help is already offered us, as fruit is in the flower. If we destroy the flower, we shall never see the fruit, which the influence of the sun and of the nourishment of the earth would have produced. Now man is sufficient to himself to fall; drawn from nothingness, he is by nature defectible. He is sufficiently assisted by God so that he falls only through his own fault, which thus deprives him of a new help. This is the great mystery of grace. We have elsewhere explained what St. Thomas and his best disciples teach about this mystery. [4]

---

[1] John 15: 5.

[2] Phil. 2: 13.

[3] See I Cor. 4: 7.

[4] *God, His Existence and His Nature,* II, 365 ff. It is not necessary that our failure precede the refusal of efficacious grace, in priority of time; priority of nature is sufficient, in the order of material causality, according to the principle of the mutual relations of causes explained by St. Thomas (Ia IIae, q.113, a.8 ad 1um; cf. Ia IIae, q.109, a.1, a.8, 9, 10). It is God who anticipates us by His grace when He justifies us, and it is we who are the first to abandon Him when we lose divine grace: "God will not desert the justified, unless He is first deserted by them." Council of Trent, Sess. VI, chap. 2.

With him and St. Augustine we must submit our intelligence before this divine obscurity, and as Bossuet says, "confess these two graces (sufficient and efficacious), one of which leaves the will without excuse before God, and the other does not permit the will to glory in itself." [5] Is this not in conformity with what our conscience tells us? According to this doctrine, all that is good in us, naturally or supernaturally, has its origin in the Author of all good. Sin alone cannot come from Him, and the Lord allows it to happen only because He is sufficiently powerful and good to draw from it a greater good, the manifestation of His mercy or justice.

This teaching of the great doctors of grace lifts our mind to a lofty contemplation of God's action in the innermost depths of our heart. To prove this, we have only to demonstrate that this doctrine should lead those who understand it well to profound humility, to almost continual interior prayer, to the perfection of the theological virtues and of the corresponding gifts of the Holy Ghost. Besides, we find it in the writings of all the great masters of the spiritual life. Considering the importance and the difficulty of the problem, we shall affirm nothing in this article except according to the very words of Scripture, as the greatest doctors explain them.

This doctrine leads first of all to profound humility. Ac-

[5] Bossuet, *Œuvres complètes*, 1845, I, 643. Cf. the general index of Bossuet's works for references to "grace" (resistance to grace). See particularly *Défense de la tradition*, Bk. XI, chaps. 19–27: Demonstration of the efficacy of grace by the permission of sins into which God allows the just to fall in order to humble them. Permission of the triple denial of St. Peter: "Peter was justly punished for his presumption by the withdrawal of an efficacious help which would have effectively hindered his denial." Bossuet shows that such is the doctrine not only of St. Augustine but of St. John Chrysostom, of Origen, of St. Gregory the Great, and of St. John Damascene, since they say that Peter was deprived of help, a statement which cannot apply to sufficient grace, for without this grace he would have been utterly powerless to avoid the sin. The statement applies to an efficacious help which would have made him effectively avoid this fall. From all of which we see that sufficient grace indeed leaves our will without excuse before God, and that the efficacious grace which St. Peter received later does not permit us to glory in ourselves.

cording to this doctrine man has as his own, as something coming exclusively from himself, only his sin, as the Council of Orange declared.[6] He never performs any natural good act without the natural aid of God, or any supernatural good act without a grace which solicits or attracts him, and also efficaciously moves him to the salutary act. As St. Paul says: "Not that we are sufficient to think anything of ourselves as of ourselves; but our sufficiency is from God."[7]

Even holy souls that have reached a high degree of charity are always in need of an actual grace in order to merit, to advance, to avoid sin, and to persevere in goodness.[8] They should say: "For the thoughts of mortal man are fearful, and our counsels uncertain,"[9] "Thy will be done on earth as it is in heaven . . . and lead us not into temptation." After striving greatly, they should admit: "We are unprofitable servants,"[10] for the Lord might have chosen others who would have served Him much better. In all truth we should say, according to the teaching of St. Thomas, that there is no sin committed by another man which I might not commit in the same circumstances by reason of the infirmity of my free will, and of my own weakness (the Apostle Peter denied his Master three times). And if actually I have not fallen, if I have persevered, this is doubtless because I worked and struggled, but without divine grace I should have done nothing.[11] "Not to us, O Lord, not to us; but to Thy name give glory";[12] "as the potter's clay is in his hand, to fashion and order it . . . so man is in the hand of Him that made him."[13] "Thy hands have made me and formed me";[14] "Thou hast redeemed us

[6] Canon 22: "No one has anything of his own except his deceitfulness and his sin." Denzinger, no. 195.
[7] See II Cor. 3: 5
[8] Cf. Ia IIae, q. 109, a. 2, 8, 9, 10.
[9] Wis. 9: 14.
[10] Luke 17: 10.
[11] Cf. Del Prado, O.P., *De gratia*, III, 151.
[12] Ps. 113: 1.
[13] Eccles. 33: 13; Jer. 18: 6.
[14] Ps. 118: 73.

to God, in Thy blood." [15] "If I have not perished, it is because of Thy mercy." [16] "Into Thy hands I commend my spirit." [17] "This," says St. Augustine, "is what must be believed and said in all piety and truth, so that our confession may be humble and suppliant, and that all may be attributed to God." [18] Such is true humility. "Or what hast thou that thou hast not received? And if thou hast received, why dost thou glory, as if thou hadst not received it?" [19]

The saints, considering their own failures, say to themselves that if such and such a criminal had received all the graces the Lord bestowed on them, he would perhaps have been less unfaithful than they. The sight of the gratuity of the divine predilections confirms them in humility. They recall our Lord's words: "You have not chosen Me: but I have chosen you."

This doctrine leads also to continual intimate prayer, to profound thanksgiving, to the prayer of contemplation.

It leads to intimate prayer; for this is a very secret grace that must be asked. We must ask not only the grace which solicits and excites the soul to good but also that grace which makes us will it, which makes us persevere, which reaches the depths of our heart and of our free will; that grace which moves us in these depths, so that we may be delivered from the concupiscence of the flesh and the eyes, and from the pride of life. God alone saves and snatches us from these enemies of our salvation. At the same time He does not wound our liberty, but establishes it by delivering us from the captivity of these things of earth.

Thus Scripture teaches us to pray: "Have pity on me, O Lord, according to Thine infinite mercy. Be propitious to a sinner. Help my unbelief. Create a clean heart in me, and

15 Apoc. 5: 9.
16 Lam. 3: 22.
17 Ps. 30: 6; Luke 23: 46.
18 *De dono perseverantiae,* chap. 13.
19 See I Cor. 4: 7.

renew a right spirit within me. Convert me, O Lord, make me return to Thee, and I shall return.[20] Thy will be done on earth as it is in heaven." Give me Thy sweet and mighty grace in order that I may truly accomplish Thy holy will. As St. Augustine says: "Lord, give what Thou dost command, and command what Thou pleasest."

Thus again the Church prays in the Missal: "Lord, direct toward Thyself our rebellious wills; grant that unbelievers, who are unwilling to believe, may have a will to believe. Apply our hearts to good works. Give us good will. Convert us and draw us strongly to Thyself. Take from us our heart of stone and give us a heart of flesh, a docile and pure heart. Change our wills and incline them toward what is good." [21]

Such is the holy confidence of the prayer of the Church because she is sure that God is not powerless to convert the most hardened sinners. What should a priest do who cannot succeed in converting a dying sinner? Persuaded that God can convert this guilty will, above all the priest will pray. If, on the contrary, he imagines that God holds this will only from without, by circumstances, good thoughts, good inspirations, which remain external to the consent to salutary goodness, will not the priest himself delay too long in the use of superficial means? Will his prayer possess that holy boldness which we admire in the saints, and which rests on their faith in the potent efficacy of grace?

Likewise prayer should be, in a sense, continual, since our soul needs a new, actual, efficacious grace for every salutary act, for each new merit. With this in mind, we clearly see the profound meaning of our Lord's words: "We ought always to pray, and not to faint." [22] This truth is fully realized only in the mystical life, in which prayer truly becomes, as the fathers say, "the breath of the soul," which hardly ceases any

20 Lam. 5: 21.
21 On these prayers of the Church, cf. St. Augustine, *Epist. ad Vital.*, 217 (*al.* 107), and Bossuet, *Défense de la tradition*, Bk. X, chap. 10.
22 Luke 18: 1.

more than that of the body. The soul constantly desires grace, which is like a vivifying breath renewing it and making it produce constantly new acts of love of God.

Such ought to be the prayer of petition. And we ought also to thank God for all our good actions, since without Him we could have done nothing. This is what makes St. Paul say: "Pray without ceasing. In all things give thanks; for this is the will of God in Christ Jesus concerning you all." [23] "Speaking to yourselves in psalms and hymns and spiritual canticles, singing and making melody in your hearts to the Lord; giving thanks always for all things, in the name of our Lord Jesus Christ, to God and the Father." [24]

This doctrine of the intrinsic efficacy of grace leads also directly to the prayer of contemplation, which considers chiefly the profound action of God in us to mortify and to vivify, and which is expressed by the *fiat* of perfect abandonment. In contemplation we see realized in the intimate depths of souls the words of Scripture: "Thou are great, O Lord, forever. . . . For Thou scourgest, and Thou savest: Thou leadest down to hell, and bringest up again." [25] "Thy word, O Lord, which healeth all things." [26] To utter a perfect *fiat* to this intense and hidden work of grace in us, even when it crucifies and seems to destroy all, is the most secret but also the most fruitful co-operation in God's greatest work. It is the prayer of Jesus in Gethsemane and that of the Blessed Virgin at the foot of the cross.

Lastly, this doctrine reminds us that even for prayer efficacious grace is necessary. "Likewise the Spirit also helpeth our infirmity. For we know not what we should pray for as we ought; but the Spirit Himself asketh for us with unspeakable groanings. And He that searcheth the hearts, knoweth what the Spirit desireth; because He asketh for the saints

---

[23] See I Thess. 5: 17–18.
[24] Ephes. 5: 19–20.
[25] Tob. 13: 2.
[26] Wis. 16: 12.

according to God." [27] This mystery is verified especially in the mystical union, often obscure and painful, in which the soul learns by experience what great need we have of grace in order to pray, as also to do good. But, says St. John of the Cross,[28] souls that have reached a certain degree of union "obtain from God all that they feel inspired to ask of Him, according to the words of David, 'Delight in the Lord, and He will give thee the request of thy heart' " (Ps. 36: 4). Moreover, every humble, confident, persevering prayer by which we ask what is necessary or useful for our salvation is infallibly efficacious, because our Lord uttered such a promise and because God Himself caused this petition to well up in our hearts. Resolved from all eternity to grant us His benefactions, He leads us to ask them of Him.[29]

This doctrine of the powerful efficacy of grace leads finally to great heights in the practice of the theological virtues. This it does because it is intimately bound up with the sublime mystery of predestination, the grandeur of which it fully preserves. St. Paul, in the Epistle to the Romans, tells us: "And we know that to them that love God, all things work together unto good, to such as, according to His purpose, are called to be saints. For whom He foreknew, He also predestinated to be made conformable to the image of His Son; that He might be the first-born amongst many brethren. And whom He predestinated, them He also called. And whom He called, them He also justified. And whom He justified, them He also glorified. What shall we then say to these things? If God be for us, who is against us?" [30] St. Paul teaches the same doctrine in the Epistle to the Ephesians.[31]

---

[27] Rom. 8: 26–27.
[28] *The Dark Night of the Soul*, Bk. II, chap. 20.
[29] Cf. IIa IIae, q.83, a.2; St. Augustine, *Enchirid.*, chap. 32; Bossuet, *Défense de la tradition*, Bk. XII, chap. 38.
[30] Rom. 8: 28–31.
[31] St. Paul also says in the Epistle to the Ephesians, 1: 3–6, 11–12: "Blessed be the God and Father of our Lord Jesus Christ, who hath blessed us with spiritual blessings, in heavenly places, in Christ: as He chose us in Him

St. Augustine [32] and St. Thomas [33] have explained these words of St. Paul without lessening their real meaning. Bossuet, their disciple, sums them up with his usual mastery by saying: "I do not deny the goodness of God toward all men, or the means which in His general providence He offers them for their eternal salvation. The Lord does not will that any should perish, but that all should return to penance.[34] But however great His designs may be on everyone, He fixes a certain particular gaze of preference on a number that is known to Him. All those on whom He gazes in this way, weep for their sins and are converted in their time. That is why Peter burst into tears when our Lord looked at him benignly. Peter's repentance was the result of the prayer which Christ had offered for the stability of his faith; for it was necessary, first of all, to rekindle his faith, and then to strengthen it that it might endure to the end. The same is true of all those whom His Father has given Him in a special manner. Of these He said: 'All that the Father giveth to Me shall come to Me. . . . Now this is the will of the Father who sent Me: that of all that He hath given Me, I should lose nothing; but should raise it up again in the last day' (John 6: 37, 39).

"And why does He make us penetrate these sublime truths? Is it to trouble us, to alarm us, to cast us into despair,

---

before the foundation of the world, that we should be holy and unspotted in His sight in charity. Who hath predestinated us unto the adoption of children through Jesus Christ unto Himself: according to the purpose of His will: unto the praise of the glory of His grace, in which He hath graced us in His beloved Son. . . . In whom we also are called by lot, being predestinated according to the purpose of Him who worketh all things according to the counsel of His will. That we may be unto the praise of His glory, we who before hoped in Christ."

[32] *De praedestinatione sanctorum,* chaps. 3, 6–11, 14, 15, 17; *De dono perseverantiae,* chaps. 1, 6, 7, 12, 16–20, 23; *De correptione et gratia,* chaps. 9, 12, 13, 14. See also on these texts, Del Prado, *De gratia et libero arbitrio,* III, 555–564; II, 67–81, 259; and Bossuet, *Défense de la tradition,* Bk. XII, chaps. 13–20.

[33] *In Ep. ad Rom.* 8: 28; *In Ep. ad Ephes.,* I, no.5; Ia, q.23.

[34] Cf. II Pet. 3: 9.

to disturb us and make us question whether or not we are of the elect? Far be it from us to indulge in such thoughts, which would make us penetrate the secret counsels of God, explore, so to speak, even into His bosom, and sound the profound abyss of His eternal decrees. The design of our Savior is that, contemplating this secret gaze which He fixes on those whom He knows and whom His Father has given Him by a certain choice, and recognizing that He can lead them to their eternal salvation by means which do not fail, we should thus learn first of all to ask for these means, to unite ourselves to His prayer, to say with Him: 'Deliver us from evil' (Matt. 6: 13); or, in the words of the Church: 'Do not permit us to be separated from Thee. If our will seeks to escape, do not permit it to do so; keep it in Thy hands, change it, and bring it back to Thee.' " [35]

This prayer assumes its full value in the plenitude of the life of faith, which is the mystical life; faith, as practical as sublime, in the wisdom of God, in the holiness of His good pleasure, in His omnipotence, in His sovereign dominion, in the infinite value of the merits of Jesus Christ, and in the infallible efficacy of His prayer.

Faith in the wisdom of God. "O the depth of the riches of the wisdom and of the knowledge of God! How incomprehensible are His judgments, and how unsearchable His ways! . . . Or who hath first given to Him, and recompense shall be made him? For of Him, and by Him, and in Him, are all things: to Him be glory forever. Amen." [36]

Faith in the holiness of the divine good pleasure. "I confess to Thee, O Father, Lord of heaven and earth, because Thou hast hid these things from the wise and prudent, and hast revealed them to little ones. Yea, Father; for so hath it seemed good in Thy sight." [37] Jesus spoke in the same man-

---

[35] Bossuet, *Méditations sur l'Évangile*, Part II, 72d day.
[36] Rom. 11: 33–36.
[37] Matt. 11: 25–26.

ner to the Pharisees: "Murmur not among yourselves. No man can come to Me, except the Father, who hath sent Me, draw him; and I will raise him up in the last day." [38]

Faith in the divine omnipotence. God can convert the most hardened sinners. "The heart of the king is in the hand of the Lord: whithersoever He will He shall turn it." [39] "For it is God who worketh in you, both to will and to accomplish, according to His good will." [40] "My sheep hear My voice; and I know them, and they follow Me. And I give them life everlasting; and they shall not perish forever, and no man shall pluck them out of My hand. That which My Father hath given Me, is greater than all: and no one can snatch them out of the hand of My Father. I and the Father are one." [41]

Faith in the sovereign dominion of the Creator. "Behold as clay is in the hand of the potter, so are you in My hands, O house of Israel." [42] "Or hath not the potter power over the clay, of the same lump, to make one vessel unto honor, and another unto dishonor? What if God, willing to show His wrath, and to make His power known, endured with much patience vessels of wrath, fitted for destruction, that He might show the riches of His glory on the vessels of mercy, which He hath prepared unto glory?" [43]

Faith in the infinite value of the merits and of the prayer of Jesus. "The Father loveth the Son: and He hath given all things into His hands." [44] "Amen, amen I say unto you: He that believeth in Me, hath everlasting life." [45] "I have manifested Thy name to the men whom Thou hast given Me out of the world. Thine they were, and to Me Thou gavest them;

[38] John 6: 43–44.
[39] Prov. 21: 1.
[40] Phil. 2: 13.
[41] John 10: 27–30.
[42] Jer. 18: 6.
[43] Rom. 9: 21–23.
[44] John 3: 35.
[45] John 6: 47.

and they have kept Thy word. . . . I pray for them. . . . Holy Father, keep them in Thy name whom Thou hast given Me; that they may be one, as We also are. . . . While I was with them, I kept them in Thy name. Those whom Thou gavest Me have I kept; and none of them is lost, but the son of perdition, that the Scripture may be fulfilled. . . . I pray not that Thou shouldst take them out of the world, but that Thou shouldst keep them from evil. . . . And not for them only do I pray, but for them also who through their word shall believe in Me. . . . Father, I will that where I am, they also whom Thou hast given Me may be with Me; that they may see My glory which Thou hast given Me, because Thou hast loved Me before the creation of the world." [46]

This act of serene and invincible faith in the infinite merits of Christ ravishes the heart of God, who at times allows everything to seem outwardly lost, that He may give His children the opportunity to prove their faith in Him by such an act.

This doctrine of grace leads us also to an entirely supernatural hope composed of confidence in the divine mercy and abandonment to it. The formal motive of hope is, in fact, the infinitely helpful divine mercy (*Deus auxilians*). That this virtue of hope may be divine and theological, we must hope in God and not in the power of our free will. "He that trusteth in his own heart is a fool; but he that walketh wisely, he shall be saved." [47] Considering our weakness, we must "with fear and trembling work out our salvation," [48] and "he that thinketh himself to stand, let him take heed lest he fall." [49] But, considering God's infinitely helpful goodness, we must say to Him: "In Thee, O my God, I put my trust; let me not be ashamed." [50] "Into Thy hands I commend my

[46] John 17: 6, 9, 11, 12, 15, 20, 24.
[47] Prov. 28: 26.
[48] Phil. 2: 12.
[49] See I Cor. 10 :12.
[50] Ps. 24: 2.

spirit." [51] "O taste, and see that the Lord is sweet; blessed is the man that hopeth in Him." [52] "Preserve me, O Lord, for I have put my trust in Thee." [53] "In Thee, O Lord, have I hoped, let me never be confounded." [54] "Behold, God is my savior, I will deal confidently, and will not fear: because the Lord is my strength, and my praise, and He is become my salvation." [55] "I can do all things in Him who strengtheneth me." [56]

Such is the abandonment which Christ wishes us to learn. It has no quietism in it, as Bossuet so well explains. He says: "We must abandon ourselves to the divine goodness. This does not mean that we need not act and work, or that, in opposition to God's command, we may yield to unconcern or to rash thoughts. Rather, while acting to the best of our ability, we must above all abandon ourselves to God alone for time and for eternity. . . .

"A proud man fears that his salvation will be uncertain unless he keeps it in his own hand, but he is deceived. Can I rely on myself? I feel that my will escapes me at every moment. If Thou, O Lord, didst wish to make me the sole master of my fate, I should decline a power so dangerous to my weakness. Let no one tell me that this doctrine of grace and preference leads good souls to despair. How mad for me to think I can be reassured by being hurled back on myself and delivered up to my inconstancy! To this, O my God, I do not consent. I find assurance only in abandoning myself to Thee. And in this abandonment I find even greater trust, for those to whom Thou dost give this confidence in entire abandonment, receive in this gentle impulse the best mark we can have on earth of Thy goodness. Increase this desire in me; and by this means

[51] Ps. 30: 6.
[52] Ps. 33: 9.
[53] Ps. 15: 1.
[54] Ps. 30: 2.
[55] Is. 12: 2.
[56] Phil. 4: 13.

put into my heart the blessed hope of being at last among the chosen number. . . . Heal me and I shall be healed; convert me and I shall be converted." [57]

In the painful, passive purifications of the spirit, souls are often tempted against hope and are troubled about the mystery of predestination. In this temptation all created helps fail them, and they must hope heroically against all hope for this single, pure reason, namely, that God is infinitely helpful and does not abandon the just unless they desert Him, that He does not let them be tempted beyond their strength aided by grace, that He sustains them by His all-powerful goodness, as He said to St. Paul: "My grace is sufficient for thee; for power is made perfect in infirmity." "Gladly, therefore," says the great Apostle, "will I glory in my infirmities, that the power of Christ may dwell in me. For which cause I please myself in my infirmities, in reproaches, in necessities, in persecutions, in distresses, for Christ. For when I am weak, then am I powerful." [58]

We ought in great difficulties to think of this formal motive of hope: God our helper; for He comes efficaciously to our assistance by the grace that urges us to the practice of goodness, and in a gentle and powerful way causes it to be accomplished.[59] "But the salvation of the just is from the Lord, and He is their protector in the time of trouble. And the Lord will help them and deliver them: and He will rescue them from the wicked, and save them, because they have hoped in Him." [60]

Lastly, this doctrine of the efficacy of grace confirms our charity toward God and souls. This charity is a friendship based on God's communication to us of the divine life through grace. Therefore the more intimate and efficacious the grace which is given us, the more we should love God and corre-

[57] Bossuet, *Médit. sur l'Évangile,* Part II, 72d day.
[58] See II Cor. 12: 9, 10.
[59] Cf. *Catechism of the Council of Trent,* chap. 45, "On temptation."
[60] Ps. 36: 39 f.

spond to His love. "Not as though we had loved God, but because He hath first loved us." [61] The Master Himself said to His Apostles: "You have not chosen Me: but I have chosen you; and have appointed you, that you should go, and should bring forth fruit: and your fruit should remain: that whatsoever you shall ask of the Father in My name He may give it you." [62] And in the exercise of the apostolate, because he believed in the potent efficacy of grace, St. Paul wrote: "Who then shall separate us from the love of Christ? Shall tribulation? or distress? or famine? or nakedness? or danger? or persecution? or the sword? . . . But in all these things we overcome, because of Him that hath loved us. For I am sure that neither death, nor life, nor angels, nor principalities, nor powers, nor things present . . . nor any other creature, shall be able to separate us from the love of God, which is in Christ Jesus our Lord." [63] Christ said to His heavenly Father: "Those whom Thou gavest Me have I kept. . . . Father, I will that where I am, they also whom Thou hast given Me may be with Me. . . . And I have made known Thy name to them, and will make it known; that the love wherewith Thou hast loved Me, may be in them, and I in them." [64]

These words of our Lord are fully realized on earth only in the mystical life, the prelude to the life of heaven. And the great theology of St. Augustine and St. Thomas on grace thus reaches the loftiest orthodox mysticism, if care is taken not to lessen its meaning.

No power is gentler than the infallibly efficacious grace of God. It diffuses itself gently in the soul which begins to will; the more the soul wills and the greater its thirst for God, the more it will be enriched. When God becomes more exacting and wishes pure crystal where there has been only sin, then He will give His grace in abundance that the soul may correspond

[61] See I John 4: 10.
[62] John 15: 16.
[63] Rom. 8: 35, 37–39.
[64] John 17: 12, 24, 26.

to His demands. He Himself said: "I am come that they may have life, and may have it more abundantly." [65] The purified soul ends by praising the power of God: "The right hand of the Lord hath wrought strength. I shall not die, but live: and shall declare the works of the Lord." [66]

We are not surprised to find this doctrine in the works of the greatest masters of the spiritual life.

St. Bernard says: "Grace is necessary to salvation, free will is equally so; but grace in order to give salvation, free will in order to receive it. . . . Therefore we should not attribute part of the good work to grace, and part to free will. It is performed in its entirety by the common and inseparable action of both; entirely by grace, entirely by free will, but springing completely from the first in the second." [67]

St. Bonaventure is of the same opinion: "Devout souls do not seek to attribute to themselves in the work of salvation some part that does not come from God. They recognize that all issues from divine grace." [68]

Tauler speaks of the efficacy of grace as St. Thomas does.

In *The Imitation of Christ* we read: "Never esteem thyself to be anything because of thy good works. . . . Of thyself thou always tendest to nothing: speedily art thou cast down, speedily overcome, speedily disordered, speedily undone. Thou hast not whereof to glory, but many things for which thou oughtest to account thyself vile; for thou art much weaker than thou art able to comprehend." "For I am nothing and I knew it not. If I be left to myself, behold I become nothing but mere weakness; but if Thou for an instant look upon me, I am forthwith made strong, and am filled with new joy." "From Me, as from a living fountain, the small and the great, the poor and the rich, do draw the water of life; and

[65] John 10: 10.
[66] Ps. 117: 17.
[67] *De gratia et libero arbitrio*, chaps. 1 and 14. Cf. *Dict. Théol.* art. "Saint Bernard," col. 776.
[68] See *II Sent.*, dist. 26, q.2.

they that willingly and freely serve Me, shall receive grace for grace. . . . Thou oughtest, therefore, to ascribe nothing to thyself, nor attribute goodness unto any man, but give all unto God, without whom man hath nothing. I have given thee all, and My will is to have all again. . . . This is the truth whereby vainglory is put to flight, and if heavenly grace enter in and true charity, there will be no envy or narrowness of heart, neither will self-love busy itself. For divine charity overcometh all things and enlargeth all the powers of the soul." "O most blessed grace, that makest the poor in spirit rich in virtues. . . . Come Thou down unto me, come and replenish me early with Thy comfort, lest my soul faint for weariness and dryness of mind. . . . This alone and by itself is my strength; this alone giveth advice and help; this is stronger than all enemies, and wiser than all the wise. . . . Without this, what am I but a withered branch and an unprofitable trunk, meet only to be cast away? Let Thy grace, therefore, O Lord, always go before and follow me, and make me continually intent on good works." "I am to be praised in all My saints; I am to be blessed above all things, and to be honored in all whom I have thus gloriously exalted and predestined without any merits of their own.[69] . . . These all are one through the bond of love. . . . They love Me more than themselves. . . . For being ravished above self and self-love, they are wholly absorbed in the love of Me, in whom also they rest with full fruition." [70]

Whenever St. Teresa touches on the question of grace, her doctrine is similar to that of St. Augustine and St. Thomas.[71]

---

[69] We find the same doctrine in St. Thomas, Ia, q.23, a.5.

[70] Bk. IV, chap. 4, no. 2; chap. 8, no. 1; chap. 9, no. 2; chap. 55, no. 5; chap. 58. These passages are from *The Imitation of Christ* (edited by Brother Leo, F.S.C., 1926). They are quoted by permission of The Macmillan Company, publishers.

[71] The directing thought of St. Teresa is found in St. Paul's words, "It is God who worketh in you, both to will and to accomplish, according to His good will" (Phil. 2: 13). In chapter 21 of her *Life* she writes: "Why His Majesty doeth this is, because it is His pleasure, and He doeth it according to His pleasure:

St. John of the Cross always assumes the truth of this doctrine.[72]

St. Francis de Sales states this doctrine in the following terms: "The chains of grace are so powerful, and yet so sweet, that though they attract our heart, they do not shackle our freedom. . . . Our yielding to the impulse of grace is much

---

even if the soul be without the fitting disposition, He disposes it for the reception of that blessing which He is giving to it." After examining why a certain soul reaches contemplation and perfection more rapidly than another, she concludes: "In short, the whole matter is as His Majesty wills. He gives His grace to whom He pleases" (*Life*, chap. 22). "God bestows His favors when He pleases, after the manner He pleases, and on whom He pleases. Being Master of His goods, He can bestow them thus without wronging anyone" (*The Interior Castle*, fourth mansion, chap. 1).

In the account of her conversion (*Life*, chaps. 8, 9), she says: "I used to pray to our Lord for help; but, as it now seems to me, I must have committed the fault of not putting my whole trust in His Majesty, and of not thoroughly distrusting myself. . . . There was no one to give me life, and I was not able to take it. He who could have given it me had good reasons for not coming to my aid, seeing that He had brought me back to Himself so many times, and I as often had left Him. . . . I implored Him to strengthen me once for all, so that I might never offend Him any more. . . . I had a very great devotion to the glorious Magdalene. . . . I seem to have made greater progress; for I was now very distrustful of myself, placing all my confidence in God. It seems to me that I said to Him then that I would not rise up till He granted my petition. I do certainly believe that this was of great service to me, because I have grown better ever since" (*Life*, chap. 9). "Now our Lord set me at liberty, and gave me strength also to use it" (*Life*, chap. 24). As someone has well said, in the face of this formidable mystery, against which so many heresies have arisen, and over which there have been so many sad controversies, even among true children of the Church, the Seraphic Virgin bows with serenity and gratitude. "O my God," she exclaims, "well is it for me that Thou didst not leave such a wretch as myself at liberty to fulfil or to frustrate Thy will. Mayest Thou be blessed forever, and may all creation praise Thee" (*The Way of Perfection*, chap. 32). "The more difficult things are to understand, the more devotion they inspire in me, and this in proportion to their difficulty" (*Life*, chap. 28).

72 *The Spiritual Canticle*, Part IV, stanza 38: "On that day of eternity, that is to say, before creation, and according to His good pleasure, God predestined the soul to glory, and the degree that it would occupy there. From that moment this glory became the property of the soul, and that in so absolute a manner that no vicissitude either temporal or spiritual can radically remove it; for what God has given gratuitously to the soul cannot fail to remain its property forever." In *The Ascent* (Bk. II, chap. 5): "God disposes freely of this degree of union (mystical), as He disposes freely of the degree of the beatific vision." In the *Prayer of the Inflamed Soul*, he says again: "For if Thou dost await my works, O Lord, in order thus to grant me what I ask, give them to me, perform them in me, and join thereto the pains Thou art willing to accept from me."

more the effect of grace than of our own will, and resistance to
its inspirations is to be attributed to our will alone. . . . 'If
thou didst know the gift of God.' " [73]

Good spiritual authors, no matter to what theological school
they belong, are led to the same doctrine by the loftiness of the
subjects with which they deal.[74]

All the difficulties of the mystery of grace are solved practically by humility. Bossuet says: "Behold a terrible danger
for human pride. Man says in his heart: I have my free will.
God made me free, and I wish to make myself just. . . . In
my free will, which I cannot harmonize with this abandonment to grace, I wish to find something to cling to. Proud foe,
do you wish to reconcile these things, or rather to believe that
God reconciles them? He reconciles them in the way He
wishes, without releasing you from your action and without
ceasing to demand that you attribute to Him all the work of
your salvation, for He is the Savior, and He said: 'I am the
Lord; and there is no savior besides Me' (Is. 43: 11). Believe
firmly that Jesus Christ is the Savior, and all difficulties will
vanish." [75]

As is evident in the passages quoted from the writings of St.
John of the Cross, this great doctrine of St. Paul, St. Augus-

[73] *Treatise on the Love of God*, Bk. II, chap. 12. The author says in the same
chapter: "Grace is so gracious and so graciously seizes on our hearts to draw
them, that it in no way offends the liberty of our will; it touches powerfully
but yet so delicately the springs of our spirit that our free will suffers no violence from it."

[74] Father Grou, S.J. (*Maximes spirituelles*, 2d maxim) writes as do the most
faithful disciples of St. Thomas: "Grace alone can free us from the slavery of
sin and assure us true liberty; whence it follows that the more the will subjects
itself to grace, the more it will do all that depends on it to become absolutely,
fully, and constantly dependent, the more free it will be. . . . Thus for the
will all consists in putting itself in the hands of God, in using its own activity
only to become more dependent on Him. . . . Is not our salvation incomparably more certain in God's hands than in our own? And fundamentally what
can we do to save ourselves except what God enables us to do?" Cf. also Father
de Caussade, S.J., *L'abandon à la Providence*, Bk. III, chaps. 1, 2; and Father
Lallemant, S.J., *La doctrine spirituelle*, 4th principle, "La docilité au Saint-
Esprit," chaps. 1, 2.

[75] Bossuet, *Elévations sur les mystères*, 18th week, 15th elevation.

tine, and St. Thomas, manifestly turns souls toward the loftiest mystical union, which is none other than the fulness of the life of faith. This truth will become clearer in the two following chapters, where we will treat of the nature of Christian perfection and of what constitutes the essence of mystical contemplation.

# CHAPTER IV

## The Full Perfection of Christian Life

### ARTICLE I

*Christian Perfection, or the Beginning of Eternal Life*

Can Christian perfection, its nature and conditions, be discussed without in any way lessening its essential sublimity? Is it possible to reach an understanding of the Master's words: "Be you therefore perfect, as also your heavenly Father is perfect"? [1] If we ask the Apostle St. John this question, he will answer us in Christ's very words, that Christian life, particularly Christian perfection, is the beginning of eternal life.

In the Fourth Gospel, the Savior says on several occasions: "He that believeth in the Son, hath life everlasting." [2] In other words, not only will he have eternal life later on if he perseveres; but he who believes has it already in a sense, because the life of grace, even on earth, is the beginning of eternal life, as St. Thomas states repeatedly.[3] As a seed is defined only by the plant that springs from it, or the aurora by the day that it heralds, so we can conceive the life of grace only by considering, first of all, the life of glory, of which it is the seed. For the same reason, we cannot determine what Christian perfection is without speaking first of eternal life, of which it is the prelude.

We will consider eternal life in the first part of this article; in the second part we shall see how the life of grace on earth

---

[1] Matt. 5: 48.

[2] John 3: 36; 5: 24, 39; 6: 40, 47. Cf. 6: 55 ff., and the *Commentary of St. Thomas on the Gospel of St. John* dealing with these passages.

[3] *Summa*, IIa IIae, q.24, a.3 ad 2um. "Grace is nothing else but the beginning of glory in us." Cf. Ia IIae, q.69, a.2; *De veritate*, q.14, a.2.

is essentially the same as the life of heaven; the same also through charity, which will never cease. We shall also see how the life of grace differs from that of heaven through faith and hope, which must disappear in order to give way to the positive possession of God by vision.

In the following articles, with St. Thomas as our teacher, we will study what in this life principally constitutes Christian perfection, properly so called; what its relations are with the gifts and the virtues, and with the precepts and counsels. Thus we shall see all that Christian perfection requires.

### ETERNAL LIFE IN ITS COMPLETE DEVELOPMENT

"Now this is eternal life: that they may know Thee, the only true God, and Jesus Christ, whom Thou hast sent." [4] St. John explains this passage by saying: "Dearly beloved, we are now the sons of God; and it hath not yet appeared what we shall be. We know that, when He shall appear, we shall be like to Him: because we shall see Him as He is." [5] St. Paul says: "We see now through a glass in a dark manner: but then face to face. Now I know in part; but then I shall know even as I am known." [6] We shall see face to face, that is, immediately, such as He is in Himself, God "who inhabiteth light inaccessible" [7] to all natural, created and creatable knowledge.

The Church teaches us expressly that "the souls of the blessed in heaven have an intuitive and direct vision of the divine essence without the intermediary of any previously known creature. The divine essence manifests itself directly and openly in perfect clarity. The souls of the blessed enjoy it continually and will enjoy it forever. Such is eternal life," [8] to which the "light of glory" [9] must raise us.

[4] John 17: 3.
[5] See I John 3: 2.
[6] See I Cor. 13: 12.
[7] See I Tim. 6: 16.
[8] Denzinger, *Enchiridion*, no. 530.
[9] *Ibid.,* no. 475.

We are therefore called to see God not merely by the reflection of His perfections in material creatures, or by His marvelous radiation in the world of pure spirits, but to see Him without any intermediary, more clearly indeed than we see here on earth the persons with whom we speak; for God, being entirely spiritual, will be intimately present in our intellect, which He will illumine at the same time that He gives it the power to endure His dazzling splendor.[10]

Between Him and us there will not be even the intermediary of an idea, for no created idea can represent being as it is in itself, pure, infinitely perfect act, uncreated, eternally subsistent thought, light of life, and source of all truth.[11] And we shall not be able to express our contemplation by any word, even by any interior word. This contemplation, superior to every finite idea, will absorb us in God, and will remain ineffable, just as in this life we lose the gift of speech when the sublime ravishes us. The Deity, such as it is in itself, can be expressed only by the consubstantial Word, which is the uncreated Word, "the brightness of eternal light, and the unspotted mirror of God's majesty, and image of His goodness."[12]

By reason of its object, this face to face vision of God infinitely excels the most sublime philosophy, and also the loftiest natural knowledge of the angels. We are called to see all the divine perfections together, identified in their common source, the Deity; to grasp how the tenderest mercy and the most inflexible justice proceed from one and the same infinitely generous and infinitely holy love, love of the supreme good. This good, wishing to communicate itself as much as possible and possessing an incontestable right to be loved above all, thus wonderfully unites justice and mercy in all the works of God.[13] We are called to see how this love, even in its

---

[10] St. Thomas, Ia, q.12, a.5.
[11] Cf. Ia, q.12, a.2.
[12] Wis. 7: 26.
[13] See Ia, q.21, a.4.

freest good pleasure, is identical with pure wisdom; how in this love there is nothing that is not wise, and in this wisdom nothing that is not converted into love. And we are called to see how this love is identical with the supreme good, loved from all eternity; how divine wisdom is identical with the first truth always known; how all these perfections harmonize and are but one in the very essence of Him who is.

We are called to contemplate the intimate life of God, the Deity itself, absolute purity and sanctity; to lose our gaze in its infinite fecundity, blossoming into the three divine Persons; to see the eternal generation of the Word, "splendor of the Father and figure of His substance"; to gaze in endless rapture upon the ineffable procession of the Holy Ghost, that torrent of spiritual flame, term of the common love of the Father and of the Son, the bond uniting Them eternally in the most absolute diffusion of Themselves.

Who can tell the love and joy that will be born in us of this vision? If we are delighted here below by the reflection of the divine perfections shared by creatures, by the fairy magic of the material world, by the harmony of sounds and colors, by the azure of a cloudless sky above a sunlit sea, which makes us think of the tranquil ocean of being and of the infinite light of divine wisdom; if we are lost in wonderment at the splendors of the world of souls revealed to us by the lives of the saints; what will we feel when we see God, the eternally subsistent flash of wisdom and of love, whence proceeds all the life of creation? We speak of a flash of genius to designate a sudden illumination of the mind. What shall we say of the uncreated light of God? For us it remains hidden only because of its excessive splendor, as too strong a ray of sunlight seems like darkness to the weak eye of an owl.

The joy born of such a vision will be that of so strong and absolute a love of God that nothing will ever destroy it or even diminish it. This love, necessarily following the beatific vision of God, the sovereign good, will be absolutely spontaneous, but will no longer be free. The infinite Good, by presenting Himself to us in this way, will quench our insatiable thirst for happiness, and will fill and satisfy the capacity of our power to love, "which will necessarily adhere to Him." [14] Our will, by reason of its nature, will turn toward Him with all its inclination and strength. It will no longer have any energy to suspend its act, which will be ravished from it, in a way, by the infinite attraction of God seen face to face. In regard to all finite good, our will remains free; it can even yield or not yield to the attraction and to the law of God as long as we do not see His infinite goodness directly. But when His glory appears to us, our desires will then be gratified and we will no longer be able not to correspond to His love. "I shall be satisfied when Thy glory shall appear." [15]

This love will be composed of admiration, respect, gratitude, and especially friendship, with a simplicity and a depth of intimacy that no human affection can have. It will be a love by which we will rejoice especially that God is God, infinitely holy, just, and merciful; a love by which we will adore all the decrees of His providence in view of His glory, which will radiate in us and through us.

Such must eternal life be in union with all those who died in charity, and particularly with those whom we have loved in the Lord.

Eternal life, therefore, consists in knowing God as He knows Himself, and in loving Him as He loves Himself. But, if we penetrate more deeply into this matter, we see that this divine knowledge and love are possible only if God, so to speak, deifies us in our very soul. In the natural order, man is capable of intellectual knowledge and of an enlightened love superior to sensible love only because he has a spiritual soul. In like manner we will be capable of a divine knowledge and of a supernatural love only if we have received a participation in

[14] See Ia, q. 82, a. 2.
[15] Ps. 16: 15

the very nature of God, of the Deity; only if our soul, the principle of our intellect and will, has been, in a sense, deified or transformed into God, as iron plunged into the fire is transformed, so to speak, into fire, without ceasing to be iron. The blessed in heaven can share in the essentially divine operations only because they participate in the divine nature, the principle of these operations; only because they have received this nature from God, somewhat as a son on earth receives his nature from his father.

From all eternity God the Father necessarily engenders a Son equal to Himself, the Word. To Him He communicates all His nature, without dividing or multiplying it; He gives Him to be "God of God, light of light." Out of pure goodness, He has willed to have in time other sons, adopted sons, according to a sonship not only moral and figurative, but very real, which makes us truly participate in the divine nature, in its intimate life. "This sonship by adoption," says St. Thomas, "is thus really a participated likeness of the eternal sonship of the Word." [16] St. John exclaims: "Behold what manner of charity the Father has bestowed upon us, that we should be called and should be the sons of God." [17] We are "born of God"; [18] and St. Peter says that we are "partakers of the divine nature." [19] "Whom He foreknew, He also predestinated to be made conformable to the image of His Son; that He might be the first-born amongst many brethren." [20]

Such is the essence of the glory that God reserves for His children: "Eye hath not seen, nor ear heard, neither hath it entered into the heart of man, what things God hath prepared for them that love Him." [21]

The elect truly belong to the family of God; they enter

16 See IIIa, q.3, a.8; in *In Ep. ad Rom.*, 8: 29.
17 See I John 3: 1.
18 John 1: 13.
19 See II Pet. 1: 4.
20 Rom. 8: 29.
21 See I Cor. 2: 9.

heaven in the cycle of the Blessed Trinity who dwells in them. The Father engenders His Word in them; the Father and the Son breathe forth love in them. Charity likens them to the Holy Ghost; the beatific vision makes them like the Word, who renders them like the Father of whom He is the image. In each of them the Trinity, known and loved, dwells as in a living tabernacle; and furthermore, they are in the Trinity, at the summit of being, of thought, and of love.

Such is the goal of all Christian life, of all spiritual progress. In it there is no concern for earthly interests, or for the development of our personalities (a poor formula, foolishly repeated by many Christians who forget the true grandeur of their vocation). Revelation tells us we must tend infinitely higher. God has predestined His elect to become conformable to the image of His Son. The world, in its wisdom, rejects this doctrine; its philosophers refuse to listen to it. Then the Lord calls the humble, the poor, the infirm,[22] to share in the riches of His glory: "I confess to Thee, O Father, Lord of heaven and earth, because Thou hast hid these things from the wise and prudent, and hast revealed them to little ones." [23]

### BEGINNING OF ETERNAL LIFE

How can we attain so lofty an end as eternal life? Spiritual progress can tend to this end only because it presupposes in us the seed of glory, that is, a supernatural life identical in its essence with eternal life. The seed contained in the acorn could not become an oak unless it had the same nature as the oak, unless it contained the same life in a latent state. A child could not become a man unless he had a rational soul, unless reason were slumbering in him. Similarly a Christian on earth could not become one of the blessed in heaven unless he had already received divine life.

[22] Luke 14: 21. "Then the master of the house, being angry, said to his servant: Go out quickly into the streets and lanes of the city, and bring in hither the poor and the feeble and the blind and the lame."
[23] Matt. 11: 25.

If we wish to understand the nature of the seed contained in the acorn, we must consider this nature in its perfect state in the fully developed oak. In the same way, if we wish to know the life of grace, we must contemplate it in its supreme development; in glory which is its consummation.

Fundamentally the life of grace and the life of glory are the same supernatural life, the same charity, with two differences. Here on earth, God is known only in the obscurity of faith, not in the clarity of vision. In addition, we hope to possess God in an inamissible manner; but as long as we are on earth, we can lose Him through our own fault.

In spite of these two differences, it is the same life. Our Lord said to the Samaritan woman: "If thou didst know the gift of God. . . . Whosoever drinketh of this water shall thirst again; but he that shall drink of the water that I will give him, shall not thirst forever. But the water that I will give him, shall become in him a fountain of water, springing up into life everlasting." [24] In the Temple on the last day of the Feast of Tabernacles, Jesus stood and cried in a loud voice: "If any man thirst, let him come to Me, and drink. He that believeth in Me, as the Scripture saith, Out of his belly shall flow rivers of living water." [25] As St. John adds, He said this of the Spirit, which they should receive who believe in Him. On several occasions Jesus repeats: "He that believeth in the Son, hath life everlasting." [26] "He that eateth My flesh and drinketh My blood, hath everlasting life: and I will raise him up in the last day." [27] "The kingdom of God cometh not with observation. Neither shall they say: Behold here, or behold there. For lo, the kingdom of God is within you." [28] It is hidden in you as the grain of mustard seed; as the leaven that causes the loaf to rise; as the treasure buried in the field.

[24] John 4: 10, 13 f.
[25] John 7: 37.
[26] John 3: 36; 6: 40, 47.
[27] John 6: 55.
[28] Luke 17: 20 f.

And how are we to know that we have already received this life which should last forever? St. John expounds the matter for us at length.[29] "We know that we have passed from death to life, because we love the brethren. He that loveth not, abideth in death. Whosoever hateth his brother is a murderer. And you know that no murderer hath eternal life abiding in himself." [30] "These things I write to you, that you may know that you have eternal life, you who believe in the name of the Son of God." [31]

And in truth, Christ said in His sacerdotal prayer: "Now this is eternal life: that they may know Thee, the only true God, and Jesus Christ, whom Thou hast sent." [32] Through supernatural faith this knowledge has its beginning; and through living faith, or faith vivified by charity, Christ "dwells in us and we in Him," [33] a statement that St. John himself explains by saying: "God hath given to us eternal life. And this life is in His Son. He that hath the Son, hath life. He that hath not the Son, hath not life." [34]

Since this is true, what does death become for the true Christian? A passage from the supernatural life which is as yet imperfect to the plenitude of this life. In this sense we must understand our Lord's words: "Amen, amen I say to you: If any man keep My word, he shall not see death forever." In amazement the Jews answered: "Now we know that Thou hast a devil. Abraham is dead, and the prophets; and Thou sayest: If any man keep My word, he shall not taste death forever. . . . Whom dost Thou make Thyself?" [35] At the

---

[29] This point is well explained in the beautiful exegetical study of Father J. B. Frey, S.Sp., "Le Concept de 'Vie' dans S. Jean," which appeared in the review *Biblica*, 1920, pp. 38–58, 213–239.
[30] See I John 3: 14 f.
[31] *Ibid.*, 5: 13.
[32] John 17: 3.
[33] John 15: 4; 17: 26.
[34] See I John 5: 11 f.
[35] John 8: 51–53.

tomb of Lazarus, Christ said: "I am the resurrection and the life: he that believeth in Me, although he be dead, shall live. And everyone that liveth and believeth in Me, shall not die forever." [36] And again to the Jews: "Your fathers did eat manna in the desert and are dead. This is the bread that came down from heaven. . . . He that eateth this bread shall live forever." [37]

The liturgy expresses the same thought in the mass for the dead: "For Thy faithful, O Lord, life is changed, not lost." [38]

Sanctifying grace, received in the essence of the soul, is, therefore, by its nature imperishable. It should last forever and blossom into eternal life.[39] Moreover, among the theological virtues is one, charity, which ought not to disappear. "Charity never falleth away," says St. Paul. . . . "And now there remain faith, hope and charity, these three: but the greatest of these is charity." [40] Indeed some saints on earth have a far greater degree of charity than certain of the blessed in heaven, but without having as much continuity in the act of love. St. John while on earth had a degree of charity superior to that possessed by the soul of a little child who died immediately after baptism.[41] The gifts of the Holy Ghost also

[36] John 11: 25 f. See also John 4: 14; 8: 51; 10: 28; 13: 8.

[37] John 6: 49, 59.

[38] Preface of the mass for the dead.

[39] Cf. the Carmelites of the Salamanca School, De gratia, disp. IV, dub. 6, nos. 107, 109; dub. 7, no. 141; Sanctifying grace is the same habitus, which, having received its final perfection, is called glory or grace consummated.

[40] See I Cor. 13: 8, 13; and St. Thomas, Ia IIae, q.67, a.6. Charity differs from faith and hope in that it does not imply any imperfection, and that it can love God either in the obscurity of faith or in the clarity of vision.

[41] As the Carmelites of Salamanca show (De caritate, disp. VII, dub. 4, no. 66), theologians commonly admit that the charity of a just man living on earth can equal that of one of the blessed in heaven. The reason for this is that the charity of each of the blessed in heaven has a determined degree beyond which it will never progress. But this degree can be attained and even surpassed by a just soul here on earth. It is certain that the Blessed Virgin, while still on earth, had a charity which far surpassed that of every soul in heaven and that of the angels. But the charity which an adult possesses on earth is always inferior to that which he will have in heaven, where nothing will hinder the impulse of his love. Cf. Ia, q.117, a.2 ad 3um.

subsist in heaven.[42] The life of grace is therefore the same as that of the blessed in heaven.

True, we do not attain God in the clarity of vision, yet it is He that our faith attains. The grace of faith makes us adhere to the uncreated, revealing Truth. We believe in God's word, not in that of St. Peter or of St. Paul,[43] and this word reveals to us "the deep things of God." [44] Our faith is thus "the substance (or the principle, the seed) of things to be hoped for," [45] which we shall contemplate in heaven. This faith, in spite of its obscurity, infinitely surpasses the keenest natural intuitions and even the most sublime natural knowledge of the loftiest angel. St. Paul declares: "Though we or an angel from heaven, preach a gospel to you, besides that which we have preached to you, let him be anathema." [46]

So long as hope has not given place to the definitive possession of God, the supernatural life of grace and charity can be lost, but solely because we can grow weak and fail to co-operate. Sanctifying grace, considered in itself, and the charity which is in us are of themselves incorruptible, like living water that would always remain pure, unless the vase containing it should happen to break. "For God who commanded the light to shine out of darkness hath shined in our hearts. . . . But we have this treasure in earthen vessels, that the excellency may be of the power of God, and not of us." [47] We can, alas, lose charity, because of the fickleness of our free will; but, be our weakness what it may, the love of charity considered in itself "is strong as death, jealousy as hard as hell, the lamps thereof are fire and flames. Many waters cannot quench charity, neither can the floods drown it." [48] It is this love which daily snatches souls from the demon, from the se-

[42] Cf. Ia IIae, q.68, a.6.
[43] See I Thess. 2: 13.
[44] See I Cor. 2: 10.
[45] Heb. 11: 1.
[46] Gal. 1: 8.
[47] See II Cor. 4: 6 f.
[48] Cant. 8: 6 f.

ductions of the world; it is this love which has triumphed over persecutions and the most frightful torments. If we allow ourselves to be penetrated by it, we are invincible.

This love of charity is the same as that which subsists in heaven. It presupposes that we are born "not of blood, nor of the will of the flesh, nor of the will of man, but of God"; [49] that we are not only the servants of God, but His children and friends according to an adopted sonship, which is as real as grace. But the reality of grace differs from that of the flesh, since grace is given to us to last forever.

We now see clearly why revelation teaches us that the Blessed Trinity dwells in every soul in the state of grace as in a temple where it is known and loved. In heaven the Trinity dwells in the souls of the blessed as in a living tabernacle where it never ceases to be glorified. But since the life of grace and of charity is the same in its essence as that of heaven, we must admit, as revelation teaches us, that even on this earth the Blessed Trinity dwells in just souls: "If anyone love Me," says Christ, "he will keep My word, and My Father will love him, and We will come to him, and will make Our abode with him." [50] "And he that abideth in charity, abideth in God, and God in him." [51] "But when He, the Spirit of truth, is come, He will teach you all truth." [52] "Know you not," says St. Paul to the Corinthians, "that you are the temple of God, and that the Spirit of God dwelleth in you?" [53] "Or know you not, that your members are the temple of the Holy Ghost, who is in you, whom you have from God; and you are not your own?" [54] "For you are the temple of the living God." [55]

This indwelling of the Blessed Trinity in us is attributed to the Holy Ghost because charity, which will remain in heaven,

[49] John 1: 13.
[50] John 14: 23.
[51] See I John 4: 16.
[52] John 16: 13.
[53] See I Cor. 3: 16.
[54] *Ibid.*, 6: 19.
[55] See II Cor. 6: 16.

likens us more particularly to the Spirit of love; whereas faith, which will be replaced by vision, likens us as yet only imperfectly to the Word, the figure of the Father and splendor of His substance. The Blessed Trinity is none the less entirely in us as the life of our life, the soul of our soul; occasionally it makes itself felt by us especially by the gift of wisdom,[56] and thus prepares us in the obscurity of faith for the life of heaven.

"Eternal life begun," says Bossuet,[57] "consists in knowing by faith (a tender and affectionate knowledge which inclines the soul to love); [58] and eternal life consummated consists in

---

[56] Cf. St. Thomas, Ia, q.43, a.3: "For God is in all things by His essence, power, and presence, according to His one common mode, as the cause existing in the effects which participate in His goodness. Above and beyond this common mode, however, there is one special mode belonging to the rational creature wherein God is said to be present as the object known is in the knower, and the beloved in the lover. And since the rational creature by its own operation of knowledge and love attains to God Himself, according to this special mode, God is said not only to exist in the rational creature, but also to dwell therein as in His own temple. . . . Again, we are said to possess only what we can freely use or enjoy, but to have the power of enjoying the divine Person can only be according to sanctifying grace. Moreover, the Holy Ghost is possessed by man, and dwells within him in the very gift itself of sanctifying grace. Hence the Holy Ghost Himself is given and sent."

*I Sent.*, Dist. XIV, q.2, a.2 ad 3um: "Any knowledge whatsoever does not suffice to indicate that there is a mission (and indwelling of the Holy Ghost). There must be a knowledge which proceeds from a gift attributed to that person, from a gift which unites us to God according to the mode proper to that person, that is to say, by love. Moreover, this knowledge is quasi-experimental." It presupposes, then, the presence of God who thus makes Himself felt by us as the principle which vivifies us. This explanation, while allowing the mystery to subsist, is considerably cleared up if we recall that charity is the same virtue in heaven and on earth; in the quality of perfect friendship charity, even on earth, demands real union with God, loved above all. God, who is pure spirit, not being by His nature in one place, is not separated from us by space. He is in us, as in all things, as first preserving cause. For several Thomists, if, by an impossibility, He were not already thus present in us, He would become so by charity. Cf. B. Froget, O.P., *De l'habitation du Saint-Esprit dans les âmes justes*, 3d ed., pp. 156–71, and Ia, q.43, a.3; IIa IIae, q.27, a.4; see Gonet, Salmanticenses, Billuart. John of St. Thomas has a different opinion about this hypothesis, "by an impossibility" mentioned above. His opinion, however, seems less probable.

[57] *Méditations sur l'Évangile*, Part II, 37th day; *In Joan.*, 17: 3: "Now this is eternal life: that they may know Thee, the only true God, and Jesus Christ, whom Thou hast sent."

[58] *Ibid.*

seeing openly and face to face. Jesus Christ gives us both the one and the other because He merits this life for us, and is its principle in all the members whom He animates."

Such is the life of grace and of charity; it is infinitely superior to genius, to the gift of miracles, to the knowledge of the angels.[59] In particular such should be Christian perfection, the true nature and conditions of which we can now more easily determine without lessening them. We have already seen the nature of conformity to the only Son of God, a progressive conformity that should render us like Christ Jesus in His hidden, apostolic, and suffering life, before making us share in His glorious life, the seed of which we already possess: "He that believeth in the Son, hath life everlasting." [60]

We shall now note two important consequences of this doctrine.

1) Since sanctifying grace is the beginning of eternal life, and since every just soul enjoys habitual union with the Blessed Trinity dwelling in it, the mystical union, or the actual, intimate, and almost continual union with God, such as is found here on earth in holy souls, appears as the culminating point on earth of the development of the grace of the virtues and of the gifts, and as the normal, even though rather infrequent, prelude to the life of heaven.[61] This mystical union belongs, in fact, to the order of sanctifying grace; it

[59] See I Cor. 13: 1 ff.
[60] John 3: 36.
[61] Cf. St. John of the Cross, *The Ascent of Mount Carmel*, Bk. II, chap. 5: "The greater love is, the more intimate is union; and this means that the conformity of the will with God's will is more perfect. The will, wholly conformed, realizes in its totality union and the supernatural transformation in God.

"This doctrine makes it clear that if the soul is occupied with creatures or with its faculties, either by attraction or by habitual dispositions, it thereby lacks preparation for such a union. The reason for this is that the soul does not offer itself entirely to God, who wishes its supernatural transformation. It must, therefore, concern itself solely with the rejection of obstacles, natural dissimilarities, in order that God, who already communicated Himself naturally, according to nature, may communicate Himself supernaturally by grace." This teaching confirms the doctrine which we defended earlier in this work on the relations between ascetical and mystical theology.

proceeds essentially from "the grace of the virtues and of the gifts" and not from graces *gratis datae,* which are transitory and in a sense exterior (as miracles and prophecy) and which may accompany it. The mystical life is Christian life, which has, so to speak, become conscious of itself. It does not give us the absolute certainty that we are in the state of grace, a certitude which, according to the Council of Trent, would presuppose a special revelation, but as St. Paul says: "The Spirit Himself giveth testimony to our spirit, that we are the sons of God." [62] He makes us know this, observes St. Thomas, "by the filial love which He produces in us." [63]

2) As the life of grace is essentially ordained to that of glory, the normal, although in fact quite rare, summit of its development should be a very perfect disposition to receive the light of glory immediately after death without passing through purgatory; for it is only through our own fault that we will be detained in that place of expiation, where the soul can no longer merit. Now this very perfect disposition to immediate glorification can be nothing other than an intense charity coupled with the ardent desire of the beatific vision, such as we find them particularly in the transforming union, after the painful passive purifications which have delivered the soul from its blemishes. Since nothing unclean can enter heaven, in principle a soul must undergo these passive purifications at least in a measure before death while meriting and progressing, or after death without meriting or progressing.[64]

[62] Rom. 8: 16.

[63] *In Ep. ad Rom.,* 8: 16, and Ia IIae, q.112, a.5. B. Froget, O.P., *De l'habitation du Saint-Esprit dans les âmes justes,* p. 183.

[64] This does not mean that in fact the transforming union must be reached before death in order to avoid purgatory. Certainly some souls—for example, the souls of children who have died immediately after baptism—go directly to heaven without having attained on earth this degree of intimate union. But here, considering a question of principle rather than of fact, what we mean and will explain farther on, is that the transforming union is the normal prelude of the beatific vision; it is a normal summit. The first of these two words should not make us forget the second; nor the second, the first. Many of those who die immediately after baptism or religious profession are far from being

These consequences, to which we will return, disclose the grandeur of the Christian perfection which can be realized on earth, and they contain the loftiest and most practical teaching.

## ARTICLE II

*Christian Perfection Consists Especially in Charity*

In our treatment of Christian perfection, we have considered the end toward which it is essentially ordained, and from this point of view we have defined it as the beginning of eternal life in our souls, or eternal life begun in the obscurity of faith. Perfection in this life is the development of grace, which has been defined as the seed of glory. Of the three theological virtues that we possess, one, charity, should endure forever.

With St. Thomas Aquinas as our guide,[1] we must now consider in what Christian perfection especially and chiefly consists here on earth; what its relations are with the virtues and gifts of the Holy Ghost, and with the precepts and the counsels.

We shall see that Christian perfection consists especially in charity: primarily in charity toward God; and secondarily in charity toward our neighbor. We will then study the charity of the perfect in contrast with that of beginners and of proficients, and shall see what are the degrees of perfect charity, even to heroism and sanctity. This will lead us to a consideration of the relations of the charity of the perfect with the other virtues, with the passive purifications of the soul, and with the gifts of the Holy Ghost, which are the principles of contemplation. By this method we shall clearly see the diffi-

---

perfect. If they had continued to live, they would have committed faults, which would have required the purification of which we are speaking.

[1] *Summa*, IIa IIae, q.184. We will follow the order of the articles of this question, supplementing them by such articles of the treatise on charity as bear directly on this subject.

culty and grandeur of evangelical perfection considered in all its loftiness, as it is proposed to us by our Lord in the eight beatitudes at the beginning of the Sermon on the Mount.

In the second place, we will treat of the relations of perfection thus defined with the precept of love and with the counsels; and lastly, we shall see in what varying degrees the obligation to tend to perfection binds all Christians, whether clerics, religious, or seculars. This is, with several additions, the order followed by St. Thomas in his exposition of the subject.[2]

## ERRONEOUS OR INCOMPLETE DOCTRINES ON THE ESSENCE OF PERFECTION

To solve the question as to what especially constitutes Christian perfection, St. Thomas asks, by way of objection, whether it consists mainly in wisdom, or in fortitude, or in patience, or in the aggregate of the virtues. Such different conceptions do, in fact, present themselves more or less explicitly to the mind.

The Greek thinkers considered that perfection lay especially in wisdom, so much esteemed by the philosopher; in that higher view of all things viewed in their first cause and last end, a view which perceives the harmony of the universe and should direct our whole life.

Today theosophists make perfection consist in a "consciousness of our divine identity," in the intuition of our divinity. Theosophy presupposes pantheism; it is the radical negation of the supernatural order and of all Christian dogmas, although it often preserves the terms of Christianity while giving them an entirely different meaning. It is a very perfidious imitation and corruption of our asceticism and mysticism.[3]

Some Christians would be inclined to say that perfection

[2] *Summa*, IIa IIae, q. 184.
[3] Cf. Father Mainage, O.P., *Les principes de la théosophie*, 1922.

consists principally in contemplation, which has its origin in the gift of wisdom. To prove their contention they would cite St. Paul's text: "In malice be children, and in sense be perfect." [4] "We speak wisdom among the perfect. . . . The spiritual man judgeth all things. . . . We have the mind of Christ." [5] Reading these inspired texts in too natural and too hasty a manner, some will perhaps expect to reach perfection rapidly by the assiduous perusal of the great mystics without, however, sufficiently concerning themselves with the practice of the virtues which these authors recommend, and also without keeping clearly in mind the fact that true contemplation must be entirely penetrated by supernatural charity and forgetfulness of self.[6]

From a lower point of view, some might even think that the study of theology and of its related sciences is the most important thing in the life of the priest, of the apostle, because he must fight against error and illumine minds. One might thus be led to consider practically as secondary in a sacerdotal and apostolic life the celebration of mass and union with God; yet this union is the very soul of the apostolate. Without being actually aware of it, how many make perfection consist in what they call the full development of their personality. They seek it chiefly in a broad, nicely balanced human culture that is "well informed" on actual problems and careful to grasp those phases of Christianity which are most attractive to a lofty nature. But they have only a superficial knowledge of it, and they are given up to a practical naturalism devoid of any vivifying influence on souls. Those among them who, in the course of time, are deeply touched by the grace of God, perceive their peculiar mistake and understand that to build

---

[4] See I Cor. 14: 20.

[5] *Ibid.*, 2: 6, 15 f.

[6] Perfection does not consist especially in contemplation, which is an intellectual act, as we shall see farther on. Perfection consists in charity. However, the loving contemplation of God is here below the most efficacious means to attain the perfection of charity; and it is a means united to the end.

on the intellect alone is to build on sand, as St. Thomas says when commenting on our Lord's expression, "like a foolish man that built his house upon the sand." [7] Unless vivified by the love of God, "knowledge puffeth up," says St. Paul, "but charity edifieth." [8] This it does because it makes us live not for ourselves, as he does who seeks only the full development of his own personality, but for God: "Charity, properly speaking, makes us tend to God, by uniting our affections to Him, so that we live, not for ourselves, but for God." [9]

Another equally imperfect tendency is opposed to this ultra-intellectualism. Natures inclined to action are by this very tendency led to make perfection consist chiefly in outward activity, in fortitude, or the courage that must be shown in such activity, or in patience when circumstances are unfavorable. For the heroes of antiquity, the perfect man is first and foremost the strong, the brave man. If this conception is transposed into the supernatural order, St. James' words will be quoted: "Patience hath a perfect work." [10] This is, in fact, the great virtue which demonstrates the sanctity of the martyr. But this patience is inspired and controlled by a higher virtue.

According to an analogous tendency, some might be led to make perfection consist especially in austerity, fasting, penitential practices; from this point of view, the most austere religious orders would be the most perfect. A certain love of austerity, not unmixed with pride, such as we find in the Jansenists, might thus be developed, which would then become false zeal and bitterness. Charity would be sacrificed to it,[11] and virtue would be made to consist in what is hard rather

---

[7] Matt. 7: 26.
[8] See I Cor. 8: 1.
[9] St. Thomas, IIa IIae, q.17, a.6 ad 3um.
[10] Jas. 1: 4
[11] It can aptly be said: "The best thing that one can do with the best of things is to sacrifice it," on condition, however, that we safeguard the hierarchy of the gifts of God and of the virtues, and that we do not sacrifice something superior to what is inferior.

than in what is good and in the order willed by God.[12] This error would confound the means with the end, or even invert the order of the means to the end, which is union with God. Austerity ought to be proportioned to this end; it is not the end.[13] The same must be said of humility, which prostrates us before God that we may with docility receive His influence, which should lift us up to Him.[14]

Others might be led to make perfection consist especially in the interior and exterior worship due to God, in acts of the virtue of religion, in the faithful accomplishment of exercises of piety, and in the devotion which animates them. This opinion approaches the truth; yet this view does not suf-

---

[12] St. Thomas says in substance that the reason of greater virtue consists in the good rather than in the difficult; although the difficulty springing from the magnitude of the work increases merit. Ia IIae, q.114, a.4 ad 2um; IIa IIae, q.155, a.4 ad 2um; q.123, a.12 ad 2um. The principle of merit resides in charity. Moreover, it is more meritorious to accomplish easy things with great charity than to perform very difficult acts with less charity. Thus many tepid souls carry their cross without great merit, whereas the Blessed Virgin merited more by the easiest acts of charity than all the martyrs together in their torments.

[13] On this subject, St. Thomas (IIa IIae, q.188, a.7 ad 1um) says: "This saying of our Lord does not mean that poverty itself is perfection, but that it is the means of perfection. Indeed, as shown above, it is the least of the three chief means of perfection, since the vow of continence excels the vow of poverty, and the vow of obedience excels them both. Since, however, the means are sought, not for their own sake, but for the sake of the end, a thing is better, not for being a greater instrument, but for being more adapted to the end. Thus, a physician does not heal the more, the more medicine he gives, but the more the medicine is adapted to the disease. Accordingly, it does not follow that a religious order is the more perfect according as the poverty it professes is more perfect, but according as its poverty is more adapted to the end, both common and special."

[14] Cf. St. Thomas, IIa IIae, q.161, a.5 ad 2um: "Just as the orderly assembly of virtues is, by reason of a certain likeness, compared to a building, so again that which is the first step in the acquisition of virtue is likened to the foundation, which is first laid before the rest of the building. . . . Humility holds the first place inasmuch as it expels pride, which God resisteth, and makes man open to receive the influx of divine grace. Hence it is written (Jas. 4: 6): 'God resisteth the proud and giveth grace to the humble.' In this sense humility is said to be the foundation of the spiritual edifice." But it is, nevertheless, inferior to the virtues which unite us immediately to God; that is, to the theological virtues and also to the intellectual virtues, such as wisdom, and to legal justice. Cf. Ibid.

ficiently discern the superiority of the theological virtues which, more than the others, unite us to God because they are immediately specified by Him. The virtue of religion is inferior to them because it is immediately concerned not with God Himself but with the worship due Him.[15] From this point of view, one might perhaps be more attentive to worship and to the liturgy than to God Himself; to the figures than to the reality; to the manner of reciting an Our Father or a Gloria than to the sublime meaning of these prayers. The service of God would take precedence over the love of God.

Others, although few in number, might be tempted to see perfection in the solitary life, especially if the soul is there favored with visions and revelations. Aristotle says in the first book of his *Politica:* "He who lives in solitude and no longer communicates with men, is either a beast or a god." And the Holy Ghost Himself, by the mouth of the prophet Osee, says of the chosen people, the figure of the interior soul: "I will allure her, and will lead her into the wilderness: and I will speak to her heart." [16] But does it follow that love of solitude is the essence of perfection? If this were true, how could fervent Christians who are detained in the world by their duties attain perfection? What of the apostles and priests consecrated to the ministry, who cannot withdraw to a Thebaid? St. Thomas believes that, "solitude, like poverty, is not the essence of perfection, but a means thereto." [17]

St. Francis de Sales says: "Everyone paints devotion according to his own passion and fancy. He that is addicted to fasting, thinks himself very devout if he fasts, though his heart be at the same time full of rancor. . . . Another accounts himself devout for reciting daily a multiplicity of prayers, though he immediately afterwards utters the most disagree-

---

[15] Cf. IIa IIae, q.81, a.5: Why is not the virtue of religion a theological virtue, but only the first of the moral virtues? Because its object is the worship due to God and not God Himself.

[16] Osee 2: 14.

[17] *Summa,* IIa IIae, q.188, a.8.

able, arrogant, and injurious words amongst his domestics and neighbors. Another cheerfully draws an alms out of his purse to relieve the poor, but cannot draw meekness out of his heart to forgive his enemies. Another readily forgives his enemies, but never satisfies his creditors, but by constraint. These, by some, are esteemed devout, when, in reality, they are by no means so." [18] Each one is inclined to judge according to his individual aptitude and tastes, and then to seek a justification of his views.

To avoid this fault, some make perfection consist in the ensemble of the Christian virtues, and they invoke St. Paul's words: "Put you on the armour of God, that you may be able to stand against the deceits of the devil . . . that you may be able to resist in the evil day, and to stand in all things perfect." [19] It is certain that all the Christian virtues are necessary for evangelical perfection: faith, hope, charity, and the moral virtues, among which the most important is the virtue of religion, which is justice in regard to God. But all these virtues are regulated like the functions of an organism. Is there not one among them which dominates all the others, which inspires them, commands them, animates or informs them, and makes their efforts converge toward one supreme end? And is it not in this directing virtue that perfection especially consists? Therefore, must not the other virtues be subordinated to this directing virtue?

### TRUE SOLUTION: PERFECTION CONSISTS CHIEFLY IN CHARITY

To solve the question thus proposed, we will consider the teaching of Scripture, and then that of theology.

St. Paul teaches, and all Christian tradition follows him: "Put ye on therefore, as the elect of God, holy and beloved, the bowels of mercy, benignity, humility, modesty, patience:

[18] *Introduction to a Devout Life*, chap. 1.
[19] Eph. 6: 11, 13.

bearing with one another. . . . But above all these things have charity, which is the bond of perfection. And let the peace of Christ rejoice in your hearts, wherein also you are called in one body." [20] It is this virtue of charity which corresponds to the two greatest precepts, which are the end of all the others and of the counsels: "Thou shalt love the Lord thy God with thy whole heart, and with thy whole soul, and with all thy strength, and with all thy mind: and thy neighbor as thyself." [21]

St. Paul is so firmly convinced of this superiority of charity over all the other virtues, over the gifts, and over graces gratuitously bestowed, that he writes: "If I speak with the tongues of men and of angels, and have not charity, I am become as sounding brass or a tinkling cymbal. And if I should have prophecy and should know all mysteries, and all knowledge, and if I should have all faith, so that I could remove mountains, and have not charity, I am nothing. And if I should distribute all my goods to feed the poor, and if I should deliver my body to be burned, and have not charity, it profiteth me nothing." [22] I do not fulfil the first commandment of God; I do not conform my will to His; I remain turned away from Him.

Moreover, charity in a way implies all the virtues which are subordinated to it, and which appear as so many modalities or aspects of the love of God. This is what St. Paul says in the same epistle: "Charity is patient, is kind: charity envieth not, dealeth not perversely; is not puffed up; is not ambitious, seeketh not her own, is not provoked to anger, thinketh no evil; rejoiceth not in iniquity, but rejoiceth with the truth; beareth all things, believeth all things, hopeth all things, endureth all things." [23] To this we must add with the great Apostle: "Charity never falleth away: whether prophe-

[20] Col. 3: 12–15.
[21] Luke 10: 27.
[22] See I Cor. 13: 1 ff.
[23] *Ibid.*, 13: 4–7.

cies shall be made void, or tongues shall cease, or knowledge shall be destroyed. For we know in part, and we prophesy in part. But when that which is perfect is come, that which is in part shall be done away. . . . We see now through a glass in a dark manner; but then face to face. Now I know in part; but then I shall know even as I am known. And now there remain faith, hope, and charity, these three: but the greatest of these is charity." [24] It will subsist eternally, when faith and hope shall have disappeared in order to give way to the vision and the definitive possession of God. In addition, according to St. Paul, in the measure with which we love God, we know Him with that sweet knowledge, which is divine wisdom: "Being rooted and founded in charity, you may be able to comprehend with all the saints, what is the breadth, and length, and height, and depth: to know also the charity of Christ, which surpasseth all knowledge, that you may be filled unto all the fulness of God." [25] Finally, St. Paul says, on several occasions, that by charity we become the temples of the Holy Ghost.

The Apostle St. John teaches the same doctrine: "God is charity: and he that abideth in charity, abideth in God, and God in him." [26] "He that loveth not, knoweth not God: for God is charity." [27] "We know that we have passed from death to life, because we love the brethren. He that loveth not, abideth in death." [28]

St. Peter expresses the same thought: "But before all things have a constant mutual charity among yourselves: for charity covereth a multitude of sins." [29] Our Lord Himself said of Magdalen: "Many sins are forgiven her, because she hath loved much."

[24] *Ibid.*, 13: 8–13.
[25] Eph. 3: 17–19.
[26] See I John 4: 16.
[27] *Ibid.*, 4: 8.
[28] *Ibid.*, 3: 14.
[29] See I Pet. 4: 8.

The full value of this teaching of Holy Scripture, commented on by the fathers, is brought home to us through the clarifying light of theology. St. Thomas proves that Christian perfection consists especially in charity: "A thing is said to be perfect in so far as it attains its proper end, which is the ultimate perfection thereof." [30] Take for example, the soldier who knows how to fight, the physician who knows how to heal, the learned teacher who has the art of communicating his knowledge. We must not, however, confound these particular ends of the soldier, the doctor, and the teacher with the universal end of man and of the Christian. "Now," continues St. Thomas, "it is charity that unites us to God, who is the last end of the human mind, since he that abideth in charity abideth in God, and God in him (I John 4: 16). Therefore the perfection of the Christian life consists chiefly in charity." [31]

Farther on, the holy doctor adds: "Perfection is said to consist in a thing in two ways: in one way, primarily and essentially; in another, secondarily and accidentally. Primarily and essentially the perfection of the Christian life consists in charity; principally as to the love of God, secondarily as to the love of our neighbor, both of which are the matter of the chief commandments of the divine law. . . . Now the love of God and of our neighbor is not commanded according to a measure, so that what is in excess of the measure be a matter of counsel." [32] We shall return later to the question of the counsels of poverty, chastity, and obedience, but it is clear even now that they are subordinated to charity. No less certainly the first object of this theological virtue is God Himself. Our neighbor is the secondary object of it, and he must be loved for the sake of God, whom he is to glorify eternally with us by participating in His beatitude.

[30] *Summa*, IIa IIae, q. 184, a. 1.
[31] *Ibid.*
[32] *Summa*, IIa IIae, q. 184, a. 3.

Charity thus conceived is truly "the bond of perfection," as St. Paul says, because if man is rendered perfect by all the virtues, charity unites them all, inspires them, rules them, animates them, or informs them, and assures their perseverance by making their acts converge toward the last end, toward God loved above all. Charity not only binds us to God, but, in a sense, it also binds all the virtues, and makes them all one.[33]

In addition, because charity thus unites us to our last end, it cannot co-exist with mortal sin, which turns us away from that end. Therefore charity is inseparable from the state of grace, or of divine life, while faith and hope can be found in a sinful soul in a state of mortal sin. This is the explanation of St. Paul's statement: "If I should have all faith, so that I could remove mountains, and have not charity, I am nothing." [34] Without charity we abide in death, says St. John. This also explains St. Peter's words: "Charity covers a multitude of sins."

Lastly, since charity has none of the imperfections of faith and of hope, it will subsist eternally; even here on earth charity attains God directly, and that is why it makes us the temples of the Holy Ghost.[35] Hence perfection consists especially in charity. Not only does it assemble all our powers, inspire our patience and perseverance, but it also unites souls and leads them to unity in truth.

### THE OBJECTION OF INTELLECTUALS: WHY IS CHARITY SUPERIOR TO OUR KNOWLEDGE OF GOD

Some people, especially intellectuals, will offer an objection to this great traditional doctrine. Is not the intellect, they will say, man's first faculty, the one that directs all the others,

---

[33] Cf. St. Thomas, in his *Commentary on the Epistle to the Colossians*, 3: 14; *Summa*, IIa IIae, q.23, a.6–8.

[34] See I Cor. 13: 2.

[35] *Summa*, IIa IIae, q.27, a.4; Ia, q.43, a.3.

that primarily distinguishes us from animals? Must we not
conclude that the perfection of man lies especially in the intellectual knowledge he can have of all things considered
in their beginning and their end; and therefore, that the
perfection of man lies in the knowledge of God, the supreme
rule of human life?

St. Thomas has certainly not failed to recognize this aspect
of the problem of perfection. He himself admits that the intellect is superior to the will which it directs. The intellect
has, in fact, a simpler, more absolute, more universal object,
being in all its universality and consequently all being; the
will, on the other hand, has a more restricted object, the
good, which is a modality of being, and which in everything
is the perfection that renders it desirable. As good supposes
being, the will presupposes the intellect and is directed by it.
It is, then, by the intellect, the highest of his faculties,[36] that
man differs specifically from animals.

St. Thomas also admits that in heaven our blessedness will
consist essentially in the beatific vision, in the intellectual and
immediate vision of the divine essence; for it is chiefly by this
vision that we will take possession of God for eternity. Beatific
love will be only the necessary consequence of this immediate
knowledge of the sovereign good. As the properties of an object spring from its essence, our immutable love of God and
the joy of possessing Him will necessarily follow the beatific
vision, which will thus be the essence of our beatitude.[37]

The Angelic Doctor could not better affirm the superiority
of the intellect over the will, in principle, and in the perfect
light of heaven. Why does he now tell us that Christian per-

---

[36] See Ia, q.82, a.3.

[37] "And so it is with an intelligible end. For at first we desire to attain an
intelligible end. We attain it (God) through His being made present to us by
an act of the intellect; and then the delighted will rests in the end when attained. So, therefore, the essence of happiness consists in an act of the intellect:
but the delight that results from happiness pertains to the will. In this sense
St. Augustine says (*Conf.*, X, 23) that happiness is joy in truth, because, to wit,
joy itself is the consummation of happiness."

fection in this life consists especially in charity, which is a virtue of the will, and not in faith, or in the gift of wisdom, or in contemplation, all of which belong to the intellect?

He himself has given us a profound answer to this question, and an answer of prime importance in ascetical and mystical theology. He tells us in substance [38] that although one faculty may by its very nature be superior to another, as sight is to hearing, it is possible that an act of the second may be superior to an act of the first, as the hearing of a sublime and very rare symphony is of a higher order than the sight of an ordinary color. Thus, although the intellect by its very nature (*simpliciter*) may be superior to the will which it directs, because it has a simpler, more absolute, more universal object, yet in certain circumstances (*secundum quid*) and with relation to God, the intellect in this life remains inferior to the will; in other words, here on earth the love of God is more perfect than the knowledge of God; while it is better to know inferior things than to love them. A profound observation on which one cannot meditate too much.

And whence comes this superiority of the love of God over the knowledge we have of Him on earth? "The action of the intellect consists in this," says St. Thomas,[39] "that the idea of the thing understood is in the one who understands; while the act of the will consists in this—that the will is inclined to the thing itself as existing in itself. And therefore the Philosopher says (*Metaph.* VI) that good and evil, which are objects of the will, are in things, but truth and error, which are objects of the intellect, are in the mind." It follows that in this life our knowledge of God is inferior to the love of God, since, as the Angelic Doctor says,[40] in order to know God we, in a way, draw Him to us, and in order to represent Him to ourselves we impose on Him the bounds of our limited ideas.

---

[38] See Ia, q.82, a.3.
[39] *Ibid.*
[40] *Ibid.*

On the other hand, when we love Him, we raise ourselves toward Him, such as He is in Himself.

It is better, therefore, to love God than to know Him, although love always presupposes a certain knowledge and is directed by it. On the other hand, it is better to know inferior things than to love them. By knowing them we raise them, in a way, to our intelligence; whereas by loving them, we stoop toward them, and we might become subservient to them as the miser is to his treasure. It is better to know the properties of gold than to love it. This is one of the principal doctrines of the tract on man left us by St. Thomas.

The holy doctor repeats this teaching in the tract on charity [41] when he asks: "Whether God can be loved immediately in this life?" He answers: "Knowledge of God, through being mediate, is said to be enigmatic, and falls away in heaven. . . . But charity does not fall away. . . . Therefore the charity of the way adheres to God immediately. The reason for this is that the act of a cognitive power is completed by the thing known being in the knower, whereas the act of an appetitive power consists in the appetite being inclined toward the thing itself. . . . We must assert that to love, which is an act of the appetitive power, even in this state of life, tends to God first, and flows on from Him to other things, and in this sense charity loves God immediately, and other things through God." This love should extend to our neighbor, who should be loved for the love of our common Father. "For knowledge begins from creatures, tends to God, and love begins with God as the last end, and passes on to creatures." [42]

By this we see the superiority of charity as compared with faith and hope. "But faith and hope attain God indeed in so far as we derive from Him the knowledge of truth or the acquisition of good, whereas charity attains God Himself

[41] See IIa IIae, q.27, a.4.
[42] *Ibid.*, ad 2um.

that it may rest in Him, but not that something may accrue to us from Him. Hence charity is more excellent than faith or hope, and consequently, than all the other virtues, which have not God directly for their object." [43] In this way it is explained that charity, unlike faith and hope, is inseparable from the state of grace and from the indwelling of the Blessed Trinity in us: "He that abideth in charity abideth in God, and God in him." [44]

In virtue of the same principle enunciated by St. Thomas, we see again that charity is superior to all knowledge in this life, even to contemplation, which proceeds from the gift of wisdom. This quasi-experimental knowledge of God also imposes on Him, in fact, the limits of our ideas, and it draws its savor from the very love which inspires it. It is charity that establishes in us a sympathy with divine things, which are thereby rendered desirable. [45] The gifts of the Holy Ghost thus find their remote rule in the theological virtues; they are ruled immediately by divine inspirations according to a superhuman mode, and from this point of view they add a new perfection to the theological virtues. Nevertheless they remain subordinated to them by nature, [46] and their fruits are the very fruits of charity—joy and peace.

All this shows us the profound meaning of St. Paul's expression, "Charity is the bond of perfection." Not only does charity unite us to God more than do the other virtues, but it unites them all by inspiring them and by ordering all their acts to a final end which is its own object, to God loved above all. Therefore it is called the mother of all the virtues. With this interpretation in mind, St. Augustine could say: "Love, and do what you will." And indeed you may, provided you

[43] See IIa IIae, q.23, a.6.
[44] See I John 4: 16.
[45] See IIa IIae, q.45, a.2, 4.
[46] "The theological virtues are more excellent than the gifts of the Holy Ghost, and regulate them. Hence . . . the seven gifts never attain perfection . . . unless all that they do be done in faith, hope, and charity" (Ia IIae, q.68, a.8).

love the Lord in very truth, more than yourself and above all things. How can we love Him thus unless we observe His commandments, the first of which, that of love, is the beginning and end of all the others?

We must conclude with all theologians that the perfection of Christian life consists especially in charity, in an active charity, which actually unites us to God, and is fruitful in every type of good work.[47] This virtue should, without a doubt, hold the first place in our souls.

### PERFECTION IS A PLENITUDE

From what we have just said, must we conclude that the other virtues, important as they are, such as faith, hope, the virtue of religion, prudence, justice, fortitude, patience, temperance, mildness, and humility, do not contribute toward the essence of perfection, and belong to it only accidentally as instruments, or secondary means? Some theologians have thought so.[48] We believe, however, with Father Passerini, O.P., who among Thomists has most profoundly commented on the article of St. Thomas which we are now explaining, that such is not the thought of the holy doctor. St. Thomas himself says: "Primarily and essentially the perfection of the Christian life consists in charity, principally as to the love of God, secondarily as to the love of our neighbor, both of which are the matter of the chief commandments of the divine

---

[47] Some theologians (for example, Suarez) teach that perfection consists formally in the virtue of charity, antecedently and concomitantly in its acts. Father Passerini, O.P., we think, states the opinion of the Thomistic school. He teaches that perfection, to which the state of perfection is ordered, consists formally in the acts of charity and antecedently in the virtue, as in the principle of perfect operation. The reason for this is that perfection consists in actual union with God, *mihi adhaerere Deo bonum est*. It is found, therefore, in active charity or in the activity of charity, which in truly perfect souls should be morally continual or unceasing. Virtue is ordered to its act as to its perfection; and we tend not only to be able to love God perfectly, but to love Him in fact by avoiding all sin as much as possible. Life consists especially in the act of living.

[48] Cajetan, on IIa IIae, q. 184, a. 1, and Suarez, on the same article.

law. . . . Secondarily and instrumentally, however, perfection consists in the observance of the counsels. . . . For the commandments, other than the precepts of charity, are directed to the removal of things contrary to charity, with which, namely, charity is incompatible, whereas the counsels are directed to the removal of things that hinder the act of charity, and yet are not contrary to charity." [49] It follows, as Passerini shows, that perfection consists essentially not in charity alone, but also in the acts of the other virtues which are of precept and which are ordered by charity.[50] Thus the acts of faith, hope, religion, and prayer, attendance at mass, and reception of holy communion, belong to the very essence of perfection, which is a plenitude. To use St. Paul's word, charity is the bond of this plenitude. We can, therefore, truthfully say with St. Thomas, that perfection consists particularly in charity,[51] and principally in the love of God.[52] Just so, the body and soul constitute the very essence of man, although this essence is chiefly constituted by the rational soul, which distinguishes man from animals. Such is the place of charity in the Christian life. St. Thomas rightly says: "Christian life consists chiefly in charity, which unites the soul to God." Unlike faith and hope,

---

[49] See IIa IIae, q. 184, a. 3.

[50] Passerini, O. P., *De statibus hominum* (on IIa IIae, q. 184, a. 1), p. 20, no. 8: "Actual perfection consists essentially not in the act alone of charity, but also in the acts of the other virtues ordered by charity according as they are of precept." Cf. *Ibid.*, pp. 22–27, 49, 54. "Actual perfection consists chiefly and principally in charity alone, because charity perfects simply, and the other virtues relatively. . . . Furthermore, actual perfection is formally in charity alone, which is the bond of perfection. . . . Yet other virtues pertain to the essence of perfection just as matter to the essence of a natural composite" (p. 21, no. 10). "The acts of the other virtues as they are of counsel, are accidents of perfection" (p. 23, nos. 20 ff.). By this distinction between what is of counsel and what is of precept in the virtues inferior to charity, Passerini introduces a precision which Cajetan had forgotten, and clearly expresses the thought of St. Thomas which, as we shall see in regard to article 3, was not understood by Suarez.

[51] Particularly (*specialiter*) is the term used by St. Thomas when he treats the question *ex professo* (IIa IIae, q. 184, a. 1). He says elsewhere (*De perfectione vitae spiritualis*): "Spiritual life consists principally in charity."

[52] "Principally as to the love of God, secondarily, as to the love of our neighbor" (IIa IIae, q. 184, a. 3).

charity absolutely excludes mortal sin, and requires the state of grace or of life.

Does it follow that every soul in the state of grace is perfect? As yet it has perfection only in the broad sense of the term (*perfectio substantialis*), which excludes mortal sin; but not for that reason alone has it perfection, properly so called (*perfectio simpliciter*), which ascetical and mystical theology speak of and which interior souls, especially those consecrated to God in the religious state, aspire to.

In the following article we shall see in what this perfection, properly so called, consists—the perfection of charity, or the charity of the perfect, in contradistinction to that of beginners and to that of proficients. But already we catch a glimpse of the inexpressible grandeur of charity even in the soul that has just been snatched from mortal sin, and that is beginning to walk in the way of perfection. This soul has truly passed from death to life, to the life which ought never to end.

## ARTICLE III

*The Full Perfection of Charity Presupposes the Passive Purification of the Senses and of the Spirit*

We have seen that Christian perfection consists chiefly in charity. Quite evidently, the possession of this virtue, the state of grace, is not sufficient for the attainment of perfection, properly so called, which ascetical and mystical theology speaks of and which all interior souls, particularly those consecrated to God in the religious state, aspire to. "Not as though I had already attained, or were already perfect," says St. Paul, "but I follow after, if I may by any means apprehend." [1] This perfection consists precisely in the charity of the perfect, which is superior to the charity of beginners and of souls that are making progress. In this article we are going to treat of

[1] Phil. 3: 12.

this charity of the perfect, and we will consider it both in its essence and in its integrity, or its normal plenitude.

We are here concerned with the summit of charity in its normal development, the fundamental law of which, quite different from that of our fallen nature, is the law of grace, which regenerates us progressively, and the consummation of which is eternal life.

All spiritual writers admit three phases in this development of charity: (1) That of beginners whose main effort is strife against sin. For this reason, it is called the purgative way. (2) That of those who are making progress in the virtues by the light of faith and of contemplation. It is often called the illuminative way. (3) That of the perfect, who live especially in union with God through charity. It is called the unitive way. These three degrees constitute the infancy, adolescence, and adult age of the spiritual life.[2]

These general terms are commonly accepted, but they have not exactly the same meaning for all theologians. Beginning in the seventeenth and eighteenth centuries, a number of authors have admitted two unitive ways; the one ordinary and ascetical, the other called "extraordinary," passive, and mystical, which cannot be reached without a special vocation. From this point of view, souls can generally be perfect, and even reach the lofty perfection required for beatification, without having received any mystical grace. Others maintain, according to the traditional doctrine, that there is only one unitive way, and that its full, normal development is the perfect mystical union, or the transforming union.[3] In their opin-

---

[2] Cf. St. Thomas, Ia IIae, q.24, a.9; *II Sent.*, Dist. IX, 2 ad 8um. In the latter text, St. Thomas, speaking of the purgative, the illuminative, and the unitive ways, observes that all who truly lead souls to perfection, also illumine them and purify them, but the reverse is not true. He who purifies them from sin, may not always be able to illumine them and *a fortiori* may be unable to lead them to perfection, to divine union.

[3] Certain authors merely say rather timidly: "To have an ensemble of the unitive life, the mystical state must be joined thereto." Thus Father Meynard, O.P., expresses his opinion in his *Traité de la vie intérieure*, I, 464 note, 22–28.

ion, this way belongs in its essential quality to the order of sanctifying grace, or "the grace of the virtues and of the gifts," and not to the lower order of graces *gratis datae,* such as the gift of prophecy or that of miracles, which sometimes accompany it. We touched on this question when we discussed the relations between ascetical and mystical theology.[4]

The authors of whom we have just spoken appeal to tradition previous to the seventeenth century, and in particular to St. John of the Cross. Therefore we must closely examine his doctrine on this subject, that we may see how it should be interpreted and what its relations are with earlier tradition.

### I. DOCTRINE OF ST. JOHN OF THE CROSS ON THE PERFECTION OF CHARITY

This great saint speaks of the three ways, purgative, illuminative, and unitive, in several of his works, notably in *The Ascent of Mount Carmel* (Bk. I, chap. 1), *The Dark Night of the Soul* (Bk. I, chaps. 1, 14), and *The Spiritual Canticle* (stanzas 1, 4, 6, 22, 26). According to him the illuminative way, or the way of souls that are making progress, begins with the cessation of meditation and the beginning of infused or mystical contemplation. Treating of this contemplation, he says: "Souls begin to enter this dark night (*passive*) when God Himself disengages them little by little from the state of beginners, that in which one meditates, and introduces them into the state of proficients, which is that of contemplatives. They must pass through this way to become perfect, that is, to attain the divine union of the soul with God." [5]

This ascent is not without suffering, as St. John of the Cross warns us in *The Ascent of Mount Carmel:* "To attain the divine light and the perfect union of the love of God—I speak of what can be realized in this life—the soul must pass through the dark night. . . . Ordinarily, when chosen souls

---

[4] Cf. *supra,* chap. 2, art. 2.
[5] *The Dark Night of the Soul,* Bk. I, chap. 1.

strive to attain this state of perfection, they encounter such darkness, endure such severe physical and moral sufferings, that human science is unable to penetrate them, and human experience to represent them." [6]

Not without difficulty does one succeed in completely conquering selfishness, sensuality, laziness, impatience, envy, unjust judgment, impulses of nature, natural haste, self-love, foolish pretensions, and also self-seeking in piety, the immoderate desire for sensible consolations, intellectual and spiritual pride; in a word, all that is opposed to the spirit of faith and confidence in God; [7] that one may succeed in loving God perfectly with all one's heart, soul, strength, and mind, and one's neighbor (enemies are included under this title) as oneself; in short, to remain firm and patient and to persevere in charity, whatever may happen, when the expression of the Apostle is verified, that "all that will live godly in Christ Jesus, shall suffer persecution." [8]

To reach this perfection, the mortification or active purification of the senses and of the spirit is not all that is necessary: "In spite of all its generosity, the soul cannot completely purify itself, so that it will be even slightly fit for divine union in the perfection of love. God Himself must put His hand to the work, and purify the soul in this fire that is hidden from it, according to the mode and manner which we shall explain in what follows." [9]

First of all, the soul is weaned from sensible consolations, which at a certain time have their value, but which become an obstacle when they are sought for their own sake. Hence the necessity of the passive purification of the senses, which establishes the soul in sensible aridity and leads it to a spiritual life which is much more detached from the senses, the imagination, and reasoning. By the gifts of the Holy Ghost, the

6 *The Ascent of Mount Carmel,* Prologue.
7 *The Dark Night of the Soul,* Bk. I, chaps. 1–7.
8 See II Tim. 3: 12.
9 *The Dark Night of the Soul,* Bk. I, chap. 3.

soul at this time receives an intuitive knowledge, which despite a very painful darkness initiates it profoundly into the things of God. Occasionally it makes the soul penetrate them more deeply in one instant than months and years of meditation would have done. Resistance to temptations, which frequently present themselves in this night of the senses, requires heroic acts of chastity and patience.[10] This period has justly been compared to that of teething in children who have just been weaned. In fact, at this stage the soul is prepared to receive a stronger food, the spiritual graces which are bestowed on it. These are far more precious than the preceding graces, but they disconcert the soul by giving no satisfaction to its desire for sensible graces.

After treating of this purification, St. John of the Cross observes: "The soul has, therefore, gone forth; it has begun to penetrate into the way of the spirit, which is followed by proficients and advanced souls, and which is also called the illuminative way, or the way of infused contemplation."[11] This text is very important, for St. John here speaks expressly of infused contemplation and not of acquired contemplation.[12]

But to reach the perfection of charity, the passive purification of the senses does not suffice: "On leaving the state of

[10] As St. John of the Cross says, in *The Dark Night of the Soul* (Bk. I, chap. 8): "The passive purification of the senses is common. It takes place in the greater number of beginners." Consequently we are surprised to see the night of the senses placed in the last chapter consecrated to the perfect, or to the unitive way, in a plan of ascetical and mystical theology (published in the *Revue d'ascétique et de mystique,* January, 1921, p. 35). According to St. John of the Cross, the night of the senses ordinarily takes place much earlier.

[11] *The Dark Night of the Soul,* Bk. I, chap. 14.

[12] The saint speaks of infused contemplation also in the first text cited (*The Dark Night of the Soul,* Bk. I, chap. 1), and even in *The Ascent* (Bk. II, chap. 13). When he uses the word "contemplation," he is speaking of contemplation properly so called, or infused contemplation, which is more or less passive at the beginning. These correspond to the first supernatural prayers of St. Teresa, those of passive recollection and of quiet (fourth mansion). She describes the night of the spirit in the sixth mansion. We mention these texts *infra* (chap. 5, art. 3, no. 2).

beginners, the soul remains more often than not immobile in the exercises proper to the advanced for an indeterminate period, which may last for years. Like the prisoner who has just left his narrow prison, the soul is more at ease in divine things and finds more satisfaction in them. . . . Neither the imagination nor the powers of the soul preserve any longer, in fact, their former attachment to discursive prayer [13] and to spiritual effort because the soul now tastes without any intellectual effort a very calm and affectionate contemplation accompanied by spiritual delights. . . . The purification of the soul is, however, not yet complete and cannot be so, since the principal one, which is that of the spirit, is still lacking. . . . The soul has still, therefore, to undergo dryness, darkness, and anguish, often far more severe than the preceding experiences." [14] The necessity of this passive purification of the spirit could not be more clearly affirmed. In one way or another, it must be undergone for the attainment of perfect purity of soul.

In this period there are no longer any deliberate venial sins, but there are still the imperfections peculiar to the advanced, imperfections that are incompatible with the full perfection of charity. "The stains of the old man still remain in the spirit, though it does not suspect their presence, nor scarcely perceives them. They must, however, yield to and be removed by the strong soap and lye of the passive purification of the spirit, without which the purity required for union will still be lacking. These proficients suffer also from dullness of mind and from the natural rudeness which every man contracts by sin. They are subject to distractions and to dissipation of mind. . . . The devil often dupes many by imaginary visions and false prophecies which lead to presumption. . . . This matter is inexhaustible, and these imperfec-

---

[13] Discourse or reasoning is no longer found in the knowledge proceeding from the gifts of the Holy Ghost, which at this point intervene more and more. See St. Thomas, IIa IIae, q.8, 45.

[14] *The Dark Night of the Soul*, Bk. II, chap. 1.

tions are so much the more incurable because these proficients consider them spiritual perfections. Therefore he who wishes to make progress must, of necessity, pass through the purification of the spiritual night. . . . Therein only can the soul find suitable and adequate means for uniting itself to God." [15]

The perfect are, therefore, not only those who have imposed on themselves exterior and interior mortifications, but who have passed through the purifications of the senses and of the spirit. The soul which has not passed through this crucible is not yet cleansed from its blemishes.

Speaking of the night of the spirit, St. John of the Cross observes: "How often on this way exaltation and depression succeed one another, and how often, too, is prosperity enjoyed for a moment and then followed by storms and trials. . . . These fluctuations are ordinary in the contemplative state. Before attaining the state of definitive peace, rest is unknown; life is a constant succession of ascents and descents. As the state of perfection consists in the perfect love of God and contempt of self, it cannot be conceived without its two parts, the knowledge of God and the knowledge of self. From this we see how necessary it is that the soul have a preliminary formation in both. This is why God at times lifts the soul up by making it taste its own greatness, and at times humbles it by showing it its baseness. This movement of ascent and descent can, therefore, be stopped only when the perfect habit of the virtues is acquired, when the soul has reached union with God." [16]

To resist temptations against the theological virtues which present themselves rather frequently in the night of the spirit, the soul must make heroic acts of faith, hope, and charity, which notably augment the intensity of these virtues. At the same time the illuminations of the gift of understanding en-

[15] *The Dark Night of the Soul*, Bk. II, chap. 2.
[16] *The Dark Night of the Soul*, Bk. II, chap. 18.

lighten the soul on the unknown depths of the mysteries of faith, on the fathomless perfections of God, on the nothingness of creatures, on the infinite gravity of mortal sin, on the ineffable abasement of Christ, to such an extent that the incarnation and the Eucharist seem absolutely impossible. The understanding, which is still too feeble, is bewildered and helpless like a man who does not know how to swim and who, upon being cast into the open sea, believes himself on the point of drowning. Therein lies the purifying action of God, opposed to the temptation of the demon, which is often simultaneous and which the Lord makes serve His ends.

Once this passive purification of the spirit is completed, souls are normally ready to enter heaven immediately after death: "Because of their perfect purification by love, they are not obliged to pass through purgatory." [17] They have had their purgatory in this life and in a fitting manner; that is, while meriting; whereas after death souls, which by their fault must be purified, no longer merit. We will treat more at length of the nature of these purifications in chapter 6, article 2.

According to St. John of the Cross, the full perfection attainable in this life is found only in the transforming union, or the spiritual marriage. "Then, in fact, the soul is no longer disturbed by the demon, nor by the world, nor by the flesh, nor by the appetites; it can then utter the words of the Canticle, 'For winter is now past, the rain is over and gone. The flowers have appeared in our land.' " [18] This state represents the full development of charity; perfect love accepts

---

[17] *Ibid.*, chap. 20. There are doubtless souls that avoid purgatory, without having passed through the passive purifications of the spirit; for example, those who died immediately after baptism, and religious who died immediately after their solemn profession; but if these had continued to live, they would have fallen into many imperfections, which would have necessitated the purifications mentioned here by St. John of the Cross. He does not consider accidental cases, but what is ordinarily required to attain a lofty perfection in this life, and in heaven, a proportionate degree of glory.

[18] *The Spiritual Canticle,* Part III, st. 22 to the end.

any work or suffering whatever for God, and even finds a holy joy in suffering.[19] It does not fear death, but desires it. It attributes nothing to self, but refers all to God, and is transformed so to speak in Him, according to St. Paul's expression, "He who is joined to the Lord, is one spirit." [20] "It is, in short, God Himself who communicates Himself to the soul by an admirable glory and transforms it in Himself. Then there takes place the perfect union of the soul and God, who are as intimately united as glass and sunlight, as coal and fire, as starlight and sunlight. Nevertheless, such a union is neither as essential nor as complete as that of heaven." [21]

When charity is perfected, all the Christian virtues reach their perfect development. "They are intertwined, closely united to each other, which renders their resistance stronger by reason of their mutual support. From this union there results a whole which constitutes the complete perfection of the soul, a compact ensemble, a solidarity, which excludes the possibility of any weak spot which might facilitate the entrance of the devil or things of the world into the soul." [22]

Finally, "the soul possesses the seven gifts of the Holy Ghost according to the entire perfection compatible with life here below." [23] "The operations of the soul in union come from the divine Spirit. . . . They alone, as a result, are perfectly harmonious . . . without ever being untimely. . . . The Spirit of God reveals to these souls what they should know, reminds them of what they should remember, . . . causes them to forget whatever deserves to be forgotten, to love what is worthy of their love, and to love nothing that is not found

[19] *Ibid.,* st. 24.
[20] See I Cor. 6: 17.
[21] *The Spiritual Canticle,* st. 26. This teaching of St. John of the Cross on the spiritual marriage, the acme of the development of the mystical life, does not differ from that of the other saints who have commented on the *Canticle of Canticles.* These commentaries become truly the light of life only for souls that are in the way of this perfect union. On this subject, see the last work of Father Arintero, O.P., *Cantar de los Cantares, Exposición mística.*
[22] *The Spiritual Canticle,* st. 24.
[23] *Ibid.,* st. 26.

in God. Thus, all the first movements of the powers in such souls are divine, and we must not be surprised that the movements and operations of these powers are divine because they are transformed in the divine Being." [24]

According to St. John of the Cross, the illuminative and the unitive ways belong, therefore, to the mystical life, properly so called. This is without doubt a very lofty conception of what the full development of "the grace of the virtues and of the gifts" ought to be, of what the intimacy of divine union should normally become in an interior soul after a life spent in great fidelity to the Holy Ghost.

Needless to say, this conception of the unitive or perfect life far surpasses what many modern writers on asceticism call the ordinary unitive way. In their opinion, this way does not presuppose the painful passive purifications, at least not those of the spirit, which belong to the mystical states.[25] There is a considerable difference between souls which have valiantly passed through these great trials and those which have not as yet undergone them. In the following article we will seek the source of this divergence between the ascetical teachings of these modern writers and the doctrine of St. John of the Cross.

The problem is a serious one. Is not the ideal of perfection notably lessened by maintaining that we can reach the full, normal development of Christian life without passing under one form or another through the passive purifications, which

[24] *The Ascent of Mount Carmel*, Bk. III, chap. 1. It would be manifestly an error to believe that *The Ascent of Mount Carmel* deals only with the ascetical way, and that the contemplation mentioned therein is not infused or mystical contemplation. Cf. Bk. II, chap. 13. But in *The Ascent* the soul learns what it must do, while in *The Dark Night of the Soul* it learns how it should allow itself to be formed by God. Cf. Father Gabriel of Jesus, C.D., "¿La Subida del Monte Carmelo es ascética o es mística?" in *La Vida Sobrenatural*, 1923, p. 24. The author holds the same opinion as we do.

[25] For example, Father Naval in his recent *Cursus theologiae asceticae et mysticae*, pp. 240–259, demands for the ordinary unitive life only the contemplation which is called acquired. According to him, the soul reaches this state without having undergone the strongest passive purifications of the senses, and without having experienced those of the spirit.

belong to the mystical order, and without being raised to infused contemplation, that dark and secret initiation into the mystery of God present in us? Are not the impulse and the great aspirations of the interior life suppressed under the pretext of avoiding illusion, of following the common way, the beaten paths? Is this not equivalent to proposing to souls a comfortable illuminative and unitive way, which is of a nature to give them an illusion just the opposite of those which they wish to avoid? Under pretext of combating one form of presumption, is this not yielding to another? Is this not leading souls to believe that they are on the point of attaining perfection, that they are already in the unitive life, when perhaps as yet they are only among the beginners and have only a faint notion of the true illuminative life, that of the proficients? Is this not also exposing them to complete divergence from the right road when the painful passive purifications come, during which they will think they are retrogressing, while in truth these trials are the narrow gate leading to true life? "How narrow is the gate, and strait is the way which leads to life, and few there are that find it" (Matt. 7: 14). It would be well to consider the words of St. John of the Cross on this subject, which we have quoted in the preceding pages. As yet we have only proposed the question. Finally, it is well to remember the saying of St. Thomas Aquinas: "The servant of God ought always to aspire without ceasing to more perfect and holier things." [26]

## ARTICLE IV

*According to Tradition the Full Perfection of Christian Life Belongs to the Mystical Order*

According to St. John of the Cross, the full perfection of Christian life belongs clearly to the mystical order, and is

[26] *In Ep. ad Hebraeos,* 6: 1, lect. 1.

truly realized only in the transforming union. However, many modern writers on asceticism hold an entirely different opinion. Whence comes this divergence?

Father Poulain's explanation is well known. He says: "All the ascetic writers speak of the three ways, the purgative, the illuminative, and the unitive, and they make them correspond, approximately at all events, to the terms: way of beginners, of proficients, and of the perfect. Some allow mysticism to play no part here; others at the most, place it only at the end of the third way. St. John of the Cross also employs these six terms, but gives them a meaning peculiar to his teaching. He looks at matters from the special point of view of mysticism, and places it in the second and third way . . . : 'The way of the spirit, which is that of proficients, is also called the illuminative way, or the way of infused contemplation' (*The Dark Night of the Soul*, Bk. I, chap. 14). Certainly this language is very different from that of other spiritual authors." [1]

The language of St. John of the Cross, to be sure, differs notably from that of many modern writers on asceticism. Some of the latter distinguish not merely three ways, but six; three ascetical and three mystical.[2] Is this not placing a materialistic interpretation on everything under the pretext of being more precise? Tradition has always spoken of only three ways, not six; but materially they appear in an imperfect manner or in their plenitude, according to the spiritual condition of the subject.[3] Although St. John of the Cross clarifies on several points the language of the great doctors who preceded him, nevertheless he teaches the same doctrine as they do.

---

[1] A. Poulain, S.J., *The Graces of Interior Prayer*, chap. 31, no. 45.

[2] In this division there would be the purgative-ascetical way, the illuminative-ascetical way, and the unitive-ascetical way below the three corresponding mystical ways.

[3] Thus the same doctrine explained to several students is clearly understood by one of them, less clearly by another.

Is a less elevated doctrine found in the spiritual works of the fathers, of St. Augustine, Dionysius, St. Bernard, St. Bonaventure, St. Thomas, Tauler, Louis de Blois, Dionysius the Carthusian, the author of *The Imitation,* St. Francis de Sales, and, in a general way, in the works of the saints who have spoken of the perfect life considered in its plenitude? We cannot find in their works, any more than we can in those of St. John of the Cross, mention of a twofold unitive life; the first ordinary, and the second extraordinary by its very nature and, as such, inaccessible to the majority of interior souls.

How can we, then, explain the divergence which we have just pointed out? While certain authors are especially concerned with beginners and with souls that have only a relative perfection in view, St. John of the Cross writes "for those who are determined to pass through nudity of spirit," especially for contemplative souls. He proposes to them the loftiest perfection attainable in this life, and the most efficacious and direct means to reach it. He himself states this fact in the prologue of *The Ascent of Mount Carmel.*[4] This explains the apparent exaggeration of his insistence on mortification. It explains also his very lofty idea of the illuminative and of the unitive ways, which he presents to us in their plenitude, which is found only in the mystical life. Some modern writers on asceticism give us, on the contrary, only an inferior and a diminished idea of them; for if these two ways appear in the course of the ascetical life, it can only be in a manner that is still very imperfect.

We find here something similar to that which occurs in intellectual culture. For many, adequate theological training is given by a manual that can be studied in three years, and that one does not feel impelled to reread, because all it contains is quickly exhausted. Who can claim that the perfection of theo-

---

4 "Both groups will find a substantial doctrine in this book, but it is on condition that they decide to pass through nudity of spirit. I confess, however, that in this treatise I have had in mind especially some members of our holy order."

logical culture is found in such a study? Others can satisfy the demands of their minds only by the profound study of St. Thomas and of his principal commentators. This study is neither an extraordinary undertaking nor a luxury for them; it is necessary for the training of their minds. They realize that even if they spend all their lives teaching the *Summa theologica*, written though it is for novices, they will never exhaust it, and will never arrive at a complete grasp of its breadth, height, and depth; to do so, would require an intellect equal to that of the master. "To comprehend is to equal," said Raphael. To study the tract on grace, some will consecrate three months to it and scarcely ever return to it; others understand that the work of a lifetime would not suffice to penetrate what the doctors of the Church wished to tell us about this great mystery.

Thus, from the spiritual point of view, many souls are quickly, even too quickly, satisfied by a very relative perfection, which seems altogether insufficient to others. The latter feel a need for the eminent exercise of charity and of the gifts of the Holy Ghost. Certain very passionate temperaments and extremely vigorous intellects seem to find peace only in a lofty perfection, even that described by St. John of the Cross. With still greater reason, this is true of souls which received early in life a superior attraction of grace. They will find rest only after the painful purifications, in the transforming union, in which they will no longer be disturbed by the devil, the flesh, and the world.

Why should we not believe that St. John of the Cross has preserved in its essentials the true and very lofty traditional conception of Christian perfection, or of union with God? Should we not believe, on the contrary, that some modern writers on asceticism have impoverished tradition by confounding the full normal development of the life of grace on earth with what is only its prelude? This is the opinion of some contemporary theologians who consider the mystical life necessary to full perfection, to that required, for example, for beatification.[5] They add that the other opinion, while claiming to combat presumption, might cause some souls to believe they have reached the unitive life, when, as a matter of fact, they are far from it. As a result, the ideal of perfection, the aim of the religious life, might be lowered and souls deprived of one of the greatest stimulants to an increasingly fervent and more generous life in closer union with God.

The true view seems to us to be the latter; namely, that there are not two unitive ways, the one ordinary and the other extraordinary by its nature, to which all fervent souls could not aspire, but only one unitive way, which, by an ever more perfect docility to the Holy Ghost, leads to a more intimate mystical union. This way is extraordinary in fact because of the small number of souls that are completely docile, but it is not extraordinary in itself or by its nature, like miracles or prophecy. On the contrary, it is in itself the perfect order, the full development of charity, actually realized in truly generous souls, at least at the close of their lives, if they live long enough. It may well be that, for lack of proper direction or favorable surroundings, or again by reason of a nature given to exterior activities, certain generous souls would reach the mystical life only after a much longer time than the ordinary span of life.[6] But these are accidental circumstances and, however frequent they may be, they do not affect the fundamental law of the full development of the life of grace.[7] St. John of the Cross makes this point very clear when, at the begin-

[5] Cf. Father Arintero, O.P., *La Ciencia tomista*, May, 1919. The expression "full perfection" shows that we are speaking not only of its essence but of its integrity. Thus to have five fingers on each hand belongs to the integrity of the human body, without being of its essence.

[6] Cf. De la Taille, S.J., *L'oraison contemplative*, 1921.

[7] The same is true in the physical order. A cedar will not attain its normal height if it is not planted in suitable ground, or if certain exterior circumstances are lacking. Similarly, from an intellectual point of view, by reason of a lack of serious foundation, of favorable environment, or because of an unreceptive temperament, certain laborious minds never attain their full normal development.

ning of his works, he says they are written "in order to help the many souls which are in great need of assistance. After the first steps in the path of virtue, when the Lord wishes to make them enter the dark night in order to lead them to divine union, there are some that go no further. Occasionally, it is the desire which is lacking, or they are not willing to let themselves be led therein. At times, it is because of ignorance, or because they vainly seek an experienced guide capable of leading them to the summit." [8]

This summit is not reached without infused contemplation; and certainly infused contemplation is not the fruit of our personal effort, for it surpasses the human mode of the Christian virtues. We do not have it when we wish it; it comes from a special grace, from an inspiration and illumination to which the gifts of the Holy Ghost render us docile. Though we do not have this inspiration when we wish it, we can hold ourselves ready to receive it; we can ask it, and merit it, at least in the broad sense of the word "merit." Every soul in the state of grace has, in fact, received the gifts of the Holy Ghost which develop with charity. As a general rule, the Holy Ghost moves us according to the degree of our habitual docility.[9]

"The conclusion is clear," says the holy doctor, "that, as soon as the soul has succeeded in carefully purifying itself of sensible forms and images, it will bathe in this pure and simple light, which will become for it the state of perfection. In truth, this light is always ready to penetrate us. Its infusion

---

[8] *The Ascent of Mount Carmel,* Prologue.

[9] Cf. John of St. Thomas, commentary on Ia IIae, q.68, *De donis Spiritus Sancti,* disp. XVIII, a. 2, no. 31: "The actual inspiration of the Holy Ghost is not within our power, but it is within our power to have our heart always ready to obey, in order that we may be easily moved by the Holy Ghost."

The Carmelite theologians and those of the Dominican school teach that all souls should aspire to supernatural or infused contemplation, and that this contemplation can be merited at least *de congruo:* "All ought to aspire to supernatural contemplation." This thesis is defended by Philip of the Blessed Trinity, *Theol. myst.* (1874), II, 299, 311; by Anthony of the Holy Ghost, *Directorium mysticum* (1732), p. 99; by Vallgornera, O.P., *Theol. mystica* (Berthier ed.), I, 428; by Father Meynard, O.P., *Traité de la vie intérieure,* II, 131.

is prevented by the forms and veils of creatures, which en-
velop and hamper the soul. Tear aside these veils . . . and
little by little, without delay, rest and divine peace will over-
whelm your soul with admirable and profound views on God,
which are enfolded in divine love." [10]

We shall demonstrate that this doctrine of St. John of the
Cross, while clarifying that of the great doctors who preceded
him, remains perfectly conformable to their teaching, and
that it is contained in the evangelical beatitudes. These propose to us Christian perfection in all its grandeur, and are
certainly not inferior in elevation to what the author of *The
Spiritual Canticle* has written.

Thus we begin to see the answer which should be made to
three questions already proposed:

1) What characterizes the mystical life? A special passivity
or the predominance of the gifts of the Holy Ghost, having a
superhuman mode specifically distinct from the human mode
of the Christian virtues, without, however, being confounded
with graces *gratis datae,* such as prophecy. These last are in
no way necessary to the mystical life; they are in a certain
sense exterior, and given especially for the benefit of one's
neighbor.[11]

[10] *The Ascent of Mount Carmel*, Bk. II, chap. 15. This is true in principle.
However, we must keep in mind predestination, about which St. John of the
Cross writes: "It is true that souls, whatever their capacity may be, can have
attained union, but all do not possess it in the same degree. God disposes freely
of this degree of union as He disposes freely of the degree of the beatific vision"
(*The Ascent*, Bk. II, chap. 5). From the fact that all the just are not predestined
to glory and do not infallibly attain it, one cannot claim that it is not the normal consummation of grace as well as of the mystical union in this life. We
must not confound vocation and predestination: "Many are called, but few
are chosen." This difference should, however, be noted: it is through his own
fault only that an adult fails to attain salvation, while he may fail through no
fault of his own to attain contemplation.

[11] This doctrine stands out as a happy medium between and a culminating
point above two opinions which are contrary to each other. The first opinion
reduces mystical contemplation to an act of living faith more intense than other
acts of faith, and this because it fails to understand the specific distinction between the virtues and the gifts, established by St. Thomas, Ia IIae, q.68, a.1-3.
The second opinion seems to elevate the mystical life greatly, though in reality

2) When does the mystical life begin in the course of the spiritual life? Normally with the passive purification of the senses, and the prayer of passive recollection which St. Teresa speaks of in the fourth mansion.[12]

3) Is a special vocation necessary to reach the mystical life? In principle, no. "The grace of the virtues and of the gifts" suffices in itself by its normal development to dispose us to the mystical life, and mystical contemplation is necessary for the full perfection of Christian life.[13] But in fact, for lack of certain conditions which at times are independent of our will, even generous souls would attain contemplation only after a longer space of time than the ordinary span of life; just as some minds, which are capable of a superior intellectual development, never reach it for lack of certain conditions. And lastly, in some who are more fitted for the active life, the gifts of action dominate.[14]

This teaching antedates that of St. John of the Cross. It will be interesting to recall the chapter of *The Imitation* on "True Peace" (Bk. IV, chap. 25). It is certainly not inferior to the doctrine we have just set forth, and it is addressed to all souls to show them an ideal of perfection which they may aspire to without presumption. We quote some passages. "Peace is what all desire, but all do not care for the things that pertain to true peace. My peace is with the humble and gentle of heart; in much patience shall thy peace be. . . . Direct thy

---

it reduces it, because it does not see clearly enough the profound difference which exists between the gifts of the Holy Ghost (supernatural by their essence and their mode, and present in all souls in the state of grace) and the graces *gratis datae*, which are not generally supernatural by their very essence, but only by their mode (*quoad modum*); which do not necessarily presuppose the state of grace, and which are, so to speak, not only actually but essentially exterior and extraordinary. Cf. Ia IIae, q.3, a.5.

[12] See *supra*, chap. 5, art. 2.

[13] See chap. 6.

[14] It may be conceded that materially and in fact there are two unitive ways, although formally and in principle there is only one, now perfectly, now imperfectly, realized. We must not elevate a material or actual distinction into a formal or essential distinction.

whole attention to please Me alone, and neither to desire nor to seek anything besides Me. . . . The spiritual progress and perfection of a man consist in these things . . . in giving thyself up with all thy heart to the divine will, not seeking thine own interest either in great matters or in small, either in time or in eternity. So shalt thou keep one and the same demeanor always giving thanks both in prosperity and adversity, weighing all things in an equal balance. Be thou so full of courage and so patient in hope, that when inward comfort is withdrawn thou mayest prepare thy heart to suffer even greater things; and do not justify thyself, as though thou oughtest not to suffer such and so great afflictions, but justify Me in whatsoever I appoint, and cease not to praise My holy name. Then thou walkest in the true and right way of peace, and thou shalt have a sure hope to see My face again with great delight. Now, if thou attain to the full contempt of thyself, know that thou shalt then enjoy abundance of peace, as great as is possible in this thy state of sojourning."

This peace is the fruit of an eminent charity and of the gift of wisdom which makes us see everything, whether agreeable or painful, in relation to God, the beginning and end of all things. St. Augustine says that the beatitude of the peacemakers corresponds to this gift.

And this is why, in the same book of *The Imitation*,[15] the disciple asks for the superior grace of contemplation, saying: "O Lord, I stand much in need of yet greater grace if it be Thy will that I should attain to that state where neither man nor any creature shall be a hindrance to me. . . . He desired to fly freely that said, 'Who will give me wings like a dove, and I will fly and be at rest?' (Ps. 54: 7.) . . . A man ought, therefore, to mount above all creatures and perfectly renounce himself, and in ecstasy of mind perceive that Thou, the Creator of all things, hast nothing amongst creatures like unto Thee. Unless a man be set free from all creatures, he cannot

15 Bk. IV, chap. 31.

wholly attend unto divine things and therefore are there so few contemplative, because few can wholly withdraw themselves from things created and perishing. To obtain this there is need of much grace to elevate the soul and carry it away above itself, and unless a man be uplifted in spirit and be freed from all creatures and wholly united unto God, whatsoever he knoweth and whatsoever he hath are of small account."

This remarkable chapter [16] is not less sublime than the chapters of St. John of the Cross on the transforming union. Properly speaking, it belongs to the mystical order, in which alone the true perfection of the love of God is to be found.[17]

[16] See the commentary on this passage by Father Dumas, S.M., in his excellent book, *L'Imitation de Jésus-Christ: introduction à l'union intime avec Dieu*, pp. 360-370.

[17] The mistress of novices in a French Carmelite convent recently wrote us the following letter on this subject: "I have been a religious for many years, and for a long time mistress of novices. In my opinion, many souls remain at the door of the true life because they lack instruction and are deluded in believing that meditation alone is a sure state. Ordinarily when one enters our monasteries with the required dispositions (and it ought to be the same in all cloisters), and when one strives seriously to acquire the virtues, the soul is, in a very short time, subjected by God to aridity and powerlessness, the prelude of the passive purifications. It is almost impossible to make those who have been trained according to the method of reasoned meditation believe that this state is good, and that it is made to lead them to the divine union. They do not understand the teaching of St. John of the Cross: 'To apply oneself at this time to the comprehension and the consideration of particular objects, were they ever so spiritual, would be to place an obstacle in the way of the general, subtle, and simple light of the spirit; it would be to overcloud one's spirit' (*The Ascent of Mount Carmel*, Bk. II, chap. 15).

"The contrary is true of souls that submissively accept these first trials. In a short time they enjoy peace, and then the knowledge of how to find God in this darkness. As a result of this knowledge, they make rapid progress. Those who cling to meditation are still waiting after thirty and more years of religious life for someone to lift them up and show them what they are still seeking. They lead a colorless and dull spiritual life. In the contemplative life the secret of happiness is in knowing how to live this life under the eye of God.

"May I continue to teach that contemplation, properly so called, in its divers degrees, always comes from God and that it is infused? One of the reasons, which has always led me to believe this, is that a soul, after making a little progress in prayer, is content only when it feels that all it has and all it experiences comes to it directly from God and not from self. Every soul that is even slightly contemplative, instinctively seeks to rid itself of everything personal and places no value on it. I clearly understand acquired contemplation which follows a fasci-

The saints use such language as this when they speak of perfect love, of the intimate knowledge of God and of ourselves which it presupposes, and of the signs by which it may be recognized.

God Himself used such words as these when speaking to St. Catherine of Siena: "I must now tell thee the sign that gives evidence that the soul has reached perfect love. This sign is the same as that which was seen in the Apostles after they had received the Holy Ghost. They left the Cenacle and, freed from all fear, they announced My word and preached the doctrine of My only Son. Far from fearing suffering, they gloried in it. . . .

"Those who passionately desire My honor and who hunger for the salvation of souls hasten to the table of the holy cross. Their only ambition is to suffer and to bear a thousand fatigues for the service of their neighbor. . . . They bear in their bodies the wounds of Christ, and the crucified love which burns them bursts forth in the contempt they feel for themselves, in the joy they experience in opprobrium, in the welcome they give to the contradictions and the pains that I grant them, wherever they may come from, and in whatever manner I may send them. . . .

"They run ardently in the way of Christ crucified. They follow His doctrine, and nothing can slacken their course, neither injuries nor persecutions nor the pleasures which the world offers them and would wish to give them. With unshakable fortitude they pass all this by, equipped as they are with a perseverance which nothing can trouble, their hearts transformed by charity, tasting and enjoying this nourish-

---

nating study or an interesting book; this is merely admiration called forth by the discovery of truth. But in prayer the subjects are always practically the same. How can one then persist for a time and habitually in this undertaking without the grace of infused contemplation? Is a person not on the road to this contemplation as soon as he wills to accept the purifications which lead to it?"

The substance of this letter seems to us the same as the doctrine of St. John of the Cross, who holds that contemplation, properly so called, is infused. See chap. 5, arts. 2–6.

ment of the salvation of souls, ready to bear all things for them. This is the incontestable proof that the soul loves God perfectly and without any selfish motive. . . . If the perfect love each other, it is for My sake. If they love their neighbor, it is for Me, in order to give honor and glory to My name. That is why suffering always finds them strong and persevering. . . . In the midst of injuries, patience shines forth and proclaims its royalty.

"To these souls I give the grace of a consciousness of My continual presence,[18] while to others I give it from time to time; not that I withdraw My grace from them, but rather the feeling of My presence. . . . These souls are plunged into the burning flames of My charity, purified of everything that is not I, stripped of all self-will and consumed with love of Me. Who then could withdraw them from Me and from My grace? . . . They always experience My divine presence in them, and I never deprive them of this feeling. . . . Moreover, their bodies are frequently raised from the earth by reason of this perfect union. . . . The body remains, as it were, motionless, broken by the love of the soul to such an extent that it would die, did not My goodness gird it with strength. . . . Furthermore, I interrupt this union for a time in order to permit the soul to remain united to the body. St. Paul complained of this body to which he was enslaved, because it hindered him from the immediate enjoyment of My divinity. He groaned because he was among mortals who continually offend Me, because he was deprived of the sight of Me, deprived of seeing Me in My essence." [19]

The sober, theological language of St. Thomas Aquinas is no less sublime when he treats of the question: "Whether anyone can be perfect in this life."

"The divine law," he answers, "does not prescribe the im-

---

[18] These words clearly indicate the mystical union, and even the perfect mystical union.

[19] St. Catherine of Siena, *Dialogue*, chaps. 74, 78, 79, *passim*.

possible. Yet it prescribes perfection, according to Matt. 5: 48, 'Be you . . . perfect, as also your heavenly Father is perfect.'

"The perfection of the Christian life consists in charity. Now, perfection implies a certain universality because the perfect is that which lacks nothing. Hence we may consider a threefold perfection. . . . Absolute perfection consists in loving God as much as He is lovable. Such perfection as this is not possible to any creature; for God alone can love Himself in this way, that is to say, infinitely. Another perfection consists in loving God to the extent of our power, so that our love always actually tends to God. Such perfection as this is not possible in this life, but we shall have it in heaven. Finally, there is a third perfection which consists in loving God not as much as He is lovable, nor in always actually tending to Him, but to the exclusion of whatever is opposed to the love of Him. 'The poison which kills charity,' says St. Augustine, 'is cupidity or covetousness. When this is destroyed, perfection exists.' On earth this perfection can exist, and that in two ways. Man may exclude from his affection all that is contrary to charity, and which would destroy it, such as mortal sin. This is necessary to salvation. Secondly, man may exclude from his affection not only what is contrary to charity, but also whatever hinders his love from being directed completely toward God. Without this perfection, charity can exist, for instance, in beginners and in proficients." [20]

It is this last perfection which is peculiar to the perfect. They still commit venial sins through frailty or surprise, but they avoid deliberate venial sin and also slight, conscious, and voluntary imperfections. They are very faithful to the inspirations of the Holy Ghost, whether these inspirations remind them of a duty, even though quite unimportant, or of a simple counsel.[21] Moreover, instead of being content to make acts of charity which are comparatively weak for the

[20] *Summa*, IIa IIae, q.184, a.2.
[21] *Summa*, Ia IIae, q.68, a.2.

degree of supernatural life to which they have attained (*actus remissi*), the perfect frequently make acts which are at least as intense as their degree of charity. By these acts they merit an immediate and notable increase of this virtue.[22] Having ten talents, they take good care not to act as if they had only two. Moreover, they receive communion with great fervor of will; they hunger for the Eucharist.[23] Ever tending toward great things by reason of the virtue of magnanimity,[24] they show a profound humility in their confessions, as also in their whole life, and, in their own opinion, they are the least of men.[25] They are meek and humble of heart, as well as firm and strong. In them "prudence scorns the things of the world for the contemplation of divine things; it directs all the efforts of their souls toward God. Temperance abandons, in so far as nature can bear it, whatever the body demands. Fortitude prevents the soul from becoming frightened in the face of death and the supernatural. Finally, justice leads the soul to enter fully on this wholly divine way." [26] Higher still, according to St. Thomas, are the virtues of the soul that has been completely purified. They are those of the great saints in this life, and of the blessed in heaven.

In the perfect, the prayer of desire is almost continuous. They understand our Lord's saying that we must pray always. Their faith has become loving contemplation; [27] their hope, invincible confidence.[28]

St. Thomas states that, "while beginners strive above all to flee sin, to resist the movements of concupiscence . . . and proficients direct their principal efforts toward advancing in the practice of charity and of the other virtues, . . . the perfect tend, above all, to unite themselves with God, to adhere

[22] *Summa*, IIa IIae, q.24, a.6.
[23] *Summa*, IIIa, q.80, a. 10.
[24] *Summa*, IIa IIae, q.129, a.3 ad 4um.
[25] *Summa*, IIa IIae, q.161, a.6, On the Degrees of Humility.
[26] *Summa*, Ia IIae, q.61, a.5.
[27] *Summa*, IIa IIae, q.8, a.4, 7; q.45; q.180, a.6.
[28] *Summa*, IIa IIae, q.18, a.4; q.129, a.6.

to Him, to enjoy Him. They desire to die in order to be with Christ." [29]

We find that St. Thomas expresses a no less sublime idea of what the love of one's neighbor should be in the perfect: "There are, likewise, three degrees in charity toward one's neighbor. In the first degree, our charity, without excluding anyone, extends positively only to our friends and to those who are known to us. Then it wishes well to strangers and does good to them, and finally, to our enemies. The last, says St. Augustine, is characteristic of the perfect.

"This progress in the extension of charity is accompanied by like progress in the intensity of this virtue. This growing intensity displays itself in the things which a man despises for the sake of his neighbor. He finally reaches a point where he despises not only exterior goods, but bodily afflictions and ultimately death itself, according to our Lord's expression, 'greater love than this no man hath, that a man lay down his life for his friends.' Last of all, the progress of fraternal charity is manifested by its effects, so that a man will surrender for his neighbor not only his temporal but also his spiritual goods, and even himself, according to the words of St. Paul: 'But I most gladly will spend and be spent myself for your souls; although loving you more, I be loved less.' " [30] St. Bonaventure teaches the same doctrine.[31]

St. Thomas teaches that to these three degrees of charity correspond three degrees in the moral virtues,[32] and also in the gifts and in contemplation.[33] A more sublime idea of Christian perfection can hardly be conceived. This conception

---

[29] *Summa,* IIa IIae, q.24, a.9.

[30] *Summa,* IIa IIae, q.184, a.2 ad 3um.

[31] St. Bonaventure, *De gradibus virtutum,* chap. 1; *De triplici via vel incendium amoris.*

[32] *Summa,* Ia IIae, q.61, a.5. Manifestly the perfection of the virtues of the purified soul, described by St. Thomas, belongs to the mystical order.

[33] *Summa,* IIa IIae, q.180, a.6. Dionysius the Carthusian, *De donis,* tr. II, a.15, has well described these three degrees of the gifts; the third certainly belongs to the mystical order.

excludes everything that would hinder the soul from belonging completely to God. To adhere to Him, to aspire eagerly to the beatific vision, to love effectively and in particular even our enemies, to scorn death for the glory of God and for the salvation of souls, such is the perfect age of the spiritual life.

An examination of the early doctors, who first spoke of the three ways (the purgative, the illuminative, and the unitive) and of the corresponding degrees of charity, shows that they used these terms in a broad sense, which has been preserved by St. John of the Cross, and not in the narrow acceptation of these terms, which has become current among several modern writers on asceticism. Evidently the distinction of the three ways owes its origin to the doctrine of Christian contemplation as formulated by St. Augustine and Dionysius. Pourrat recognizes this fact in his recent work, *La spiritualité chrétienne*,[34] when he says: "The doctrine of the three stages, the purgative, the illuminative, and the unitive, . . . was gradually generalized and applied to the ordinary Christian life"; that is, in the course of time these expressions were often used in a diminished sense. At the beginning they were understood in their loftiest acceptation, which did not designate something extraordinary in itself, or something miraculous, but something of eminent degree, the perfect order, or the full development of the supernatural life here below.

Dionysius often speaks of these three ways, especially throughout chapter five of his book, *The Ecclesiastical Hierarchy*. "God," he says, "first purifies the souls in which He dwells, then He illumines them, and finally leads them to divine union. . . . In the same way, in the Church the power of purifying belongs to the diaconate, . . . the power of illuminating, to the priesthood, and that of perfecting, to the episcopate."[35] St. Thomas later repeats this doctrine and makes it his own.[36]

[34] P. 349, no. 1.
[35] *Ibid.*, no. 7.
[36] See *IV Sent.*, d.4, q.1, a.1, q.3, and *II Sent.*, d.9, q.1, a.2, c. and ad 8um.

In his *Mystical Theology*,[37] Dionysius shows more explicitly what he understands by these words, which he uses so frequently: "As for thee, O well beloved Timothy, in thy desire to reach mystical contemplation strive without wearying to detach thyself both from the senses and from the operations of the understanding, from all that is sensible and intellectual, and from all that is or is not, in order to raise thyself by unknowing, as much as it is possible to do so, to union with Him, who is above all being and all knowledge; that is to say, to raise thyself by detachment from self and from all things, stripped of all and untrammeled, to that supernatural, transluminous way of the divine darkness." This is exactly the same doctrine and the terms are the same as those which in a later age St. John of the Cross often used.

St. Augustine employs the same language when he discusses contemplation in the *Confessions*,[38] in the *Soliloquies*,[39] in *De beata vita,* and in *De quantitate animae.*[40] In particular in this last named work,[41] when he is describing the various degrees of the life of the soul, after considering the vegetative, the sensitive, and the intellectual life, or the knowledge of

---

This entire article, which is entitled "Whether one angel purifies another," should be read to see how exactly St. Thomas, following Dionysius, takes the words purgation, illumination, and union. Cf. also the general index of the works of St. Thomas, called *Tabula aurea,* under the heading *Illustratio.* An idea of what he understands by the illuminative life can be obtained by reading what he says of the gift of understanding, *III Sent.,* d.34, q.1, a.1, c: "The gift of understanding, as Gregory says, illumines the mind in regard to things that are heard, so that man, even in this life, receives a foretaste of the future manifestation." This illumination of the gift of understanding gives us a foretaste of the beatific vision.

[37] Chap. 1, no. 1.
[38] Bk. IX, chap. 10.
[39] Bk. I, chaps. 1, 12, 13.
[40] These works are found in Migne, PL, Vol. XXXII. Pourrat has clearly brought out these texts in *La spiritualité chrétienne,* pp. 332-44. Their meaning would be clearer, in our opinion, if they were more closely related to those quoted in the preceding chapter of the same work, which is entitled "The Spiritual Doctrine of St. Augustine." St. Augustine's mysticism is certainly not separated from his spiritual doctrine. We do not see why Pourrat has dealt with them separately in two distinct chapters.
[41] *De quantitate animae,* Bk. I, chap. 33.

the sciences, he studies the degrees of the spiritual life: (1) The struggle against sin, the very difficult work of purification, during which entire confidence must be placed in God. This purification, he says, leads to true virtue, which shows all the grandeur of the soul, its incomparable superiority over the world of bodies. (2) The entrance into the light, which is possible only to those who are purified, for infirm eyes cannot endure the light which a pure and healthy eye desires. (3) Contemplation and divine union, which permit us to enjoy the sovereign good: "How shall I describe the joys and the foretastes of eternal serenity which the soul experiences in the intellectual vision and the contemplation of truth? Some great and incomparable souls have related these marvels. . . . We know that they have seen them and still see them." [42]

St. Augustine describes this contemplation in the *Confessions* [43] when he relates his meeting with his mother at Ostia. In the following phrases he indicates his conception of the contemplative state: "He who would silence in himself the tumult of the flesh, who would close his eyes to the spectacles offered by the earth, the waters, the air, and the firmament, who would impose silence on his very soul, suppressing self, . . . he who would no longer hear these creatures . . . and to whom God alone would speak directly . . . in an entirely spiritual manner. . . . Were this rapture to continue and this contemplation alone to absorb him who would enjoy it, . . . would not this state of things be the fulfilment of the expression found in the Gospel: 'Enter thou into the joy of the Lord'?" [44]

It is not surprising that, to reach such contemplation and divine union, the full purification, spoken of by St. John of the Cross, is necessary. St. Augustine himself insists upon it, and it would be an error to separate his asceticism from his

---

[42] *Ibid.*
[43] Bk. IX, chap. 10.
[44] Certainly he is speaking here of infused and, indeed, of lofty contemplation.

mysticism. The first leads to the second, as adolescence does to maturity. The three ways that he speaks of, in terms quite similar to those used by later great masters, correspond to the three degrees of charity which he mentions elsewhere, that of beginners, of proficients, and of the perfect.[45]

According to St. Augustine, a soul must, in fact, possess great charity to be numbered even among the proficients. We may say that a Christian is not of that number until he has undergone the trial of criticism and contradiction on the part of people who cannot bear to have anyone surpass them in virtue.[46] The perfect charity, which St. Augustine speaks of in *The Canticle of the Degrees* [47] and in the *Confessions*,[48] presupposes that one is ready to die for his brethren, and cannot be conceived as existing without that intimate and penetrating knowledge of God which is mystical contemplation. The gift of wisdom grows with charity; the supernatural organism of grace, of the virtues, and of the gifts develops at the same time.

Therefore we conclude that St. John of the Cross, in his description of the three ways (the purgative, the illuminative, and the unitive) and in his account of the three corresponding degrees of charity, agrees perfectly with St. Augustine, Dionysius, St. Thomas Aquinas, and also with St. Bernard, St. Bonaventure, and the true disciples of these great masters. He clarifies their teaching on several points, but he does not alter it. His lofty conception of the illuminative and unitive ways

---

[45] Cf. St. Augustine, *De natura et gratia*, chap. 70, nos. 82, 84. *Commentary on the First Canonical Epistle of John* (Tract. V, 4) "As soon as charity is born it takes food . . . , after taking food, it waxes strong . . . and when it has become strong it is perfected. . . . If a man be ready even to die for his brethren, charity is perfect in him." St. Thomas quotes this classic text in IIa IIae, q.24. a.9, sed c.

[46] *Enarr. in psalm.*, CXIX, no. 3. See Pourrat, *La spiritualité chrétienne*, p. 313.

[47] *Enarr. in psalm.*, LXXXIII, no. 10.

[48] *Confessions*, XIII, 8.

is therefore entirely traditional. He does more than depict them in an inferior or embryonic form, as do several modern writers on asceticism. He shows them to us in their plenitude; thus considered, they belong to the mystical order.

In company with this great master, who is the faithful echo of tradition, we must hold that the full perfection of charity in this life cannot exist without mystical contemplation, without the full development of the gifts of understanding and of wisdom, which grow with charity. The entire supernatural organism should develop at the same time. This development is not anything extraordinary in itself; it is the full harmony, the perfect order, of the life of grace which has attained here on earth the summit of its normal development. This grace, called by St. Thomas "the grace of the virtues and of the gifts," [49] is entirely distinct, as we have seen, from the graces *gratis datae,* such as prophecy or the gift of miracles.[50]

This is what makes St. John of the Cross exclaim: "O souls created for such glories, and called to them, of what are you thinking? With what are you occupied? How mediocre are your aspirations, and how wretched your pretended good! How sad is the blindness of your soul! You are blind to the most dazzling light and deaf to the powerful voices which solicit you. By allowing yourselves to be led on by what you consider happiness and glory, you do not see that you remain plunged in your wretchedness and your mediocrity, and you render yourselves ignorant and unworthy of the treasures destined for you." [51]

All should say with the psalmist: "As the hart panteth after the fountains of water; so my soul panteth after Thee, O God. My soul hath thirsted after the strong living God; when shall I come and appear before the face of God?" [52]

49 *Summa,* IIIa, q.62, a.2.
50 St. Thomas, Ia IIae, q.111, a.5.
51 *The Spiritual Canticle,* IV, st. 39.
52 Ps. 41: 3.

RELATIVE PERFECTION. HEROISM AND SANCTITY

Mystical theologians [53] have remarked that even among the perfect we should distinguish between those who are beginning to live a perfect life, those who are making progress in this life by heroism of virtue, and those who reach full perfection or sanctity.

Immediately after the passive purification of the senses, the soul already possesses a relative perfection. It generally avoids deliberate venial sins and enjoys a very calm and loving contemplation of God,[54] described by St. Teresa in the fourth and fifth mansions. But it still has many imperfections to remove.

Especially during the passive purifications of the spirit and their concomitant trials, heroic virtues, particularly those of faith, hope, and charity, are practiced, as St. John of the Cross shows,[55] and as St. Teresa describes them at the beginning of the sixth mansion.

Finally, when the soul has passed through and beyond the passive purifications of the spirit, it reaches the full perfection of the interior life, described by St. John of the Cross in *The Living Flame* and in the third part of *The Spiritual Canticle;* by St. Teresa in the seventh mansion; and by St. Bernard in the higher of the ten degrees of charity which he enumerates.[56] Because of this distinction made even among the perfect, we have in this present work, as a rule, purposely spoken of the full perfection of Christian life, and not only of that lesser, relative perfection discussed in several works on asceticism which do not deal with the mystical life, properly so called.

Is not this full perfection truly the summit of the normal

---

[53] Notably Joseph of the Holy Ghost, in his *Cursus theol. scolastico-mysticae,* in which he considers the perfect according to the teaching of St. John of the Cross.

[54] Cf. St. John of the Cross, *The Dark Night of the Soul,* Bk. II, chap. 1.

[55] *Ibid.*

[56] St. John of the Cross explains them: *The Dark Night of the Soul* (Bk. II, chap. 20), following a short work attributed to St. Thomas.

development of the life of grace? The word "normal" should not make us forget the word "summit," and vice versa. To understand it clearly, we must remember that Christian life requires of all souls heroism of virtue (according to the preparation of the mind); that is, in the sense that every Christian must be ready, with the help of the Holy Ghost, to accomplish heroic acts when circumstances require them. Martyrdom in certain cases is of precept and not only of counsel, for we must all prefer torments and death to abjuration, and we must love God more than life. Otherwise how should we be conformed to Christ crucified and sealed with His countenance? [57] Christians who habitually fulfil their duties must hope that, if they ask with humility, trust, and perseverance, the Holy Ghost will grant them the strength to remain faithful even in torture, should they have to undergo such a trial. Our Lord told His disciples not to fear those who kill the body, and He assured them that the Holy Ghost would inspire them on occasion with what they should say. Considering the matter from a purely human point of view, should we not say that every citizen ought to be ready, if necessary, to die heroically in defense of his country?

Moreover, every Christian ought to prefer the supernatural good, the salvation of his neighbor, to his own natural good. Charity counsels him to assist, even at the risk of his life, a soul in extreme spiritual need. This obligation is stricter for a priest who has charge of souls and for a bishop in regard to his flock. Although the latter is not obliged to have the virtues in a heroic degree, he must be ready, if the occasion arises, to give his life for the faithful of his diocese.

Therefore it must be conceded that Christian charity should in its daily progress tend normally to the heroic degree, which permits the prompt and even joyful performance of most

[57] On this point, cf. St. Thomas on the question of martyrdom, IIa IIae, q.124, a.1 ad 3um.

difficult acts for God and our neighbor. Every soul that has undergone the passive purifications of the spirit feels strongly inclined to this heroic degree of charity.

These purifications lead finally to true sanctity, which is perfect purity, immutable union with God,[58] and also the intimate harmony of all the virtues, even of those which to all appearances are most opposed: the perfect accord of great fortitude and unalterable meekness, of rigorous justice and tender mercy, of the loftiest and simplest wisdom with all-embracing prudence. This is truly sanctity before God, although it may not always be manifested by definite signs to the Church. Only in this sanctity is found the full perfection of Christian life, a perfection truly superior to the relative perfection which is mentioned by several authors on asceticism and which is only the entrance into the way of the perfect.

Evidently we are speaking not merely of the essence of perfection, but of its normal integrity; as, for example, to have good eyes belongs, if not to the essence of the human body, at least to its integrity. Similarly, as will become more and more evident, infused contemplation belongs, if not to the essence of Christian perfection, at least to its integrity. This contemplation, very manifest in the perfect who are more fitted to the contemplative life, is diffuse in the other perfect in whom dominate especially the gifts of the Holy Ghost which relate to action—the gifts of fear, fortitude, counsel, and knowledge, united to the gift of piety, under a less visible influence of the gifts of wisdom and of understanding.[59]

## ARTICLE V

*Perfection and the Precept of the Love of God*

### A. IS THE FIRST PRECEPT WITHOUT LIMIT?

The twofold precept of love is strictly formulated in the

[58] *Summa,* IIa IIae, q.81, a.8.
[59] Cf. *infra,* chap. 5, art. 6.

Gospel of St. Luke: [1] "Thou shalt love the Lord thy God with thy whole heart, and with thy whole soul, and with all thy strength, and with all thy mind: and thy neighbor as thyself." After weighing the meaning of each of these terms and considering the insistence with which the word "all" is repeated, we might ask with St. Thomas whether the precept of the love of God has a limit; and, if it has, whether it follows that beyond this limit there is only a counsel of charity in which perfection would consist.

Some have thought so and have insisted that even to observe this precept perfectly, we need not possess a high degree of charity. Higher perfection, which suppresses deliberate venial sin and voluntary imperfections, is only of counsel. It is not included under the precept, but goes beyond it. Perfection would thus consist especially in the accomplishment of certain counsels of charity, superior to the first precept itself. [2]

This may seem true if we consider matters superficially. In

[1] Luke 10: 27.

[2] This opinion is expressed by Suarez, De statu perfectionis, chap. 11, nos. 15, 16. He admits that St. Thomas and before him St. Augustine seem to teach clearly that the perfection of Christian life is not only counseled, but commanded, by the first precept, as an end toward which one must tend. But he himself replies in the negative: "Respondeo nihilominus, si proprie et in rigore loquamur, perfectionem supererogationis non solum non praecipi, ut materiam in quam obligatio praecepti cadat, verum etiam neque per modum finis in praeceptis contineri." Thus he admits above the precept of the love of God, which in his opinion is limited, counsels of charity superior to those of poverty, chastity, and obedience. Perfection, according to him, consists essentially in these counsels of charity, instrumentally in the other three. Cf. ibid., no. 16.

This doctrine of Suarez is criticized at length by the great canonist Passerini, O.P., who was a profound theologian and most faithful to St. Thomas. Cf. his De hominum statibus et officiis, on IIa IIae, q.184, a.3, p. 50, no. 70, and p. 57, no. 106, where he shows that this doctrine of Suarez is opposed to that of St. Augustine and of St. Thomas, which was accepted by St. Antoninus, Cajetan, and Valentia. This will be easily understood by reading the article quoted from the Summa theologica, which we are going to translate. We will then, in a footnote, briefly answer the objections of Suarez.

St. Thomas has also occasionally (e. g., In Ep. ad Phil., chap. 3, lect. 2) used the expression "perfection of supererogation," but in a different sense from that in which Suarez uses it. Cf. G. Barthier, O.P., Perfection chrétienne et perfection religieuse, I, 229. When St. Thomas uses this phrase, he simply means that the three counsels of poverty, chastity, and obedience are not obligatory.

stating the problem, St. Thomas carefully notes it in his objection: "All are obliged to observe the precepts in order to obtain salvation. If, therefore, the perfection of Christian life consisted in the precepts, it would follow that perfection would be necessary to salvation and that all would be obliged thereto, which is false." [3] This is a specious objection. As we shall see, St. Thomas solves it by showing, as St. Augustine does, the grandeur of the precept of the love of God, which is superior to all the counsels. It is surprising to find that modern theologians, and not the least among them, as a result of their failure to comprehend the doctrine of the greatest masters on this fundamental point of spirituality, have turned this objection into a thesis.

Instead of being content with appearances and the material side of things, we will consider the deep meaning and extent of the precept. As a basis for this discussion, we will follow as exactly as possible the text of a little known article of St. Thomas, "Whether perfection consists in the observance of the commandments or of the counsels." [4]

"It is written in Deuteronomy: 'Thou shalt love the Lord thy God with thy whole heart,' [5] and in Leviticus: 'Thou shalt love thy neighbor as thyself.' [6] Our Lord adds: 'On these two commandments dependeth the whole law and the prophets.' [7] Now the perfection of charity, according to which Christian life is perfect, consists precisely in this, that we love God with all our hearts and our neighbor as ourselves. It would seem, therefore, that perfection consists in the fulfilment of the precepts. To understand it clearly, it must be observed that perfection consists necessarily and essentially in one thing, secondarily and accidentally in another.

---

[3] *Summa*, IIa IIae, q.184, a.3 ad 2um: "Whether perfection consists in the observance of the precepts or of the counsels."
[4] *Summa*, IIa IIae, q.184, a.3.
[5] Deut. 6: 5.
[6] Lev. 19: 18.
[7] Matt. 22: 40.

"Necessarily and essentially, the perfection of Christian life consists in charity; primarily in the love of God, and secondarily in the love of our neighbor. This charity is the object of the two chief precepts of the divine law. Now it would be a mistake to imagine that the love of God and of our neighbor is the object of a law only according to a certain measure, that is to say, up to a certain degree, after which it would become the object of a simple counsel. No, the message of the commandment is clear and shows what perfection is: 'Thou shalt love the Lord thy God with thy whole heart.' The two expressions *all* and *entire* or *perfect* are synonymous. Similarly, it is said: 'Thou shalt love thy neighbor as thyself'; and each one loves himself, so to speak, without limit (*maxime*).[8] This is so, because, according to the teaching of the Apostle, 'The end of the commandment is charity.' [9] Now, the end does not present itself to the will in a fragmentary manner, but in its totality. In this it differs from the means. Either one wishes it or one does not wish it. One does not wish it by halves, as Aristotle observes.[10] Does a doctor seek only half the cure of a sick person? Obviously no. What he measures is the medicine, but not health, which he wishes without measure. Manifestly, therefore, perfection consists essentially in the precepts. Moreover, St. Augustine says, in his book *De perfectione justitiae:* 'Why, therefore, should this perfection not be prescribed to man, although he cannot have it (fully) in this life?' " [11]

This is so much the more true because the end in question is not an intermediary end, such as health, but the ultimate end, God Himself, who is infinite good. St. Thomas says: "We

---

[8] In this sense, that everyone ought by charity to wish for himself salvation, eternal life, and not only an inferior degree of glory, but eternal life without fixing any limit; for we do not know to what degree of glory God wishes to raise us.

[9] See I Tim. 1: 5.

[10] See *I Polit.*, chap. 3.

[11] See IIa IIae, q.184, a.3. St. Augustine means that even the perfection of heaven falls under the precept of the love of God, not as something to be realized immediately, but as the end toward which one must tend. It is thus that Cajetan explains it (commentary on IIa IIae, q.184, a.3).

can never love God as much as He ought to be loved, nor believe and hope in Him as much as we should." [12] Moreover, the theological virtues differ from the moral virtues in that they do not essentially consist in a happy mean. Their object, their formal motive, their essential measure, is God Himself, His infinite truth and goodness. If, from one point of view, these supreme virtues are a happy mean,[13] it is accidental and on the part of the human subject, not of the divine object. For example, the proficient can and should love God more than the beginner, yet without being able to love Him as the perfect do, or as the blessed in heaven.[14]

Finally, another reason why the precept of love has no limit is that our charity ought always to grow even until death, for we are travelers on the road to eternity. The way to eternity is not made to be used as a place of rest and sleep, but rather to be traveled. The lazy are those who rest along the road instead of pushing on to their goal. The traveler who has not yet reached the fixed term of his pilgrimage is commanded and not only counseled to advance, just as the child must grow according to the law of nature until he has reached maturity. Now, when it is a question of walking toward God, it is not

[12] *Summa,* Ia IIae, q.64, a.4: Whether the theological virtues observe the mean.

[13] For example, faith between infidelity and credulity; and hope between presumption and despair.

[14] Likewise, from this secondary and accidental point of view, on the part of man, and not of God, hope is found between despair and presumption. The presumptuous man does not hope too much in God—that is impossible; but he hopes for a good which exceeds his condition—for example, pardon without true repentance. In the same way, credulity does not consist in believing too much in God, but in believing as if revealed by Him, what is only invention or human imagination (Ia IIae, q.64, a.4). On the other hand, the moral virtue which rules a passion ought essentially to constitute a happy mean between the excess and the absence of this passion. Thus the virtue of fortitude is essentially a rational, happy mean, between cowardice and temerity; a happy mean, moreover, which, by reason of its rationality, stands out as a culminating point above these irrational forms of human action. To forget, as Epicurus does, that the rational, happy mean must thus be a summit, and to wish to make the essentially theological virtues consist in a mean as the moral virtues do, is the peculiarity of mediocrity or of tepidity, erected into a system under pretext of moderation.

by the movement of our bodies that we advance, but rather by the steps of love or charity, as St. Thomas says. Therefore we ought daily in this way to draw nearer to God, without placing a limit on the progress of our charity. We have no right to say that we will love God so much and no more. Such a restriction of charity would fail to observe the first commandment, which is measureless: "Thou shalt love the Lord thy God with thy whole heart, and with thy whole soul, and with all thy strength, and with all thy mind."

Does it follow that perfection in no way consists in the evangelical counsels? In the passage we have quoted above, St. Thomas replies: "Secondarily and instrumentally, however, perfection consists in the observance of the counsels; in other words, they are only precious instruments to attain it. In fact, all the counsels, like the commandments, are ordained to charity, with one difference however. The commandments, other than the two great precepts of love, are intended to remove whatever is contrary to charity, whatever might destroy it; while the end of the counsels is to remove whatever hinders or prevents the perfect exercise of charity without, however, being opposed to it, as for example, marriage, the necessity of being occupied with secular affairs, and things of this sort. This is what St. Augustine teaches (*Enchiridion,* chap. 21): 'Precepts . . . and counsels . . . are well observed when one fulfils them in order to love God, and one's neighbor for God, in this world and in the next.' "

This is why Abbot Moses says: "Fasts, vigils, meditation on Holy Scripture, nudity, and the privation of external goods, are not perfections, but instruments or means of perfection. It is not in them that perfection consists, but by them that one attains it." [15]

This is what our Lord had in mind when He said to the rich young man: "If thou wilt be perfect, go sell what thou hast, and give to the poor, and thou shalt have treasure in heaven:

[15] *Conferences of the Fathers,* Bk. I, chap. 7.

and come, follow Me." [16] As St. Thomas observes (*loc. cit.,* ad 1um), by these words our Lord indicates, first of all, the road which leads to perfection: "Go sell what thou hast, and give to the poor"; then He adds in what this perfection consists: "and follow Me," in spirit through charity. As St. Ambrose says,[17] "He orders him to follow, not with the steps of the body, but with devotion of the soul." The counsels are, therefore, instruments or means to attain perfection, but they do not constitute it essentially. Perfection is found in the fulfilment of the supreme and limitless precept of the love of God and of our neighbor.

Let us return to the difficulty pointed out at the beginning of this article. The following objection is raised: "All are bound to the observance of the commandments, since this is necessary for salvation. Therefore, if the perfection of Christian life consists essentially in the commandments, it follows that perfection is necessary for salvation and that all are obliged to be perfect, which is manifestly false. Moreover, imperfect charity already observes the precepts. It seems, therefore, that perfect charity consists essentially in observing the counsels."

To these two difficulties St. Thomas (*ibid.,* ad 2um and 3um), following St. Augustine, offers a profound reply showing the sublimity of the precept of love, which only the saints observe in its fulness: "As St. Augustine says in *De perfectione justitiae,*[18] the perfection of charity is prescribed to man in this life because 'one runs not in the right direction unless one knows whither to run. And how shall we know this, if no commandment declares it to us?' But the matter of the precept (of love) can be fulfilled in different ways. Moreover, he who does not fulfil it in the most perfect manner does not for that reason transgress the precept. To avoid this transgression,

---

[16] Matt. 19: 21.
[17] *In Luc.,* 5: 27.
[18] Chap. 8.

it is enough to fulfil the law of charity to a certain extent as beginners do.

"The perfection of divine love falls entirely within the object of the precept; even the perfection of heaven is not excluded from it, since it is the end toward which one must tend, as St. Augustine says.[19] But one avoids the transgression of the precept by putting into practice a little love of God.

"Now, the lowest degree of the love of God consists in loving nothing more than God, or contrary to God, or equally with God, and he who has not this degree of perfection nowise fulfils the commandment. There is another degree of charity, which cannot be realized in this life, and which consists in loving God with all our strength, in such a way that our love always tends actually toward Him. This perfection is possible only in heaven, and therefore the fact that one does not yet possess it, does not entail a transgression of the commandment. And in like manner the fact that one has not attained the intermediate degrees of perfection, does not entail a transgression, provided only that one reaches the lowest degree."

But evidently he who remains in this lowest degree does not fulfil the supreme commandment in all its perfection. He does not accomplish fully what the law of love demands: "Thou shalt love the Lord thy God with thy whole heart, and with thy whole soul, and with all thy strength, and with all thy mind."

It would, therefore, be a great illusion to think that only imperfect charity is prescribed, and that the higher degrees of this virtue are only of counsel. They fall under the precept, if not as something to be realized immediately, at least as that toward which we must tend, as the Thomists say. Even the charity of heaven is prescribed as the end toward which the soul in this life must always strive and even run, as St. Paul says,[20] without losing the time granted to it. Purgatory is for

19 *Ibid.,* and *De Spiritu et littera,* chap. 36.
20 See I Cor. 9: 24: "Know you not that they that run in the race, all run indeed, but one receiveth the prize? So run that you may obtain."

those who have not well enough employed their time of trial on earth.[21] This great doctrine seems subtle at first glance merely because of the objection that might embarrass the mind. In reality, it is quite conformable to what common sense in the natural order tells us. "Thus, in fact," observes St. Thomas,[22] "man, even from birth, has a certain essential perfection by which he belongs to the human species, and is quite superior to the animal; but he has not, as yet, the perfection of maturity, the full development of the body and of the faculties of the soul. In like manner, there is a certain perfection of charity which is none other than its very essence: to love God above all things, and to love nothing contrary to Him. But there is also, even in this life, another perfection of charity which one attains only by spiritual progress, analogous to natural growth. To reach this perfection, the Christian abstains even from lawful things, so as to fulfil more freely his duties toward God."

The analogy is evident. To belong to the human race, it is enough to be a child, but that is not sufficient to be a fully developed man. Further, by virtue of a necessary law, a child must grow under pain not of remaining a child but of becoming a deformed dwarf. Likewise it suffices to have a very low degree of charity in order to avoid the transgression of the precept of love, but that does not suffice for the perfect fulfilment of this first precept, which is superior to all the others and to all the counsels. Moreover, if the beginner does

---

[21] Cajetan (commentary on IIa IIae, q.84, a.3) says on this subject: "The perfection of charity is prescribed as an end. We must will to attain the complete end; but precisely because it is an end, if we are to avoid failing in the matter of the precepts, it suffices that we be in the state to attain this perfection some day, even though only in eternity. Whoever possesses even the weakest degree of charity, and thus makes progress heavenward, is in the way of perfect charity, and thereby avoids the transgression of the commandment which is necessary for salvation." But whoever dies in the state of grace without having sufficiently utilized the time of life, will have to pass through purgatory in order to be profoundly purified therein. There he will experience the ardent desire for the vision of God.

[22] *Summa*, IIa IIae, q.184, a.4 ad 3um.

not grow in charity, he will not remain a beginner, but will become an abnormal creature and, as it were, a dwarf from the spiritual point of view. For example, he has faith and piety which are, so to speak, embryonic, coupled with a highly developed literary, scientific, or professional culture. The disproportion is evident; balance is altogether lacking. Objections arise, disconcert the soul, and put it to rout. For lack of development, the divine seed which is in the soul runs the risk of dying, as we learn in the parable of the sower.[23] In the spiritual life these abnormal souls are certainly not the true mystics and saints, but the retarded and the lukewarm.

This point of doctrine is evidently of primary importance in the spiritual life, but, strange to say, it is often misunderstood or at least forgotten. The perfection of charity is not only counseled, it is prescribed as the end toward which every Christian should tend, if not by the practice of the counsels, at least by their spirit while continually growing in charity. Pope Pius XI recalled this doctrine in his encyclical on the spiritual doctrine of St. Francis de Sales. The rejection of this doctrine is the suppression of the final cause in the question we are considering.[24]

---

[23] Matt. 13: 4–6: "And whilst he soweth some fell by the wayside, and the birds of the air came and ate them up. And other some fell upon stony ground, where they had not much earth; and they sprung up immediately, because they had no deepness of earth. And when the sun was up, they were scorched: and because they had not root, they withered away."

[24] This truth has been clearly stated by Cardinal Mercier in his *La vie intérieure, appel aux âmes sacerdotales* (1919), p. 98. He draws this conclusion: "We are all called to ascend the summits of perfection, to ascend from that spiritual condition in which the fear of losing charity is the ordinary and predominating motive of conduct, to that state in which the soul more willingly allows itself to be guided by the purpose of progress in virtue; to ascend even higher, even to complete detachment from created things and to the spirit of union with God alone for Himself alone. In regard to this ascent, there are in the world, and at times among the clergy, sad and profound prejudices, which we ought all to apply ourselves to extirpate. I repeat, everyone is called to the fulness of evangelical perfection. . . . To all it is said: 'Be ye therefore perfect as also your heavenly Father is perfect' (Matt. 5: 48). 'To all the faithful,' says the Catechism of the Council of Trent, Part II, *De matrimonii sacramento*,

When a soul, after living for a long time in the state of mortal sin, returns to God, it should do more than simply take care not to fall again and avoid the occasions of evil; it should ascend higher. The precept of love has no limit; it does not stop at a certain degree, beyond which there is only a counsel, but it commands us to grow continually in charity without ever stopping. God, who is infinitely good, deserves to be loved without measure, continually more and more "with all our heart, and with all our soul, with all our strength, and with all our mind." Only the saints perfectly observe this great law, which is the soul of Christian life.[25]

## B. THREE CONSEQUENCES OF THE PRECEPT OF THE LOVE OF GOD

Three important consequences result from this lofty doctrine of the precept of the love of God which teaches that the first precept, superior to all the others and to all the counsels,

---

'pastors must recommend the perfect life . . . the source of the most complete happiness that man can taste in this life.' The liturgy asks for all souls the grace 'not to allow themselves to be tossed about by the fluctuations of the world, but to keep their hearts fixed on Him who alone can render us truly happy' " (prayer for the fourth Sunday after Easter).

[25] Perhaps some will object that the precept does not impose an act of charity every minute, and therefore such an act of charity, not being obligatory, is only a matter of counsel. Passerini answers correctly (*op. cit.*, p. 50, no. 72) that this act is not obligatory, as something to be fulfilled immediately, but it is obligatory as an intermediary end toward which we must tend.

Some insist that we are not bound by precept to make each act of charity more intense than the preceding one, for what falls under the precept is the substance of the act and not its more or less perfect mode. This is of precept, at least in so far as it is an end which we should try to attain, for man should aspire to love God ever more and more. St. Thomas explains the matter (Ia IIae, q.100, a.10, ad 2um): "If he who honors his parents is obliged to honor them by a motive of supernatural charity, this act does not spring from the particular commandment, 'Honor thy father and thy mother,' but from the supreme commandment, 'Thou shalt love the Lord with thy whole heart.' " Thus what falls under the inferior precept is the substance of the act, but the mode of the act is commanded by the supreme precept. Cf. IIa IIae, q.44, a.1 ad 1um. In addition under the precept of charity falls the mode, which is expressed by the words "with all thy heart" (IIa IIae, q.44, a.4 ad 1um), and also the order of charity (*ibid.*, a.8).

has no limit; that by it the perfection of the Christian life is not only counseled, but commanded, to all; and that it is commanded not as something to be realized immediately, but rather as the end toward which everyone should tend according to his condition.

Since the charity of a Christian should increase until death, any halt in its development is in opposition to the law of the love of God. This is the explanation of the expression used by several fathers of the Church: "In the way of salvation, he who does not advance, goes back." If life does not ascend, it descends. The soul cannot live without love. If it fails to make progress in the love of God, it falls back into self-love. This is the danger of imperfect acts (*actus remissi,* as the theologians say) which proceed from charity, but are inferior in intensity to our degree of that virtue.

Three points are to be noted in regard to these acts: (1) These acts are still meritorious but, according to St. Thomas and the best theologians, they do not immediately obtain an increase of charity. They will obtain it only when we make a more fervent act, equal or superior to the degree of our virtue; just as in the natural order a virtuous friendship grows only through more generous acts.[26] (2) Acts of charity relatively too feeble for our degree of virtue show even a deficit, in this sense that the soul ought always to progress instead of remaining stationary; just as a child ought always to grow in order not to be stunted. (3) Lastly, these acts dispose us to positive retrogression, for by reason of their weakness they permit the rebirth of disordered inclinations, which lead to venial sin, and may end by overcoming us or leading us to spiritual death. Does the virtue of charity thus directly diminish? Not directly in itself; but its radiation, its influence, become weakened as a result of the obstacles that gradually accumulate

---

26 Cf. St. Thomas, IIa IIae, q.24, a.6 ad 1um; *ibid.,* ad 2um; also Ia IIae, q.114, a.8 ad 3um. On this point, consult also the commentators of St. Thomas, *Tract on charity.*

about it, as the light of a lantern which, while keeping its intensity, sheds less and less light in proportion as its chimney becomes dimmed and soiled with the splashing mud of the road.[27]

In the same way, a retarded soul falls back like an intelligent man who ceases to apply his mind to study. If, possessing five talents, he acts as though he had only two or even four, he does not sufficiently increase the treasure entrusted to him. He is thereby guilty of negligence and spiritual laziness, that hinder him from perfectly observing the precept of love, the fundamental law of Christian life. From all this, we see that a meritorious act which is too weak is an imperfection disposing to venial sin, as the latter disposes to mortal sin.

The proficient who is satisfied to act like a beginner ceases to make progress and becomes a retarded soul. People do not give sufficient thought to the fact that the number of these souls is considerable. Many indeed think of developing their intellect, of expanding their knowledge, their exterior activity or that of the group to which they belong (in which there may be not a little selfishness), and yet scarcely think of growing in supernatural charity, which ought to have first place in us, and ought to inspire and vivify our entire life, and associate us intimately with the great life of the Church and that of Christ. And many retarded souls end by becoming lukewarm, cowardly, and careless, especially when their natural bent is toward skepticism and raillery. In the

[27] Theologians commonly teach, with St. Thomas (IIa IIae, q.24, a.10), that the virtue of charity, although it may be lost by mortal sin, does not directly diminish in itself by venial sin, or by the cessation of acts. Venial sin is, in fact, a disorder that has to do with the means, without affecting the final end, which is the object of charity. And as this virtue is infused, and not acquired by the repetition of acts, it is not directly increased by them, nor diminished by their cessation.

But this inactivity and venial sins indirectly diminish charity because they hinder its application or influence and permit the formation of bad habits, which are obstacles to the radiation of charity. These obstacles deserve a lessening of God's actual, special graces, and they dispose finally to mortal sin.

end they may become hardened and, as a result, it is often more difficult to bring them back to a fervent life than to bring about the conversion of a great sinner.[28]

Certain modern writers do not devote enough thought to the considerable number of retarded souls that are in the so-called category of proficients. They then describe the illuminative way by being too easily satisfied with showing what it is rather generally in fact, that is, notably inferior to infused contemplation, which thus appears as an extraordinary grace. St. John of the Cross, who follows the teaching of the greatest masters, has, on the contrary, shown what it ought to be if it is to correspond fully to its great name. Considering the matter from this higher point of view, we are not surprised that he makes the illuminative way (that of proficients) begin with the passive night of the senses or the beginning of infused contemplation, which then appears in the normal development of the interior life.[29]

This first consequence of the precept of the love of God—he who does not advance, falls back—shows that the progress of charity ought to be continual. It thus opens up great perspectives.

A second result of the precept of the love of God is that every Christian, each according to his condition, must strive for the perfection of charity. For each and every one it is a general obligation, and is not reserved to religious and clerics.

Because of his vows, a religious must tend to perfection by

28 For a discussion of retarded and lukewarm souls, cf. Saudreau, *Degrés de la vie spirituelle,* 5th ed., I, 46, 49.

29 "Souls begin to enter this dark night (passive) when God Himself frees them little by little from the state of beginners, that division of the spiritual life in which one meditates, and introduces them into the state of proficients, which is that of contemplatives. They must pass through this way in order to become perfect, in other words, to attain the divine union of the soul with God" (*The Dark Night of the Soul,* Bk. I, chap. 1). "The soul has therefore gone forth; it has begun to penetrate into the way of the spirit, followed by the proficients and the advanced. This way is also called the illuminative way, or the way of infused contemplation" (*ibid.,* chap. 14).

practicing the counsels of poverty, chastity, and obedience, and by keeping the rule of his order. This special obligation places him in the state of perfection without at once making him perfect. It is identical with that of the observance of the vows,[30] the transgression of which in a grave matter is a mortal sin. In the way of progress, as marked out for him by his rule, the religious can never set a limit. He must always aspire to greater perfection.

Although a secular priest is not in the state of perfection, nevertheless he must tend to perfection on account of the holy orders he has received. Even if he has not the care of souls, he is obliged to a greater inward holiness than that required of a religious who is not a priest. "By holy orders," says St. Thomas, "a man is appointed to the most august ministry of serving Christ Himself in the sacrament of the altar. This requires a greater inward holiness than that which is required for the religious state." [31]

The ordinary Christian must strive for the perfection of charity according to the general obligation of the first commandment. How shall he do this? By avoiding mortal and venial sin, by having the spirit of the counsels, without binding himself to practice those which do not correspond to his

[30] Cf. Salamanticences, *Theol. moralis,* Vol. IV, "De statu religioso."

[31] St. Thomas, IIa IIae, q. 184, a.8. "A man must possess inward perfection in order to exercise worthily the acts of the priesthood" (*ibid.,* a.6). In a.8: "If one compares the religious priest who has care of souls with the secular priest who also has care of souls, they are equal in order and office or function, but the first is superior to the second in his state of life, since he is in a state of perfection. If the religious priest has not care of souls, he is more excellent than the secular priest in state, less excellent in office, and equal in order" (*ibid.,* a.8). The holy doctor adds that the goodness or perfection of the religious state, in which one pledges one's whole life, is more excellent than that of the office of parish priest, which does not bind for life. As to the difficulty of persevering in good, it is greater for the priest who lives in the world because of the obstacles to be found there. In the religious life there is another difficulty, that which comes from the dignity of the work to be accomplished, the practice of obedience, of poverty, and the austerity of observances. Now, this second difficulty increases merit, which is not always true of the difficulty springing from exterior obstacles, for it may be that one does not love virtue sufficiently to put away these obstacles and leave secular life. Cf. *ibid.,* ad 6um.

condition, and by thus growing in charity until death.[32] If a Christian follows this way generously, he will be called not only in a remote manner, but in a proximate and even efficacious manner, to a very high perfection, to which he can attain though married. All ought, therefore, to grow in charity, each according to his state in life, whether it be that of a simple layman, a secular priest, or a religious; in other words, each according to his condition, whether it be that of beginner, proficient, or perfect.[33] It was with this meaning that our Lord said to all: "Be you therefore perfect, as also your heavenly Father is perfect." [34] This call is not merely to the perfection of the angels, but to that of God Himself, since we have received a participation not only in the angelic nature but in the divine nature, and since this participation, sanctifying grace, is the beginning of eternal life, that will develop into glory in which we shall see God as He sees Himself, and love Him as He loves Himself.

In the same sense, St. Peter wrote for all the faithful: "As newborn babes, desire the rational milk without guile, that thereby you may grow unto salvation; if so be you have tasted that the Lord is sweet. Unto whom coming, as to a living stone, rejected indeed by men, but chosen and made honorable by God: be you also as living stones built up, a spiritual house, a holy priesthood, to offer up spiritual sacrifices, acceptable to God by Jesus Christ." [35] "But grow in grace, and in the knowledge of our Lord and Savior Jesus Christ." [36] St. Paul also teaches us: "But doing the truth in charity, we may in all things grow up in Him who is the head, even Christ." [37]

---

[32] We read in the *Dialogue* of St. Catherine of Siena, chap. 47: "Inasmuch as the counsels are bound up in the commandments, no one can observe the latter who does not observe the former, as least in thought, that is to say, that they possess the riches of the world humbly and without pride."

[33] Cf. St. Thomas, *In Ep. ad Hebr.*, 10: 25.

[34] Matt. 5: 48.

[35] See I Pet. 2: 2.

[36] See II Pet. 3: 18.

[37] Eph. 4: 15.

"Therefore, we also . . . cease not to pray for you, and to beg that you may be filled with the knowledge of His will, in all wisdom, and spiritual understanding: that you may walk worthy of God, in all things pleasing; being fruitful in every good work, and increasing in the knowledge of God: strengthened with all might, according to the power of His glory, in all patience and long-suffering with joy." [38] "Wherefore, leaving the word of the beginning of Christ, let us go on to things more perfect" (Heb. 6: 1).

Commenting on this last text of St. Paul, St. Thomas observes: "In regard to his judgment of himself, a man ought not to consider himself perfect, but he ought always to be like a pilgrim who continues on his way and ever tends higher, as the Apostle states: 'Not as though I had already attained, or were already perfect' (Phil. 3: 12). In regard to the progress to be made, man ought always to strive to attain perfection: 'Forgetting the things that are behind, and stretching forth myself to those that are before' (*ibid., 3: 13*). As St. Bernard says, not to advance in the way of salvation is to fall back. . . . To be sure, this does not mean that all are obliged to that perfection, in a certain sense exterior, which consists, for example, in voluntary poverty and virginity. . . . But all ought to strive for the inward perfection of charity . . . for if a man did not wish to love God more, he would fail in that which charity requires." [39] "He who would not always wish to become better, would not be able to avoid contempt for that which is worthy of all respect." [40]

---

[38] Col. 1: 9–11.

[39] St. Thomas, *In Ep. ad Hebr.*, 6: 1.

[40] "As far as exterior acts are concerned, because he is not obliged to the doubtful good, man is not obliged to the best; but as far as his desire is concerned, he is obliged to the best, whence he who does not always wish to be better, cannot without contempt refrain from wishing it" (St. Thomas, *In Matth.*, 19: 12). The same idea is expressed in IIa IIae, q.186, a.2 ad 2um: "All, both religious and secular, are bound, in a certain measure, to do whatever good they can; for to all without exception it is said: 'Whatsoever thy hand is able to do, do it earnestly' (Eccles. 9: 10). Yet there is a way of fulfilling this precept, so as to avoid sin, namely, if we do what we can as required by the conditions of our

St. Francis de Sales, quoting these words of Scripture, teaches the same doctrine: [41] " 'And he that is just, let him be justified still: and he that is holy, let him be sanctified still.' [42] 'But the path of the just, as a shining light, goeth forward and increaseth even to perfect day.' [43] 'So run that you may obtain.' [44] If you follow Christ, you will always run, for He never stopped, but continued the course of His love and obedience 'unto death, even to the death of the cross.' " [45]

According to this same law, the progress of charity in the Blessed Virgin, who was preserved from every stain of sin, was continual in this life. It was not even interrupted by sleep, for the infused knowledge which she had received kept the superior part of her soul always on the alert and her meritorious acts did not cease, any more than did the beating of her heart.[46] The initial plenitude of grace, which she had received from the instant of her immaculate conception, was thus multiplied by every act of charity, each one more intense than the preceding, and incessantly multiplied according to a marvelous progression which we could never calculate.[47]

What a prodigious acceleration in the progress of divine love takes place when there is nothing in the soul to arrest its growth! Reason is overawed in the presence of this masterpiece of God. Is it credible? Indeed, so much so that if we look about us, we find even in the material world a semblance of this wonderful law of the spiritual life; namely, every ma-

---

state of life; provided there be no contempt of doing better things, which contempt sets the mind against spiritual progress."

[41] *Treatise on the Love of God*, Bk. III, chap. 1.

[42] Apoc. 22: 11.

[43] Prov. 4: 18.

[44] See I Cor. 9: 24.

[45] Phil. 2: 8. On the general obligation of every Christian to strive according to his condition for more perfect charity, see Passerini, *De statibus hominum*, p. 758, no. 13; G. Barthier, O.P., *De la perfection chrétienne et de la perfection religieuse* (1907), I, 315–73; P. A. Weiss, O.P., *Apologie des Christenthums*, Vol. V, Index: "Vollkommenheit."

[46] Cant. 5: 2: "I sleep but my heart watcheth."

[47] Cf. E. Hugon, O.P., *Marie mère de la divine grâce*, pp. 112–24.

terial body falling freely in space takes on a uniformly accelerated movement, the speed of which grows in proportion to the time of the fall.[48]

This is a particular case of the law of universal gravity, which is analogously applied in the spiritual order. If bodies attract each other in the direct ratio of their mass, and in the inverse ratio of the square of their distance, similarly souls are so much the more drawn by God as they are nearer to Him by the intensity of their supernatural charity. Were a soul always to remain faithful, the progress of the love of God encountering no obstacle would thus be uniformly accelerated, and would be just so much more intense as the initial speed or the first grace was greater. This gives us a glimpse of what this progress must have been in the soul of the Blessed Virgin, in whom the initial grace was superior to that of all the saints and angels together, as the diamond is worth more than all other precious stones. Mary was also able to avoid not only every venial sin, but all taken collectively, and she never produced acts inferior to her degree of charity; consequently the progress of the love of God never encountered in her the slightest obstacle or the least retardation.

St. Thomas, who knew that bodies fall more rapidly as they approach the earth,[49] also noted this acceleration of the progress of charity in the souls of the saints in the measure in which they drew nearer to God: "Those," he says, "who are in the state of grace ought to grow the more in it as they draw closer to the end."[50] This is the way he understood the expression in the Epistle to the Hebrews:[51] "Comforting one an-

[48] Thus, in five seconds the initial speed multiplied by the time increases according to the following progression: 20, 20 x 2, 20 x 3, 20 x 4, 20 x 5, or 20, 40, 60, 80, 100.

[49] *In I de Coelo*, lect. 17. St. Thomas explains this fact by the Aristotelian theory of the natural place. See also Ia IIae, q.35, a.6, where he says that, contrary to violent movement, every natural motion is more intense at the end than at the beginning, for it approaches the end which agrees with the nature of the motion and which attracts it as an end.

[50] St. Thomas, *In Ep. ad Hebraeos*, 10: 25.

[51] *Ibid.*

other, and so much the more as you see the day approaching," so much the more as we approach the end of the journey.

There is a third consequence of the precept of the love of God, namely, since the perfection of charity falls under the precept as the end toward which one must tend, assuredly actual graces are progressively offered to us proportionate to the end to be attained. Knowing this, how is it possible that we should not hope to attain this end and how can we make it a matter of humility not to pretend to ascend so high? Our Lord Jesus Christ continually repeats: "*Sursum corda,*" and He adds: "Without Me you can do nothing." If you ascend, do not take the glory to yourself. It is I who carry you, who lift you up, who constantly give you life, and I wish to give it to you in ever greater abundance so that you may correspond ever more perfectly with the commandment of My Father. Perfect charity, as it exists in the transforming union, appears thus more and more as the summit of the normal development of the grace of baptism. It seems quite difficult now to admit possible discussion on this point.[52] And to think that contemplative souls have suffered so greatly because they willed to doubt God's munificence on behalf of the baptized soul! Rightly their hearts protested against the doubts raised by their souls. In what gentle harmony everything is bound up and united in God's truth! How calm must the soul of a

[52] In virtue of the principle set forth in this article, it can be explained why Thomistic theologians (such as Philip of the Blessed Trinity, Vallgornera, and Anthony of the Holy Ghost) maintain not only that all may laudably desire infused contemplation and the union of fruition, but that all should desire it. At first glance this statement seems exaggerated, and it would be so if they were speaking of a special obligation (which may exist for a contemplative religious). They speak only of a general obligation based on the first precept, which makes it everyone's duty to tend toward the perfection of heaven and consequently toward what is normally found even in a very lofty degree on the way to heaven, toward that which is the normal prelude of the beatific vision. This explains the theses that these theologians also formulate in their mystical theology in the chapters on infused contemplation and the union of fruition: "All should aspire to supernatural contemplation. All, and most especially souls consecrated to God, should aspire and tend to actual fruitive union with God." These two theses have already been pointed out and will be referred to again.

St. Augustine or a St. Thomas have been, living habitually in the peace-giving contemplation of the being and unity of God! What love burst forth also from the sweet knowledge of the supreme precept and of the grace offered to fulfil it ever more fully! However sublime the degree to which divine mercy raises a soul in this life, it ought always to say that it would be its own fault if it did not ascend higher in the time remaining to it on earth. The same profound mystery exists in regard to the degree of sanctity and the degree of glory as in regard to salvation. It is the goodness of God that awakens our goodness, that saves us and makes us advance. It is a creature's own ill will that condemns him, or at least delays him on the way of eternity: "Destruction is thy own, O Israel; thy help is only in Me." [53] The depths of humility open up for the contemplative soul at the same time as the abyss of the divine mercy into which it is more and more deeply plunged. To wretchedness which humbly petitions, infinite mercy from its height stoops to give us the strength always to fulfil more perfectly the first precept, which is the generating law of all our life. This is the burden of Psalm 41: "My soul is troubled within myself; therefore will I remember Thee. . . . Deep calleth on deep, at the noise of thy flood-gates. . . . With me is prayer to the God of my life. . . . Hope thou in God, for I will still give praise to Him: the salvation of my countenance, and my God!" [54] The great poetry of the psalms has been revealed to us in order to be understood. To understand it well, however, and to make it vibrate in the depths of the soul, should we not have received infused contemplation, which raises the mind and the heart even to the fountain of living water and to the light of life? This contemplation and its degrees are the subject of the following pages.

[53] Osee 13: 9.
[54] Ps. 41: 7, 9, 12.

# CHAPTER V

## Contemplation and Its Degrees

Since we have determined in the light of revelation and also in that of experience what the full perfection of the Christian life should be, we must now examine the second part of the problem and see whether this full perfection truly supposes infused or mystical contemplation. With this end in view, after recalling what prayer in general and common prayer should be, we will consider: (1) the different meanings of the words, "contemplation," "ordinary," and "extraordinary"; (2) the description of mystical contemplation and its degrees according to the most authoritative saints; (3) what infused contemplation does not essentially require; (4) what constitutes contemplation and from what principle it proceeds. From the consideration of these points, we shall see whether contemplation is extraordinary in itself, as a miraculous favor is, or whether it belongs to the full, normal development of the life of grace on earth.

## ARTICLE I

### Prayer in General and Common Prayer

First of all, we must have a correct idea of prayer in general and recall what St. Augustine and St. Thomas teach about the prayer of petition.[1]

#### I. THE PRAYER OF PETITION

We seem at times to believe that prayer is a force, with its first principle in ourselves, by which we try to bend the will

1 See IIa IIae, q.83, a.2.

of God with persuasion. Immediately we are confronted with this difficulty, often formulated by unbelievers and in particular by deists, namely, that no one can move or bend the will of God. God is without doubt goodness which asks only to give itself, mercy ever ready to come to the help of him who suffers and implores; but He is also perfectly immutable being. The will of God is from all eternity as inflexible as it is merciful. No one can boast of having enlightened God, of having made Him change His will. "I am the Lord and I do not change." The order of the world and the course of human events are, by His providential decree, mightily and gently, as well as irrevocably, determined in advance. Must we conclude that our prayer can accomplish nothing, that it comes too late, and that, whether we pray or not, what is going to happen will happen?

We have our Lord's words in the Gospel: "Ask, and it shall be given you; seek, and you shall find; knock, and it shall be opened to you." Prayer is not a force with its first principle in ourselves; it is not an effort of the human soul trying to do violence to God to make Him change His providential dispositions. At times these human ways of expression are used metaphorically. In reality, the will of God is absolutely immutable; and precisely in this immutability lies the source of the infallible efficacy of prayer.

Basically it is very simple. True prayer, by which we ask for ourselves with humility, confidence, and perseverance, the gifts necessary for our sanctification, is infallibly efficacious, because God, who cannot contradict Himself, has decreed that it should be so, and because our Lord has promised it.[2]

It is puerile even to conceive of a God who would not have foreseen and willed from all eternity the prayers we address to Him, or of a God who would incline before our will and change His designs. Not only all that happens has been foreseen and willed, or at least permitted, in advance by a provi-

2 *Summa*, IIa IIae, q.83, a.15.

dential decree, but the way things happen, the causes that produce events, all have been determined from all eternity by Providence. In all orders, physical, intellectual, and moral, in view of certain effects, God has prepared the causes that must produce them. For material harvests, He has prepared the seed; to make parched soil fertile, He willed abundant rainfall. He raises up a great military leader to bring about a victory which will be the salvation of a people. To give the world a man of genius, He prepares a superior intellect served by a better brain, by special heredity, by a privileged intellectual environment. To regenerate the world in its most troubled periods, He decided there should be saints. And to save humanity, divine Providence prepared from all eternity the coming of Jesus Christ. In all orders, from the lowest to the highest, God disposes causes in view of certain effects which they are to produce. For spiritual as well as material harvests, He has prepared the seed, without which the harvest will not be obtained.

Prayer is precisely a cause ordained to produce this effect, the obtaining of God's gifts necessary or useful for salvation. All creatures live by the gifts of God, but only intellectual creatures take cognizance of this fact. Stones, plants, and animals receive without knowing that they do so. Man lives by the gifts of God, and he knows it. If the carnal man forgets this fact, it is because he does not live as a man. If the proud will not admit it, that is because pride is the greatest foolishness. Existence, health, strength, the light of understanding, moral energy, the success of our undertakings, all are the gift of God; but especially is this true of grace, which leads us to salutary good, makes us accomplish it, and persevere therein.

Is it surprising that divine Providence wills that man should ask for alms, since man understands that he lives only on alms? Here as elsewhere, God wills first of all the final effect, then He ordains the means and the causes which are to produce it. After deciding to give, He decides that we shall pray in order to receive; just as a father, who purposes in advance to grant a favor to his children, resolves to make them ask for it. The gift of God is the result; prayer is the cause ordained to obtain it. It has its place in the life of the soul, that it may receive the good things necessary or useful for salvation, as heat and electricity have their place in the physical order.

Jesus, who willed to convert the Samaritan woman, said to her, for the purpose of leading her to pray: "If thou didst know the gift of God . . . thou perhaps wouldst have asked of Him, and He would have given thee living water . . . springing up into life everlasting."

From all eternity God foresaw and permitted the falls of Mary Magdalen, but He had His designs on her and willed to restore life to that dead soul. He decided, however, that this life would be restored to her only on condition that she desired it. He also decided to give her a very strong and gentle actual grace that would make her pray. This is the source of the efficacy of prayer. Because Magdalen prayed, sanctifying grace was given to her; but certainly, without prayer she would have remained in her sin. It is, therefore, as necessary to pray if we are to obtain God's assistance which we need for the observance of the divine law and for perseverance in it, as it is necessary to sow seed if we are to reap grain.

Consequently we should not say: "Whether we prayed or not, whatever was going to happen, would happen." This would be as silly as to say: "Whether we sow or not, once summer has come, if we are to have wheat, we shall have it." Providence has to do not only with the result, but also with the means to be employed. It safeguards human liberty by a grace as sweet as it is strong. "Amen, amen I say to you: if you ask the Father anything in My name, He will give it you."

Prayer is not, then, a weak force with its first principle in us. The source of its efficacy is in God and the infinite merits of Jesus Christ. It descends from an eternal decree of God; it springs from redeeming love, and it reascends to the divine mercy. A jet of water cannot rise unless the water descends from an equal height. Likewise, when we pray it is not a question of persuading God, of inclining Him, of changing His providential dispositions; it is simply a question of raising our will to the level of His will so as to will with Him what He has decided to give us, the good things useful to our sanctification and salvation. Prayer, instead of tending to bring down the Most High to us, is an elevation of our soul to God. Dionysius compares the man who prays to a sailor who, in order to land, pulls a cable fastened to a rock on the shore. This rock, which rises above the water, is motionless; to the man in the boat, however, the rock appears to be advancing; although in reality, only the boat is moving. Likewise, it seems to us that the will of God bends when our prayer is heard and granted; yet it is our will alone that ascends. We begin to will in time what God has willed for us from all eternity.

Prayer is not in opposition to the divine government; rather it thus co-operates with that government. There are two of us who will, instead of one. When a sinful soul, for which we have long prayed, is converted, it is God who converts it, but we have been the associates of God in this work. From all eternity, He decided to produce this salutary effect in that soul only with our co-operation.

The Church has defined, as a point of doctrine against the Pelagians and semi-Pelagians, that we cannot form a true prayer without an actual grace. We ask only for what we desire, and it is a question here of desiring what God wishes for us in the way in which He wishes it; in other words, it is a question of making our will conform to His. To do that He must draw us, and we must allow ourselves to be attracted by Him. "No man," says our Lord, "can come to Me, unless the Father who hath sent Me, draw him," and St. Paul says: "Not that we are sufficient to think anything of ourselves, as of ourselves, but our sufficiency is from God" (II Cor. 3: 5).

A sinner is deprived of sanctifying grace and in that state is incapable of meriting; but he can pray. An actual grace suffices; it is offered to all, and only those are deprived of it who refuse it.[3] At the moment this grace is granted him, a sinner should fall on his knees. If he does not resist, he will be led from grace to grace, even to conversion and salvation. With humility, confidence, and perseverance, a Christian must throughout his life ask God for the supernatural energy which he needs to obtain heaven.

From all this we see what prayer can obtain for us. Heaven is the goal of the life of the soul. To this supreme end God subordinates whatever He is pleased to grant us, for He gives us both corporal and spiritual things only for the conquest of a blessed eternity.

Therefore prayer can obtain for us only the things that help in the attainment of our last end, eternal life. Beyond that it can do nothing. It is too lofty to obtain for us temporal success without regard or relation to our salvation. We must not expect such a result from it.[4]

There are two types of goods which advance us on our way to heaven: spiritual goods, which bring us there directly; and temporal goods, which can be indirectly useful for salvation in the measure in which they are subordinated to the first. Spiritual goods are grace, virtues, and merits. Prayer is all-powerful in obtaining for a sinner the grace of conversion, and for a just man the actual grace necessary for the accomplishment of his duties as a Christian. Prayer is supremely efficacious in obtaining for us a livelier faith, a more confident hope, a more ardent charity, and a greater fidelity to our vocation. The first petition in the Lord's prayer is that the name of God be sanctified, glorified by a radiant faith; that His king-

---

[3] Man, though in himself he does not suffice to desire and will salutary good, is sufficient in himself to fail, and to fail freely. God often lifts him up again. This, however, is not always the case. Therein lies a mystery.

[4] See IIa IIae, q.83, a.5, 6.

dom may come is the object of our hope, and that His will may be done and accomplished with love and a more fervent charity. Prayer is all-powerful in obtaining our daily bread, not only the food of the body but that of the soul, the supersubstantial bread of the Eucharist and the dispositions necessary for a good communion. It is efficacious in obtaining for us the pardon of our faults, with the interior disposition to pardon our neighbor. Likewise it is efficacious in making us triumph over temptation; "Watch and pray that you enter not into temptation," said our Lord. He has also told us that, to be delivered from evil and from the spirit of evil, we must pray; "This kind is not cast out but by prayer and fasting." [5]

Obviously prayer must be sincere. To ask for grace to overcome a passion without avoiding the occasions of sin, to ask for the grace of a happy death without trying to lead a better life, is not to formulate a true prayer, a true desire; it is scarcely indeed a vague wish. Prayer must also be humble, since it is the petition of a beggar. It must be confident, trusting in the mercy of God, never doubting His infinite goodness. It must be persevering to show that it springs from a profound desire of the heart.[6] Occasionally God seems not to hear us immediately, that He may try our confidence and the strength of our good desires, as Jesus tried the confidence of the woman of Canaan by severe words that appeared to be a refusal: "I was not sent but to the sheep that are lost of the house of Israel. . . . It is not good to take the bread of the children, and to cast it to the dogs." Under divine inspiration, the woman of Canaan answered; "Yea, Lord; for the whelps also eat of the crumbs that fall from the table of their masters. Then Jesus answering, said to her: O woman, great is thy faith: be it done to thee as thou wilt. And her daughter was cured from that hour." [7]

[5] Matt. 17: 20.
[6] *Summa*, IIa IIae, q.83, a.15 ad 2um.
[7] Matt. 15: 22, 24–28.

If we have truly prayed with perseverance and if, in spite of our supplications, God leaves us to grapple with temptation, we should recall the example of St. Paul, who also asked repeatedly to be delivered from the sting of the flesh which tormented him. And he received this reply: "My grace is sufficient for thee." With the Apostle, believing that this struggle is profitable for us, let us not cease to ask for grace, which alone can keep us from weakening. Let us thus learn our indigence, that we are really poor and that it is fitting for a poor man to ask for aid. All his life a Christian must ask for the supernatural energy necessary to work out his salvation. The human soul cannot attain heaven unless it is propelled by God.[8] Once it is launched on its way, it must fly. Prayer is like the beating of the wings of a little bird which has been thrown out of its nest and needs help.

As regards temporal blessings, prayer can obtain for us everything that in some way or other will assist us on our voyage to eternity: food, health, strength, prosperity. Prayer can obtain all, on condition that we ask first and foremost for grace to love God more: "Seek ye first the kingdom of heaven, and all these things will be added unto you." [9] Is prayer inefficacious because we have not succeeded in some undertaking? If we have prayed truly, we have not asked for this temporal favor in itself, but only in the measure in which it would be useful to our salvation. If we have not obtained it, that is because we are to be saved without it. Our prayer is not lost; we have not obtained this temporal favor which was useless to us, but we have obtained or will obtain another more precious grace.

Humble, trusting, persevering prayer, by which we ask for the things necessary for salvation, is infallibly efficacious by virtue of our Lord's promise.[10] God indeed commands us to

---

[8] See Ia, q. 23, a. 1.
[9] See IIa IIae, q. 83, a. 6.
[10] See IIa IIae, q. 83. a. 15 ad 2um.

work for our salvation. He adds: "Without Me (without My grace) you can do nothing"; "ask, and you shall receive." He promises that if we ask this grace of Him, He will give it to us. What is more, He causes this prayer to spring up in our hearts, and inclines us to ask Him for what He wills from all eternity to grant us. If such a prayer were not infallibly efficacious, salvation would be impossible. God would be commanding us to do something impossible of realization, and contradiction would exist in Him who is supreme truth and supreme goodness. A simple soul immediately understands Christ's words: "Ask, and it shall be given you; seek, and you shall find; knock, and it shall be opened to you." "And which of you, if he ask his father bread, will he give him a stone? or a fish, will he for a fish give him a serpent? . . . If you then, being evil, know how to give good gifts to your children, how much more will your Father from heaven give the good Spirit to them that ask Him?" [11] Prayer is the breath of the soul.

Prayer is a more powerful force than all physical energies taken together, more powerful than money, than learning. Prayer can accomplish what all material things and all created spirits cannot do by their own natural powers. According to Pascal: "All bodies, the firmament and its stars, the earth and its kingdom, are not equal to the least of spirits. . . . By assembling all material things one could not succeed in producing even a small thought. This is impossible and belongs to another order. . . . All material bodies together and all spirits, and all that they produce are not worth the slightest movement of charity, which belongs to an infinitely more elevated order." [12] Prayer can obtain grace for us which will make us produce this act of charity.

Prayer thus plays an infinitely greater rôle in the world than the most amazing discovery. Who would presume to compare the influence exercised by an eminent scholar like

[11] Matt. 6: 7; Luke 11: 9, 11, 13.
[12] *Pensées* (Havet ed.), art. 17, 1.

Pasteur with that exercised through prayer by a St. Paul, a St. John, a St. Benedict, a St. Dominic, or a St. Francis?

Each immortal soul is worth more than the entire physical world. It is like a universe, since by its two superior faculties, intellect and will, it dwells on all things, even the Infinite. Prayer assures two things to souls striving to attain to God: supernatural light, which directs them; and divine energy, which urges them on. Without prayer darkness reigns in souls; they grow cold and die like extinguished stars. It is essential to trust in this force which is of divine origin; to keep in mind whence it comes and whither it goes. It descends to us from eternity by a decree of infinite goodness, and it is to eternity that it again ascends.

### II. COMMON PRAYER

Prayer is an elevation of the soul to God, by which we will in time what God from all eternity wills that we should ask of Him, namely, the different means of salvation, especially progress in charity. "Seek ye first the kingdom of God and His justice, and all these things will be added unto you." But we feel the need of a more intimate prayer in which our soul, in deeper recollection, may come into contact with the Blessed Trinity dwelling in us. This we desire that we may receive more abundantly from the interior Master that light of life which alone can make us penetrate and taste the mysteries of salvation, and reform our character by supernaturalizing it, by making it conformable to Him who invites us to seek peace of soul in humility and sweetness. This intimate prayer is mental prayer. This is the prayer that prepares for infused contemplation. We will briefly consider how to attain to this acquired prayer and how to persevere in it.

Our Lord tells us in the Gospel: "And when ye pray, you shall not be as the hypocrites that love to stand and pray in the synagogues and corners of the streets, that they may be

seen by men. . . . But thou when thou shalt pray, enter into
thy chamber, and having shut the door, pray to thy Father in
secret, and thy Father who seeth in secret, will repay thee." [13]
St. Teresa says simply: "Mental prayer is nothing else, in my
opinion, but being on terms of friendship with God, frequently conversing in secret with Him who, we know, loves
us." [14] Truly simple Christian souls are acquainted with spontaneous, intimate prayer. A certain peasant, questioned by the
Curé of Ars, gave an excellent definition of it. The Curé,
noticing that he remained silent, without even moving his
lips, during long periods of adoration, asked him what he said
to our Lord during those hours of recollection. "Oh, I don't
say anything to Him," replied the peasant; "I look at Him,
and He looks at me." [15] This is that interior prayer which was
so often the prayer of the Christians of the catacombs and of
all the saints, long before modern treatises on meditation.

What is more simple than prayer? Its spontaneity is sometimes lost by the use of methods that are too complicated.
They may be useful to beginners, but they are apt to provoke
an excessive reaction in many souls. The latter, wearied by
this complexity, sometimes sink into a pious reverie without
any real profit. The truth, here as elsewhere, is above these
two extreme errors and lies in a happy medium. A method is
useful in the beginning, especially as a means of preventing
distractions. But if we are to keep it from becoming an obstacle rather than a help, it must be simple; instead of break-
ing the spontaneity and continuity of prayer, it must simply
describe the elevation of the soul toward God. It must merely
indicate the essential acts which compose this movement.

What are these acts? Evidently prayer is more than an act
of the intellect like a simple study. Speculative souls, curious
about the things of God, are not for that reason contemplative

---

[13] Matt. 6: 5 f.
[14] *Life of St. Teresa by Herself,* chap. 8.
[15] It is true that the prayer of this peasant was already contemplation.

souls or prayerful souls. In their reflections they may experience a pleasure far surpassing that of the senses; but this pleasure often comes merely from their knowledge, and not from charity. They are moved by a love of knowledge much more than by the love of God. This pleasure sometimes increases their pride and self-love. Study and speculation do not necessarily suppose the state of grace and charity, and do not always assist in developing this state. Prayer, on the contrary, must proceed from the love of God and must end in Him. The contemplation of God is desired out of love for Him, and the contemplation of His goodness and beauty increases love. Moreover, love of God in this life, as we have seen, is more perfect than the knowledge of God. Charity is more perfect than faith, because knowledge in a way draws God down to us and, as it were, reduces Him to the measure of our ideas; whereas love draws us toward God, elevates us to Him, unites us to Him. And, as long as we are deprived of the beatific vision, it is charity especially which unites us to God and constitutes the bond of perfection. Consequently this virtue must have the first place in our soul. The soul must lift itself to God on the wings of the intellect and the will aided by grace. Therefore prayer is a movement of supernatural knowledge and love.

What are the essential acts of prayer? That it may be the lifting up of the whole soul to God, prayer must be preceded by an act of humility and must proceed from the three theological virtues, which unite us to God, animate the virtue of religion, and obtain for us the illuminations and inspirations of the Holy Ghost. The soul flies, so to speak, like a bird by the effort of its wings, but the breath of the Holy Ghost sustains this effort and often carries the soul higher than it could go by its own virtues. We will consider these different acts of prayer. In the perfect they are often simultaneous and continuous; but, in describing them, we will enumerate them one after the other as they appear in beginners.

Prayer should begin with an act of humility, a fundamental virtue, for every prayer should be humble. When we begin to converse with God, we should recall what we are. Of ourselves we can do nothing and less than nothing, since our sins are a disorder inferior to nothingness itself. The basic virtue of humility removes pride, which is the chief obstacle to grace. Humility does not crush us; it leads us to adoration and reminds us that in a very fragile vessel we bear an infinitely precious treasure, sanctifying grace and the Trinity dwelling in us. We do well to think of this truth at the outset so that our prayer may not proceed from vain sentimentality, but from grace itself which is infinitely superior to our emotions. We should humbly adore the Blessed Trinity who vivifies us interiorly. Adoration is one of the first acts of the virtue of religion, which is quite naturally joined to that of humility.[16]

This act of humility should be followed by an act of faith, a very simple, wordless, deep, and prolonged act on some fundamental truth, such as: God, His perfections, His goodness; our Lord, the mysteries of His life, passion, and glory; or again our great duties, sin, our vocation, the duties of our state in life, our last end. These subjects should recur frequently. On feast days the liturgy suggests the subject. For this consideration of faith, some words of the Gospel or of the divine office suffice. St. John of the Cross taught his disciples to spend very little time on the representation of figures formed in the imagination, but to elevate themselves by discursive acts to the consideration of the mystery itself in the light of faith: for example, to the consideration of what constitutes the price of Christ's sufferings, His redeeming love which is of infinite value. It is not necessary to reason much, because the simple act of theological faith is superior to reasoning. It becomes more and more a simple gaze which ought to be accompanied by admiration and love. This faith, which is higher than all philosophical or theological speculation,

16 See IIa IIae, q.84.

makes us adhere infallibly and supernaturally to the mysteries which the elect contemplate in heaven. In this sense it is, as St. Paul says, "the substance of things to be hoped for." Its obscurity does not hinder it from being infallibly certain. It is the first light of our interior life. I believe what God has revealed, because He has revealed it. This *Credo* seems at times to become a *Video*. We see from afar the fountain of living water.

This act of faith in the divine truth which is being considered gives rise naturally to an act of hope. We desire beatitude, the peace promised by God to those who follow Jesus Christ. We see clearly, however, that by our own natural strength we shall not be able to realize this supernatural ideal. Then, turning to the infinitely helpful goodness of God, we ask His grace. This is supplication, the ordinary language of hope, the formal motive of which is the divine help, *Deus auxilians*.[17] After uttering its *Credo,* the soul is led spontaneously to say; *desidero, sitio, spero.* Having seen from afar the fountain of living water, we desire to attain it that we may drink long draughts from it: "As the hart panteth after fountains of living water, so doth my soul pant after Thee, O God." [18]

The act of hope in its turn disposes us to an act of charity; for confidence in God's help makes us reflect that He is good in Himself and not only because of His favors.[19] Then spontaneously an act of charity arises in us, at first under an affective form. If in this act our feelings offer us their inferior assistance, we should accept it. It may indeed be useful, on condition that it remains subordinated; but it is not necessary, since it disappears in aridity. We are here speaking of a calm but profound affection which is surer and richer than superficial emotions. It expresses itself somewhat in this manner: My

[17] Hope thus leads to the prayer of petition, which is an act of the virtue of religion. Cf. IIa IIae, q.83, a.3.
[18] Ps. 41: 1.
[19] Cf. Ia IIae, q.62, a.4.

God, I no longer wish to lie by telling Thee that I love Thee. Grant that I may love Thee and please Thee in all things. *Diligo*.

This affective charity should finally become effective charity. It may take this form of expression: I wish to conform my will to Thine, O good God; to break whatever renders me the slave of sin, of pride, of selfishness, of sensuality. I wish, O Lord, to participate more and more fully in the divine life Thou dost offer me, for Thou didst come that we might have life in abundance. Increase my love; Thou dost ask only to give, and I in turn wish to receive as Thou desirest me to do, in trial as well as in consolation, whether Thou dost come to me to associate me with the joyful or the sorrowful mysteries of Thy earthly life, for all lead to eternal life which will unite us forever. I resolve today to be faithful to Thee in this matter which I have so often neglected. *Volo*.

In this culminating point of prayer, the knowledge of faith and the love of hope and charity tend under the divine influence to fuse into a gaze of supernatural love. As we shall see, this gaze is nascent contemplation, an eminent source of action; it is Christian contemplation dwelling on God and our Lord, as an artist's contemplation dwells on nature, and that of a mother on the face of her child.

This loving contemplation supposes an inspiration of the Holy Ghost. His gifts, especially the gift of wisdom, which we received in baptism and which increases in us with charity, render us particularly docile to these good inspirations. Thus the Holy Ghost answers the prayer which He inspired. From time to time, He makes Himself felt by us as the soul of our soul, the life of our life; He "asketh for us with unspeakable groanings," as St. Paul says. It is He who makes us cry "Abba, Father" to our Father in heaven and, after letting us taste the beauty and riches of the mysteries of salvation, gives us a quasi-experimental knowledge of His presence and leads us to that fountain of living water which is Himself; there we may drink the light of life without the intermediary of human reasoning, even though it is always in the obscurity of faith. "Taste and see that the Lord is sweet." [20] How the Gospel fulfils our aspirations, surpasses them, and elevates them!

The knowledge of truths about the historic life of Christ which are preserved in our memory is superseded by a living, and as it were experimental, knowledge of God's action in us, of the actual influence of Christ's humanity which transmits all grace to us, and of the presence of the Blessed Trinity in our souls. [21] Prayer thus introduces us into the intimacy of love. Nothing is better able to correct our defects of character, give us a keen desire to resemble our Lord, lead us to imitate Him in everything, and arouse the highest virtues in us. Some characters will succeed in reforming themselves only by the loving contemplation of the divine Master; for we imitate those whom we love, without being conscious of doing so.

Prayer is "the intercourse of friendship by which the soul often converses alone with God, knowing that it is loved by Him." "My Beloved to me, and I to Him." The acts of humility, faith, hope, and charity, and the influx of the gifts of the Holy Ghost tend, in proportion as the soul grows, to fuse into a gaze of ardent love. Consequently methods useful at the beginning must increasingly give place to docility to the Holy Ghost, who breathes where He will.

Prayer tends to become a prolonged spiritual communion: "I look at our Lord, and He looks at me." As the fathers have said, it is truly the repose of the soul in God, or the respiration of the soul which breathes in the truth and beauty of God by faith and breathes out love. What it receives from God under the form of grace, it returns to Him as adoration. This prayer,

---

[20] Ps. 33: 9.

[21] The Word and the other two Persons of the Blessed Trinity dwell in us: "If anyone love Me, he will keep My word, and My Father will love him, and We will come to him, and will make Our abode with him." The humanity of Jesus is, as St. Thomas shows (IIIa, q.48, a.6), the physical, instrumental cause of all the graces we receive, after meriting them for us here on earth.

as we shall see farther on, is a disposition to contemplation. For the moment it will suffice to quote St. Teresa: "Those who are able thus to enclose themselves within the little heaven where dwells the Creator of both heaven and earth . . . may feel sure that they are travelling by an excellent way, and that they will certainly attain to drink of the water from the fountain, for they will journey far in a short time. They resemble a man who goes by sea,[22] and who, if the weather is favorable,[23] gets in a few days to the end of a voyage which would have taken far longer by land. These souls may be said to have already put out to sea." [24]

This method, or rather this very simple manner of making prayer, by recalling the necessity of the acts of the three theological virtues, makes it possible to unite the simplicity of prayer, as described by the ancient writers, with what is useful in the teaching of more recent masters. It is easy to make acts of faith, hope, and charity on all subjects. But if no subject attracts us, and if, on the other hand, we do not feel ourselves sufficiently united to God to avoid loss of time and to flee distractions, we will do well to follow St. Teresa's advice and meditate as slowly as possible on the Our Father. This is the greatest of prayers; composed by our Lord, it contains all possible petitions in a perfect order. We often recite it during the day, but so rapidly as not to taste all it contains. It is the true conversation of the soul. Let us say it with Christ who taught

22 This expression shows that this prayer is in our power, at least in its beginning, as the context makes evident.

23 This is the symbol of the breath of the Holy Ghost. Prayer then becomes infused, as we shall see farther on.

24 *The Way of Perfection,* chap. 28. When we speak of so-called acquired contemplation (chap. 5, art. 2), we shall quote at length from this chapter of St. Teresa in which she treats of the acquired prayer of recollection, which disposes to supernatural recollection and to quiet, which is spoken of in the fourth mansion, chaps. 1, 3.

The passage from acquired prayer to infused contemplation is well described in the little work where Bossuet treats of the prayer which he calls the prayer "of simplicity or of the simple presence of God." The first phase of this prayer is acquired; the second infused, as we shall see more clearly farther on.

it to us. The first three petitions correspond exactly, as St. Thomas says, to the three acts of faith, hope, and charity, which we have pointed out.

*Our Father who art in heaven.* Thou art also in us, for our souls are a heaven which is still in darkness.

*Hallowed be Thy name.* Glorified, that is, recognized and adored *(gloria est clara notitia cum laude)*. May Thy word be accepted by a living and unshakable faith. *Credo.*

*Thy kingdom come.* This is the object of our hope, which rests especially on Thy infinitely helpful goodness. May this reign be more and more established in me and round about me. *Sitio, spero.*

*Thy will be done on earth as it is in heaven.* May our will, like that of the saints in heaven, be comfortable to Thine. This is the greatest desire of affective and effective charity, which also asks for the daily bread of the Eucharist, and the forgiveness of sins. This charity also forgives the offenses committed by our neighbor, and it makes us ask to be kept from sin in the future. It is the elevation of the soul to God; in the morning before work, at night before sleep, and as often as possible during the day, at least by some short ejaculation.

If at times we are not table to meditate on the Our Father in this simple manner and cannot succeed in freeing ourselves from distractions, finding only aridity, it is well for us to practice affective prayer. This prayer consists simply in willing to be in that condition so as to love our Lord more than ourselves; willing to remain thus abandoned to His divine will, accepting our powerlessness and uniting ourselves to Christ in the abandonment which He experienced while on earth, in Gethsemane and on the cross, and which He still experiences in the Blessed Sacrament. This prayer, which sometimes resembles a purgatory, is not inertia; on the contrary, it is distinguished from it by the vigilance of love. It is very fruitful, since merit has its source in charity, and the end of prayer is not so much the forming of lofty considerations as the uniting of our souls to God, in Christ Jesus, in our sufferings as well as in our joys. Many intimate friends of our Lord are for many years associated in this manner with the sufferings of His heart. He makes them share in the sorrowful life which He led on earth before communicating to them His glorious life for eternity. A Christian soul is thus led to the "love of God even to the despising of self," or at least to forgetfulness of self and absorption in the glory of God and the salvation of souls.

### III. HOW TO ATTAIN TO A LIFE OF PRAYER AND PERSEVERE IN IT

We have demonstrated what common prayer, which tends to become more and more simple, should be. How can one attain to this prayer and persevere in it? First of all, we must confess that even common prayer depends chiefly on the grace of God, and consequently the soul prepares for it less by mechanical processes than by humility. God gives His grace to the humble. "Unless you be converted, and become as little children, you shall not enter into the kingdom of heaven." [25] It is the little ones that God is pleased to instruct interiorly; humble souls like the peasant of Ars. In addition to the cultivation of humility, we must prepare ourselves for a life of prayer by mortification and detachment from sensible things and from self. Evidently, if our minds are preoccupied with worldly affairs and our souls disturbed by too human an affection, by jealousy, rash judgment, and the memory of wrongs we have suffered from others, we shall not be able to converse with our Lord. If in the course of the day we have criticized our superiors, in the evening we cannot feel united to God.

It is evident that all inordinate inclinations must be mortified so that charity may take the first place in our souls and

[25] Matt. 18: 3.

rise spontaneously to God. On all occasions, in suffering or in consolation, we must form the habit of raising our hearts to God and of blessing the coming hour. Silence must reign in our souls, and our passions must be suppressed, if we are to hear the interior Master who speaks in a low voice as friend to friend. If we are habitually concerned with ourselves, how shall we taste the sweetness of the Trinity, the incarnation, the redemption, and the Eucharist?

All this work may be called a remote preparation for prayer. It is, however, far more important than the immediate preparation and the choice of a subject. The purpose of the immediate preparation is merely to stir up the fire of charity, which ought never to be extinguished in us and which must be nourished by a continual generosity. In this way very simple and fervent souls may reduce the immediate preparation to a minimum and may often during manual labor make fervent mental prayer of habitual conformity to the will of God.

It is not sufficient to attain to a life of prayer; we must persevere in it. By persevering effort the soul is sure to make great gain; without it, everything may be lost. Perseverance is not an easy task, for we must struggle against self, against spiritual laziness, and against the devil who inclines us to discouragement. Even among the far advanced, how many souls have turned back when deprived of the first consolations they received. St. Catherine of Genoa, who devoted herself to prayer from the age of thirteen and made great progress in it, abandoned the interior life after five years of sufferings. For five years she neglected the interior life. But one day she felt keenly the frightful emptiness of her soul, and the desire for prayer revived in her. God received her back instantly. After fourteen years of terrible penance, she was granted the assurance that she had fully satisfied the divine justice. "If I should turn back," she used to say, "I should wish someone to tear out my eyes, and even that would not seem sufficient punishment."

Other souls, after struggling for a long time, become discouraged, says St. Teresa, when they are within a few steps of the fountain of living water. They fall back and, since without prayer they no longer have the strength to carry the cross, they lapse into a superficial life in which others might perhaps be saved, but in which they run the risk of being lost because their powers will carry them to excesses. The measureless love of God permitted and even asked excess of them; but this same excess, if indulged outside of God, would be their ruin. For certain souls of a naturally lofty turn, mediocrity is impossible; either they give themselves wholly to God, or wholly to themselves in opposition to God. They wish to enjoy their ego and their abilities and, as a result, run the risk of setting up self instead of God as their absolute end. The angels can know only ardent charity or unpardonable mortal sin. Venial sin, according to St. Thomas, is impossible for them because "from their very nature they can have no inordinateness in respect of the means, unless at the same time they have an inordinateness in respect of the end, and this is a mortal sin." [26] Angels or devils, very holy or very wicked, for them there is no other alternative. Certain souls have something angelic about them; for them it is very dangerous not to persevere in prayer, or at least to be at prayer only bodily without any act of true love. This amounts to the abandonment of the interior life, perhaps ruin.

The saints tell us that, if we are to persevere, we must, first of all, hope in our Lord who calls all devout souls to the living waters of prayer. On this point we will consider particularly the testimony of St. Teresa.[27] In the second place, we must humbly allow ourselves to be led along the road which our Lord has chosen for us.

1) We must hope, with trust in our guide. We fail in this

[26] *Summa,* Ia IIae, q.89, a.4.
[27] Cf. chap. 5, a.2, 3. We shall see that St. Teresa understands by "drinking from the fountain of living water" infused contemplation, which is given to us by the Holy Ghost. He Himself is the fountain.

confidence when, after the first aridity, we say that prayer is not for us. We might just as well say with the Jansenists that frequent communion is not for us, but only for a few great saints. Our Lord calls all souls to this intercourse of friendship with Him. As He says, He is the good shepherd who leads His sheep to the eternal pastures that they may feed on every word of God. In the midst of these pastures is the fountain of living waters which Jesus spoke of to the Samaritan woman, who was, nevertheless, a sinner; "If thou didst know the gift of God, and who He is that saith to thee, Give Me to drink, thou perhaps wouldst have asked of Him, and He would have given thee living water. . . . He that shall drink of the water that I will give him, shall not thirst forever. But the water that I will give him, shall become in him a fountain of water springing up into life everlasting." [28] At Jerusalem on a certain festival day, Jesus stood in the Temple and cried out to all: "If any man thirst, let him come to Me, and drink. He that believeth in Me, as the Scripture saith, Out of his belly shall flow rivers of living water." [29] Later on our Lord explains that this fountain of living water is the Holy Ghost, the Comforter, whom He will send to us and who will make us penetrate and taste the intimate meaning of the gospel.

According to St. Paul, the Holy Ghost dwells in us by charity. Therefore He is in every soul in the state of grace. He dwells in the soul not to remain idle, but rather to make Himself its interior master by His seven gifts, which develop in proportion as charity grows in the soul. The growth of charity should continue until death, without any assigned limit. Our failure better to understand the holy inspirations of the interior Master is probably due to the fact that we listen to ourselves, that we are not humble enough and desirous of the reign of God in our souls.

2) The second element necessary for perseverance in prayer

[28] John 4: 10, 13 f.
[29] John 7: 37 f.

is that we allow ourselves to be led by the road that our Lord has chosen for us. The great highway is the road of humility and conformity to the divine will. All should pray as the publican did. Along this road, however, are stony spots and level stretches, some sections covered with grass, others burned by the sun, and still others shady. The good Shepherd leads His sheep as He judges best: some by the way of parables, others by that of reasoning, before bringing them to simple intuition in the obscurity of faith. He leaves some souls for a long time in difficult spots for the purpose of inuring them to hardships. Our Lord raises Marys to contemplation sooner than He does Marthas. The former find in contemplation interior sufferings unknown to the latter; but these, if they are faithful, will reach the living waters and will quench their thirst according to their desires.

We will now consider what these living waters are, because they are the symbol of contemplation.

## ARTICLE II

*Meaning of "Contemplation," "Ordinary," "Extraordinary"*

### I. SO-CALLED ACQUIRED CONTEMPLATION AND INFUSED CONTEMPLATION

Contemplation in general, such as may exist in a non-Christian philosopher, for example, in Plato or Aristotle, is a simple, intellectual view of the truth, superior to reasoning and accompanied by admiration, *simplex intuitus veritatis,* as St. Thomas says.[1] An example of this contemplation is the admiring knowledge of that supreme truth of philosophy, namely, that at the summit of all composite and changeable beings there exists absolutely simple and immutable being itself, the principle and end of all things. It has not received existence; it is of itself existence, truth, wis-

[1] *Summa,* IIa IIae, q. 180, a. 1, 6.

dom, goodness, love, just as, in the physical order, light of itself is light and has no need to be illumined; just as heat of itself is heat. Reason by its own strength, with the natural help of God, may rise to this contemplation.

The contemplation of the faithful is, on the contrary, founded on divine revelation received through faith. Although faith is an infused gift of God received at baptism, several theologians admit in the faithful a so-called "acquired" contemplation. They generally define it as a simple and loving knowledge of God and of His works which is the fruit of our personal activity aided by grace. They usually agree that this so-called "acquired" contemplation exists in a theologian at the end of his research, in the synthetic view which he reaches; or in a preacher who sees his entire sermon in one thought, and in the faithful who listen attentively to this sermon, grasp its order, admire its unity and, as a result, taste the great truth of faith which they see in its radiation.

In these cases we have a certain contemplation which is, with the help of grace, the fruit of human activity, of our reflection, or of the meditation of the author we are reading or the preacher we are listening to. Grace and the theological virtues certainly enter in. Even the gifts of the Holy Ghost exercise a latent influence. But if well ordered human activity were lacking, the soul would not reach this contemplation, which is therefore called "acquired." A poorly prepared sermon, lacking order, vigor, or unction, will produce the contrary effect and will weary most of the hearers. In an order quite superior to philosophical speculation, many of the faithful can by reading and meditation experience the deep meaning of these words of God: "I am who am . . . God is a spirit, and they that adore Him, must adore Him in spirit and in truth. . . . God is charity: and he that abideth in charity, abideth in God, and God in him."

Since the loving contemplation of God is not the fruit of human activity aided by grace, it cannot be called acquired, but rather must be called infused. For example, in a poorly arranged, lifeless sermon, that merely tires most of the listeners, the preacher may, however, quote an expression of our Lord which profoundly seizes a soul, captivates it, and absorbs it for an hour.[2] That is an example of contemplation which is not the fruit of the preacher's human activity or of personal reflection; it springs from a manifest divine inspiration. It is called infused. Why? Not only because it springs from infused virtues; this was the case also with so-called "acquired" contemplation. Nor is it called "infused" in this sense, that the very act of contemplation is infused or directly produced by God alone in us; it would then no longer be a vital, free, and meritorious act. It is called infused and also passive in this sense, that it is not in our power to produce this act at will, like an ordinary act of faith. We can only receive the divine inspiration with docility, and dispose ourselves to it by pious recollection. "This infused or passive contemplation is in us without our deliberation, though not indeed without our consent." [3]

This infused contemplation is also called supernatural because it is so by its very nature (*reduplicative ut sic*) not only as regards the substance of the act, like the act of infused faith, but as regards the mode, which in this case is the superhuman mode of the gifts of the Holy Ghost, a mode no longer latent, but manifest. This essentially infused contemplation begins with what St. Teresa calls the prayer of passive recollection,[4] and what St. John of the Cross calls the passive night of the senses; in other words, at the beginning of the mystical life, strictly so called. Whence it follows that essentially mystical contemplation is that which is manifestly passive, in the sense

---

2 We suppose that this absorption does not spring from the fact that the soul has on previous occasions often meditated on these words of our Lord. Infused contemplation, however, is not always received unexpectedly; we can dispose ourselves to receive it.

3 See what St. Thomas says about operating grace, Ia IIae, q. 111, a. 2.

4 St. Teresa, *The Interior Castle*, fourth mansion, chap. 3.

we have indicated,⁵ if it lasts and becomes frequent as in the mystical state.

All we have just said about the meaning of the words "acquired contemplation" and "infused contemplation" is rather generally accepted. But the expression "acquired contemplation" is not found in the writings of the great masters. According to them contemplation, properly so called, is infused, and they simply call it contemplation. St. John of the Cross says: "Contemplation is a science of love; it is an infused, loving knowledge of God." ⁶ St. Teresa,⁷ St. Francis de Sales,⁸ and St. Jane de Chantal hold the same opinion.

Canon Saudreau ⁹ observes that Thomas of Jesus (1564–1627), in his book *De contemplatione divina*,¹⁰ was the first Carmelite to speak of an acquired contemplation as a degree of prayer intermediate between affective meditation and infused contemplation. He adds: "The same author, in the prologue of his first work,¹¹ divided prayer into two classes: acquired prayer (meditation) and infused prayer (contemplation). This division is correct and entirely conformable to the doctrine of St. Teresa. This prologue, found in the editions of 1610, 1613, 1616, and 1623, was suppressed in the later editions of 1665 and 1725, undoubtedly because the doctrine exposed therein does not conform to that which recognizes a non-mystical contemplation."

At the beginning of the seventeenth century, glosses were introduced into the works of St. John of the Cross to defend

---

⁵ Dom Vital Lehodey, *Les voies de l'oraison mentale*, 5th ed., p. 205.
⁶ *The Dark Night of the Soul*, Bk. II, chap. 18. It is infused contemplation which is discussed at the beginning of *The Dark Night of the Soul*, Bk. I, chap. 1, and also in *The Ascent of Mount Carmel*, Bk. II, chap. 13.
⁷ *The Interior Castle*, fifth mansion, chap. 1; seventh mansion, chap. 4. *The Way of Perfection*, chaps. 17, 19, 20, 21, 25, 27, 31. See *infra* in this chapter, art. 3.
⁸ *Traité de l'amour de Dieu*, Bk. VI, chap. 7.
⁹ *État mystique*, 2d ed., pp. 109, 357.
¹⁰ Published in 1620.
¹¹ *Grados de oración*, 1609.

them against unjust charges of illuminism. These glosses often attenuated the meaning of the terms.[12] Indeed certain authors maintained that the saint had treated only of acquired contemplation, which is inferior to the infused contemplation spoken of by St. Teresa. The meaning of these terms was not clearly fixed at this time.[13] Some even claimed that acquired contemplation is the summit or the term of the normal development of the interior life, and that infused contemplation is absolutely extraordinary, like graces *gratis datae*, and that consequently it could not be desired without presumption. This was in particular the teaching of Anthony of the Annunciation, C.D.; [14] but on this point he was not followed by the Carmelite theologians, as may be clearly seen from what another well-known Discalced Carmelite, Joseph of the Holy Ghost,[15] says of him.

These difficulties and divergences explain the reservations of certain authors. In their eagerness to preserve St. Teresa's teaching, they are reluctant to admit a degree of prayer which she probably did not mention. And in fact we would be creating a degree of prayer not referred to by St. Teresa and would be opposing her explicit teaching, if by acquired contemplation we meant a prayer distinct from simplified affective prayer, a prayer in which the intelligence would be completely absorbed by its object, and which the soul would attain by the suppression of all rational activity. As a matter of fact, the saint repeatedly opposes the total suppression of rea-

[12] Father Andrew of the Incarnation, C.D., undertook in 1574 to restore the true text of the saint's writings, but he did not publish his work. Only recently Father Girard, C.D., gave us a critical edition which contains 55 corrections in Book I, 207 in Book II, and 71 in Book III. Several problems of textual criticism remain to be solved. Cf. *La vie spirituelle*, March, 1923, p. 154.

[13] At this time the expression infused or supernatural contemplation was not yet clearly understood by all. By these terms some apparently indicated contemplation united to certain graces *gratis datae* which St. Teresa received abundantly and which she often mentioned.

[14] *Disceptatio mystica*, tr. 2, q.4, a.8, no. 34.

[15] *Cursus theol. scol.-mysticae* (1721), II, 224, 236.

soning and thought as long as one has not received infused contemplation.[16]

Such is not, however, the Carmelite theologians' conception of acquired contemplation. Their detailed descriptions of it show that the prayer they have in mind corresponds to what St. Teresa in *The Way of Perfection* (chap. 28) calls "the (acquired) prayer of recollection," a prayer in which intellectual activity is simplified, but not suppressed. These theologians call this prayer contemplation because the act of simple intellectual intuition is frequent and predominant in it, and meditation, on the other hand, is reduced. This conception removes the substance of the difficulty, and the question becomes one of terminology.

As a rule the Carmelite theologians who admit the existence of acquired contemplation have been right in refusing to see in it the normal term of spiritual progress on this earth. According to them, in generous souls truly faithful to the Holy Ghost, it is a proximate disposition to receive infused contemplation normally.[17] Different opinions have been brought forward as to the time when infused contemplation begins; certain authors link quiet, and even spiritual intoxication, with acquired contemplation. But anyone who reads carefully the third chapter of the fourth mansion,[18] will see that contemplation begins with the prayer of supernatural recollection, which we cannot obtain for ourselves by our own activity aided by grace and which almost always precedes the supernatural prayer of quiet. This supernatural recollection is quite different from the acquired prayer of recollection, which is the fruit of our activity, and which St. Teresa

[16] *Life,* chap. 12, p. 81; *The Interior Castle,* fourth mansion, chap. 3, pp. 108 f.

[17] This is the teaching of Thomas of Jesus, Philip of the Holy Ghost, Anthony of the Holy Ghost, Dominic of Jesus, and Joseph of the Holy Ghost. They agreed on this point with the Dominicans, John of St. Thomas (cf. his *Catechism*) and Vallgornera.

[18] St. Teresa, *The Interior Castle.*

speaks of.[19] It is altogether untenable to say that acquired contemplation is that in which we can place ourselves by our own industry, and to include in it supernatural recollection, quiet, spiritual intoxication, and mystical sleep. And if the expression "acquired contemplation" is applied to what St. Teresa, when treating of acquired prayer, calls "the prayer of recollection," [20] her doctrine is kept without preserving her terms; because in her writings, as we shall see later on, the word "contemplation" designates infused contemplation.

It would be difficult to improve on St. Teresa's description of the essential difference separating the last acquired prayer from the first infused prayer, and the passage from one to the other. Speaking of "the (acquired) prayer of recollection," which has often since been called "affective prayer," she says: "This kind of prayer has many advantages. It is called 'recollection,' because by its means the soul collects together all the faculties and enters within itself to be with God.[21] The divine Master thus comes more speedily than He otherwise would to teach it and to grant it the prayer of quiet. . . . Those who are able thus to enclose themselves within the little heaven of their souls where dwells the Creator of both heaven and earth, and who can accustom themselves not to look at anything nor to remain in any place which would preoccupy their exterior senses, may feel sure that they are travelling by an excellent way and that they will certainly attain to drink of the water from the fountain,[22] for they will journey far in a

19 *The Way of Perfection*, chap. 28.

20 *Ibid.*

21 The words "by its means the soul collects together all the faculties and enters within itself," denote manifestly an acquired prayer. Everyone agrees on this point.

22 St. Teresa does not mean that, without going beyond this acquired prayer of recollection, a person will slake his thirst at the fountain of living water, which she always proposes to her daughters as the goal of their course. For she has declared clearly in *The Way of Perfection* (chap. 19): "I do not call prayer made by thinking over a subject, 'living water.' " From what is said in *The Way of Perfection* (chap. 19), evidently the living water is the image of contemplation, which is given to us by the Holy Ghost.

short time. They resemble a man who goes by sea and who, if the weather is favorable,[23] gets in a few days to the end of a voyage which would have taken far longer by land.[24] These souls may be said to have already put out to sea, and though they have not quite lost sight of *terra firma*, still they do their best to get away from it by collecting their faculties." [25]

In the following chapter St. Teresa states clearly the nature of this last acquired prayer and shows in it a disposition to receive infused contemplation. She says: "I advise whoever wishes to acquire this habit (which, as I said, we have the power to gain) not to grow tired of persevering in trying gradually to obtain the mastery over herself. . . . I know that, with His help, if you practise it for a year, or perhaps for only six months, you will gain it. Think what a short time that is for so great an advantage as laying this firm foundation, so that if our Lord wishes to raise you to a high degree of prayer, He will find you prepared for it, since you keep close to Him. May His Majesty never allow us to withdraw from His presence. Amen." Speaking of this acquired prayer of recollection, she says: "You must understand that this is not a supernatural state, but something which, with the grace of God, we can desire and obtain for ourselves.[26] This 'grace' is always implied whenever I say, in this book, that we are able to do anything, for without it we can do nothing—nothing—nor could we, by any strength of our own, think a single good thought. This is not what is called silence of the powers; it is a recollection within the soul itself." [27]

On the contrary, the supernatural recollection described in *The Interior Castle*,[28] is not in our power with the help of God, and does not depend on our will. St. Teresa says it is a

---

[23] This is the symbol of the Holy Ghost, who breathes where He will.
[24] Symbol of prayer which remains discursive.
[25] *The Way of Perfection*, chap. 28.
[26] Father Bañez noted on the original: "By supernatural she means that which is not left to our choice with the ordinary grace of God."
[27] *The Way of Perfection*, chap. 29.
[28] Fourth mansion, chap. 3.

prayer which almost always precedes the supernatural prayer of quiet: "This is a recollection which also seems supernatural to me. It neither consists in placing oneself in a dark corner nor in closing one's eyes; it in no way depends on exterior things. And yet, without wishing to do so, one closes one's eyes and desires solitude. Then the palace of prayer of which I have just spoken is built, so it seems to me, but without the labor of human art. . . . The King, who holds His court within it, seeing their good will, out of His great mercy is kind enough to recall them to Him (the senses and the powers). Like a good Shepherd, He makes them hear His voice, and He plays so sweetly on His pipe, that they scarcely hear it. He invites them to desist from their wanderings and return to their former dwelling. This piping of the Shepherd has such power over them, that forsaking the exterior things which captivated them, they re-enter the castle. I think I never put this matter so clearly before.

"When God bestows this grace, it helps greatly to seek God in oneself. . . . But do not fancy that this recollection can be obtained by the work of the understanding, by forcing yourself to think of God dwelling within you, or by that of the imagination by picturing Him as present in your soul. This is a good practice and a very excellent kind of meditation because it is founded on the indisputable truth that God dwells within us. It is not, however, the prayer of recollection, for by the divine assistance everyone can practice it. What I mean is quite a different thing. Sometimes even before they have begun to think of God, the powers of the soul find themselves within the castle. . . . Here this act does not depend on our will; it takes place only when God sees fit to give us this grace. In my opinion His Majesty only bestows this favor on those who have renounced the world. . . . He thus specially calls them to devote themselves to spiritual things. Moreover, I am convinced that if they allow Him power to act freely, He will bestow still greater graces on those whom

He thus evidently calls to a higher life." The saint adds that if God has not yet granted this grace, she cannot well understand "how we are to stop thinking, without doing ourselves more harm than good." [29]

Supernatural recollection is manifestly a mystical prayer, the beginning of infused contemplation. It would be difficult to show more definitely how it differs from the acquired prayer of recollection, often called simplified affective prayer. St. Teresa also clearly indicates how the transition is made from one to the other. [30]

This transition is also described by Bossuet, but he does not show so plainly the distinction between the last acquired prayer and the first infused prayer. [31]

[29] *Life*, chap. 12. The saint expresses the same opinion in this earlier work.

[30] *La vie spirituelle*, October, 1922, contains an excellent article entitled "La doctrine de sainte Thérèse; les oraisons communes," by a Carmelite nun. But in the *Études Carmélitaines* (1920–22), the author of several articles on acquired contemplation gives this name to the prayers of supernatural recollection, quiet, mystical sleep, and spiritual intoxication. Without intending to do so, he strays from the thought of St. Teresa and forgets that she expressly declared that these supernatural prayers are not within our power; they cannot, therefore, be called acquired. The saint's text is very clear on this point. If these prayers are called acquired because they are often preceded by a preparation which disposes us to receive them, then it would be necessary to admit an acquired rapture, for this grace is often given "at the end of a long mental prayer" (*Life of St. Teresa*, chap. 18). To avoid all confusion on this point, it will suffice to note the difference established by St. Teresa between supernatural recollection (fourth mansion, chap. 3) and the acquired prayer of recollection (*The Way of Perfection*, chap. 28).

[31] The prayer of simplicity, described by Bossuet in his famous work on the subject, seems to be acquired in its first phase and infused in its second; it is clearly the transition from one to the other. "The soul, leaving off reasoning, makes use of a sweet contemplation which holds it peaceful, attentive, and susceptible to the divine operations and impressions which the Holy Ghost communicates to it. (It is here with this communication that the prayer becomes infused.) It does little and receives much; its work is sweet and nevertheless more fruitful. As it more nearly approaches the source of all light, grace, and virtue, its capacity is greatly increased. . . . God becomes the sole Master of its interior, and He operates therein more particularly than is usual; the less the creature works, the more powerfully God operates. Since the operation of God is a repose, the soul becomes in a certain way like to Him in this prayer, and also receives marvelous effects from it . . . the divine influences which enrich it with every virtue. . . . This same light of faith, which keeps us attentive to God, will cause us to discover our slightest imperfections and to conceive a great

If the phrase "acquired contemplation" is applied to the last of the acquired prayers, called by St. Teresa "the prayer of recollection," [32] the saint's doctrine is kept, but not her terms; for, like all great mystics, by the word "contemplation" she means infused contemplation. We can easily become convinced of this by reading the sections of her works where she begins to use this word.[33] Evidently also St. John of the Cross is speaking of infused contemplation in *The Dark Night of the Soul* [34] when he describes God's action and our passivity. The contemplation he describes in his earlier work, *The Ascent of Mount Carmel*, is not specifically different. In this study he sets forth the part we can take in it and shows that, though we cannot procure infused contemplation by our efforts, we can place obstacles in its way, or, on the contrary, dispose ourselves for it and favor its exercise. The Discalced Carmelite, Nicholas of Jesus Mary,[35] was quite right in his opinion that, beginning with Part I, Bk. II, chapter 13, of *The Ascent of Mount Carmel*, infused contemplation is clearly meant.[36] St. Francis de Sales,[37] the Carmelites, John of Jesus Mary, C.D.,[38] and Michael de la Fuente [39] also place

---

sorrow and regret for them." *Manière courte et facile pour faire l'oraison en foi et de simple présence de Dieu.*

[32] *The Way of Perfection*, chap. 28.

[33] *The Way of Perfection*, chaps. 18–21, 25, 27, 33. *The Interior Castle*, fourth and fifth mansions. These texts will be quoted later in the present chapter (art. 2).

[34] Bk. II, chap. 18: "Contemplation is a science of love; it is an infused loving knowledge of God." Cf. Bk. I, chap. 1.

[35] *Elucidatio phrasium mysticarum operum Joannis a Cruce*, Part II, chap. 4.

[36] *The Ascent of Mount Carmel*, Bk. II, chap. 15: "In this state God communicates himself to the soul remaining passive, as the light to one who keeps his eyes open and does nothing to receive it. For the soul which thus receives supernaturally infused light understands all while remaining passive."

[37] *Treatise on the Love of God*, Bk. VI, chap. 7. Immediately after having discussed meditation, without speaking of acquired contemplation, St. Francis de Sales describes the different degrees of infused contemplation, as St. Teresa does, beginning with supernatural recollection which is not in our power. And he considers this transition normal: "Contemplation is the term to which all these means are directed" (Bk. VI, chap. 6).

[38] *Theologia mystica*, chap. 3.

[39] *Las tres vidas*, Introduction, and III, 4.

infused contemplation immediately after meditation, without mentioning acquired contemplation as a special degree of prayer.

Spiritual writers of the Middle Ages expressed the same teaching. We find in particular that St. Bonaventure,[40] Tauler, and Louis de Blois [41] mean infused contemplation by the words *contemplatio divina,* or quite simply *contemplatio.* Moreover, authors on all sides who are anxious to return to traditional terminology think that contemplation, properly so called, is infused.[42]

If by the expression "acquired contemplation" something other than simplified affective prayer, called by St. Teresa the "(acquired) prayer of recollection," [43] is meant, and if the supernatural prayers that are beyond our power (which she describes in the fourth and fifth mansions) are classed in this group, then violence is offered to her words and opposition to the authorities we have just quoted. Moreover, numerous difficulties, the chief of which we shall point out, would be encountered.

1) It is explicable that there may be a certain acquired contemplation at the end of a captivating study or reading when the soul is suspended in admiration of the divine truths which it discovers or which are proposed to it. Thus the philosopher and the theologian have it as the fruit of their study. It may also exist in a simple Christian while he is listening to a good sermon, or at the end of meditation. During the psalmody or during mass and the liturgical chant it may exist in souls that are accustomed to meditation on divine things but that have not yet received the grace of infused contemplation. The variety of the divine office favors a certain activity of the superior and inferior faculties, inclining us to taste the word of God. But in the prayer of the simple

40 *La théol. myst. de S. Bonaventure,* by Lompré, O.F.M., 1921.
41 *Institutio spiritualis,* chap. 12.
42 Saudreau, *État mystique* (2d ed.), pp. 103, 357.
43 *The Way of Perfection,* chap. 28.

presence of God, where the object known is almost always the same, if the soul is really captivated in its superior faculties, this state is no longer the fruit of human activity, for one is not captivated at will. It is the result of a special grace of light and attraction which is the germ of infused contemplation.

2) It may be said that the soul remains captivated by the intensity of its love, without anything new in the consideration of the object attracting it. But this intense love normally supposes a lively and penetrating knowledge of the goodness of God and is a proximate and immediate disposition to receive the grace of infused contemplation. This consideration leads Father Arintero to think that so-called acquired contemplation is rare in prayer, or at least that it lasts but a short time in generous souls; for when the soul reaches this stage, God, finding it disposed to receive the action of the Holy Ghost, gives it a beginning of infused contemplation.[44]

3) Acquired contemplation excludes distractions, or ceases when they begin. This is what happens to a philosopher or theologian. As the great mystical writers commonly teach, initial contemplation is often accompanied by distractions of the imagination, yet it lasts in spite of these ramblings. St. Teresa explains this at length when she speaks of quiet.[45] This initial contemplation is not, therefore, the fruit of the activity of our intellect directing the imagination, but the effect of a special inspiration of the Holy Ghost fixing our mind in spite of the movement of the inferior faculties.

4) Those who admit acquired contemplation as a special state of prayer between simplified affective prayer and infused contemplation say there is in acquired contemplation an influence of the gifts of the Holy Ghost, latent as yet, but more marked than in discursive meditation. It seems difficult to distinguish this influence from that which produces initial infused contemplation, or incompletely passive prayer, called by

44 *Cuestiones místicas* (2d ed.), pp. 291-311.
45 *The Interior Castle*, fourth mansion.

St. Teresa [46] supernatural recollection and quiet. Since the latter is not in our power, it cannot be called acquired.

5) Finally, St. Teresa observes with great insistence in the same passage, when speaking of supernatural recollection, which is the beginning of infused contemplation, that as long as anyone has not received this gift, he must "be careful not to check the movement of the mind . . . and to remain there like a dolt." [47] If she admitted acquired contemplation as an intermediate state of prayer between simplified affective meditation [48] and initial infused contemplation, she would grant that the soul can "stop the deliberation of the mind" before receiving "supernatural" or passive "recollection." If anyone were to do this, in St. Teresa's opinion he would be guilty of thrusting himself into the mystical ways, as do the quietists, who in reality remain there "like dolts."

To acquired contemplation, which the quietists continually recommended to everybody, they applied what the saints say about infused contemplation. This mistake was one of their principal errors. They presumptuously thrust themselves into the mystical or passive ways and they "remained there like dolts," to use St. Teresa's expression.[49] In the twenty-third proposition of Molinos, which has been condemned, it is evident that he applied the term *contemplatio acquisita* to that which he continually recommended and which, according to his teaching, precedes infused contemplation, which he considered a very special favor. At any rate, he simulated the passive state before the hour willed by God.

As Father Dudon, S.J., has justly observed,[50] Molinos be-

---

[46] *The Interior Castle*, fourth mansion.

[47] *Idem.*, fourth mansion, chap. 3.

[48] The saint called this the (acquired) prayer of recollection.

[49] Cf. Denzinger, no. 1243, 23d proposition of Molinos.

[50] *Le quiétisme espagnol, Michel de Molinos*, 1921, p. 260: "There is no contemplation worthy of this name other than passive contemplation . . . and God in His common providence favors with it those who, by the heroic generosity of their virtue, show that they are worthy to be treated as privileged friends." "Certain doctors of the twentieth century teach, as Molinos did, a

lieved that St. John of the Cross, in *The Ascent of Mount Carmel,* spoke only of acquired contemplation. From this contemplation, wrongly termed acquired, he took the rule of passivity and made from it an acquired passivity also. By applying this passivity to a prayer which in reality was ascetical, he introduced it into all of asceticism, which thereafter was, so to speak, suppressed.

In consideration of all these reasons, we do not believe that so-called acquired contemplation is a special state of prayer, distinct from simplified affective prayer, called by St. Teresa "the (acquired) prayer of recollection." [51] What the great mystics understand by "contemplation" is undoubtedly infused contemplation.

## II. THE ORDINARY AND THE EXTRAORDINARY IN THE SUPERNATURAL LIFE

In order to learn whether infused or characteristically mystical contemplation is extraordinary or whether it is ordinarily granted to the perfect, we must clearly define these terms.[52]

In the supernatural life whatever is outside the normal way of sanctity and not at all necessary to attain it, is, strictly speaking, essentially, or by its nature, extraordinary.[53] For example, graces *gratis datae,* such as the gift of prophecy, of tongues, of miracles, the gift of expressing the loftiest mysteries of religion (*sermo sapientiae*),[54] are in no way necessary

---

contemplation intermediate between meditation and passive contemplation. . . . One can and must prove this fact without instituting against the writers in question the slightest prosecution of tendency" (p. 265).

[51] *The Way of Perfection,* chap. 28.

[52] It would be suitable to define ordinary first, if the present difficulties did not bear exactly on this word.

[53] This is true at least of the holiness generally required for entrance into heaven immediately after death; for no one goes to purgatory except through his own fault, by reason of negligences which could have been avoided.

[54] This is the meaning which St. Thomas gives to the grace *gratis data* called *sermo sapientiae,* the highest degree of the gift of wisdom. This degree not only makes one contemplate the loftiest mysteries, but renders the recipient of it

for personal holiness. They are granted primarily for the good of others, although they may secondarily help in the sanctification of him who receives them, if he uses them with charity. The beatific vision, received in a transitory manner before death, as St. Paul seems to have received it (according to the opinion of St. Augustine and St. Thomas), is with even greater reason essentially extraordinary. A miraculous conversion, which without any previous preparation instantly purifies the soul and introduces it immediately into the mystical life, such as the conversion of St. Paul, is also essentially extraordinary. Likewise the grace of the transforming union or of the spiritual marriage granted from childhood, that is, at the age of six or seven, to certain saints, is manifestly extraordinary. Less elevated mystical graces bestowed on souls still very imperfect, before they have the dispositions ordinarily required,[55] are extraordinary in a lesser degree.

On the contrary, in the supernatural life whatever belongs to the normal way of sanctity and in the majority of cases is absolutely or morally necessary to attain it, is essentially ordinary.[56] In other words, whatever in the supernatural life is accomplished in accordance with even the superior laws of its full development, is ordinary in itself, though these laws are infinitely more elevated than those of our nature. This is why the beatific vision after death, although entirely supernatural, is not an extraordinary gift; it is the normal crowning of the life of grace, such as God has gratuitously willed it for us all. But we are not to conclude that the majority of men will reach this very high end. "Many are called, but few are

---

capable of manifesting them to others and of directing his neighbor. Cf. IIa IIae, q.45, a.5.

[55] Among extraordinary graces we may place interior words and visions, even if they are directly ordered to the sanctification of the soul that receives them. They are not then graces *gratis datae*, but concomitant phenomena of the mystical life; accessory and passing phenomena which in the majority of cases are not necessary to reach sanctity.

[56] This definition is given by Father Arintero in his *Cuestiones místicas,* 2d ed., p. 45.

chosen." The elect in heaven will evidently be an élite, as the name indicates, but an élite chosen from men of all classes, to which we should all eagerly desire to belong.[57] Likewise here on earth, the summit in the normal development of the life of grace, no matter how elevated, should not be called essentially extraordinary (per se), although it may be rare or extraordinary in fact, like the perfect generosity which it supposes. This summit is called sanctity, even lofty sanctity, which implies heroic virtues. Before reaching it, we can have a certain perfection, but it is not yet the full perfection to which the life of grace is essentially ordained. Just as a distinction is made between beginners, proficients, and the perfect, so among the latter a distinction [58] must be drawn between those who have just entered upon the unitive way, those who are more advanced in it, and finally those who have reached the plenitude of perfection, lofty sanctity, which alone deserves to be called the culminating point in the development of the life of grace.

It follows, then, that whatever in the majority of cases is either absolutely or morally necessary to attain this summit is not essentially extraordinary. On the contrary, these things belong to and make up the plenitude of the normal order willed by God. In studying this point, we must take care not to confound what is eminently useful for reaching sanctity in the majority of cases with what is observed in the majority of pious souls, with what is common among them; for many of them are still far from the goal. Consequently, without admitting that the mystical prayers are essentially extraordinary, we can

[57] St. Thomas observes on this subject (Ia, q.23, a.7 ad 3um): "Since eternal happiness, consisting in the vision of God, exceeds the common state of nature, and especially in so far as it is deprived of grace through the corruption of original sin, the fewer will be saved. In this, however, appears the mercy of God that He has chosen some for salvation, from which very many in accordance with the common cause and tendency of nature fall short."

[58] This is particularly the teaching of St. John of the Cross, as Joseph of the Holy Ghost observes several times in his great *Cursus theologiae mysticoscolasticae.* Cf. *supra,* chap. 4, art. 4.

distinguish them from the common forms of prayer, because the former suppose in fact an eminent or superior grace.[59]

The passive purifications of the senses and of the spirit (a mystical state) and infused contemplation, even in its highest degree, which is realized in the transforming union, are, as St. John of the Cross teaches,[60] generally necessary to the perfect purification and sanctification of the soul. Therefore they should not be called essentially extraordinary, although in fact they may be quite rare because of the common mediocrity of souls. These passive purifications seem extraordinary to us because they are so painful and take our nature by surprise; they are an anticipated purgatory. Very generous souls ought normally to suffer their purgatory on earth while meriting, rather than after death without meriting. If we go to purgatory after death, it will be our own fault, it will be because we have neglected graces that were granted us or offered us during life. Purgatory after death, frequent though it may be, is not according to the order arranged by God for the full development of the supernatural life, since immediately after death it is radical to the order established by Him that the soul should possess God by the beatific vision. Hence the precise reason why the soul suffers so greatly in purgatory is because it does not see God. We will consider, by a study of the writings of the saints, what in their opinion is the normal way to holiness here on earth.

## ARTICLE III

### Description of Infused Contemplation and its Degrees According to St. Teresa

We might have borrowed the description of mystical contemplation and its degrees from authors other than St.

---

[59] Cf. Dom Vital Lehodey, *Les voies de l'oraison mentale*. Cf. also the *Treatise on the Love of God* by Father Surin, S.J.

[60] *The Dark Night of the Soul*, Bk. I, chap. 3; Bk. II, chap. 1.

Teresa.[1] We have chosen St. Teresa because she clarifies several points, because her description has become classical, and also because those who consider infused or mystical contemplation an essentially extraordinary favor declare that they base their doctrine on her teaching.

When we read *The Life of St. Teresa*, written by herself, or her *Interior Castle*, we seem at first to come into contact with an inaccessible spiritual world, quite above what every interior soul may legitimately desire. True, she often deals with extraordinary phenomena: visions, which make us anticipate even here on earth the life of heaven, and revelations or interior words, which the majority of devout souls have never heard. These extraordinary phenomena, which strike us at the first reading, may, if we give our attention entirely to them, hide from us instead of manifesting to us what is most profound and elevated in her life; in other words, the full development in her of the Christian virtues that we ought all to have, but that in many souls remain mean, colorless, and without vigor.

But when St. Teresa's work is read in an effort to see in it the perfect development of that spiritual organism which exists in every just soul, we cannot fail to recognize that she clearly shows how the grace of the virtues and the gifts received at baptism ought to develop when obstacles have been removed. When read with this intention, the more or less extraordinary exterior manifestations of the supernatural life fade into the background.

We do not sufficiently grasp the value of the treasure that every true Christian bears in a fragile vase. Our human eyes see only the vase. We forget that sanctifying grace, which is in us, is the beginning of eternal life, *semen gloriae, inchoatio vitae aeternae.*[2] We forget practically that it is a real and formal participation in the intimate life of God, and that some

---

[1] For example, Dionysius, Richard of St. Victor, St. Bonaventure, Tauler, Ruysbroeck, Louis de Blois, St. John of the Cross, and St. Francis de Sales.

[2] St. Thomas, IIa IIae, q.24, a.3 ad 2um.

day it absolutely must either die forever in us or flower into glory by making us see God as He sees Himself, and love God as He loves Himself. Such is our destiny; for each of us only one inevitable alternative exists—eternal life or eternal death. Therein lies our wealth and our nobility. By grace we are of God, born of God,[3] and even here on earth our supernatural life is basically the same as that of heaven, just as the vegetable life hidden in the acorn is the same as that of the vigorous oak that springs from it; as the intellectual life slumbering in a child is the same as that of an adult who has reached the full development of reason.

Sanctifying grace deifies our souls. To elevate our faculties, it brings forth in them the supernatural virtues, especially the theological virtues, faith, hope, and charity, the last of which must endure forever. This entirely supernatural life is incomparably superior to a miracle perceived by the senses, which is only a sign.[4] It is also superior to the natural life of created and creatable angels, since it is a participation in the very life of God.[5] With this supernatural treasure which divinizes all our energies, we receive the Author of grace, the Holy Ghost who was sent to the Apostles on Pentecost, and who was given to us by confirmation with the seven gifts, which dispose us to receive His divine inspirations. Christ addressed us all when He said: "The Holy Ghost, whom the Father will send in My name, He will teach you all things, and bring all things to your mind, whatsoever I shall have

[3] John 1: 13.

[4] A miracle (for example, life restored to a dead body) is natural in its essence and supernatural only in the mode of its production. Hence it is very inferior to grace, which is essentially supernatural. The same must be said of the prophetic announcement of a future and free occurrence in the natural order. This is what theologians mean when they say that the life of grace is essentially supernatural, *quoad substantiam,* while miracles and prophecies are supernatural only as to the mode of their production, *quoad modum,* or preternatural.

[5] The angels themselves must have received the life of grace to be able to merit the beatific vision, which infinitely surpasses the powers and claims of their nature. Cf. St. Thomas, Ia, q.62, a.2.

said to you . . . He will teach you all truth." [6] "His unction," says St. John, "teacheth you of all things." [7]

This supernatural life remains anemic and weak and is without radiance in many Christians because they are too absorbed by worldly things. Instead of living with God, their divine and interior Guest, their Father and Friend, who is closer to them than they are to themselves, they scarcely ever raise their minds and hearts to Him. In the souls of the saints, on the contrary, this supernatural life appears in all its vigor, and it is this life especially which we should consider in them more than the extraordinary, miraculous, and inimitable gifts by which their sanctity is outwardly manifested.

We will therefore consider union with God in the souls of the saints, which is the basis of their life; in what this union consists; and what are its degrees. To do this, we will follow St. Teresa step by step, using her own words; for in our opinion the best commentary consists in bringing together her various writings on one subject, and in allowing these texts to throw light on one another.

I. THE MYSTICAL STATE IN GENERAL: PREPARATION;
GENERAL CALL AND INDIVIDUAL CALL; NATURE
OF THE MYSTICAL STATE

1) St. Teresa shows that at first the soul, which seeks to unite itself to God present in it, must ordinarily raise itself above sensible things by its own efforts aided by grace, by making frequently acts of humility, faith, hope, and charity, which are suggested to it by the Our Father.[8] To penetrate revealed truths, it meditates on them, making use of a book if necessary;

---

[6] John 14: 26; 16: 13.
[7] See I John 2: 27.
[8] *The Way of Perfection,* chaps. 21–27; *The Interior Castle,* second and third mansions.

it brings them together and from them draws practical consequences which lead it to turn more and more fully toward
God. This is the human work of the understanding which
rather rapidly becomes simplified, like reading in the case
of a child who no longer needs to spell. Meditation thus becomes a very simple, affective prayer, an active recollection
which is a preparation or disposition to receive the grace of
contemplation.[9] The soul has so far succeeded in drinking only
"the water of sensible devotion which . . . has run its course
over the earth and always contains a certain amount of
mud." [10] The divine truth it attains is still mingled with
human considerations.

2) There is, however, a fountain of living water of which
our Lord spoke to the Samaritan woman: great indeed are
"the benefits of drinking of this fountain of living water." [11]
This is the figure of contemplation, which is given to us by
the Holy Ghost. Whatever the obstacles to be found on the
road leading to this source, we must "be courageous and not
grow weary. . . . Remember, our Lord invited 'Any man.' [12]
He is truth itself; His word cannot be doubted. If all had not
been included He would not have addressed everybody, nor
would He have said: 'I will give you to drink.' He might have

[9] *The Way of Perfection*, chap. 28. This important text we here quote in
part, as follows: "This kind of prayer has many advantages. It is called 'recollection' because by its means the soul collects together all the faculties, and
enters within itself to be with God. The divine Master thus comes more speedily than He otherwise would to teach it and to grant it the prayer of quiet. . . .
Those who are able thus to enclose themselves within the little heaven where
dwells the Creator of both heaven and earth . . . may feel sure that they
are travelling by an excellent way and that they will certainly attain to
drink of the water from the fountain. . . . These souls may be said to have
already put out to sea." In chapter 29, St. Teresa clearly points out the nature of this active recollection: "You must understand that this is not a
supernatural state, but something which, with the grace of God, we can
desire and obtain for ourselves." Father Bañez noted on the original: "By
*supernatural* she means what is not left to our choice with the ordinary grace
of God."
[10] *Ibid.*, chap. 29.
[11] *Ibid.*, chap. 19.
[12] Matt. 11: 28: "Come to Me all you . . ."

said: 'Let all men come, for they will lose nothing by it, and I will give to drink to those I think fit for it.' But as He said, unconditionally: 'If any man thirst, let him come to Me,' I feel sure that, unless they stop halfway, none will fail to drink of this living water. May our Lord, who has promised to grant it us, give us grace to seek it as we ought, for His own sake." [13] This is the general and distant call; as yet it is not the individual and proximate call.[14] In other words, if we are humble, generous, and faithful in the practice of the virtues and of common prayer, a time will come when the Holy Ghost, dwelling in us to enlighten and sanctify us, will take over more fully the direction of our life and ask us to be entirely docile to His divine inspirations. Then will begin for us a more intimate union with God, called by St. Teresa supernatural prayer [15] and quite generally today the "mystical state."

3) What essentially characterizes this mystical life is an infused and loving knowledge of God; in other words, it is an infused light and an infused love coming to us from the Holy Ghost and from His gifts in order to make us grow in

---

[13] *The Way of Perfection*, chap. 19.

[14] On this general and distant call of all interior souls to the living waters of infused contemplation, see also *The Way of Perfection*, chap. 20: "The last chapter seems to contradict what I said, when in order to console those who were not contemplatives, I told them that God had made many ways of reaching Him. . . . His majesty, being God, knows our weakness and has provided for us. He did not say: 'Let some men come to Me by drinking this water, but let others come by some other means.' His mercy is so great that He hinders no one from drinking of the fountain of life. May He be forever praised. . . . Indeed He calls us loudly and publicly to do so. . . . You see, sisters, there is no fear you will die of drought on the way of prayer. . . . Take my advice: do not loiter on the road, but struggle manfully, until you perish in the attempt." St. Teresa says further (*The Way of Perfection*, chap. 21): "I maintain that this is the chief point: in fact, that everything depends on their having a great and a most resolute determination never to halt until they reach their journey's end, happen what may, whatever the consequences are, cost what it will, let who will blame them . . . whether the earth itself goes to pieces beneath their feet."

[15] This superior life is in fact doubly supernatural, not only in its essence, as common Christian life, but by the divine mode of knowing and loving, which is inspired by the Holy Ghost.

charity.[16] In certain souls it is love which dominates, in others light. Since we love only what we know, and since we cannot love ardently what we know but poorly, every soul ought to be very enlightened if it is to be inflamed with love. In this state the soul is no longer inclined to meditate by itself, to reason on the great truths of faith so as to arouse itself to acts of love of God. It receives "a supernatural recollection" which it could never acquire by its own efforts and "which does not depend on our will."[17] It is no longer the soul recollecting itself, it is God who recollects it and draws it toward the inner sanctuary. This is the beginning of contemplation, properly so called; it is infused since we cannot procure it for ourselves by our activity aided by grace. St. Teresa, in opposition to the quietists, says that, if we have not as yet received this gift, we should be careful not "to stop the movement of our thoughts . . . and to remain there like blockheads."[18] This recollection and the quiet which

[16] It will be seen from the texts which follow why we cannot admit that in St. Teresa's opinion mystical contemplation is an immediate perception of God in Himself and not in His effects, or a knowledge by infused ideas similar to that of the angels, which completely excludes the possibility of reasoning. Mystical contemplation would thus become not only an eminent grace, but a miraculous grace; it would be properly speaking extraordinary and, contrary to what St. Teresa says, all interior souls could not aspire to it as to the fountain of living water. On this point, consult the following article in this chapter. St. Teresa's texts, which we have brought together here, answer the objections made to our teaching on this subject in the *Revue d'ascétique et de mystique*, July, 1922, p. 272.

[17] *The Interior Castle*, fourth mansion, chap. 3, pp. 104–13.

[18] *The Interior Castle*, fourth mansion, chap. 3. St. Teresa's remark concerns the individual, proximate call to infused contemplation. Evidently she does not admit, after the acquired prayer of recollection (described in *The Way of Perfection*, chap. 28, and afterward called simplified, affective prayer) and before the beginning of infused contemplation which we are here considering, an intermediate state that can rightly be called acquired contemplation. If she admitted it, she would grant that the soul "can stop the movement of thought" before receiving the grace of supernatural recollection.

If the term "acquired contemplation" is applied to the last of the acquired prayers, which is simplified, affective prayer, called by St. Teresa the prayer of (acquired) recollection (*The Way of Perfection*, chap. 28), the saint's doctrine is kept, but not her terms; for, like all the great mystics,

follow are "a supernatural state to which no effort of our own can raise us." [19] "As for disposing oneself to it, that can be done, and that is without doubt an important point." [20] Psalmody, for instance, disposes the soul to contemplative prayer and also makes the soul desire it.

During this passive recollection, "when our Lord suspends the understanding and makes it cease from its acts, He puts before it that which astonishes and occupies it: so that, without making any reflections, it shall comprehend in a moment more than we could comprehend in many years with all the efforts in the world." [21] In contemplation "the soul understands that the divine Master is teaching it without the sound of words." [22] "It was not by way of vision; I believe it was

---

by contemplation she understands infused contemplation, which we cannot obtain for ourselves by our own efforts. Cf. *The Way of Perfection*, chaps. 18–21, 25, 27, 31; *The Interior Castle*, fourth and fifth mansions.

If, on the contrary, the term "acquired contemplation" is applied to any other than the acquired prayer of recollection, and if anyone should desire to introduce it into the category of supernatural prayers described in the fourth and fifth mansions, he would be doing violence to the words of St. Teresa and to her doctrine, since she expressly states that we cannot by our own industry aided by grace place ourselves in the supernatural prayers of (passive) recollection, quiet, spiritual intoxication, and mystical sleep.

We need not here interpret the saint's teaching, but merely read what she has written. If it were necessary to apply "acquired" to these supernatural prayers, which are not in our power, because we can dispose ourselves to receive them, and if the qualification "infused" or "mystical" were refused them because some preparation is brought to them, then we would have to refuse this title also to rapture which she speaks of in her *Life*, chap. 18. She says: "The truth is that, in the beginning, this almost always happens after much mental prayer." To be logical, we would have to speak of an acquired rapture and even of an acquired transforming union.

Quite in harmony with St. Teresa's teaching is that of the Carmelites, John of Jesus Mary (*Theol. mystica*, chap. 3) and Michael de la Fuente (*Las tres vidas*, Introduction), who place infused contemplation immediately after simplified, affective prayer, or the acquired prayer of recollection. St. Francis de Sales does the same in *The Love of God* (Bk. VI, chap. 7).

19 *The Way of Perfection*, chap. 31.

20 *Relation* LIV to Father Rodriguez Alvarez, p. 295. See what is said also on the work of the mind, analogous to that of a *noria* (water wheel), disposing to the supernatural prayer of quiet which we cannot procure for ourselves by our personal effort. Cf. *Life*, chap. 14.

21 *Life*, chap. 12.

22 *The Way of Perfection*, chap. 25.

what is called mystical theology. . . . The understanding
stands as if amazed at the greatness of the things it understands; for God wills it to understand that it understands
nothing whatever of that which His Majesty places before
it." [23] "The presence of God is frequently felt, particularly
by those who have attained to the prayer of union and of
quiet, when we seem, at the very commencement of our
prayer, to find Him with whom we would converse, and when
we seem to feel that He hears us by the effects and the spiritual
impressions of great love and faith of which we are then
conscious, as well as by the good resolutions, accompanied
by sweetness, which we then make. This is a great grace from
God; and let him to whom He has given it esteem it much,
because it is a very high degree of prayer; but it is not vision.
God is understood to be present there by the effects.[24] He
works in the soul: that is the way His Majesty makes His
presence felt." [25]

Under this infused light, "the soul is inflamed with love
without comprehending how it loves." [26] "This very sweet
love of our God enters our soul with an extreme gentleness;
it fills it with pleasure and joy [27] without its being able to
understand how or where this good was introduced into it." [28]
It is therefore clearly an infused love like the light it supposes;
it is, as the Thomists say, the fruit of an operating grace by
which the soul is vitally and freely moved by God without
deliberate movement on its own part.[29] "When God will make
you drink this water (of contemplation) . . . you will under-

[23] *Life*, chap. 10.
[24] God is therefore not perceived in Himself or immediately, as certain
interpreters of St. Teresa have claimed. She speaks as St. Thomas does (Ia,
q.94, a.1 ad 3um; IIa IIae, q.5, a.1; q.97, a.2 ad 2um).
[25] *Life*, chap. 27, where St. Teresa distinguishes between mystical prayer
and the visions that sometimes accompany it.
[26] *The Way of Perfection*, chap. 25.
[27] Nevertheless it continues in the dryness of the dark night.
[28] *Pensées sur le Cantique*, chap. 4.
[29] St. Thomas, Ia IIae, q.111, a.2.

stand that the true love of God, when it is in its vigor, that is to say entirely free from earthly things and soaring above them, is master of all the elements and of the world itself." [30] "The prayer of quiet is a little spark of the true love of Himself, which our Lord begins to enkindle in the soul," [31] and this fire "purifies the soul of the dross and the wretchedness into which its faults have plunged it." [32] This infused knowledge and love, which are the superior exercise of the theological virtues under the influence of the Holy Ghost, constitute the essential foundations of the mystical life. The Holy Ghost alone can give us this knowledge and love of God, which have a superhuman mode exceeding our personal efforts aided by grace. [33] St. John of the Cross expresses the same doctrine when he says: "Contemplation is a science of love, an infused and loving knowledge of God." [34] "This obscure contemplation . . . is mystical theology which the doctors call secret wisdom, communicated according to the doctrine of St. Thomas, by the infusion of love into the soul. [35] This communication is made secretly . . . our faculties are incapable of acquiring it; it is the Holy Ghost who pours

[30] *The Way of Perfection*, chap. 19.

[31] *Life*, chap. 15.

[32] *The Way of Perfection*, chap. 19.

[33] In fact, St. Teresa says in her *Life* (chap. 14) that to make people understand what a supernatural prayer is she would have to speak of the particular assistance which the soul sees, in a way, with its own eyes in this prayer. She does not speak of infused ideas.

[34] *The Dark Night of the Soul*, Bk. II, chap. 18. By thus defining contemplation, St. John of the Cross shows that in his opinion contemplation, properly so called, is infused; it is of this infused contemplation that he speaks constantly. Moreover, the Carmelite, Nicholas of Jesus Mary, in his *Elucidatio phrasium myst. operum Joannis a Cruce* (Part II, chap. 4), is right in saying that infused contemplation is discussed not only in *The Dark Night of the Soul* but also in *The Ascent of Mount Carmel*, Bk. II, chap. 13. Cf. *Études Carmélitaines*, July, 1912, pp. 263, 270.

[35] Cf. IIa IIae, q. 180, a. 1. From this quotation, taken from St. Thomas by St. John of the Cross, we can clearly see how greatly mistaken people are who claim today that the Angelic Doctor did not speak of essentially mystical contemplation in his *Summa*.

it into the soul." [36] Under its influence the three theological virtues are exercised in the highest degree.[37] If this infused and loving contemplation lasts a certain time, it is called a state of prayer; a passive state, or at least one that is more passive than active, in this sense that we cannot produce it, but only dispose ourselves for it.

## II. THE DEGREES OF THE MYSTICAL STATE; FROM THE FOURTH TO THE SEVENTH MANSIONS

In this section we will consider particularly the growing intensity of charity, of living faith, and of the corresponding gifts in the mystical state. St. Thomas studied this intensity from an abstract and theoretical point of view; [38] St. Teresa described it from experience and in its loftiest forms. To show this growing intensity of the mystical state, St. Teresa insists on its progressive extension to the different faculties of the soul, which are gradually suspended or captivated by God. First of all, the will is seized and held, then the intellect and the imagination; finally in ecstasy, the exercise of the exterior senses is suspended. St. Teresa knows, however, that the suspension of the imagination and of the senses is only a concomitant and accidental phenomenon,[39] sign of a greater

[36] *The Dark Night of the Soul*, Bk. II, chap. 17; and chap. 5.
[37] *The Ascent of Mount Carmel*, Bk. II, chaps. 6, 7.
[38] *Summa*, IIa IIae, q.24.
[39] *The Interior Castle*, fifth mansion, chap. 1, p. 120. When St. Teresa begins to discuss the prayer of union, which follows quiet, and which is sometimes accompanied by a beginning of ecstasy, she says to her daughters: "The majority may be said at least to gain admittance into these rooms. I think that certain graces I am about to describe are bestowed on only a few; but if the rest only arrive at the portal, they receive a great boon from God, for 'many are called, but few are chosen.'" Farther on in the fifth mansion, chap. 3, she says: "God has many ways of enriching the soul and bringing it to these mansions (which means, to the supernatural prayer of union) besides what might be called a shortcut." We shall see later on what she means by this shortcut: not the mystical state as has been believed at times, but the ecstatic state or a beginning of ecstasy. Moreover, in the fifth mansion, chap. 3, St. Teresa also speaks of a union of conformity to the divine will, which is not a degree of prayer but an excellent disposition not

intensity of knowledge and love of God, since it generally ceases in the most perfect mystical state, the transforming union.[40] The mystical state, complete in regard to its extension, is not therefore necessarily the most intense or the most elevated.[41] St. Teresa does not overlook this fact; but this extension, which is at first progressive, then restrained and rather easy to determine and describe, may give some light on the growing elevation of the mystical state, if it is joined to another sign which is more profound, one on which St. John of the Cross strongly insisted. This more profound sign is found, first of all, in the passive purification of the senses, then in that of the spirit, both of which denote progress in

---

to have any self-will, a disposition which one can have without having received a beginning of ecstasy.

[40] *The Interior Castle*, seventh mansion, chap. 3.

[41] This has been clearly explained by Saudreau, *État mystique*, 2d ed., p. 89. Precisely because of this we regret to see in the same work (p. 46) that he applies the term "extraordinary" to the prayers of the fifth and sixth mansions which are accompanied by ecstasy. They are not extraordinary in their essence, but only in certain concomitant and accidental phenomena. Saudreau recognizes this (p. 51) when he says as we do: "God can conduct the soul even to the transforming union without granting it raptures." He is certainly right in distinguishing the mystical state from what he calls the extraordinary phenomena of angelic order (p. 180). The objections which have been raised against him lately on this point (*Revue Apologétique*, June 15, 1922) are not well founded. Father Poulain himself clearly distinguished the mystical state from the visions which may accompany it.

Father Lallemant, S.J., rightly observes in his *Doctrine spirituelle* (VII Principe, chap. 4, art. 7): "According to some writers the degrees of contemplation are: first, the recollection of all the powers; second, semi-rapture; third, complete rapture; fourth, ecstasy. This division does not, however, so much express the essence of contemplation as its accidents; for a soul may sometimes have without rapture a more sublime light, a clearer knowledge, a more excellent operation of God, than another that is favored with extraordinary raptures and ecstasies. The Blessed Virgin was raised higher in contemplation than all the angels and saints together, and yet she had no raptures." Some of the saints, as Bernadette at the Grotto of Lourdes, have had them in childhood, and then fewer of them in later years. This observation contains something analogous to what is ordinarily said about science: its progress in extension is not a certain sign of its progress in penetration. Several persons have a rather extended knowledge of a science without possessing a profound or elevated knowledge that enables them to grasp with a glance the whole science in its first principles. Cf. St. Thomas, Ia IIae, q.52.

the intensity of the knowledge and love of God. St. Teresa did not neglect this second sign.

A third and still more decisive indication arises from the fact that virtue normally increases with prayer. The increasingly intimate action of God must be judged especially by this sign rather than by the passive purifications. These, in fact, depend greatly on the obstacles that grace encounters, and also on the types of temperament and on morbid dispositions. Although these passive purifications are inseparable from the development of the mystical life, they cannot measure it with as great certainty as can progress in virtue. Progress in virtue, not as man judges it, but rather as it appears in the sight of God, the only judge of souls, corresponds to the growing intensity of infused contemplation and of the love of God. St. Teresa has noted this in an admirable manner.[42] Pope Pius X praised her especially for this, saying: "The degrees of prayer enumerated by the saint are so many superior ascents toward the summit of perfection."

At first, in the prayer of quiet "the will alone is made captive" [43] by the mysterious light received, which manifests to it the goodness of God present in it, as a little child enjoys the milk which is given to it.[44] Better still, it is like the gushing forth of the living water which Jesus spoke of to the Samaritan woman: "The water flows from the very fountain itself, which is God, . . . it wells up from the most intimate depths of our being with extreme peace, tranquillity, and sweet-

---

[42] Besides the texts that we shall quote, see what the saint says in her *Life* about the progress of virtue corresponding to the prayers symbolized by the four manners of watering: second water, the flowers (of the virtues) are about to appear (chap. 15); third water, the flowers bloom; the virtues draw from this prayer much greater vigor than from the preceding, which is that of quiet (chaps. 16 f.); fourth water, "this is the time of resolutions, of heroic determinations, of the living energy of good desires, of the beginning of hatred of the world, and of the most clear perception of its vanity. The soul makes greater and higher progress than it ever made before in the previous states of prayer; and grows in humility more and more" (chap. 19).

[43] *The Way of Perfection*, chap. 31, p. 179.

[44] *Ibid.*, p. 183.

ness. . . . Hardly has this celestial water begun to flow from its source . . . , when one experiences a great interior dilation and increase. The soul then receives inexpressible spiritual benefits and indeed is incapable of understanding what it receives at that moment." [45] In this state, however, the understanding, memory, and imagination are not captivated by the divine action. Sometimes they act as the auxiliaries of the will and engage in its service; at other times their contribution serves only to trouble it. St. Teresa says: "Often during this prayer you will not know what to do with your understanding and memory (which never cease to be agitated). . . . But when the will enjoys this quiet, it should take no more notice of the understanding than it would of an idiot." [46]

This quiet is often interrupted by the aridities and trials of the passive night of the senses [47] and by temptations against patience and chastity which oblige the soul to a salutary reaction. This greatly strengthens the moral virtues which have their seat in the sensitive appetites. The effects of the prayer of quiet are a greater virtue, especially a greater love of God and ineffable peace, at least in the superior part of the soul. [48]

If the soul is humble and generous, [49] it will be raised to a higher degree. In simple union, God's action is strong enough to absorb completely the activity of the interior faculties of the soul; all this activity is directed toward Him and no longer goes astray. God seizes and captivates the will, and also the

45 *The Interior Castle*, fourth mansion, chap. 2.
46 *The Way of Perfection*, chap. 31; *The Interior Castle*, fourth mansion, chap. 1.
47 *The Way of Perfection*, chap. 24, 34, 38. *The Interior Castle*, third mansion, chap. 1; fourth mansion, chap. 1. Cf. St. John of the Cross, *The Dark Night of the Soul*, Bk. I.
48 *Life*, chap. 15.
49 *The Interior Castle*, fifth mansion, chap. 1. The saint observes that it is no longer sufficient to follow one's rule attentively; besides, one must be very docile to the inspirations of the Holy Ghost, who becomes more exacting in proportion as He gives more and wishes to give more.

thoughts, memory, and imagination. Furthermore, the soul is usually no longer troubled by distractions. God suspends the natural action of the intellect "in order better to impress on us true wisdom." [50] The memory and imagination are likewise arrested in their natural operations and intimately united to God in a way suitable to them. The soul no longer seeks with effort to draw the salutary water which refreshes and purifies it; it receives this water simply, like rain falling from heaven.[51] "God does not leave us any share other than that of an entire conformity of our will to his." [52] "How beautiful is the soul after having been immersed in God's grandeur and united closely to Him for but a short time! Indeed, I do not think it is ever as long as half an hour!" [53] The soul has, so to speak, changed form, by dying entirely to the world, like the silkworm which becomes a white butterfly.[54]

St. Teresa observes that this prayer of union is frequently incomplete, without suspension of the imagination and memory, which at times wage a veritable war on the intellect and will.[55] Here, as in the prayer of quiet, no more attention should be paid to the imagination than to a madman.[56] St. Teresa speaks of this incomplete mystical union in *The Interior Castle* [57] when she says: "Is it necessary, in order to attain to this kind of divine union, for the powers of the

[50] *Ibid.*

[51] The first way of watering, by drawing water from a well by main strength, is a picture of meditation (*Life*, chap. 11); the second way, with the *noria* (water wheel), symbolizes the prayer of quiet in which there is still some activity, even though this is a supernatural prayer (*Life*, chap. 14); the third way of watering, by water flowing from a river or fountain, corresponds to the sleep of the powers (*Life*, chap. 16); the fourth water, which is rain, symbolizes the prayer of union (*Life*, chap. 18).

[52] *The Interior Castle*, fifth mansion, chap. 1.

[53] *Ibid.*, chap. 2.

[54] *Ibid.* It must be observed that by this transformation this insect reaches adult age; by an analogous transformation the soul reaches the adult age of the supernatural life.

[55] *Life*, chap. 17.

[56] *Ibid.*

[57] Fifth mansion, chap. 3.

soul to be suspended? No. God has many ways of enriching the soul and bringing it to these mansions besides what might be called a 'shortcut.' " [58]

The effects of the prayer of union are most sanctifying. The soul experiences a great contrition for its faults, an ardent desire to praise God, and strength to face every trial so as to serve Him. It is bitterly grieved at the loss of sinners, and thus it sees what the sufferings of Christ must have been during His earthly life.[59]

At this time, a period of trial generally comes, described by St. Teresa at the beginning of the sixth mansion, and called by St. John of the Cross the passive night of the soul. "There is an outcry raised against such a person by those amongst whom she lives. . . . They say she wants to pass for a saint, that she goes to extremes in piety. Persons she thought were her friends desert her, making the most bitter remarks of all. . . . She suffers scoffing remarks of all sorts . . . and the worst of it is, these troubles do not blow over but last all her life." But the soul enlightened by God is "strengthened rather than depressed by its trials; experience

---

[58] This shortcut and the delights found in it have at times been thought to be infused or mystical contemplation; but it is only the suspension of the imagination and memory, or a beginning of ecstasy, which sometimes accompanies mystical union and greatly facilitates it. Cf. Arintero, O.P., *Evolución mística*, p. 639, and *Cuestiones místicas*, pp. 325 ff.; Father Garate, S.J., *Razón y Fe*, July, 1908, p. 325. Saudreau rightly observes in *Les degrés de la vie spirituelle* (5th ed.), II, 101: "Apropos of this passage (fifth mansion, chap. 3), the new translators of St. Teresa say that according to her teaching there are two ways leading to the state of union, the mystical way and the non-mystical way. St. Teresa says nothing of the sort; if she did, she would be contradicting her own constant teaching (cf. *The Way of Perfection*, chaps. 18–21). She says—and the new translation shows this to be the original text—merely that the soul enters this fifth mansion either by union, which is a beginning of ecstasy, or without it. It may be that the soul has not this ecstatic union, and yet has received very precious mystical graces." We repeat that the passive prayer of union is not extraordinary in its basis or in its very essence, even though certain of its accidental or concomitant phenomena may be so. For a discussion of St. Teresa's word "shortcut," cf. Philip of the Blessed Trinity, *Theol. myst.*, III, 71; Anthony of the Holy Ghost, *Direct. myst.*, Tract. IV, Disp. I, sec. 4; Vallgornera, O.P., *Theol. myst.*, II, 137.

[59] *The Interior Castle*, fifth mansion, chap. 2.

having taught it the great advantages derived from them. . . .
Moreover, the soul conceives a special tenderness for these
people who make it suffer." "Our Lord now usually sends
severe illnesses.[60] . . . The rest would seem trifling in comparison, if one could relate the interior torments met with
here, but they are impossible to describe. . . . A confessor
who dreads and suspects everything. . . . Interior anguish
of the soul at the sight of its own wretchedness. . . . It
believes that God permits it to be deceived in punishment
for its sins. This suffering becomes almost unbearable, especially when such spiritual dryness ensues that the mind
feels as if it had never thought of God nor ever will be able
to do so. When men speak of Him, they seem to be talking
of some person heard of long ago. . . . The understanding
is so obscured that it is incapable of discerning the truth; it
believes all that the imagination puts before it, besides credit-
ing the falsehoods suggested to it by the devil. Our Lord
doubtless gives the devil leave to tempt it, and even to make
it think that God has rejected it. . . . During this tempest,
the soul is incapable of receiving any comfort. The only
remedy is to wait for the mercy of God who, when the soul
least expects it, delivers it from all its sufferings by a single
word addressed to it, or by some unforeseen happening. Then
it seems as if there had never been any trouble and the soul
praises the Lord, for it is He who has fought for it and
rendered it victorious. The soul sees clearly that the conquest
was not its own. . . . Then it recognizes perfectly its weakness and how little we can do of ourselves when the Lord
withdraws His help. It no longer needs to reflect in order
to understand this truth." [61]

[60] *Ibid.*
[61] *The Interior Castle,* sixth mansion, chap. 1. St. Teresa understood thus by
experience the great doctrine of St. Augustine and St. Thomas on efficacious
grace, as Dominic Bañez expounded it. Generally souls which pass through the
night of the soul can no longer admit any other doctrine, even though previously they have been inclined toward the contrary opinion, according to
which grace is rendered efficacious by our good consent.

"Since these troubles come from above, no earthly comfort can avail. This great God wishes us to acknowledge His sovereignty and our misery. . . . The best means . . . to succeed in bearing this anguish is to perform external works of charity and to hope for everything from the mercy of God. He never fails those who hope in Him. . . . The exterior sufferings caused by the devils are more unusual . . . and all the sufferings which they may cause are slight in comparison with those which I have just described." [62] Farther on, St. Teresa speaks of a still more painful purification of love which occurs at the entrance to the seventh mansion, "as the purification of purgatory introduces the soul into heaven"; [63] but then the soul, while bearing this suffering, is aware that it is an eminent favor.

After passing through these interior sufferings, the soul receives such a knowledge of God's grandeur that frequently partial or complete ecstasy follows.[64] Union with God is so perfect that it suspends the operations of the exterior senses; all the activity of the soul is ravished toward God, and consequently ceases to function in regard to the exterior world.[65] If at times a scholar, like Archimedes, is so absorbed by speculation that he no longer hears words spoken to him, with greater reason is this true of the contemplative soul when a very strong grace, making it experience God's infinite grandeur, absorbs it in this blessed contemplation.[66]

[62] *The Interior Castle,* sixth mansion, chap. 1.

[63] *Ibid.,* chap. 11.

[64] *The Interior Castle,* sixth mansion, chap. 5. Father Joret, O.P., showed clearly (*La vie spirituelle,* May, 1922, p. 90) that ecstasy, which is a consequence of infused contemplation, is not properly speaking extraordinary. It is a different matter if it precedes contemplation and prepares the soul for it.

[65] This is in virtue of the principle often formulated by St. Thomas: "cum totaliter anima intendat ad actum unius potentiae, abstrahitur homo ab actu alterius potentiae" (*De veritate,* q. 13, a. 3).

[66] God then appears more and more as supreme Truth, and the soul understands the meaning of the psalmist's words: "Every man is a liar." The soul also sees why the Most High so greatly loves humility. "Because He is the supreme Truth and humility is the truth. It is most true that we have nothing good of ourselves, and that misery and nothingness are our portion" (sixth mansion,

At other times, the soul exults and cannot refrain from singing the praises of God. This is a very desirable grace: "May His Majesty frequently grant us such a prayer which is both safe and advantageous! We cannot acquire it for ourselves as it is quite supernatural. Sometimes it lasts for a whole day. . . . This jubilation plunges the soul into such a forgetfulness of itself and of all things that it is incapable of thinking or of speaking, except to offer to God praise, which is, as it were, the natural fruit of its joy." [67]

St. Teresa says, on the contrary, when speaking of visions impressed directly on the imagination: "It is not at all fitting . . . to desire them"; [68] they are extraordinary favors quite distinct from the full development of the life of grace in us. "Know that for having received many favors of this kind, a soul will not merit more glory. . . . There are many saints who never knew what it was to receive one such favor, while others who have received them are not saints at all. . . . Often for even one of these favors the Lord sends a great number of tribulations." [69]

Finally the soul is introduced into the seventh mansion, the transforming union with God, which is immediately preceded by a last and very painful purification, that of love, "where the soul dies with the desire to die." In this mansion some souls have an intellectual vision of the Blessed Trinity who dwells in us; but this vision, with a clarity that varies and is as it were intermittent, is not of the essence of the transforming union. Indeed it does not seem necessarily to

---

chap. 10). It would, therefore, be an error to believe that the just man is distinguished from the sinner by his liberty alone, and that this difference does not come from grace. "What distinguisheth thee?" says St. Paul.

[67] *The Interior Castle*, sixth mansion, chap. 6.

[68] *Ibid.*, chap. 9. In the same sense the Discalced Carmelite, Joseph of the Holy Ghost, correcting Anthony of the Annunciation, C.D., rightly observes and proves that "we can keenly desire and humbly petition God for infused contemplation, but not for ecstasy and other similar favors which sometimes accompany it." *Cursus theol. mystico-scolasticae* (1791), II, 222, 224.

[69] *The Interior Castle*, sixth mansion, chap. 9.

be linked with it.[70] Moreover, ecstasies have generally ceased; [71] and what constitutes the foundation of this eminent state is in no way miraculous, that is, the superior faculties are passively drawn to the deepest center of the soul where the Blessed Trinity dwells. Under the influence of this grace, the soul cannot doubt that the divine Persons are present in it; it is, besides, practically never deprived of Their company. "The soul recognizes by certain secret aspirations that it is God who gives it life," and that He is the Life of our life.[72] The Christian who has reached this perfect age is morally one with Him, in the sense in which St. Paul says: "He who is joined to the Lord, is one spirit." [73] As far as is possible on earth, this is the full realization of our Lord's prayer: "That they may be one, as We also are one; I in them, and Thou in Me . . . and that the world may know that Thou hast sent Me, . . . and hast loved them, as Thou hast also loved Me." [74] In the same way, rain falling into a river is so mingled with the stream that it can no longer be distinguished from it; or, to use the figure employed by St. John of the Cross: "It resembles the condition of wood when the fire has attacked it with its flames, dried it out, and finally penetrated it and transformed it into itself." [75] It is still wood,

---

70 St. Teresa speaks of it in the seventh mansion (chaps. 1, 2), and describes it as it was granted to her "in an extraordinary way." St. John of the Cross, who discussed at greater length the spiritual marriage in its relation with the theological virtues, does not say that such a vision is necessarily linked with that state. He simply points out (*Canticle*, Part III, and *The Living Flame*) the fact that in the transforming union there is a very lofty contemplation of the divine perfections. Father Poulain recognizes this. Cf. *Les grâces d'oraison* (9th ed.), chap. 19, no. 15.

71 *The Interior Castle*, seventh mansion, chap. 3: "From the moment when the Lord discloses to the soul the wonders of this mansion and gives it entrance to it, the soul loses this great weakness (of ecstasy) which was so painful to it and from which nothing could deliver it. Perhaps this comes from the fact that the Lord has strengthed it, dilated it, and rendered it capable of His operations." Thus union with God, being possible without hindering the exercise of the faculties, becomes almost constant.

72 *The Interior Castle*, seventh mansion, chap. 2.

73 See I Cor. 6: 17.

74 John 17: 22 f.

75 *The Living Flame*, st. 1, v. 4.

but incandescent wood which has taken on the properties of fire. In the same way, a flame rises almost constantly toward God from a purified heart.

The effects of the transforming union are those of the perfect exercise of the theological virtues and of the gifts, which have reached their full development. The soul is practically freed from the disorders of the passions; as long as it is under the actual grace of the transforming union, it does not commit deliberate venial sins.[76] At other times, it still occasionally commits some venial faults, which are quickly atoned for. What is outstanding in the soul is a great forgetfulness of self, a keen desire to suffer in imitation of our Lord, a true joy in persecution. Aridities and interior sufferings have ceased as well as the desire to die. These souls, inflamed with zeal for the glory of God and the salvation of their neighbor, "desire to live long years in the midst of the most severe trials in order that the Lord may be ever so little glorified by them." [77] This is truly the apostolic life (manifest or hidden), which flows from the plenitude of contemplation, to use the expression of St. Thomas.[78] It is the full perfection of Christian life, which our Lord, the Blessed Virgin, and the Apostles have exemplified in the highest degree. "God cannot bestow upon us a more precious favor than a life conformed to that of His well-beloved Son. Moreover, . . . these graces are intended to strengthen our weakness and to make us able to bear great sufferings in imitation of this divine Son." [79] The soul is thus truly spiritualized and shares in the very strength of Christ and in His immense love for God and for souls. Such is, on earth, the perfect age of the life of grace, the full realization of the first precept: "Thou shalt love the Lord thy God with thy whole heart, and with thy whole soul, and with all thy strength, and with all thy mind." [80]

---

[76] *The Interior Castle,* seventh mansion, chap. 2.
[77] *Ibid.,* chap. 3.
[78] See IIa IIae, q. 188, a. 6.
[79] *The Interior Castle,* seventh mansion, chap. 4.
[80] Luke 10: 27.

All just souls are called, at least in a general and remote manner, to this transforming union, which is the normal prelude to the life of heaven. If they are faithful to this call, and at the same time humble and generous, they will hear a more proximate and urgent invitation.[81] St. Teresa repeats this in the Epilogue to *The Interior Castle:* "In truth you cannot by your own strength, no matter how great it may seem to you, enter all the mansions. The Master of the Castle must Himself admit you. If you encounter any resistance on His part, I advise you not to try to use violence. You would so greatly displease Him that He would forever close the doors to you. He deeply loves humility; if you believe yourself unworthy to enter even the third mansion, you will soon obtain admission to the fifth. You will even be able to frequent it so assiduously and to serve Him so well, that He will admit you to the mansion which He has reserved for Himself." [82] She makes the same statement in her *Life.*[83]

In conclusion, let us point out that in St. Teresa's writings the normal way of sanctity consists in humility and abnegation, which prepare the soul for infused contemplation, highly desirable for all, and also for a more and more intimate divine union, indeed even for the transforming union, the culminating point in the normal development of the supernatural life. As for extraordinary facts, such as visions, interior words, and private revelations, however useful for the sanctification of the soul, they ought not to be desired. They are accidental, transient phenomena, whereas infused contemplation continues. They do not unite us as closely to God as do perfect

---

81 Cf. the texts from *The Way of Perfection,* chaps. 18–21, quoted in the first part of this article.

82 Cf. also St. John of the Cross, *The Spiritual Canticle,* st. 34.

83 Chap. 40: "Then He said: 'Ah, My daughter, they are few who love Me in truth; for if men loved Me, I should not hide My secrets from them.' " She observes also (*ibid.*): "There are many more women than men to whom our Lord gives these graces." To show what purity of soul is required for us to enter heaven, she says (chap. 38): "In 'all the visions I had, I saw no souls escape purgatory except three." Yet to avoid purgatory is the normal way of sanctity.

faith and the gift of wisdom which, in varying degrees, exists in all the just.[84]

What the interior soul should desire above all else is the ever deeper reign of God in it, continual growth in charity. This it should long for because the precept of love is without limit and obliges us, if not to be saints, at least to tend to sanctity, each one according to his condition,[85] and because Christ said to all: "Be ye perfect as your heavenly Father is perfect." This is the goal which St. Teresa has shown us. The greatest tribute that can be given her is that she has marvelously praised the glory of God by making us see, in her writings and in her life, God's great love for the humble, and all that He wishes to do for "souls determined to follow our Lord and to journey on, in spite of the cost, even to the fountain of living water. . . . This is the royal road which leads to heaven." [86]

## ARTICLE IV

### *What Infused Contemplation Does Not Essentially Require*

The different definitions of infused contemplation given by theologians agree on one fundamental point. Infused contemplation, they say, is, above reasoning and in the obscurity of faith, a simple and loving knowledge of God, which cannot be obtained by our personal activity aided by grace, but rather demands a manifest, special illumination and inspiration of the Holy Ghost.[1] When it lasts for a certain time, this

---

[84] *The Ascent of Mount Carmel*, Bk. II, chaps. 7, 8.

[85] Cf. St. Thomas, IIa IIae, q.184, a.3. The doctrine taught in this article is forgotten and misunderstood by many great modern theologians.

[86] *The Way of Perfection*, chap. 21.

[1] In the ascetical life, the inspiration of the Holy Ghost remains latent; but in the mystical life it is generally quite manifest. It may not be so for the soul receiving it, for in periods of trial this inspiration may remain hidden from the soul; but it is manifest at least for the spiritual director who sees that the passive night of the senses and of the spirit have as their principal cause a purifying light of mystical order.

contemplation is a state of passive prayer. Theologians generally agree on this fundamental point. We believe it is the true definition, which retains what is essential in the descriptions given by the most accepted mystics. To understand this definition well, we will show first what infused contemplation does not require. Once the ground has been cleared, we shall more easily see what really constitutes it, by seeking the principle from which contemplation proceeds.

There have been theologians who thought that more distinctive marks should be added to the definition we have just given. Some have declared that infused contemplation is given suddenly, unexpectedly, without preparation on our part, and that it is accompanied by an absolute impossibility of discursive reasoning.[2] Others, confusing it with certain accidental and concomitant phenomena, have seen in it a gratuitous grace *(gratis data),* an extraordinary gift such as prophecy.[3] According to others, it would require infused ideas similar to those of the angels and would make us see God not in an image, but as He is in Himself.[4] Some have even added that infused contemplation is not a meritorious act.[5] These

---

[2] It is thus that Honoré de Sainte-Marie, C.D., in his work, which in certain respects is very valuable, *Tradition des pères et des auteurs ecclésiastiques sur la contemplation,* 1708, Part III, Diss. 3, a. 1, sec. 2, applies the word "acquired" to all contemplative prayer which has been preceded by some work of recollection. Moreover, he even maintains that acquired contemplation, like infused, "is accompanied . . . by the prayer of quiet, by the sleep of the powers, by spiritual silence, ecstasy, rapture." He is, however, obliged to add: "Although acquired contemplation may sometimes cause ecstasy and rapture, it seems quite evident that this cannot happen without some influence of the gifts of the Holy Ghost; and thus acquired contemplation passes into infused." We read in the same chapter: "In this acquired contemplation, one never attains to what is called pure contemplation."

[3] This is what Anthony of the Annunciation, C.D., taught in his *Disceptatio mystica,* tr. 2, q. 4, a. 8, no. 34. He was later corrected on this point by Joseph of the Holy Ghost, C.D., *Cursus theol. myst.-scol.,* II, 224.

[4] Farges, *Les phénomènes mystiques,* 1921, pp. 76, 86, 94, 98, 108, 114.

[5] Bossuet, *Instruction sur les états d'oraison,* Bk. VII: "The mystical state is like prophecy, or the gift of tongues or of miracles. It resembles the kind of grace which is called a grace freely bestowed, *gratia gratis data.* . . . If we must be more explicit, we shall say that the mystical state, consisting principally in something that God operates in us, without us, and in which consequently

confusions may be easily dispelled by an examination of St. Teresa's descriptions, quoted in the preceding article. It is a simple matter to show that the definition which we have given fully suffices without the addition of other ideas.

1) Infused contemplation is not always given suddenly, unexpectedly, like rain falling from heaven. More often than not, it is granted after a certain preparation, when the soul is already recollected. Thus, according to St. Teresa (*The Interior Castle*, fourth mansion), the prayer of quiet is a "supernatural" prayer which we are incapable of procuring for ourselves by our own efforts. But she says that the soul prepares itself to receive this prayer by pious thoughts, by labor of the understanding, as one turns a *noria* (water wheel) in order to draw water.[6] On this point, it is well also to consult St. John of the Cross.[7]

2) Infused contemplation is not necessarily accompanied by an absolute impossibility to discourse or to reason, which would come from the suspension of the imagination. It is possible for this ligature not to exist, since according to the saints there are often distractions in the supernatural prayer of quiet. They also say that some souls, which are in this state, are wrong in leaving it by being willing to discourse too much.

3) Another error is to hold that infused contemplation is not a meritorious act. Although we cannot have it at will like an act of faith, we can freely consent to be moved in this way by the Holy Ghost. Consequently the act is vital and free, without in itself being deliberate and the fruit of our personal

---

there is not and cannot be any merit." This is a surprising confusion in so great a soul; it is one which led him to state in the same work (Bk. IX) that St. Francis de Sales had not experienced quiet. St. Jane de Chantal says the contrary in her *Réponses* (2d ed., 1665), pp. 508 ff. It is true that later on in his last work, in his letters of direction and pious treatises, after having examined the question more thoroughly, Bossuet spoke of contemplation and the prayer of the simple presence of God as St. John of the Cross and St. Teresa did. Cf. p. 230 note 31.

6 *Life*, chap. 14.

7 *The Ascent of Mount Carmel*, Bk. II, chap. 12.

effort. In the same way a good student, attentive to the doctrine proposed by his teacher, is passive while receiving it, for he could not have discovered it himself; but he receives it voluntarily and with facility. In infused contemplation the soul exercises this docility toward God; this docility is free and also meritorious because it proceeds from charity, the source of all merit.

4) Neither the consciousness of being in the state of grace nor a sense of delight is necessary to infused contemplation, since neither this consciousness nor this joy is found in the periods called the passive night of the senses and of the soul; yet these periods are a mystical state. As we shall see later, in the night of the senses the gift of knowledge dominates by showing us especially the vanity of created things; [8] and in the night of the soul the gift of understanding [9] manifests less the goodness of God than His infinite majesty, and by contrast our own wretchedness. Sweetness and peace, the fruit of the gift of wisdom, are experienced especially between the two nights, and much more strongly after the second. Although great consolations are to be found in the mystical life, there are also terrible interior trials lasting for months and years.

5) For the same reason the feeling of the presence of God is not essential to the mystical state. This feeling does not exist at all in the night of the spirit, during which the soul thinks it is rejected by God, and seems almost to despair of its salvation. Nevertheless the soul still possesses the loving and profound knowledge of God's infinite grandeur but is as it were crushed by it. "Then," says St. John of the Cross, purifying "contemplation consists in feeling oneself deprived of God, chastised, repulsed by Him." [10] If anyone were to admit that the essence of the mystical state is the feeling of God's

8 *Summa,* IIa IIae, q.9, a.4.
9 *Ibid.,* q.8, a.7.
10 *The Dark Night of the Soul,* Bk. II, chap. 6.

presence, he would be led to maintain, with a recent author, that the mystical state does not exist in the periods of desolation through which contemplatives pass. This view is utterly opposed to the entire doctrine set forth by St. John of the Cross in *The Dark Night of the Soul* on the infused, purifying light which gives an impression of great darkness to the soul, which is still too weak to bear it. This teaching is founded on the description given to us by the most accepted mystics. We will now devote our attention to considerations of a more abstract order.

6) Infused contemplation is certainly not a grace *gratis data,* bestowed especially in view of the sanctification of others, like prophecy or the gift of tongues, because contemplation is directly ordained to personal sanctification, and more often than not is known only to the person receiving it and to his confessor. Joseph of the Holy Ghost, C.D., is therefore quite right in saying that he cannot comprehend why Anthony of the Annunciation, C.D., in contradiction to tradition, placed infused contemplation among the graces *gratis datae* and insisted that it should not be asked of God, except with the reservations with which one may ask for the grace of miracles and the gift of prophecy.[11]

7) Infused contemplation does not require infused ideas like those of the angels. Infused ideas may indeed be found in certain mystical states as a concomitant phenomenon, for example, in intellectual visions and certain revelations. But prophecy itself, according to St. Thomas,[12] does not generally require these infused ideas; it suffices to have an infused light, which is quite a different thing, and a new co-ordination of acquired ideas. We would be greatly in error if we confounded the *impressio specierum* with the *impressio luminis;* the material element of knowledge (species or ideas) would no longer be distinguished from the formal element (the light

---

[11] Joseph of the Holy Ghost, C.D., *Cursus theol. myst.-scol.* (1721), Vol. II, Praedicabile II, disp. XI, q. 2, pp. 224, 236.

[12] *Summa,* IIa IIae, q. 173, a. 2.

which elevates the intellect and gives it the strength to perceive and to judge).[13]

Moreover, if mystical contemplation required infused species of angelic order, it would ordinarily require no cooperation on the part of the imagination. If this were true, all who are in the mystical state, even simply in quiet, would operate without the assistance of the brain, and sleep itself would offer no obstacle. They would contemplate even while asleep. Experience proves that this is true only in very special and truly extraordinary states.[14] According to St. Thomas, who follows Dionysius and St. Albert the Great in this matter, there is in infused contemplation (setting aside certain very superior intellectual visions) a certain almost imperceptible contribution on the part of the imagination; although the soul does not pay attention to images, they are not excluded.[15] In the same way, in the ordinary course of life we use a pen to write, without observing its form; when we read we see letters, but are attentive only to their meaning. A theologian, speculating on the Deity, superior to being, to unity, to the good, has only a verbal image, the word "Deity," to which he does not give any heed. At other times we may start with the image of a body so as to come to the idea of the incorporeal. St. Thomas clearly states [16] that infused contemplation is more perfect in proportion as it is freed from sensible images.

13 *Ibid.*

14 Saudreau, *État mystique*, 2d ed., p. 356.

15 St. Thomas, IIa IIae, q. 180, a. 5 ad 2um; *De veritate*, q. 18, a. 5. In this article St. Thomas shows that in the state of innocence, Adam, to whom he nevertheless attributes a very lofty mystical contemplation, did not know the angels by their very essence, in a purely spiritual manner; for he did not obtain natural knowledge and supernatural knowledge without sensible images, except perhaps in extraordinary raptures. Man, in his present state, does not know things in fact without a certain contribution on the part of the imagination, and grace perfects the intellect without changing the mode of knowing. St. Thomas cites in support of this doctrine the following quotation from Dionysius, who nevertheless had the loftiest conception of infused contemplation (*De coelesti hierar.*, chap. 1): "quod impossibile est nobis aliter lucere divinum radium, nisi varietate sacrorum velaminum circumvelatum." Cf. also *De veritate*, q. 13, a. 1.

16 *Summa*, IIa IIae, q. 15, a. 3.

Often it suffices to have the impression of a light in the imagination, or on the contrary, in the period called the dark night, the impression of darkness; or again a very confused impression suggestive of life. In any case, infused ideas, similiar to those of the angels, are not at all necessary, although they may sometimes be granted in exceptional favors.[17]

8) Notwithstanding what has recently been written,[18] it is even truer that infused contemplation does not require an immediate perception of God, which would make us know Him as He is. This immediate perception of God does not exist, in fact, in the great anxieties of the passive nights of the senses and of the soul, which are, nevertheless, mystical states and are accompanied by infused contemplation. Does this perception exist in the other phases of the mystical ascent? Nothing permits such an affirmation; on the contrary, everything leads us to think that it is impossible. The texts of St. Thomas, on which this theory claims to be based, cannot have the meaning attributed to them.[19] One writer asserts: "It is sufficient (in mystical contemplation) to know God as He shows Himself, partially, in order to know Him as He is." [20] God, however, being incapable of division, cannot show Himself partially in such a way that He would make Himself seen as He is. The divine attributes exist in Him *formaliter eminenter,* and they are only virtually distinct, because they are really identical in the eminence of the Deity. Consequently nobody can see one of them as it is, without seeing the others and without seeing the Deity itself, which, as Dionysius says,

[17] This is the common teaching. Cf. Vallgornera, *Theol. myst. S. Thomae,* I, 450; Philip of the Blessed Trinity and Anthony of the Holy Ghost.

[18] Farges, *Les phénomènes mystiques,* p. 97: "To sum up; God, the supernatural agent, is immediately perceived in His action received in the soul (infused idea), as the material agent is directly perceived in its action on the external senses, *quasi species (impressa) rei visae."*

[19] Cf. *op. cit.,* p. 98. A text is cited from the *Contra Gentiles,* Bk. III, chap. 54. But St. Thomas is there speaking of the light of glory necessary for the beatific vision, and not of an infused idea which would render possible an immediate perception of God inferior to this vision. The difference is a notable one.

[20] Farges, *Les phénomènes mystiques,* p. 98.

is *super ens et super unum*. St. Thomas states explicitly and proves that no vision inferior to the beatific vision can make us know God as He is in Himself; no created, infused idea can manifest just as He is, Him who is being itself, who is eternally subsistent intellection itself.[21] In theology the expression *sicuti est* has a formal meaning which is fulfilled only in the beatific vision.[22] Neither angels before receiving the light of glory nor Adam before his sin, knew God as He is. St. Thomas is explicit on this point.[23] He says as clearly as possible: "The vision of the blessed in heaven differs from that of creatures still in the state of trial, not as seeing more perfectly and seeing less perfectly, but as seeing and not seeing. Consequently neither Adam nor the angels in the state of trial saw the divine essence." [24]

If St. Paul, while on earth, received the beatific vision in a transitory manner when he was ravished to the third heaven, as St. Augustine and St. Thomas think he did, he certainly enjoyed an altogether extraordinary grace far above the highest mystical state described by St. Teresa.[25]

According to Farges,[26] the immediate perception of God, which would be essential to mystical contemplation, is none other than that which the angels naturally possess according to St. Thomas. But St. Thomas teaches that this natural knowledge, which an angel has of God, is not immediate. He

---

[21] See Ia, q.12, a.2.

[22] The Council of Vienne condemned this error of the Beghards: "The soul does not need the light of glory in order to see God and to enjoy Him."

[23] See Ia, q.56, a.3; q.94, a.1; IIa IIae, q.5, a.1; *De veritate*, q.18, a.1.

[24] *De veritate. loc. cit.*

[25] Even in such extraordinary graces as intellectual visions of the Blessed Trinity, of which St. Teresa speaks, intuition remains negative, *per viam negationis*, as St. Thomas teaches, *De veritate*, q.10, a.11 ad 14um: ". . . de visione intellectuali, qua sancti divinam veritatem in contemplatione intuentur; non quidem sciendo de ea quid est sed magis quid non est." In an intellectual vision of the Blessed Trinity, a vision of angelic order or by means of infused ideas, the soul sees, especially in regard to the divine essence of the Father, Son, and Holy Ghost, what they are not, rather than what they are. This vision is very superior to theological speculation, but it does not take away faith; it does not give the intrinsic evidence of the mystery, evidence which is given only by the light of glory.

[26] *Op. cit.*, pp. 99, 108.

does not say,[27] as some authors claim he does, that it excludes the *species expressa* or *verbum mentis*, but that it is not obtained through the mirror of creatures exterior to the angels. The difference is considerable. St. Thomas says: "The angel knows God naturally, in so far as he is himself (by his angelic nature) a similitude of God; but he does not see the divine essence, for no created similitude can represent it. Moreover, this angelic knowledge is related rather to specular knowledge, for the nature of the angel is like a mirror reflecting the image of God."

If, as has been said,[28] the immediate intuition of God, essential to mystical contemplation, "is at one and the same time the natural gift of the angels and the supernatural gift of contemplative mystics," it would follow that mystical contemplation would be in an order immensely inferior to that of sanctifying grace and of the theological virtues. It would not be a participation in the divine nature and life, but only a participation in the angelic life; there is a great abyss between these two. And contemplation would not attain to more than the natural knowledge of God which the devil preserves, for the fallen angel retains the integrity of his natural knowledge.[29] On the contrary, it is absolutely certain that infused contemplation, like sanctifying grace or the grace of the virtues and of the gifts, is essentially supernatural (*quoad substantiam*), as well in the angels in the state of trial as in man. By this very fact, contemplation is infinitely superior to the natural knowledge of the greatest human geniuses, and also to the natural knowledge of the highest angel, and even of creatable angels.

Evidently this theory of mystical contemplation, which seems greatly to elevate it by making it an extraordinary, angelic thing, generally inaccessible to interior souls, lowers it exceedingly by identifying it with the natural knowledge

---

[27] See Ia, q.56, a.3.
[28] Farges, *loc. cit.*
[29] See Ia, q.64, a.1.

which the devil preserves.[30] This point of view springs from the confusion, which we have pointed out several times, between the essential *(quoad substantiam)* supernaturalness of the grace of the virtues and of the gifts, and the modal *(quoad modum)* supernaturalness of miracles, prophecy, and other extraordinary facts of the same class. The difference is considerable: the resurrection of a dead person supernaturally restores natural life, which is infinitely inferior to that of grace; the life restored is not essentially supernatural, but only so by the mode of its production *(quoad modum)*. Likewise, if the natural knowledge of the angels is communicated to man by infused ideas, it is supernatural for man by the manner of its production *(quoad modum)*, but not essentially so. Hence it remains infinitely inferior to the order of grace, and it could become increasingly perfect in its order

---

[30] The reader will not be astonished that, from this point of view, Bishop Farges declares that the unitive way branches in two different directions: the ordinary or active way, and the extraordinary or passive way *(op. cit.,* p. 18). To support this statement, he appeals to an isolated text from St. Teresa's writings, the meaning of which should be determined by comparison with many other very important texts commonly quoted in favor of the contrary thesis.

The principal reason, he tells us *(op. cit.,* p. 275), why, according to St. Teresa, many souls do not pass beyond quiet, is that God does not call them higher. . . . St. Teresa, on the contrary, expresses this opinion (fifth mansion, chap. 1): "There are many called, few chosen. . . . Let us beg the Lord to grant us His grace in order that we may not be frustrated by our own fault: let us ask Him to show the way and give us the strength to dig continually until we find this hidden treasure." Cf. St. Francis de Sales, *Treatise on the Love of God,* Bk. XII, chap. 11.

Bishop Farges also appeals (p. 127) to the authority of Father Vallgornera, O.P., but he seems to forget that this Thomist, faithful to his school, teaches, as do the Carmelite theologians, that all souls should aspire to infused contemplation and that it is ordinarily granted to the perfect. It is, therefore, not essentially extraordinary (by nature). Cf. Vallgornera, *Theol. myst. S. Thomae,* I, 428; likewise Philip of the Blessed Trinity, C.D., and Anthony of the Holy Ghost, C.D.

He recognizes elsewhere *(op. cit.,* pp. 243, 257) that the passive purifications, purgatory before death, are necessary to cleanse the soul from all its blemishes. When we add to this idea the fact that these passive purifications are, as St. John of the Cross says, a mystical state, must we not conclude that the mystical state normally leads to the full perfection of Christian life, to the perfect purification of the soul immutably united to God?

without ever attaining the dignity of infused faith by which we believe in the Trinity and in the incarnation.[31] Thus the sides of a polygon inscribed in a circle can be multiplied infinitely, and the polygon will never coincide with the circle, for no matter how small each side may be, it will never become a point.

The theory of the immediate perception of God is likewise contrary to the common teaching of the mystics. St. John of the Cross tells us that even in the spiritual marriage contemplation takes place in faith. For him, as well as for St. Thomas,[32] faith and immediate, positive perception are mutually exclusive: the act of vision cannot be an act of faith. Consequently we can admit here only an obscure, negative (*per viam negationis*) intuition. According to St. Thomas, this intuition shows us better and better what God is not, that He surpasses all conception; it is to this quasi-unknown God that infused love unites us.

All mystics tell us that they perceive, not God Himself, as He is, but the effect of His action on their souls especially in the sweetness of love which He causes them to experience. Speaking of what often happens to those who have the supernatural prayer of union or that of quiet, St. Teresa writes, as we have already observed: "The presence of God is frequently felt, particularly by those who have attained to the prayer of union and of quiet, when we seem, at the very commencement of our prayer, to find Him with whom we would converse, and when we seem to feel that He hears us by the effects and the spiritual impressions of great love and faith of which we are then conscious, as well as by the good resolutions, accompanied by sweetness, which we then make. This is a great grace from God; and let him to whom

---

[31] Thus our infused faith, which is exercised by acquired ideas, differs materially from the infused faith of the angels, which is exercised by infused ideas; but it does not differ from it formally by the formal motive, or by the infused light which is likewise supernatural.

[32] *Summa,* IIa IIae, q. 1, a. 4.

He has given it esteem it much, because it is a very high degree of prayer; but it is not vision. God is understood to be present there by the effects He works in the soul: that is the way His Majesty makes His presence felt." [33] We could quote many similar texts from the greatest masters of mysticism.[34] St. Thomas teaches the same doctrine in his explanation of the classic expression of Dionysius: "Not only learning but also experiencing divine things." "There is a twofold knowledge of God's goodness or will. One is speculative. . . . The other knowledge of God's will or goodness is affective or experimental, and thereby a man experiences in himself the taste of God's sweetness, and complacency in God's will, as Dionysius says of Hierotheos (*Div. nom.*, II), that he learns divine things through experience of them. It is in this way that we are told to prove God's will, and to taste His sweetness." [35] This is the way that we know God, not immediately as He is, but by the effects which He produces in us.

## ARTICLE V

*The Essential Relation of Infused Contemplation and of The Mystical Life with the Gifts of The Holy Ghost*

We have seen what infused contemplation does not essentially require. We must now see what constitutes it formally and from what principle it proceeds. By so doing, we shall

[33] *Life*, chap. 27.

[34] Cf. Saudreau, *État mystique* (2d ed., pp. 320–48), in which he shows that the texts invoked in favor of the immediate perception of God are incomplete and have not the meaning that some writers attribute to them.

[35] *Summa*, IIa IIae, q.97, a.2 ad 2um. In the Commentary on the *Divine Names* (chap. 2), St. Thomas thus explains this passage: "Not only learning but also experiencing divine things, that is, not only receiving the knowledge of divine things in the intellect but also by loving, united to Him by affection." Likewise *De veritate*, q.26, a.3 ad 18um. See farther on (p. 306) for other texts of St. Thomas and of John of St. Thomas.

explain the definition given at the beginning of the preceding article.

According to the common teaching of theologians, infused contemplation is, above reasoning and in the obscurity of faith, a simple and loving knowledge of God which cannot be obtained by our personal activity aided by grace; but, on the contrary, it requires a special, manifest inspiration and illumination of the Holy Ghost.[1] In other words, whereas the ascetial life is characterized by the predominance of the human mode of the Christian virtues, which we exercise at will, the mystical life has as its distinctive character the predominance of the superhuman or divine mode of the gifts of the Holy Ghost; that is, an infused knowledge and love that cannot be the fruit of our personal effort.[2] To understand this doctrine clearly, we must recall the rôle and the necessity of the gifts of the Holy Ghost in our supernatural life, and in particular that of the gift of wisdom, which theologians commonly consider the superior principle of infused contemplation. The best means of learning the traditional teaching on this point is to consult St. Thomas, who has been generally followed.

I. The gifts of the Holy Ghost. Are they specifically distinct from the acquired virtues and from the infused virtues?

We have explained (supra, chap. 3, art. 2) the specific distinction between the infused virtues and the acquired virtues by their formal object. It is of faith that over and above the

---

[1] This inspiration and illumination are quite manifest, if not for the person who receives them, at least for the experienced spiritual director to whom the soul reveals itself. We will explain this later on. The soul may, in fact, be in the mystical state without knowing it. This is the case with certain very pure and simple souls who have never heard of the passive state, but who are in it, as St. Teresa remarked on more than one occasion.

[2] St. Teresa says: "Here, indeed, learning would be very much to the purpose, in order to explain the general and particular helps of grace; for there are many who know nothing about them. Learning would serve to show how our Lord now will have the soul to see, as it were, with the naked eye, as men speak, this particular help of grace" (Life, chap. 14). This is a clear statement about the special inspiration to which the gifts of the Holy Ghost make us docile.

natural virtues, which are acquired and developed by the frequent repetition of the same acts, we have received with sanctifying grace the infused virtues of faith, hope, and charity.[3] As for the infused moral virtues, such as Christian prudence, justice, fortitude, and temperance, they differ from the corresponding acquired moral virtues because they have a superior rule—in other words, not only natural reason, but reason illumined by faith; they are inspired by much loftier views.[4] It is thus that Christian temperance implies a mortification which purely natural ethics would not know; it is founded on the revealed doctrines of original sin, of the gravity of our personal sins, of their results, of our elevation to a supernatural end, and of the imitation of Jesus crucified. What a distance there is between the temperance described by Aristotle and that of which St. Augustine speaks!

The gifts of the Holy Ghost are, moreover, superior to the infused moral virtues; although they are less elevated than the theological virtues, nevertheless they bring them, as we shall see, an added perfection.[5] "In order to differentiate the gifts from the virtues," says St. Thomas,[6] "we must be guided by the way in which Scripture expresses itself, for we find there that the term employed is 'spirit' rather than 'gift.' For thus it is written (Is. 11: 2, 3): 'The spirit . . . of wisdom and of understanding . . . shall rest upon him . . .'[7] From these words we are clearly given to understand that these seven are there set down as being in us by divine in-

---

[3] Council of Trent, Sess. VI, chap. 7.
[4] See Ia IIae, q.63, a.4.
[5] *Summa*, Ia IIae, q.68, a.8.
[6] *Ibid.*, a.1.
[7] In Is. 11: 2 f., we read: "And the spirit of the Lord shall rest upon him: the spirit of wisdom, and of understanding, the spirit of counsel, and of fortitude, the spirit of knowledge, and of the fear of the Lord." This text is applied to the announced Messias, and since Pentecost, also to the living members of the mystical body of our Lord. It is in this way that the fathers understood it. Cf. *Dict. de théol. cathol.*, art. "Dons du Saint-Esprit" by Father Gardeil, O.P.: "Fondement scripturaire de cette doctrine, et enseignement des Pères," col. 1728–81.

spiration. Inspiration denotes motion from without. For it must be noted that in man there is a twofold principle of movement, one within him (the reason), the other extrinsic to him (God), as stated above (q. 9, a. 4, 6), and also by the Philosopher in the chapter on Good Fortune (*Ethic. Eudem.,* VII).

"Now it is evident that whatever is moved must be proportionate to its mover: and the perfection of the mobile as such, consists in a disposition whereby it is disposed to be well moved by its mover. Hence the more exalted the mover, the more perfect must be the disposition whereby the mobile is made proportionate to its mover: thus we see that a disciple needs a more perfect disposition in order to receive a higher teaching from his master. Now it is manifest that human virtues perfect man according as it is natural for him to be moved by his reason [8] in his interior and exterior actions. Consequently, man needs yet higher perfections, whereby to be disposed to be moved by God. These perfections are called gifts, not only because they are infused by God, but also because by them man is disposed to become amenable to the divine inspiration,[9] according to Is. 50: 5: 'The Lord . . . hath opened my ear, and I do not resist; I have not gone back.' Even the Philospher says in the chapter on Good Fortune (*Ethic. Eudem., loc. cit.*) that for those who are moved by divine instinct, there is no need to take counsel according to human reason, but only to follow their inner promptings, since they are moved by a principle higher than human reason. This then is what some say, viz., that the gifts perfect man for acts which are higher than acts of virtue."

From this we see that the gifts of the Holy Ghost are not acts or actual movements or passing helps of grace, but rather

[8] We are concerned here with what happens in the supernatural order of reason illumined by faith; it is thus in particular that infused prudence directs the infused moral virtues.

[9] "Secundum ea homo disponitur, ut efficiatur prompte mobilis ab inspiratione divina."

permanent qualities or habits, conferred on the soul in view of certain supernatural operations.

Holy Scripture, in the classic text of Isaias,[10] represents them as existing in a stable manner in the just, and it is said of the Holy Ghost: "He shall abide with you, and shall be in you." [11] The Church in her liturgy considers the "sevenfold gift," *sacrum septenarium,* as constituting an organic whole with habitual or sanctifying grace, which is often called "the grace of the virtues and of the gifts." [12] St. Gregory the Great insists on this permanence, saying: "By the gifts, without which one cannot attain to life, the Holy Ghost dwells in a stable manner in the elect; while by prophecy, the gift of miracles, and other gratuitous graces, He does not fix His dwelling in those to whom He communicates Himself." [13]

St. Thomas defines them: "The gifts of the Holy Ghost are habits (or essentially supernatural, permanent qualities) whereby man is perfected to obey readily the Holy Ghost." [14] The word "obey," used by St. Thomas, does not express a pure passivity. As the moral virtues subject our appetitive faculties to the domination of reason and thus dispose them to act well, so the gifts render us docile to the Holy Ghost, in order to make us produce those excellent works known as beatitudes.[15] In this sense we can say of the gifts: "They confer at one and the same time pliability and energy, docility and strength, which render the soul more passive under the hand of God, and likewise more active in serving Him and in doing His work." [16]

---

10 Is. 11: 2.

11 John 14: 17.

12 "Whether sacramental grace confers anything in addition to the grace of the virtues and gifts" (IIIa, q.62, a.2).

13 *Moral.,* Bk. II, chap. 56.

14 *Summa,* Ia IIae, q.68, a.3; a.2 ad 1um; *III Sent.,* D. XXXIV, q.1, a.1.

15 "The beatitudes are none but perfect works and which, by reason of their perfection, are assigned to the gifts rather than to the virtues" (Ia IIae, q.70, a.2).

16 Bishop Gay, *De la vie et des vertus chrétiennes,* first treatise.

According to these principles, the great majority of theologians hold with St. Thomas that the gifts are really and specifically distinct from the infused virtues, as the principles which direct them are distinct: that is, the Holy Ghost and reason illumined by faith. We have here two regulating motions, two different rules, which constitute different formal motives. It is a fundamental principle that habits (*habitus*) are specified by their object and their formal motive, as sight is by color and light, and hearing by sound.[17] Virtue is a habit inclining us to follow the rule of right reason, whereby we lead a good life measured by the rule of reason.[18] The gifts are higher perfections which have divine inspiration as their rule.[19] A virtue and the corresponding gift (for example, fortitude and the gift of fortitude) have the same material, but they differ in the rule which serves as a measure for their acts, and also by their mode of acting; therefore their formal object is not the same. Reason, even illumined by faith and infused prudence, directs our acts according to a human mode; the Holy Ghost, according to a superhuman mode.[20]

[17] If we confuse the virtues and the gifts, we meet with serious difficulties. It would not be possible to explain why certain gifts, such as fear, are not among the number of the virtues, and why Christ possessed the seven gifts, as Isaias (11: 2) teaches us, without having certain infused virtues such as faith, hope, and penance, which suppose an imperfection.

[18] *Summa*, Ia IIae, q.68, a.1 ad 3um.

[19] "Since the gifts are above the human mode in their action, it is fitting that the operations of the gifts should be measured by a rule other than that of human virtue, which is the Divinity itself shared by man in his manner, so that he operates no longer in a human way after the manner of man, but as though he were made God by participation" (*ibid.*, and *III Sent.*, D. XXXIV, q.1, a.3).

[20] "The gifts surpass the ordinary perfection of the virtues, not as regards the kind of works (as the counsels surpass the commandments), but as regards the manner of working, in respect of man being moved by a higher principle" (Ia IIae, q.68, a.2 ad 1um). Likewise *III*, D. XXXIV, q.1, a.1: "The gifts are distinguished from the virtues in this that the virtues accomplish acts in a human manner, but the gifts in a superhuman manner." *III*, D. XXXV, q.2, a.3: "The gift transcends the virtues in this that it operates above the human manner."

This doctrine of St. Thomas in his *Commentary on the Sentences* does not differ, in spite of what has been said, from that of the *Summa*, as can be seen from the text (Ia IIae) quoted at the beginning of this note, and from that indicated in the following note. Moreover, it is clear that when (Ia IIae, q.68, a.1)

Likewise, while faith adheres simply to revealed truths, the gift of understanding makes us scrutinize their depths. The theologian points out what is of faith and answers the sophisms of heresy by collating texts from Scripture and from the councils according to a human method of procedure, which is often very complicated. Simple souls, on the contrary, under a special inspiration of the Holy Ghost answer in a different manner, at times with an astonishing and unanswerable perspicacity which causes the theologian to exclaim: "Mirabilis Deus in sanctis suis."

The same difference exists between prudence and the gift of counsel. When a grave decision is to be made, prudence, whether acquired or infused, must take counsel, examine all the circumstances and consequences of the act to be performed; it deliberates at length, without always reaching certitude, as to what is best to choose. On the contrary, if we have prayed with humility and trust, sometimes an inspiration of the gift of counsel instantly clarifies the whole problem.[21] In a difficult situation, where two duties in apparent opposition must be harmonized, prudence is, as it were, perplexed; it hesitates, for example, about what answer to give so as to avoid a lie and keep a secret. In certain cases, only an inspiration of the gift of counsel will enable us to find the proper reply without in any way failing in the truth, and without having recourse to mental restrictions of dubious morality.[22]

---

he distinguishes the virtues from the gifts by what moves them respectively, it is a question of the powers which direct and rule (the Holy Ghost and reason) and not of pure, efficient causes which would give a more or less strong impulse without direction and formal regulation. It is manifest that the Holy Ghost directs according to a superhuman mode. The doctrine of the *Summa* clearly maintains on this point what had already been written in the *Commentary on the Sentences*. Likewise *Qu. Disp. de caritate,* q. unic., a.2 ad 7um: "The gifts perfect the virtues by elevating them above the human manner."

21 *Summa*, IIa IIae, q.52, a.2 ad 1um.

22 St. Thomas says expressly: "Prudence or *eubulia*, whether acquired or infused, directs man in the research of counsel according to principles that the reason can grasp; hence prudence or *eubulia* makes man take good counsel

II. Are the gifts of the Holy Ghost necessary to salvation?

The necessity of the gifts of the Holy Ghost, as we have seen, springs from the imperfect mode of even lofty Christian virtues in our souls. Consequently the more the soul advances toward perfection, the more the gifts must intervene; so much so indeed that their superhuman mode must end by prevailing, in an order superior not only to the processes of casuistry, but also to those of asceticism and to methods of prayer. This is the very foundation of our doctrine.

Here, in imitation of St. Thomas, we must proceed with measure. Were one to neglect to examine for himself, when possible, what should be thought, said, and done, under the pretext of abandonment to Providence, he would be tempting God.[23] But we must take into account our insufficiency with regard to the supernatural end toward which we should tend.

St. Thomas teaches that the gifts of the Holy Ghost are necessary to salvation.[24] "Of all the gifts," he says, "wisdom seems to be the highest, and fear the lowest. Each of these is necessary to salvation: since of wisdom it is written (Wis. 7: 28): 'God loveth none but him that dwelleth with wisdom'; and of fear (Eccles. 1: 28): 'He that is without fear cannot be justified.'" Because our Lord knew the profound needs of our souls, He promised us the Holy Ghost, from whom we have received the sevenfold gift.

To explain this necessity of the gifts, St. Thomas makes use of a profound reason: "The gifts are perfections of man, whereby he is disposed so as to be amenable to the prompt-

---

either for himself or for another. Since, however, human reason is unable to grasp the singular and contingent things which may occur, the result is that the thoughts of mortal men are fearful, and our counsels uncertain (Wis. 9: 14). Hence in the research for counsel, man requires to be directed by God who comprehends all things: and this is done through the gift of counsel whereby man is directed as though counselled by God" (IIa IIae, q.52, a.1 ad 1um).

[23] "If man, instead of doing what he can, were to be content with awaiting God's assistance, he would seem to tempt God" (IIa IIae, q.53, a.4 ad 1um).

[24] *Summa*, Ia IIae, q.68, a.2.

ings of God. Wherefore in those matters where the prompting of reason is not sufficient, and there is need for the prompting of the Holy Ghost, there is, in consequence, need for a gift. Now man's reason is perfected by God in two ways: first, by its natural perfection, viz., by the natural light of reason (like the acquired virtue of wisdom); secondly, by a supernatural perfection, viz., by the theological virtues. And, though this latter perfection is greater than the former, yet the former is possessed by man in a more perfect manner than the latter: because man has the former in his full possession, whereas he possesses the latter imperfectly, since we love and know God imperfectly. Now it is evident that anything that has a nature or a form or a virtue perfectly, can of itself work according to them: not, however, excluding the operation of God, who works inwardly in every nature and in every will. On the other hand, that which has a nature or form or virtue imperfectly, cannot of itself work, unless it be moved by another. Thus the sun, which possesses light perfectly, can shine by itself; whereas the moon, which has the nature of light imperfectly, sheds only a borrowed light. Again a physician, who knows the medical art perfectly, can work by himself; but his pupil, who is not yet fully instructed, cannot work by himself, but needs to receive instructions from him.

"Accordingly, as to things subject to human reason, and subordinate to man's connatural end, man can do them through the judgment of his reason (with the ordinary help that Providence gives to secondary causes). If, however, even in these things man receive help in the shape of special promptings from God (*instinctum specialem*), this will be out of God's superabundant goodness (*hoc erit superabundantis bonitatis*): hence, according to the philosophers, not everyone that had the acquired moral virtues, had also the heroic or divine virtues. But in matters directed to the supernatural end (which absolutely surpasses the forces and exigences of our reasonable nature) to which man's reason moves him, according as it is, in a manner, and imperfectly, actuated by the theological virtues, the motion of reason does not suffice, unless it receives in addition the prompting or motion of the Holy Ghost, according to Rom. 8: 14, 17: 'Whosoever are led by the Spirit of God, they are the sons of God . . . and if sons, heirs also': and Ps. 142: 10: 'Thy good Spirit shall lead me into the right land'; because, to wit, none can receive the inheritance of that land of the blessed, except he be moved and led thither by the Holy Ghost." [25] In this sense, the gifts are necessary to salvation as habitual dispositions to receive divine inspirations, just as sails are necessary on a boat that it may be responsive to the winds.

This does not mean that, without the intervention of the gifts of the Holy Ghost, a Christian is never capable of a supernatural act. But, if by mortal sin he has lost these gifts together with charity, he can still, with an ordinary actual grace, make a supernatural act of faith; and rather often the just man also acts in a supernatural manner without a special inspiration of the Holy Ghost. But, as St. Thomas says, it is not in the power of reason, even when enlightened by faith and infused prudence, "to know all things or all possible things. Consequently it is unable to avoid folly (*stultitia*) and other like things. . . . God, however, to whose knowledge and power all things are subject, by His motion safeguards us from all folly, ignorance, dullness of mind, and hardness of heart, and the rest. Consequently the gifts of the Holy Ghost, which make us amenable to His promptings, are said to be given as remedies to these defects." [26] "By the theological and moral virtues, man is not so perfected in respect of his last end, as not to stand in continual need of being moved by the yet higher promptings of the Holy Ghost." [27]

---

[25] *Summa*, Ia IIae, q.68, a.2. Cf. Cajetan's commentary on this question 68, and also that of John of St. Thomas.

[26] *Ibid.*, ad 3um.

[27] *Ibid.*, a.2 ad 2um. Some theologians have wrongly interpreted this text of St. Thomas and thought he meant to say that man needs always to be moved

III. Necessity of an increasingly perfect docility to the interior Master.

This special assistance, of which we have spoken, is so much the more necessary since the soul, in advancing, should perform more perfect works, and since the Lord wishes to conduct us to a deeper and more loving knowledge of the supernatural mysteries.[28] The infused moral and theological virtues, even when they have reached a high degree, without a special help of the Holy Ghost still operate according to the human mode of the faculties in which they are received.[29]

Faith makes us know God in a way which is still too abstract, too exterior, *in speculo et in aenigmate,* by excessively narrow formulas that must be multiplied. We should like to be able to condense them into one that would bring us into close contact with the living God and that would express for us the Light of life which more and more He ought to be for us. Hope and charity, which are directed by faith, share in this imperfection of faith. These two virtues of the will lack vitality and keep too much of the human manner as long as they are directed only by reason illumined by faith.

No matter how circumspect Christian prudence, which

for each salutary act by a special inspiration of the Holy Ghost, even in acts which are called *remissi.* They confounded ordinary actual grace with the special inspiration which is in question here. St. Thomas did not write: "Quin indigeat semper moveri," but "Quin semper indigeat moveri." St. Thomas' expression means that man is not perfected to such a degree by the theological virtues that he never needs to be inspired by the interior Master, as one might say: "This student of medicine is not so well instructed that he never needs the assistance of his master for certain operations." It is quite certain that man can make a supernatural act of faith with an actual grace, without any assistance on the part of the gifts of the Holy Ghost. This is certainly the case with a soul which, being in the state of mortal sin, has lost together with charity the gifts of the Holy Ghost, and which, nevertheless, still rather frequently makes acts of supernatural faith. Cf. Gardeil, art. "Dons," in *Dict. théol.,* col. 1779; Father Frojet, O.P., *De l'habitation du Saint-Esprit dans les âmes justes,* Part IV, pp. 407–24, clearly expresses the true thought of St. Thomas on this point.

28 Rom. 8: 14. "For whosoever are led by the Spirit of God, they are the sons of God."

29 *Summa,* Ia IIae, q.68, a.2.

rules the other moral virtues, may be, though it is quite superior to purely natural prudence, which is described by the philosophers, it still frequently remains timid, uncertain in its foresight, and too cautious to respond to all the exigencies of divine love; just as our fortitude and patience do not suffice in certain trials, or our chastity in the face of some temptations.[30] Because our supernatural virtues must be adapted to the human mode of our faculties, they leave us in a state of inferiority with respect to the supernatural end toward which we should advance with greater eagerness.

With only the virtues, even though they are supernatural, man is like an apprentice who knows fairly well what he must do, but who has not the skill to do it in a suitable manner. Consequently the master who is teaching him must come from time to time, take his hand, and direct it so that the work may be presentable. Thus, as long as our prayer is only the fruit of an assiduous meditation, it remains too human to taste truly the word of God. In meditation we drink only of water which has flowed along the ground and is mixed with mud, as St. Teresa says. That we may drink from the fountain, the Holy Ghost must, like the master of the apprentice, directly intervene, take possession of our intellect and will, and communicate to them His manner of thinking and of loving; a divine manner which alone is worthy of God, who wishes to be known as a living truth and divinely loved. As we always remain apprentices toward God, the Holy Ghost must intervene habitually in our prayer and works that they may be perfect. That is why, unlike purely gratuitous graces (*gratis datae*) such as prophecy, the gifts, which make us amenable to divine inspirations as the virtues do to the directions of reason, should be permanent in us.[31] They are in our soul what sails are on a boat. Two means can be used

---

[30] St. Thomas, *III Sent.*, D. XXXIV, q.1, a.2.
[31] "Whether the gifts of the Holy Ghost are habits" (Ia IIae, q.68, a.3).

to move a small sailboat through the water: rowing, which is slow and laborious, and sailing. A soul can make progress and can advance by the exercise of the virtues; in this it is active; or by the inspiration of the Holy Ghost, who breathes where He wills and when He wills. Here the soul is docile, acting less than it is acted upon. "The gifts of the Holy Ghost perfect man . . . for he is so acted upon by the Holy Ghost, that he also acts himself in so far as he has a free will. Therefore he needs a habit." [32] From this we see that the soul approaches perfection only by a great docility to the Holy Ghost, in which the superhuman mode of the gifts must normally prevail so as more and more to remedy what is essentially imperfect in the human mode of the virtues. This is the function of the gifts.

IV. The special inspiration of the Holy Ghost and the progress of charity.

No one questions that St. Thomas' mystical theology is found especially in his teaching about the gifts of the Holy Ghost, their relation to charity and to infused contemplation. But some persons merely read rather hastily in the *Summa* (Ia IIae, q. 68) the articles devoted to the gifts of the Holy Ghost in general, and (IIa IIae, q. 8, 9, 45) the articles that relate to the gifts of understanding, knowledge, and wisdom, without considering sufficiently their connection with what is said (IIa IIae, q. 24, a. 9) about the three degrees of charity in beginners, the proficient, and the perfect, and without recalling what St. Thomas teaches (Ia IIae, q. 111, a. 2) about operating grace, to which he attaches the special inspiration of the Holy Ghost. As a result, they fail to see clearly what is original and very deep in the Thomistic doctrine of the gifts.

This point is briefly and lucidly set forth in the most thorough treatment that has been written on the subject of

[32] *Ibid.*, ad 2um.

the gifts. We refer to the article by Father Gardeil, O.P., in the *Dictionnaire de théologie catholique*.[33] In the historical part of the article, after showing the sources for the doctrine of the gifts in Scripture and in the Greek and Latin fathers, and after mentioning the treatises of the first Scholastic theologians, Father Gardeil analyzes what has been written on the gifts by the founders of systematized theology—Alexander of Hales, St. Bonaventure, St. Albert the Great, and St. Thomas Aquinas. It is interesting to see how these four great Scholastics reacted against William of Auxerre and William of Paris, who denied the specific character of the gifts and reduced them to the virtues, thus preparing the ground for the minimist doctrine of the decadent nominalists of the fourteenth century. Father Gardeil says: [34] "These four great theologians fundamentally consecrated the ancient doctrine, which distinguished the gifts from the virtues, by considering them as *primi motus in corde* . . . but, instead of identifying the gifts and actual graces, they saw in the gifts, at least St. Thomas did, subjective dispositions to receive the most sublime actual graces. With an incomparable and magnificent synthesis, St. Thomas attached this point of doctrine to what, both in the philosophy of Aristotle and in his own theology, is most elevated and most profoundly true on the pre-eminence of the divine action. He thus brought this point of doctrine back to absolutely first principles, which, in philosophy as well as theology, govern questions about the divine action as such; that is, developing it in conformity with the inner law of the divine being. By this systematization, he assured it the indestructible solidity of every doctrine which is attached to first principles, evident in themselves or primarily revealed." [35]

[33] Vol. IV, col. 1728–81.

[34] *Loc. cit.*, col. 1776.

[35] Cf. Gardeil, *Le donné révélé et la théologie*, 1910: A comparison of the theological systems (pp. 266–86). On the question which occupies our attention, see also the introduction of the excellent work of the same author, *Les dons du Saint-Esprit dans les Saints Dominicains*.

It is our wish: (1) to show how, according to St. Thomas, the special inspiration of the Holy Ghost, to which the gifts render us docile, differs from the common, actual grace necessary to the exercise of the infused virtues; (2) to follow the growing elevation of this special inspiration, in beginners, the proficient, and the perfect, by considering especially the gifts of wisdom, understanding, and knowledge.

## THE SPECIAL INSPIRATION OF THE HOLY GHOST AND COMMON, ACTUAL GRACE

For a clear understanding of this teaching, as Father del Prado[36] remarks, we must distinguish, as St. Thomas does, the different ways in which God moves our intellect and our will, whether in the natural or in the supernatural order. St. Thomas distinguishes between three principle modes of the divine motion in the order of nature, and three others proportionately similar in that of grace. They can be expressed in the following division which we will explain:

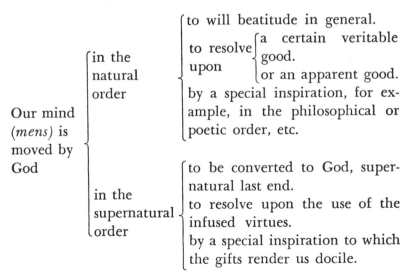

Our mind (*mens*) is moved by God

in the natural order
- to will beatitude in general.
- to resolve upon
  - a certain veritable good.
  - or an apparent good.
- by a special inspiration, for example, in the philosophical or poetic order, etc.

in the supernatural order
- to be converted to God, supernatural last end.
- to resolve upon the use of the infused virtues.
- by a special inspiration to which the gifts render us docile.

36 *De gratia et libero arbitrio,* 1907, II, 201, 225, 247.

The first mode of motion is before human deliberation,[37] the second is after or with it, the third is above it, and that in the order of nature as well as in that of grace. St. Thomas has enumerated them in Ia IIae, q. 9, a. 6 ad 3um; q. 68, a. 2, 3; q. 109, a. 1, 2, 6, 9; q. 111, a. 2; *De veritate*, q. 24, a. 15. It will suffice to translate the first of these texts which—many seem to ignore the fact—is explained by those that follow, as we shall see: "God moves man's will, as the Universal Mover, to the universal object of the will, which is good. And, without this universal motion, man cannot will anything. But man determines himself by his reason, to will this or that, which is true or apparent good. Nevertheless, sometimes God moves some specially to the willing of something determinate, which is good; as in the case of those whom He moves by grace, as we shall see later on (q. 109, a. 2; q. 109, a. 6; q. 111, a. 2)." [38]

By the first mode of divine motion in the natural order, our will is therefore moved, as to its exercise, to will good in general or beatitude, and this act, by which each one of us wishes to be happy or desires happiness, is without doubt a vital act determined upon by the will; but it is not free, in this sense that we cannot hate beatitude or prefer anything else to it.[39] We always aspire to it, and this aspiration bears thus confusedly on God, although we do not always judge that our true beatitude is to be found in Him.[40] Every man

[37] There is, properly speaking, no deliberation and election on the ultimate end; cf. Ia IIae, q.13, a.3; IIa IIae, q.24, a.1 ad 3um. We will explain this farther on.

[38] *Summa*, Ia IIae, q.9, a.6 ad 3um. See, on this text and its relation with the others which we have quoted, Del Prado, *De gratia et libero arbitrio*, I, 236; II, 228, 266.

[39] *Ibid.*, q.10, a.1, 2.

[40] "To know that God exists in a general and indefinite way is implanted in us by nature, inasmuch as God is man's beatitude. For man naturally desires happiness, and what is naturally desired by man must naturally be known to him. This, however, is not to know absolutely that God exists; as to know that someone is approaching is not the same as to know that Peter is approaching,

naturally desires to be happy, "and the source of all good consists in placing happiness where it should be, and the source of all evil lies in misplacing it." [41] This is why our Lord began His preaching with the evangelical beatitudes, which tell us, as opposed to the maxims of the world, where true happiness is to be found.

In this first act of the will, in this natural desire for happiness, there can be no sin, if the act is considered in itself independently of the acts that may follow it. We do not say that the will moves itself to this first act; strictly speaking, it moves itself to an act only in virtue of an anterior act. Thus it moves itself to choose the means in virtue of the act by which it wishes the end.[42] The question here concerns the first act in the strict sense; hence in this case the will cannot sin; it is moved by God without moving itself, although it produces this act vitally.[43]

The second mode of divine motion is that in virtue of which our free will, still in the natural order, determines upon a true good or an apparent good. This movement of our will is not only vital but free, and to produce it the will moves itself in virtue of an anterior act; hence it can sin in this case.[44] But, since God cannot by His motion be equally the cause of evil and of good, we must say that the motion by which He moves the free will to determine upon a good natural act, is not the same as that by which He is the cause

---

even though it is Peter who is approaching; for many there are who imagine that man's perfect good (which is happiness) consists in riches, and others in pleasures, and others in something else" (Ia, q.2, a.1 ad 1um).

41 Bossuet, *Méditations sur l'Évangile,* first meditation.

42 *Summa,* Ia IIae, q.9, a.3: "The intellect, through its knowledge of the principle, reduces itself from potentiality to act, as to its knowledge of the conclusions; and thus it moves itself. And, in like manner, the will, through its volition of the end, moves itself to will the means." *Ibid.,* ad 1um and Ia, q.63, a.5.

43 *Summa.,* Ia IIae, q.9, a.6, third objection and reply.

44 *Summa,* Ia, q.63, a.1 ad 4um; a.5; a.6; Ia IIae, q.79, a.1, 2.

of the physical act of sin and not of its malice.[45] The good act comes entirely from God, as from its first cause, and entirely from us as from its second cause: "What hast thou that thou hast not received?" [46] On the contrary, the evil act, considered with respect to what is disordered and evil in it, does not come from God, but only from our defectible and evilly disposed free will.[47] Just so, the gait of a lame person, in so far as the action is concerned, springs from his vital energy, but its defectiveness comes only from the malformation of his leg.[48] As opposed to the divine motion which moves to good, the motion required for the physical act of sin is accompanied by the divine permission of the disorder contained in the sin. God allows this disorder to occur for very lofty reasons of which He is the judge, but He can in no way be its cause. Indefectible principle of all good and of all order, He can no more cause the evil involved in the act of sin than the eye, seeing the color of a fruit, can perceive its taste. Moral evil is no more the object of omnipotence than sounds are the object of sight. Without being obliged thereto, God often remedies the weaknesses of our free will; He does not always do it. Therein lies a mystery.

The third mode of divine motion in the natural order is mentioned by St. Thomas [49] when he quotes the *Eudemian*

[45] Otherwise it would follow that God by His motion is no more the cause of the good act than of the sin, which would be contrary to the definition of the Council of Trent (Sess. VI, canon 6): "Si quis dixerit mala opera ita ut bona Deum operari non permissive solum, sed proprie et per se, anathema sit." If the divine share were only simultaneous or if it were an indifferent first impulse, God by this participation would no longer be the cause of the good act any more than of the sin. The reason why He would not be the cause of the sin, is that His participation would be only simultaneous and indifferent; for the same reason He would not, strictly speaking, be the cause of the good act. Cf. Ia IIae, q.79, a.2, and the Thomists on this article.

[46] See I Cor. 4: 7. As St. Thomas shows, in a commentary on this Epistle, all good things come from God, even the good determination of our free will, in so far as it is distinguished from the evil. Cf. Ia, q.23, a.5; Ia IIae, q.109, a.2.

[47] *Summa,* Ia IIae, q.79, a.1, 2.

[48] *Ibid.*

[49] "Even the Philosopher says in the chapter on Good Fortune (*Ethic. Eudem.,* loc. cit.*) that for those who are moved by divine instinct, there is no need to

*Ethics* (Bk. VII, chap. 14). In this work, which is attributed to Aristotle but was composed under his influence by one of his platonizing disciples, the author says: "Someone will ask, perhaps, whether a person's good fortune makes him desire what he should when he should. . . . Without reflecting, deliberating, or taking counsel, it happens that he thinks and wills what is most suitable. . . . To what is this due, if not to good fortune? What is good fortune itself and how can it give such happy inspirations? This is equivalent to asking what is the superior principle of the movements of the soul. Now, it is manifest that God, who is the principle of the universe, is also the principle of the soul. All things are moved by Him who is present in us. The principle of reason is not reason but something superior. What is superior to reason and intelligence except God? . . . This is why the ancients used to say: 'Happy are they who without deliberating are led to act well.' This does not come from their own will, but from a principle present in them which is superior to their intellect and to their will. . . . Under a divine inspiration, some even foresee the future."

In the *Nicomachian Ethics*, Bk. VII, chap. 1, Aristotle speaks of heroes, such as Hector, who "because of the excellence of their courage are called divine . . . , for there is something superior to human virtue in them" or to human science. Thus it was customary to say "the divine Plato," because of the superior inspiration which often animated his discourse. This inspiration is in the natural order and takes different forms, philosophical, poetical, musical, and strategic. These are the various forms of genius.

St. Thomas clearly states that this special inspiration is not at all necessary to man for the attainment of his natural

---

take counsel according to human reason, but only to follow their inner promptings, since they are moved by a principle higher than human reason. This then is what some say, viz., that the gifts perfect man for acts which are higher than acts of virtue" (*ibid.*, q.68, a.1).

last end. But he maintains that it is otherwise in the order of grace, where the gifts of the Holy Ghost and the corresponding inspirations are necessary to salvation.[50]

These three modes of divine motion, which we have defined, are transposed in the order of grace; in this order the three are normal.

1) At the moment when a sinner is justified, God as the Author of grace moves the sinner's free will to be converted to his supernatural last end. Under this divine motion and by it the sinner is made just or is justified, and begins to act no longer merely in view of happiness naturally desired, but for God supernaturally loved above all things. This supernatural motion first of all prepares the sinner to receive sanctifying grace, and justifies him through the infusion of this grace and of charity by moving him to a free act of faith, charity, and repentance.[51] In this case the free will does not, strictly speaking, move itself to this act of living faith and charity; it is moved thereto by operating grace.[52] In this act there cannot be

[50] "Accordingly, as to things subject to human reason, and subordinate to man's connatural end, man can do them through the judgment of his reason. If, however, even in these things man receive help in the shape of special promptings from God, this will be out of God's superabundant goodness: hence according to philosophers, not everyone that had the acquired moral virtues, had also the heroic or divine virtues. But in matters directed to the supernatural end to which man's reason moves him, according as it is, in a manner, and imperfectly, actuated by the theological virtues, the motion of reason does not suffice, unless it receives in addition the prompting or motion of the Holy Ghost, according to Rom. 8: 14: 'Whosoever are led by the Spirit of God, they are the sons of God'" (Ia IIae, q.68, a.2).

[51] *Summa*, Ia IIae, q.113, a.1–3, 4 ad 1um; a.5–8. Cf. Del Prado, *De gratia et libero arbitrio*, II, 240.

[52] *Summa*, Ia IIae, q.111, a.2: "First, there is the interior act of the will, and with regard to this act the will is a thing moved, and God is the mover; and especially when the will, which hitherto willed evil, begins to will good. Hence, inasmuch as God moves the human mind to this act, we speak of operating grace. But there is another, exterior act; and since it is commanded by the will, as was shown above (q.17, a.9), the operation of this act is attributed to the will. And because God assists us in this act, both by strengthening our will interiorly so as to attain to the act, and by granting outwardly the capability of operating, it is with respect to this that we speak of co-operating grace." In the same article (in reply to the second objection), St. Thomas shows how under operating grace, although the will does not move itself by virtue of an anterior act, it

sin; on the contrary, there is hatred of sin. This act is freely produced under the impulse of efficacious grace.[53] Although entirely free, this supernatural movement of the will resembles the first natural movement by which we wish happiness. Strictly speaking, man cannot move himself; that would suppose an efficacious anterior act of the same order. This anterior act does not exist, since the question here concerns the first efficacious act of love of the supernatural end.[54] This act is not preceded by personal merit; rather it opens the way of merit. It is, as it were, the threshold of the order of grace, or the first step in the execution of divine predestination.

2) The second mode of motion in this order is that by which God moves a just man to act well supernaturally by using the infused virtues as he ought. In this movement of the free will, the will is moved and moves itself by virtue of an anterior supernatural act. Here there is deliberation, properly so called, regarding the means in view of the end, and a human manner of acting under the direction of reason enlightened by faith.[55] Moreover, this grace is called co-operating

---

nevertheless freely consents to be moved: "God does not justify us without ourselves, because while we are being justified we consent to God's justification (*justitiae*) by a movement of our free will. Nevertheless, this movement is not the cause of grace, but the effect; hence the whole operation pertains to grace."

[53] "Hence if God intends, while moving, that the one whose heart He moves should attain to grace, he will infallibly attain to it" (*ibid.*, q.113, a.5; q.112, a.3).

[54] *Summa*, IIa IIae, q.24, a.1 ad 3um. Cf. Del Prado, *op. cit.*, II, 220. "Hic motus voluntatis (sub gratia operante in instanti justificationis) quamvis liberrimus, est etiam ad instar motus naturalis per modum simplicis volitionis; et homo non valet per rationem se primo determinare ad hujusmodi velle, quod excedit omnem naturalem facultatem, tam rationis, quam voluntatis. . . . Est fundamentum omnium sanctarum electionum in ordine gratiae." Cf. *ibid.*, p. 223, and I, 226–28, 236, where the author shows that on this point St. Thomas is followed more faithfully by Lemos than by Didacus Alvarez, Gonet, and Goudin, who reduce operating grace to a simple exciting grace which does not go as far as consent.

[55] Thus by infused prudence a man deliberates that he may act as is proper according to the virtues of religion, justice, fortitude, and temperance; and, when necessary, even to make acts of faith, hope, and charity. Prudence thus rules *per accidens* the acts of the theological virtues, although it does not measure them. Cf. Billuart's commentary on IIa IIae, q.81, a.5.

grace.[56] When this grace is efficacious, free will can still resist if it wishes, but it never wills to do so. In fact it cannot happen that sin is produced in the very use of grace, when man is moved by efficacious actual grace.[57] Thus he who is seated can indeed rise, but he cannot at one and the same time be seated and standing. Liberty is not destroyed because God, who is infinitely powerful and closer to us than we are to ourselves, moves our will according to its natural inclinations freely to will one thing or another.[58]

3) Lastly, the third mode of the divine motion in the order of grace is that by which God especially moves the free will of a spiritual man, who is disposed to the divine inspiration by the gifts of the Holy Ghost. Here the just soul is immediately directed, not by reason enlightened by faith, but by the Holy Ghost Himself in a superhuman manner.[59] This motion is not only given for the exercise of the act, but for its direction and specification; consequently it is called illumination and inspiration.[60] It is an eminent mode of operating grace which thus leads to the highest acts of the virtues and of the gifts:

[56] "But in that effect in which our mind both moves and is moved, the operation is not only attributed to God, but also to the soul; and it is with reference to this that we speak of co-operating grace" (Ia IIae, q.111, a.2). The will already willing the supernatural last end moves itself, under the impulse of co-operating grace, to will the means ordained to this end. Actual grace is necessary for every act of infused virtue. Cf. Ia IIae, q.109, a.9, and Hugon, *De gratia*, pp. 281–83.

[57] "If God moves the will to anything, it is incompossible with this supposition, that the will be not moved thereto. But it is not impossible simply. Consequently, it does not follow that the will is moved by God necessarily" (Ia IIae, q.10, a.4 ad 3um).

[58] "The divine will extends not only to the doing of something by the thing which He moves, but also to its being done in a way which is fitting to the nature of that thing. And therefore it would be more repugnant to the divine motion for the will to be moved of necessity, which is not fitting to its nature, than for it to be moved freely, which is becoming to its nature" (*ibid.*, ad 1um). Likewise Ia, q.19, a.8; q.83, a.1 ad 3um; *De malo*, q.6, a.1 ad 3um: "Deus movet quidem voluntatem immutabiliter propter efficaciam virtutis moventis, quae deficere non potest, sed propter naturam voluntatis nostrae, quae indifferenter se habet ad diversa, non inducitur necessitas, sed manet libertas" (*ibid.*, ad 1um).

[59] See Ia IIae, q.68, a.1–3.

[60] *Ibid.*

faith, illumined by the gift of understanding, becomes much more penetrating and contemplative; hope, enlightened by the gift of knowledge as to the vanity of all that is transitory, becomes perfect confidence and filial abandonment to Providence; and the illuminations of the gift of wisdom invite charity to the intimacy of the divine union. As the bee or the carrier pigeon, directed by instinct, acts with a wonderful certainty revealing the Intelligence which directs them, just so, says St. Thomas, "the spiritual man is inclined to act, not principally through the movement of his own will, but by the instinct of the Holy Ghost, according to the words of Isaias (59: 19): 'When he shall come as a violent stream, which the Spirit of the Lord driveth on.' And in St. Luke we find: 'Jesus . . . was led by the Spirit into the desert.' [61] It does not follow that the spiritual man does not operate by his will and his free will, but it is the Holy Ghost who causes this movement of the will and of the free will in him, as St. Paul says: 'For it is God who worketh in you both to will and to accomplish.' " [62] These words of St. Thomas are the best commentary on what he has written about operating grace.[63] Again he says: "The sons of God are led by the Holy Ghost in order that they may pass through this life which is full of temptations (Job 7: 1) and gain the victory by the grace of Christ." [64]

Although the illumination of the Holy Ghost dispenses us from deliberating, nevertheless the act remains free and meritorious, for we consent to be moved in this way, as a good student wills to profit from the lesson of his teacher and as an obedient man is perfectly and freely docile to the order given him. This third mode of divine motion thus

[61] Luke 4: 1.
[62] Phil. 2: 13: St. Thomas, *In Ep. ad Rom.*, 8: 14: "For whosoever are led by the spirit of God, they are the sons of God." Likewise, *In Comm. in Cantic.*, chap. 1.
[63] See Ia IIae, q. 111, a. 2.
[64] *In Matth.*, 4: 1: "Then Jesus was led by the Spirit into the desert."

safeguards liberty and harmonizes with the infallibility of the divine foreknowledge and of the divine decree: "The Holy Ghost . . . does unfailingly whatever He wills to do. Hence it is impossible for these two things to be true at the same time—that the Holy Ghost should will to move a certain man to an act of charity, and that this man, by sinning, should lose charity." [65]

Evidently these three modes of motion, in the natural order and also in that of grace, are distinct, according as they are before human deliberation,[66] after it (or with it), or above it.[67] But the third of these modes is rarely found in the natural order, in geniuses or heroes, whereas in the order of grace it is normal, for reason, even enlightened by faith, acts in so human a manner as not to suffice to direct us toward our supernatural last end.[68]

This doctrine of St. Thomas, confirming what he teaches on "the virtues of the purified soul," [69] is reiterated exactly in the writings of St. John of the Cross [70] where he speaks of these purified souls: "Thus ordinarily the first movements

[65] See IIa IIae, q.24, a.11.

[66] We do not actually deliberate for the purpose of desiring happiness, and if we do so to place our last end in God and not in a creature (Ia IIae, q.89, a.6), it is not deliberation, properly speaking, which bears on the means (cf. Ia IIae, q.13, a.3, and IIa IIae, q.24, a.1 ad 3um): "Charity, whose object is the last end, should be described as residing in the will rather than in the free will."

[67] See Ia IIae, q.9, a.6 ad 3um. This is the explanation of that famous ad 3um which has been the object of so many controversies. Cf. Del Prado, *De gratia et libero arbitrio*, I, 236; II, 228, 256.

[68] See Ia IIae, q.68, a.2 ad 3um: "Human reason as perfected in its natural perfection, or as perfected by the theological virtues, . . . does not know all things, nor all possible things. Consequently it is unable to avoid folly and other like things . . . ignorance, dullness of mind, and hardness of heart."

[69] "There are the virtues of those who have already attained to the divine similitude: these are called the perfect virtues. Thus prudence sees nought else but the things of God; temperance knows no earthly desires; fortitude has no knowledge of passion; and justice, by imitating the divine mind, is united thereto by an everlasting covenant. Such are the virtues attributed to the blessed, or in this life, to some who are at the summit of perfection" (Ia IIae, q.61, a.5).

[70] *The Ascent of Mount Carmel*, Bk. III, chap. 1.

of the powers in such souls are, as it were, divine. This is not to be wondered at since these powers are, in a fashion, transformed into the divine Being.[71] . . . God moves specially the powers of these souls . . . ; consequently, their works and prayers are always efficacious. Such were those of the glorious Mother of God, who from the beginning of her life, was raised to this high degree of union. There was never in her soul the impress of any created form whatsoever, capable of distracting her from God, for she was always docile to the motion of the Holy Ghost." [72]

Therefore every just man has, together with grace and the infused virtues, the seven gifts of the Holy Ghost, which are related to charity, perfect the different virtues, and with them constitute a perfect supernatural organism ready to move deliberately and also to be moved by the Holy Ghost in a manner beyond all human consideration. This is why habitual or sanctifying grace is called "the grace of the virtues and of the gifts," from the name of the infused *habitus* which spring from it, just as the faculties have their origin in the essence of the soul.[73]

This supernatural organism, according to the teaching of St. Augustine and St. Thomas, we illustrate by the synopsis on the next page, where we note the correspondence of the virtues, the gifts, and the beatitudes indicated by these two great doctors.

In this summary, in which we have brought together the teaching of Scripture and of tradition on this subject, the

---

[71] This transformation is the effect of a high degree of grace; since grace, being a participation of the divine nature, deifies us in a way. Cf. Ia IIae, q.112, a.1: "For it is as necessary that God alone should deify . . . as it is impossible that anything save fire should enkindle."

[72] St. Thomas speaks in a like manner of the Blessed Virgin's holiness (IIIa, q.27, a.4).

[73] "The grace of the virtues and gifts perfects the essence and powers of the soul sufficiently as regards ordinary conduct: but as regards certain special effects which are necessary in a Christian life, sacramental grace is needed" (IIIa, q.62, a.2 ad 1um).

Table: The grace of the virtues and of the gifts

| Virtues | Gifts | Beatitudes | Fruits of the Holy Ghost (Gal.5: 22–23) |
|---|---|---|---|
| charity | wisdom | peacemakers | charity / peace / joy / patience / benignity |
| faith | understanding | pure of heart | |
| hope | knowledge | those who weep | |
| prudence / justice | counsel | the merciful | goodness / longanimity / faith |
| (religion) | piety | the meek | |
| fortitude | fortitude | those who hunger after justice | modesty / continency / chastity |
| temperance | fear | the poor in spirit | |

theological virtues bearing directly on the end: charity, faith, hope

moral virtues bearing directly on the means: prudence, justice, (religion), fortitude, temperance

The grace of the virtues and of the gifts

virtues are set down according to the order of their hierarchy, and the corresponding gifts in like manner.[74] The gift of knowledge is placed opposite hope, inasmuch as it acquaints us with the vanity of created things and human help,[75] and thus leads us to desire the possession of God and to hope in Him. The correspondence of the beatitudes is more clearly seen if we recall the reward promised to each one.[76] The last one ("Blessed are they who suffer persecution") is not indicated, even though it is the most perfect, because it contains all the others in the midst of the greatest difficulties.[77]

The order of the gifts of the Holy Ghost is clearly seen from the outline of what St. Thomas says of them,[78] as appears in the synopsis on the next page.

From this outline we see that the gifts of the intellect, which direct the others, are superior to them.[79] They perfect the intellect in its first two operations: simple apprehension and penetration of the truth, and judgment. There is no question of the third, reasoning or discourse, because the acts dependent on the gifts are not discursive, and are superior to the human mode of reasoning. The gift of wisdom is superior to that of understanding, for wisdom judges first principles themselves by the highest Cause.[80] Here we are concerned with judgment, not only according to the perfect use of speculative reason, as in acquired wisdom, but by connaturality or sym-

---

74 This enumeration of the gifts corresponds to that made by Isaias (11: 2) except for the gifts of counsel and of fortitude, which, because of their difficult matter, are placed by Isaias before those of knowledge and of piety, though they are *simpliciter* inferior to them. Cf. Ia IIae, q.68, a.7.

75 *Summa*, IIa IIae, q.9, a.4.

76 See Ia IIae, q.69, a.3 ad 3um, and IIa IIae, q.8, a.7; q.9, a.4; q.45, a.6; q.19, a.12; q.121, a.2; q.139, a.2.

77 See Ia IIae, q.69, a.3 ad 5um. On the fruits of the Holy Ghost, cf. Ia IIae, q.70, where St. Thomas shows clearly that they proceed from the Holy Ghost, according as He disposes our souls in regard to God, to our neighbor, and to inferior things.

78 *Ibid.*, q.68, a.4; IIa IIae, q.8, a.6.

79 *Summa*, Ia IIae, q.68, a.7.

80 *Ibid.*, q.66, a.5. In the preceding outline, to simplify the arrangement wisdom was placed after understanding. It should, however, precede it.

Gifts     Virtues

The gifts

perfect

the under-
standing
enlightened
by faith

⎰ for the penetra-
⎱ tion of truth ........... understanding .. faith
  to judge ⎰ divine things ... wisdom ...... charity  ⎱ theological
         ⎨ created things .. knowledge ....hope
         ⎩ our actions ....counsel .......prudence

the will
and the
sensitive
appetites

⎰ relative to the wor-
⎱ ship due to God ........piety .........(religion)
  against the fear
  of danger ..............fortitude ......fortitude  ⎱ moral
  against disorderly                justice
  concupiscences ...........fear ...........temperance

pathy with divine things; a connaturality founded on charity, or the supernatural love of God.[81]

## GROWING ELEVATION OF THE SPECIAL INSPIRATION OF THE HOLY GHOST IN BEGINNERS, PROFICIENTS, AND THE PERFECT

All the gifts are related to charity,[82] and as infused *habitus* they grow with charity, which ought always to increase until death.[83] Consequently, as we distinguish three degrees of charity (that of beginners, of proficients, and of the perfect),[84] we make the same distinction in regard to the gifts of the Holy Ghost. This point has been especially developed by Dionysius the Carthusian in his treatise on the gifts,[85] where he shows that their first degree corresponds to strict obligation, the second to the practice of the counsels, and the third to heroic acts. We will briefly indicate these three degrees: first, in the gift of knowledge and in the gifts subordinated to it; then, in the more elevated gifts of understanding and wisdom.

The gift of knowledge makes us judge created things supernaturally, either by showing us their nothingness,[86] or by disclosing to us the divine symbolism hidden in them. In the first degree, it makes us recognize the fact that in themselves creatures are nothing and that we should not be attached to them as to our last end, but should use them solely as a means to bring us to God. In the second degree, it leads us to use creatures with moderation and with interior detachment; at

---

[81] "Wisdom denotes a certain rectitude of judgment according to the eternal law. Now, rectitude of judgment is twofold: first, on account of perfect use of reason, secondly, on account of a certain connaturality with the matter about which one has to judge . . . thus, Dionysius says (*Div. Nom.*, ii) that Hierotheus is perfect in divine things, for he not only learns, but is patient of, divine things" (IIa IIae, q.45, a.2).

[82] *Summa*, Ia IIae, q.68, a.5.

[83] *Summa*, IIa IIae, q.184, a.3.

[84] *Ibid.*, q.24, a.9; q.183, a.4.

[85] *Opera omnia*, 1908, XXXV, 157–260: *De donis Spiritus Sancti.*

[86] *Summa*, IIa IIae, q.9, a.2, 4. This gift has an important place in the passive night of the senses; from it proceeds the holy sadness of which Christ speaks in the beatitude of tears.

the same time, by the spectacle of nature, it lifts us to God.[87] In the third degree, it bestows the spirit of renunciation, carried even to the heroic practice of the counsels. It makes us see the value of humiliations and sufferings, which render us like Christ crucified and which associate us with the great mystery of the redemption. This knowledge is no longer superficial and a simple remembrance of pious reading, but a profound conviction and true participation in the divine knowledge of created things.[88] It consists particularly in the knowledge of the gravity of sin, and has as its fruit the tears of contrition. Under the direction of the gift of knowledge, the gifts of counsel, fear, piety, and fortitude are exercised.

While the gift of knowledge directs us to a general point of view (detachment from created things), that of counsel, perfecting prudence, shows us in particular the best means of attaining the end. Where prudence would hesitate, it shows us what to do or to avoid, what to say or to suppress, and what to undertake or to abandon.[89] In the first degree, it directs us in matters of strict obligation; in the second, it inclines us to the generous practice of the evangelical counsels; and in the third, it makes us undertake holy works with heroic perfection.[90] It corresponds to the beatitude of the merciful, for it counsels the works of mercy. Only the merciful really know how to give afflicted souls good advice that will encourage them.[91]

Under the direction of the gift of knowledge, the gift of fear strengthens temperance and chastity by making us avoid,

---

[87] By this gift St. Francis of Assisi trod earthly things under foot and received such a penetrating intuition of the symbolism of nature that he called all creatures his brothers and sisters, and through them was lifted to God.

[88] On these three degrees of the gift of knowledge, cf. Dionysius the Carthusian, *op. cit.*, tr. 3, a.25.

[89] *Summa*, IIa IIae, q.52, a.1, 2. It makes us more surely avoid haste, rashness, inconsiderateness, negligence, and inconstancy. Cf. IIa IIae, q.53–55.

[90] Cf. Dionysius the Carthusian, *op. cit.*, tr. 3, a.7.

[91] *Summa*, IIa IIae, q.52, a.4.

in the sight of God, the mistakes that our corrupted nature is prone to.[92] It corresponds to hope by leading us to a filial respect toward God.[93] In the first degree, it inspires horror of sin and arms us against temptation.[94] In the second, it bestows deeper filial respect for the divine Majesty, preserves us from irreverence to holy things, and also from presumption. In the third, it leads to the practice of perfect renunciation and of the mortification which St. Paul describes in the following words: "Always bearing about in our body the mortification of Jesus, that the life also of Jesus may be made manifest in our body." [95] Thus we can see how this fear, which has for its fruit the beatitude of the poor in spirit, is "the beginning of wisdom," [96] of a very lofty wisdom.

This holy fear, however, should be accompanied by the gift of piety, which fills us with a filial affection for God our Father and makes us accomplish with our whole heart and with religious eagerness all that has to do with divine worship. This gift makes us cry: "Abba (Father)," as St. Paul says.[97] It corresponds to the beatitude of the meek, since it bestows a heavenly sweetness and thus leads us to comfort our afflicted neighbor because it makes us see in him a brother or a suffering member of Christ.[98] In its highest degree, the gift of piety strongly inclines us to give ourselves entirely to the service of God, to offer Him all our acts and sufferings as a perfect sacrifice. This gift makes us realize that communion is a participation in the sacrifice of the cross perpetuated on our altars; a participation by which our Lord wishes to render our hearts like His Sacred Heart of priest and victim, and to associate us with the deepest sentiments He experienced when instituting

92 *Ibid.*, q. 19, a.9, c.; q. 141, a. 1 ad 3um.
93 *Ibid.*, a.9 ad 1um.
94 Ps. 118: 120: "Pierce Thou my flesh with Thy fear."
95 See II Cor. 4: 10.
96 Ps. 110: 10.
97 Rom. 8: 15.
98 *Summa,* IIa IIae, q. 121, a. 1 ad 3um; a. 2.

the Holy Eucharist just before He went forth to die for us.⁹⁹ Of this union with Christ the priest, St. Peter says: "Be you also as living stones built up, a spiritual house, a holy priesthood, to offer up spiritual sacrifices, acceptable to God by Jesus Christ." ¹⁰⁰

The gift of fortitude, under the same direction of the gifts of knowledge and counsel, gives us the courage to undertake great things for God and to bear crushing trials for Him. It comes to the aid of the virtue of fortitude in very difficult circumstances. This gift corresponds to the fourth beatitude: "Blessed are they who hunger and thirst after justice," and who, in spite of all obstacles, maintain unshaken confidence in the help of God. In the perfect, this gift imbues the soul with an irresistible attraction to the things of God; it leads the soul to suffer joyfully the most painful torments for God, for faith, and for justice. This gift enables humble virgins and weak children to win the crown of martyrdom.¹⁰¹ It also sustains those who pass without weakening through the bitter crucible of the passive purifications of the soul, and who experience the truth of the Scriptural expression: "Many are the afflictions of the just; but out of them all will the Lord deliver them." ¹⁰² This gift is what made St. Paul exclaim: "I exceedingly abound with joy in all our tribulation"; ¹⁰³ and also, "who now rejoice in my sufferings for you, and fill up those things that are wanting of the sufferings

⁹⁹ *Summa*, IIIa, q.79, a.2 ad 1um: "We must first suffer with Him in order that we may also be glorified afterward with Him (Rom. 8: 17)." Cf. *Officium SS. Sacramenti.* On the three degrees of the gift of piety, see also Dionysius the Carthusian, *op. cit.*, tr. 3, a.40. To the third degree of this gift, considered in relation to one's neighbor, Dionysius refers St. Paul's words: "I most gladly will spend and be spent myself for your soul; although loving you more, I be loved less" (II Cor. 12: 15).

¹⁰⁰ See I Pet. 2: 5.

¹⁰¹ *Summa*, IIa IIae, q.139, a.1, and Dionysius the Carthusian, *op. cit.*, tr. 3, a.18.

¹⁰² Ps. 33: 20.

¹⁰³ See II Cor. 7: 4.

of Christ in my flesh, for His body which is the Church." [104]
Knowledge, counsel, fear, piety, and fortitude are, as we
have seen, the inferior gifts directed to victory over sin and
to action. The soul, living habitually under the régime of
these gifts, is already in the mystical life, even though mystical
contemplation, which proceeds from the higher gifts, is not
yet clearly discerned in it. This fact is important in practice,
and should be clearly noted so as to maintain, always without
exaggeration, the exact meaning of the doctrine which we
defend, namely, the normal though eminent character of
infused contemplation. Although infused contemplation is
generally granted to the perfect, it is not always clearly characterized in them. But they are already in the mystical life
if they live habitually under the régime of the gifts which
correspond to the beatitudes of the flight from sin and to those
of the active life. This is evident from what St. Thomas says
about the first five beatitudes. [105] Thereby the soul is immediately prepared for infused contemplation, which is chiefly
the fruit of the gifts of understanding and wisdom.

The gift of understanding makes us penetrate the meaning
of revealed truths and discover the spirit beneath the letter.
While faith is a simple assent to the word of God, an assent
that exists in a believing soul even in the state of mortal sin,
this gift, which like the others is found only in the just, implies
a penetrating and progressive understanding of the mysteries
of faith, the precepts, and the counsels. It does not remove

104 Col. 1: 24. Cf. St. Thomas, *In Ep. ad Col.* 1: 24. There is nothing lacking
in the passion of Christ in itself. It has a superabundance and infinite value;
there is something lacking only in its radiation in us. This is why St. Paul says:
"I fill up those things that are wanting of the sufferings of Christ, in my flesh,"
in order to be associated in the great work of the redemption in Christ and
through Him, in order to continue His redeeming work by the application of
His merits. "Heirs indeed of God and joint-heirs with Christ: yet so, if we suffer
with Him, that we may be also glorified with Him."

105 *Summa,* Ia IIae, q. 69, a. 3, 4. See also what St. Thomas says of the active
life and its relation to the contemplative life and to the mixed or apostolic life
(IIa IIae, q. 179, 181, 182, 188, a. 4, 6).

the obscurity of faith or its merit. It never gives us, while on earth, the evidence of mysteries, properly so called, for example, those of the Blessed Trinity, the incarnation, the redemption, and predestination. But it makes us perceive more and more clearly that the obscurity of these mysteries is the very opposite to the obscurity of incoherence and absurdity, and that it comes from a light which is too strong for our weak eyes. Thus it shows us the emptiness of the objections raised against faith, and it greatly confirms the motives of credibility, or signs of revelation.[106]

In the first degree, the gift of understanding strengthens the faith of every good Christian to such an extent that illiterate persons, who cannot make a study of the motives of credibility, adhere to the word of God with a firmness which may surpass that of the faith of learned men. In the second degree, this gift discloses the consistency and sublimity of revealed mysteries. It also contributes greatly to the passive purification of the soul, by making us glimpse the infinite grandeur of God, His unfathomable perfections, the annihilations of the Word made flesh and, on the other hand, the depth of the wretchedness subsisting in us. It corresponds to the beatitude of the clean of heart.[107] In the third degree, this gift makes the soul penetrate the hidden depths of the divine mysteries; it unveils more and more the meaning of the prophecies and of our Lord's words, and in a way makes us see God; "by the gift of understanding, we can, so to speak, see God," [108] not by a positive, immediate intuition of the divine presence, but

---

[106] *Summa*, IIa IIae, q.8, a.1, 2, 4.

[107] "For cleanness is twofold. One is a preamble and a disposition to seeing God, and consists in the heart being cleansed of inordinate affections: and this cleanness of heart is effected by the virtues and gifts belonging to the appetitive power. The other cleanness of heart . . . is the cleanness of the mind that is purged of phantasms and errors . . . and this cleanness is the result of the gift of understanding" (*ibid.*, a.7).

[108] "In this life . . . the (mind's) eye being cleansed by the gift of understanding, we can, so to speak, see God." Thus, the reward of each of the eight beatitudes exists in a certain inchoative manner in Christian life on earth, which is eternal life begun, *semen gloriae* (Ia IIae, q.69, a.2 ad 3um).

by showing us more and more clearly what God is not, and how His intimate life infinitely exceeds the natural knowledge of every created and creatable intelligence.[109] Evidently the third degree of the gift of understanding, that which is normally proper to the perfect, belongs to the mystical life, strictly so called, as the principle of infused contemplation. We can easily understand this by reading the description of the third degree in the work of Dionysius the Carthusian.[110]

Lastly, whereas the gift of understanding conceives and penetrates, that of wisdom makes us judge all created things by the taste, by the affective and sweet knowledge of God, their beginning and end.[111] Although in this life wisdom remains in the obscurity of faith, without seeing God as He is *(sicuti est)*, nevertheless it contemplates Him in His intimate life in the measure in which we have an experimental knowledge of Him as the soul of our soul, the life of our life. As we take cognizance of our soul in our actions,[112] so, in a certain way, we have a quasi-experimental knowledge of God by the action He exercises in us and by the spiritual joy and peace we experience therefrom.[113] Thus St. Paul says: "For the

109 *Summa*, IIa IIae, q.8, a.7: "Again, the sight of God is twofold. One is perfect, whereby God's Essence is seen: the other is imperfect, whereby though we see not what God is, yet we see what He is not; and whereby, the more perfectly do we know in this life, the more we understand that He surpasses all that the mind comprehends. Each of these visions of God belongs to the gift of understanding; the first, to the gift of understanding in its state of perfection, as possessed in heaven; the second, to the gift of understanding in its state of inchoation, as possessed by wayfarers."

110 *De donis*, tr. 2, a.35: "Ad tertium gradum (doni intellectus) id attinet ut singulorum fidei articulorum proprias rationes ac fundamenta quis purgatissima acie valeat considerare . . . atque certissimo mentis oculo quoeat delectabiliter speculari."

111 *Summa*, IIa IIae, q.45, a.1, 2.

112 "Socrates or Plato perceives that he has an intellectual soul, because he perceives that he understands" (Ia, q.87, a.1).

113 *Summa*, IIa IIae, q.45, a.2, 5, and q.97, a.2 ad 2um, where it is stated: "There is a twofold knowledge of God's goodness or will. One is speculative. . . . The other knowledge of God's will or goodness is affectve or experimental, and thereby a man experiences in himself the taste of God's sweetness and complacency in God's will, as Dionysius says of Hierotheos (*Div. nom.*, ii) that he learns divine things through experience of them." This does not require

Spirit Himself giveth testimony to our spirit, that we are the
sons of God." [114] Such is indeed, as St. Thomas and John of
St. Thomas show, the effect of the gift of wisdom. We will
quote in a note the formulas of the Master to which one must
continually revert, as will be seen from what follows.[115]

The gift of wisdom is thus the most perfect of all; it exerts
the same influence over the other gifts as charity does on the
virtues which are subordinated to it. Wisdom is, at one and the
same time, eminently speculative and practical; [116] it appears
in some souls especially under the first form, and in others
more particularly under the second. Thus, there are saints
called to the active life, like St. Vincent de Paul, who under
a practical form have, nevertheless, a very profound mystical
union with God. It is this which makes them see constantly
in the poor, the sick, and abandoned children, the suffering

infused ideas. St. Thomas says also in Ia, Dist. 14, q.2, a.2 ad 3um: "This knowledge is quasi-experimental."

[114] Rom. 8: 16.

[115] St. Thomas (*In Ep. ad Rom.* 8: 16) says: " 'Ipse enim Spiritus testimonium
reddit spiritui nostro quod sumus filii Dei,' reddit testimonium per effectum
amoris filialis quem in nobis facit." Likewise in Ia IIae, q.112, a.5: "Without
special revelation the presence of God in us and His absence cannot be known
with certainty. . . . But things are known conjecturally by signs; and thus
anyone may know that he has grace, when he is conscious of delight in God,
and of despising worldly things, and inasmuch as a man is not conscious of any
mortal sin. And thus it is written (Apoc. 2: 17): 'To him that overcometh I will
give the hidden manna . . . which no man knoweth, but he that receiveth it,'
because whoever receives it knows, by experiencing a certain sweetness, which
he who does not receive it, does not experience." It is with this meaning, moreover, that this text of the Apocalypse is generally quoted by mystics.

John of St. Thomas explains this doctrine clearly by saying: "Sicut contactus
animae quo experimentaliter sentitur, etiamsi in sua substantia non videatur,
est informatio et animatio, qua corpus reddit vivum et animatum, ita contactus
Dei quo sentitur experimentaliter, et ut objectum conjunctum, etiam antequam
videatur intuitive in se, est contactus operationis intimae, quo operatur intra
cor, ita ut sentiatur, et experimentaliter manifestetur, eo quod 'unctio ejus
docet nos de omnibus,' ut dicitur I Joan. 4. . . .

"Haec cognitio experimentalis datur etiamsi intuitive non videatur in se
sufficit quod per proprios effectus, quasi per tactum et vivificationem sentiatur,
sicut animam nostram experimentaliter cognoscimus, etiamsi intuitive ejus
substantiam non videamus." John of St. Thomas, on Ia, q.43, disp. 17, a.3, nos.
13, 17. Also Vallgornera, *Theol. myst. D. Thomae*, Vol. II, no. 866.

[116] *Summa*, IIa IIae, q.45, a.3.

members of Christ. It is very important to note these practical forms of the mystical life if we are to understand clearly the meaning of the doctrine which we hold as traditional, and if we do not wish to apply it materially in the same way to all souls. St. Paul was thinking of this gift when he said: "Howbeit we speak wisdom among the perfect. . . . But we speak the wisdom of God in a mystery, a wisdom which is hidden. . . . So the things also that are of God no man knoweth, but the Spirit of God. . . . Now we have received . . . the Spirit that is of God. . . . The spiritual man judgeth all things; and he himself is judged of no man. . . . But we have the mind of Christ." [117] This experience of divine things gives a certitude which fills the soul with ineffable consolation.[118] The gift of wisdom thus corresponds to the beatitude of the peacemakers,[119] who, in the midst of all that might trouble them, preserve deep peace, the tranquillity of order, so as to communicate it to others. They are accustomed to contemplate all things in God, unforeseen and most painful events, as well as those that are most consoling.

This gift is bestowed on us according to the measure of our charity, by virtue of its intimate connection with charity. Moreover, we can see in it, better than in the other gifts, the three degrees corresponding to those of charity. In the first degree, wisdom shows us principally the grandeur of God's commandments and gives us an attraction to what is good. "But it is good for me to adhere to my God." [120] In the second degree, it makes us see how valuable the counsels are and how all Christians should have the spirit of the counsels, even when their condition does not permit the practice of them. Illumined by the light of contemplation, a soul which

---

117 See I Cor. 2: 6–16; and St. Thomas, IIa IIae, q.45, a.1.

118 Cf. St. Thomas on Ps. 33: 9: "O taste, and see that the Lord is sweet." "The effect of experience is twofold: one is certitude of the intellect, the other security of the affections."

119 *Summa*, IIa IIae, q.45, a.6.

120 Ps. 72: 28.

passes through the night of the spirit more and more appreciates the cross of Jesus; at times, it even finds therein a spiritual sweetness and a "peace which surpasses all understanding." In the third degree, the soul is transformed by the gift of wisdom. In the light of this gift, says St. Thomas, "the perfect aim chiefly at union with and enjoyment of God, and desire to be dissolved and to be with Christ." [121] Like St. Paul the soul takes pleasure "in infirmities, in reproaches, in necessities, in persecutions, in distresses, for Christ." [122] This is the eighth beatitude, the highest of all. [123]

Evidently this third degree of the gift of wisdom belongs to the mystical life, strictly so called, even when this degree of wisdom appears under a practical form, as it does in the saints called to the active life. Dionysius the Carthusian, following the principles of St. Thomas, brings this out in his description of this third degree. He says: "The spirit no longer rests in any created thing for itself; it is completely fixed in the contemplation of divine things, a contemplation, which is very pure, easy, and sweet, now that the passions are calmed and the soul purified . . . as far as human frailty permits. This wisdom belongs to those who can say with St. Paul (II Cor. 3: 18): 'But we all beholding the glory of the Lord with open face, are transformed into the same image from glory to glory as by the spirit of the Lord.' " [124] We ought

---

[121] *Summa*, IIa IIae, q.24, a.9: "The divers degrees of charity are distinguished according to the different pursuits to which man is brought by the increase of charity (beginners, proficients, and the perfect). . . . Man's third pursuit is to aim chiefly at union with and enjoyment of God: this belongs to the perfect who desire to be dissolved and be with Christ." Likewise *In Ep. ad Phil.* 1: 23.

[122] See II Cor. 12: 10.

[123] *Summa*, Ia IIae, q.69, a.3 ad 5um.

[124] *De donis*, tr. 2, a.15: "Quod donum sapientiae et virtus caritatis divinae proportionaliter crescunt simul." Art. 16: "And I live, now not I: but Christ liveth in me" (Gal. 2: 20). Dionysius observes here that these three degrees of the gift of wisdom correspond to the three degrees of the moral virtues explained by St. Thomas, Ia IIae, q.61, a.5, where he divides the virtues into social virtues, perfecting virtues, and perfect virtues. Cf. Dionysius, *De fonte lucis*, a.12, 13, 15, and *De cont.*, Bk. I, a.44. In these works we find a similar description of

all to desire this divine wisdom which normally increases with charity, which ought to grow continually in this life.[125]

What is extraordinary is supereminent contemplation which proceeds not only from the gifts of the Holy Ghost, but from a grace *gratis data*, like that of prophecy, or that called by St. Thomas *sermo sapientiae*. Moreover, after stating that all the just receive the gift of wisdom in the measure necessary to their own sanctification, St. Thomas adds: "Some, however, receive a higher degree of the gift of wisdom, both as to the contemplation of divine things (by both knowing more exalted mysteries and being able to impart this knowledge to others) and as to the direction of human affairs according to divine rules (by being able to direct not only themselves but also others according to those rules). This degree of wisdom is not common to all that have sanctifying grace, but belongs rather to the gratuitous graces."[126] We must also remark that these graces, like prophecy, are not precisely necessary for this act of contemplation, but they simply help to render it more complete and more perfect.[127] What would be even more extraordinary is the beatific vision granted in a transitory manner in this life, as St. Augustine and St. Thomas thought that it was granted to Moses and St. Paul.[128]

---

the gift of wisdom. In *De fonte lucis* (a.12, 15) it is clearly stated that that is properly the *contemplatio unitivae ac mysticae sapientiae* which unites us to God *tanquam prorsus ignoto* in the transluminous darkness, *per supersplendentem caliginem*, of which Dionysius the Mystic speaks, and St. Thomas after him (*In lib. de div. nom.*, chap. 1, lect. 1; chap. 7, lect. 4).

[125] Cf. Henry Suso, *L'Exemplaire*, Part I, chap. 4; Part III, chap. 1; Ruysbroeck, *Le royaume des amants*, chap. 33.

[126] *Summa*, IIa IIae, q.45, a.5; and on graces *gratis datae*, Ia IIae, q.111, a.1.

[127] Cf. Thomas of Jesus, C.D., *De contemplatione*, Bk. II, chaps. 3–5; *De oratione*, Bk. II, chaps. 1, 4; Schram, *Theol. myst.*, I, 2; chap. 4, sec. 244. "Solum probatur contemplationem secundum essentiam suam non consistere in his gratiis, sed per illas juvari accidentaliter et perfici directe in ordine ad alios, indirecte in ordine ad se. . . . Quia sermo est de contemplatione perfecta, quae supponit vel facit animam perfectam, haec nequit a solis gratiis gratis datis procedere, cum sit caritate formata, et elevata donis Spiritus Sancti." Cf. Meynard, O.P., *Traité de la vie intérieure*, Vol. II, nos. 42–46.

[128] *Summa*, IIa IIae, q.175, a.3–6.

This is the Angelic Doctor's teaching on the special inspiration of the Holy Ghost in the souls of the just, and on its progress, which usually accompanies that of charity. If we recall that, in his opinion, the perfection of charity is not only of counsel, but falls under the first precept as the end to which all must tend, each one according to his condition,[129] we shall see more and more clearly that infused contemplation, proceeding from the gift of wisdom, is truly found in the normal way of sanctity and that it is generally granted to the perfect.

We must now make a more profound study of the gift of wisdom in particular, and of its relation to faith and to infused contemplation.

## ARTICLE VI

*The Essential Character of Infused Contemplation;
How it Proceeds from The Gift of Wisdom
and from Faith*

For the reasons we have just set forth, theologians commonly teach that infused contemplation proceeds formally from the gifts of the Holy Ghost, particularly from the gift of wisdom which makes us taste the mysteries of salvation and, so to speak, see all things in God, just as acquired wisdom tries to judge everything by the supreme cause and the last end.[1] The gift of understanding also contributes to contemplation by making us penetrate these mysteries.[2] The gift of knowledge may also have a share in it by manifesting to us the emptiness and the vanity of all created things in comparison with God, or by revealing to us, in a more striking

---

[129] *Ibid.*, IIa IIae, q.184, a.3.

[1] *Summa*, IIa IIae, q.45, a.1, 2.

[2] *Ibid.*, q.8. By an illumination of this kind, our Lord opened the minds of the disciples of Emmaus to give them understanding of the Scriptures.

manner than years of meditation could, the infinite gravity of mortal sin.[3]

All tradition associates with the inspirations of the gift of wisdom that loving knowledge of God which is quite different from speculative knowledge. This loving knowledge supposes, together with the special illumination of the Holy Ghost, a living "connaturality with divine things,"[4] based on infused charity, a wholly supernatural attraction of the soul for God, who makes Himself felt by it as the life of its life. This living knowledge is an affective knowledge which becomes more lively, penetrating, and sweet because the gift of wisdom grows with charity and is related to it as the infused virtues and the other gifts are.

### 1. THE SPIRIT OF WISDOM IN SCRIPTURE

This doctrine, which is commonly accepted in the Church, is manifestly founded on what Scripture tells us of the spirit of wisdom. It was not only of the Messias that Isaias spoke when he declared: "And the spirit of the Lord shall rest upon him: the spirit of wisdom, and of understanding, the spirit of counsel, and of fortitude, the spirit of knowledge, and of godliness. And he shall be filled with the spirit of the fear of the Lord."[5] The Old Testament applies to all men the following words, which we have already quoted: "God loveth none but him that dwelleth with wisdom";[6] "for wisdom will not enter into a malicious soul, nor dwell in a body subject to sins."[7] St. John writes to the faithful: "Let the unction which

---

[3] Summa, IIa IIae, q.9. Thus the gift of knowledge, according to St. Augustine and St. Thomas, corresponds to the gift of tears: "Blessed are those who mourn" when they see, under the inspiration of the Holy Ghost, the gravity of their faults as a disease of the soul and offense against God. The other gifts, those of counsel, piety, fortitude, and fear, do not formally participate in infused contemplation, but prepare the soul for it. Contemplation may at times be accompanied by prophetic light, but it is then an extraordinary favor.

[4] Summa, IIa IIae, q.45, a.2, and John of St. Thomas, De donis, art. 4.

[5] Is. 11: 2.

[6] Wis. 7: 28.

[7] Ibid., 1: 4.

you have received from Him abide in you. . . . His unction teacheth you of all things, and is truth, and is no lie." [8] St. Paul, after stating that "the charity of God is poured forth in our hearts, by the Holy Ghost, who is given to us," [9] then adds: "For you have not received the spirit of bondage again in fear; but you have received the spirit of adoption of sons, whereby we cry: Abba (Father)." [10] "Howbeit we speak wisdom among the perfect: yet not the wisdom of this world, neither of the princes of this world that come to nought: but we speak the wisdom of God in a mystery, a wisdom which is hidden, which God ordained before the world, unto our glory: which none of the princes of the world knew; for if they had known it, they would never have crucified the Lord of glory. But, as it is written: That eye hath not seen, nor ear heard, neither hath it entered into the heart of man, what things God hath prepared for them that love Him. But to us God hath revealed them, by His Spirit. For the Spirit searcheth all things, yea, the deep things of God. For what man knoweth the things of a man, but the spirit of a man that is in him? So the things also that are of God no man knoweth, but the Spirit of God. Now we have received not the spirit of this world, but the Spirit that is of God: that we may know the things that are given us from God. Which things also we speak, not in the learned words of human wisdom: but in the doctrine of the Spirit, comparing spiritual things with spiritual. But the sensual man perceiveth not these things that are of the Spirit of God: for it is foolishness to him, and he cannot understand, because it is spiritually examined. But the spiritual man judgeth all things: and he himself is judged of no man. For who hath known the mind of the Lord, that he may instruct Him? But we have the mind of Christ." [11]

These words about the wisdom preached "among the per-

[8] See I John 2: 27.
[9] Rom. 5: 5.
[10] Ibid., 8: 15.
[11] See I Cor. 2: 6-16.

fect" are fully lived only by souls raised to mystical contemplation; especially to them the unction of the Holy Ghost "teaches all things." By Him they cry to God in their prayers; they scrutinize the deep things of God; they anticipate all He has prepared for those who love Him; they know experimentally all the riches already received; and they judge all things, whether painful or pleasurable, by referring them to the glory of God. Again St. Paul writes for all Christians: "But we all beholding the glory of the Lord with open face, are transformed into the same image from glory to glory, as by the Spirit of the Lord." [12] Only in infused contemplation is this transformation of a certainty fully realized on earth.

Without the mystical knowledge of God, how can we possess the full perfection of Christian life? "Now all good things came to me together with her." [13] As the Apostle St. James says: "But the wisdom, that is from above, first indeed is chaste, then peaceable, modest, easy to be persuaded, consenting to the good, full of mercy and good fruits, without judging, without dissimulation." [14]

The doctors of the Church, following the lead of St. Augustine and St. Gregory the Great, have interpreted these passages of Scripture as referring to the gift of wisdom, the principle of infused contemplation. The liturgy likewise brings this message to all the faithful in the *Veni Creator*.[15]

## 2. THE GIFT OF WISDOM AND INFUSED CONTEMPLATION ACCORDING TO THEOLOGY

St. Thomas, in conformity with tradition, teaches that con-

---

[12] See II Cor. 3: 18.

[13] Wisd. 7: 11.

[14] Jas. 3: 17.

[15] Cf. *Dict. théol.*, art. "Dons" by Father Gardeil, O.P., for the doctrine of the fathers. The Scriptural bases of the teaching of St. Thomas on the gifts are to be found in his commentaries on the Old and New Testament, on the passages we have just quoted, and also on the following: Ps. 41: 2; Wis. 7: 7, 22; Eccles. 15: 2; 39: 8; Is. 12: 3; 55: 1; Matt. 5: 1; John 3: 4; 4: 10; 7: 38; 14: 16–26; 16: 13 f.; Rom. 8: 26; Eph. 3: 16; 4: 30; Phil., chap. 4; I John, 4: 1–13.

templation is chiefly the fruit of the gift of wisdom. This gift is an infused disposition *(habitus infusus)* of the intellect, as contemplation is an intellectual act,[16] requiring an illumination of the Holy Ghost. But as the gift of wisdom presupposes charity, contemplation depends essentially also on charity, which makes us desire to know God better, not for the joy of knowing, but for God Himself, that we may love Him more.[17] In this act the will applies the intellect to the consideration of divine things in preference to all others (order of exercise), and also (in the order of specification), from the fact that this will is fundamentally rectified and elevated by an eminent charity, these divine things appear to us more and more conformable to our highest aspirations. By experience we learn that they fill and surpass these aspirations and never cease to elevate them. Consequently we live more and more by God, by His supreme goodness, which makes itself felt by us as the life of our life. We "taste the sweetness of God": "O taste, and see that the Lord is sweet." [18]

St. Thomas says: "Wisdom denotes a certain rectitude of judgment according to the Eternal Law. Now rectitude of judgment is twofold: first, on account of perfect use of reason, secondly, on account of a certain connaturality with the matter about which one has to judge. Thus about matters of chastity, a man after inquiring with his reason forms a right judgment, if he has learned the science of morals, while he who has the habit of chastity judges of such matters by a kind of connaturality. Accordingly, it belongs to the wisdom that is an intellectual virtue to pronounce right judgment about divine things, after reason has made its inquiry; but it belongs to wisdom [19] as a gift of the Holy

16 *Summa,* IIa IIae, q.180, a.1.

17 *Ibid.*

18 Ps. 33: 9.

19 St. Thomas says in the preceding article: "Now man obtains this judgment through the Holy Ghost . . . who searcheth all things." In this there might indeed be a simple affective knowledge through faith united to charity. That this knowledge may proceed from the gift of wisdom, there must be, moreover,

Ghost to judge aright about them on account of connaturality with them: thus Dionysius says (*Div., Nom., ii*) that Hierotheus is perfect in divine things, for he not only learns, but he is patient of divine things. Now this sympathy or connaturality with divine things is the result of charity, which unites us to God, according to I Cor. 6: 17: He who is joined to the Lord, is one spirit." [20]

Thus love makes the object loved better known, *affectus transit in conditionem objecti,* as John of St. Thomas says,[21] "for by it and by affective experience this object appears to us more and more conformable to our aspirations and intimately united to us. The intellect is thus directed toward God, as if it touched Him experimentally. In this way, love moves the understanding, by applying it to consideration (*in genere causae effectivae*), and also in an objective manner (*in genere causae objectivae*), since by this experience the object appears quite otherwise than without it" and manifests itself as supremely suitable, as Goodness itself that is felt. This is what made our Lord say: "If any man will do the will of Him (the Father); he shall know of the doctrine, whether it be of God, or whether I speak of Myself." [22] This love unites us more closely to God than abstract [23] knowledge; and by the experience it gives us, it makes us more and more keenly desire the intuitive knowledge of the life to come, the beatific vision. This true prag-

---

an inspiration of the Holy Ghost; thereby infused contemplation is distinguished from the sensible consolations acquired in meditation, as we will point out later on.

[20] *Summa,* IIa IIae, q.45, a.2.

[21] On Ia IIae, q.68, disp. 18, a.4.

[22] John 7: 17.

[23] *Summa,* Ia IIae, q.28, a.1 ad 3um: "Knowledge is perfected by the thing known being united, through its likeness, to the knower. But the effect of love is that the thing itself which is loved, is, in a way, united to the lover, as stated above. Consequently, the union caused by love is closer than that which is caused by knowledge."

However, if knowledge is absolutely immediate, if one knows God by His very essence and no longer by a likeness, as is the case in the beatific vision, then it is this knowledge which makes us take possession of God rather than love. Cf. Ia IIae, q.3, a.4.

matism, which scoffs at pragmatism, is born of supernatural charity, which supposes faith.

A soul might have affective knowledge from the simple fact that the love of charity is united to the act of faith; this is what occurs in affective, discursive prayer. But in infused contemplation there is, in addition, an inspiration and special illumination of the Holy Ghost. This subject was discussed at length in article 5 above.

When a distinction is made, as often occurs in the writings of the fathers and of theologians, between illumination and inspiration, special illumination is a grace for the intellect, inspiration a grace for the will. In this sense we speak of infused knowledge and love that we cannot produce at will. No one can set a limit to the growing intensity of the illumination which the gift of wisdom renders us apt to receive. This illumination, as we shall see, can always grow in intensity in this life, just as charity can.

This infused contemplation is obscure because it is superior both to every sensible image and to every distinct idea. This state of transluminous obscurity is indeed, in so far as the intelligence is concerned, what constitutes the foundation of the mystical state, according to the opinion of Dionysius, St. John of the Cross, and the other great spiritual teachers. It is very difficult to describe, for it is entirely supernatural and surpasses all expression. In it is something akin to a death of the understanding, which in reality is an incomparably superior new life, the true prelude of the life of heaven. St. John of the Cross should be consulted on this point, which he discusses in *The Dark Night of the Soul*. He says: "The imagination is bound, and unable to make any profitable reflections; the memory is gone; and the understanding, too, is darkened and unable to comprehend anything." [24] The faculties are, as it were, annihilated according to their human mode; here, there is a deeper and more vital communication

---

[24] Bk. II, chap. 16, sec. 1.

of the divine mode of knowing and loving. St. John of the Cross [25] quotes St. Thomas (IIa IIae, q. 180, a. 1) and adds: "This happens in a secret, hidden way in which the natural operation of the understanding and the other faculties have no share. And, therefore, because the faculties of the soul cannot attain it, and since the Holy Ghost infuses it into the soul in a way unknown to it, as the Bride declares in the Canticle, it is called 'secret.' And, it is not only the soul that is ignorant of it, but every one else, even the devil; because the Master, who now teaches the soul, dwells substantially within it where neither the devil, nor the understanding, nor natural reason can penetrate."

This is why so much difficulty is found in describing psychologically what theology calls the superhuman mode of the gifts of the Holy Ghost, especially of the gift of wisdom. Among the best descriptions are the one we have just quoted, and also the passage where St. Teresa [26] distinguishes the first infused prayer (supernatural recollection) from the last of the acquired prayers which preceded it. We quoted this description above (chap. 5, arts. 2, 3).

It is important, however, not to believe with liberal Protestantism and modernistic agnosticism that this transluminous obscurity of infused contemplation, which brings no distinct knowledge, can do without a definite *Credo,* or that it finds an obstacle in such a *Credo.*[27] On the contrary, this obscurity is at the opposite extreme from the "unstable wandering of the soul" with which sentimentality or theosophy is satisfied. To this it is somewhat opposed, as God, its object, is opposed to prime matter, which is capable of receiving all forms. In fact, infused contemplation is what gives ever more clearly

---

[25] *Ibid.,* chap. 17.

[26] *The Interior Castle,* fourth mansion, chap. 3.

[27] Every true Catholic mystic is and should be ready to give his life for the least iota of the *Credo.* Every formal heresy destroys infused faith in us and therefore charity; that is, the essential principle from which proceeds the contemplation we are speaking of.

the spirit of the words, concepts, and formulas of faith. It thus makes us, in a way, pass beyond the formulas of dogmas in order to enter into the deep things of God by believing in the mysteries as they are in Him, without its being granted us to see them. Thus conceived, this contemplation, far more profoundly than any study or meditation could, enables us to grasp the evangelical parables, the different mysteries of salvation, the unfathomable perfections of God, the supreme mystery of the Deity which contains them all, and the ineffable relations of the divine Persons.

Hence St. Thomas,[28] following Dionysius, distinguishes three principal degrees in this contemplation, according to the brilliance of the illumination of the Holy Ghost, which has an unlimited intensive progress.

1) The soul contemplates God in the mirror of sensible things of which He is the author, or in the mirror of the evangelical parables, as for instance, infinite mercy in the story of the prodigal son. The soul rises from a sensible fact toward God by a straight movement, like that of a lark soaring directly from earth toward heaven. While preaching the parable, our Lord placed His hearers in this prayer.

2) The soul contemplates God in the mirror of the mysteries of salvation, the mysteries of the Word made flesh, the incarnation, redemption, Holy Eucharist, the life of the Church; mysteries which the rosary constantly sets before our eyes to familiarize us with them. In this spiritual mirror the soul contemplates the goodness of God. It comprehends better and better the harmony of these mysteries, and passes from one to another by an oblique movement analogous to that of a bird which, being already aloft, flies from one point to another, its gaze lost in the azure depths of the sky.

3) The soul contemplates God in Himself, not as the blessed in heaven do, but in the penumbra of faith. Here the soul has risen above the multiplicity of sensible images and

[28] *Summa*, IIa IIae, q. 180, a.6.

ideas. It sees, but a little indistinctly, that God our Father, who is infinitely good, is superior to every idea we can have of Him; and it sees that His goodness surpasses everything He Himself could put into human formulas for us, as the sky includes all the stars which manifest its depths to us. The soul not only tells itself these things, which every philosopher can think, even though he be in the state of mortal sin; but, under the inspiration of the Holy Ghost, by a loving and quasi-experimental knowledge it is wholly united to this unknown God; holy and sweet ignorance, superior to all knowledge. This is the pure contemplative movement which recollects the soul in God alone above all things, as Dionysius describes it in *The Divine Names*.[29] This prayer has been compared to an eagle's circular movement high up in the air, or to the movement of a bird hovering as though suspended and seeming to be motionless. This immobility is far more perfect than the varied movement that preceded it. As a circular movement has neither beginning nor end, there is here no method, for one does not start from principles in order to reach conclusions. Under the illumination of the Holy Ghost, it is truly *simplex intuitus veritatis*, the simple intuition of divine truths in the obscurity of faith, and the impetuosity of love which mysteriously unites us to God.[30] Christ's sacerdotal prayer in the Gospel of St. John [31] gives us

[29] Chap. 4.
[30] *Summa,* IIa IIae, q.180, a.6. This contemplation, compared by Dionysius to a circular movement, consists, as he says (*loc. cit.*), "in the soul leaving exterior things so that it may enter into itself; that it may recall its intellectual faculties to unity in order that shut up, as it were, in a circle it may not go astray; then in this release from distractions, in this recollection and simplification of itself, that it may unite itself to the angels marvelously lost in unity, and allow itself thus to be led toward the beautiful and the good, toward the Deity itself, superior to the beautiful and the good." Philip of the Blessed Trinity, C.D., followed by Vallgornera, O.P., recognizes in his *Mystical Theology,* II, 66, where he discusses circular contemplation, that it is generally infused. This is the least that can be said. This contemplation differs enormously from the acquired speculation of the philosopher or from meditation on the ineffability of the divine essence.
[31] John, chap. 17.

the idea of this circular contemplation. An argument with major, minor, and conclusion must not be sought in it; on the contrary, it is composed, as it were, of luminous undulations which descend from heaven to us.

This circular contemplation no more resembles meditation or abstract speculation on the divine essence than a circumference resembles a polygon inscribed within it; in proportion as the circumference is simple, the other is complex. Very often commentaries on the works of the saints give the same impression as this polygon; in vain we would multiply its sides in an attempt to make them identical with the circle enclosing them.

As can be seen from his *Commentary on the Divine Names*,[32] St. Thomas follows Dionysius. Above symbolical theology, which speaks of God in metaphores, and above speculative theology, which is expressed in less unsuitable terms and which reasons on the divine perfections and mysteries, there is "a perfect knowledge of God, which is obtained by ignorance in virtue of an incomprehensible union. This takes place when the soul, leaving all things and forgetting self, is united to the splendors of the divine glory and is enlightened in the splendid depths of unfathomable wisdom." [33] Only a person who has received this grace can clearly understand all that these words express. St. Thomas adds: "We know God by ignorance, by a certain union with the divine which is above the nature of the mind . . . and thus knowing God, in such a state of knowledge, the soul is illumined from the very depths of divine Wisdom, which we cannot scrutinize." [34]

We attain the mysterious ocean of being, which is superior to substance, to life, and to light, only by the repose of the superior faculties, not by reasoning or by a sight of God,

---

[32] He says in the *Summa* (IIa IIae, q.180, a.6 ad 2um): "Discoursing must be laid aside and the soul's gaze fixed on the contemplation of the one simple truth."

[33] *The Divine Names*, VII, 3.

[34] *Loc. cit.*, lect. 4.

but by a most loving and intimate union, "by a sort of initiation which no master can teach." [35] Dionysius says: "We desire to enter that transluminous obscurity and to see and know, by the very fact of not seeing and not knowing, Him who is above all sight and all knowledge. For the soul truly sees and knows and supersubstantially praises the supersubstantial when it declares that the supersubstantial is nothing of that which other beings are." [36] "The good Being . . . drives away ignorance and error from all souls in which He reigns; He dispenses to them all sacred light. . . . First of all He gives them a little light; then when, having tasted it, they desire it in greater abundance, He distributes it to them with greater largess. Because they have loved much, He inundates them with this light; and He ever urges them forward in proportion to the zeal they exercise in directing their faculties toward Him." [37]

The soul cannot by its own efforts reach this infused contemplation, but it ought to prepare itself to receive it. This it should do by prayer and mortification,[38] and by setting aside the senses and reasoning: "As for thee, O well beloved Timothy, exercise thyself unceasingly in mystical contemplation. Put aside the senses and the operations of the understanding, all that is material and intellectual, all the things that exist and those that do not, and by a supernatural flight unite thyself as intimately as possible with Him who is above all being and all knowledge. For it is by this sincere, spontaneous, and total abandonment of thyself and of all things that, free and disengaged from all ties, thou wilt cast thyself into the mysterious splendor of the divine obscurity." [39]

"This intimate union, which surpasses the range of non-mystical minds, is a fusion produced by divine love . . . for

[35] *Ep.*, IX, 1.
[36] *Theol. myst.*, II.
[37] *The Divine Names*, IV, 5.
[38] *Ibid.*, III, 1.
[39] *Theol. myst.*, I, 1.

love is a unifying force." [40] It is the perfection on this earth of the "deification of the soul." [41]

"Mystical knowledge," says St. Albert the Great, [42] "does not proceed from the findings of reason, but rather from a certain divine light. The object seized by the soul (God Himself) acts so strongly on the intellect that the soul wishes at any price to be united to it. Since this object is above the grasp of the intellect, it does not make itself clearly known to it; consequently the understanding rests on something which is not determined."

This contemplation gives us a foreknowledge of the divine perfections, which are identical with each other, without excluding each other, in the eminence of the Deity. It shows us how infinite justice harmonizes with infinite mercy, without ceasing to be justice; how sovereign mercy could not exist without being identical with this justice, in appearance so contrary to it. [43] The soul is introduced into the divine darkness, which Dionysius speaks of and which Blessed Angela of Foligno so wonderfully praises, [44] by a speculative and a quasi-

[40] *The Divnie Names*, IV, 12.

[41] *Hierar. coel.*, I, 3.

[42] *In libr. de myst. theol. Dionys.* q. proem., ad 1.

[43] We have treated this question elsewhere from the speculative point of view. Cf. Garrigou-Lagrange, *God, His Existence and His Nature*, Vol. II, chap. 3, "Reconciliation of the Divine Attributes: Their Formal Existence and Their Identification in the Eminence of the Deity." "Absolute perfections are contained formally and eminently in God, and yet they are only virtually distinguished from each other. They are contained formally, which means according to their formal concept; they are contained eminently, which means according to a mode infinitely above the created mode. . . . Thus, the absolute perfections are contained formally in God and yet are only virtually distinguished from one another, or, in other words, according to a reasoned-out distinction for which there is a foundation, but consequent to the consideration of the mind" (*ibid.*, p. 196).

[44] *Le livre des visions et instructions de la B. Angèle de Foligno*, chap. 26: "One day my soul was ravished and I saw God in a light superior to every known light; in a plenitude superior to every plenitude. In the place where I was, I sought love and I no longer found it. . . . Then I saw God in a darkness, and necessarily in a darkness because He is too far above the spirit, and all that can become the object of a thought cannot express Him. . . . This is an ineffable delectation in the good which contains all, and nothing there can become the object of a word or a concept. I see nothing, I see

experimental knowledge that God in His intimate life, in what constitutes Him as such (in His nature as God) is, so to speak, superior to being, truth, good, wisdom, love, mercy, and justice; and that nevertheless these divine perfections are in Him formally in an eminent manner, without any real distinction.

How can the soul know in this way that Deity, which is common to the three divine Persons and from which they are not in reality distinct? Grace alone permits us to know it in this way, because grace is precisely a real and formal participation in this Deity, in the divine nature as such. Whereas a stone resembles God because it has existence; a plant, because it has life; and the natural man, because he is endowed with intelligence; grace makes us resemble God precisely inasmuch as He is God, in His Deity, superior to being, life, and thought. This relationship belongs to an order quite superior to a sensible miracle and to the prophecies of possible future events.[45] Such is this connaturality, this natural resemblance with God, the grace of the virtues and the gifts. It makes the just soul, as it were, an Aeolian harp which, under the breathing of the Holy Ghost, gives forth the most harmonious sounds, the sweetest as well as the most brilliant, the most piercing as well as the most solemn. As a new leitmotif, which at first is imperceptible and distant, little by little rises, approaches, envelops us, and ends by dominating all, so the mysterious harmony of the gift of wisdom rises in our soul. Its superhuman mode scarcely appears at first, and then

---

all. The more profound the darkness is, the more the good exceeds all. This is the reserved mystery. . . . The divine power, wisdom, and will, which I saw marvelously elsewhere, seems less than this. This is a whole; the others could be called parts. . . . In the immense darkness I see the Blessed Trinity. . . . That is the supreme attraction, in comparison with which all is nothing; that is the incomparable." On the same subject, cf. St. Thomas, *In De divinis Nominibus*, c. VII, lect. 4; and *I Sent.* d.8, q.1, a.1 ad 5um. It would be a gross error to confound this infused contemplation with the philosophical meditation in which one thinks that the divine essence surpasses all our concepts.

45 *Summa*, Ia IIae, q.111, a.5.

in rather a negative manner by the disappearance of the human mode of thinking. As St. John of the Cross says,[46] meditation becomes impossible or impracticable; the soul has no desire to fix its imagination on any particular interior or exterior object; it is pleased in prayer to find itself alone with God, and to fix its attention lovingly on Him. This is the beginning of the divine intimacy.

Theology, by what it teaches about the gift of wisdom, makes us know ontologically the spiritual organism of contemplation; but it leaves to mystics the description of the psychological signs that correspond to contemplation. It thus remains a superior science, distinct from the eminent art of the direction of souls, which is its application. We can see from this point of view why St. Thomas (IIa IIae, q. 180) treats contemplation in a formal manner. He determines its essence, which is analogically found in both philosophical and infused contemplation;[47] but he does not describe the different types of the latter according to the psychological and material signs that manifest it. St. Teresa is essentially descriptive; St. John of the Cross, both a mystic and a theologian, takes his place between the two. A number of authors make a mistake in wanting to discern which of these three points of view is the highest. In the great sobriety of his language, St. Thomas expresses the essence of things; without writing of mystical theology, he has given us its principles.

### III. PROGRESSIVE PREDOMINANCE OF THE DIVINE MODE OF THE GIFT OF WISDOM IN PRAYER

When we say that spiritual progress normally demands the progressive predominance of the divine mode of the gifts of the Holy Ghost in order to remedy the imperfect mode of the

[46] *The Ascent of Mount Carmel*, Bk. II, chaps. 11-13; *The Dark Night of the Soul*, Bk. I, chap. 9.

[47] Thus he treats of the essence of prudence, which is analogically found in acquired and in infused prudence, or of the essence of friendship which makes possible the definition of charity.

infused virtues, and when we add that the mystical life is precisely characterized by this predominance and by perfect docility to the interior Master, we do not mean to reserve to the mystical state the intervention of the gifts of the Holy Ghost, or to exclude the exercise of the virtues from this state. On the contrary, we have always said that, before the entrance into the mystical state, the gifts intervene in a manner that may be latent and rather frequent, or that may be manifest but rare.[48] When this intervention becomes frequent and manifest, then the mystical life begins, characterized by this predominance of the divine mode of the gifts,[49] whereas the ascetical life is characterized by the human mode of the virtues.

What we do not admit is that the gifts must enter into play every time the soul receives an actual grace; because an actual grace is required for even the most imperfect exercise of the Christian virtues, for *remissi* acts notably lower than the degree of charity we possess. In these acts no influence of the gifts is seen.[50] It would be an error to confound actual grace, at first exciting, then co-operating, which moves us to deliberate well according to the human mode, to will, and to act in consequence, with the inspiration of the Holy Ghost, to which the gifts render us docile, without our having to deliberate according to the human mode.[51] It may well be

[48] This is what theologians, particularly Thomists, generally teach. Cf. Joseph of the Holy Ghost, C. D., *Cursus theol. scol.-mysticae*, Vol. II, Disp. VII, q. 1, no. 28.

[49] On this point cf. Joseph of the Holy Ghost, *ibid.*

[50] Cf. Gardeil, *Dict. théol.*, art. "Dons," the last part of the article.

[51] St. Thomas says (IIa IIae, q.52, a.2 ad 1um): "In the gifts of the Holy Ghost, the position of the human mind is of one moved rather than of a mover." He speaks in the same manner of operating grace in order to distinguish it from co-operating grace (Ia IIae, q.111, a.2): "Hence in that effect in which our mind is moved and does not move, but in which God is the sole mover, the operation is attributed to God, and it is with reference to this that we speak of operating grace. But in that effect in which our mind both moves and is moved, the operation is not only attributed to God, but also to the soul; and it is with reference to this that we speak of co-operating grace." The inspiration of the Holy Ghost, of which we are speaking, is an operating grace

that a latent inspiration rather often accompanies human deliberation and work, just as a breeze facilitates the labor of a man who is rowing; but the divine mode of acting remains specifically distinct from the human mode. When the divine mode predominates in an act or a state to such an extent that this act and this state cannot be produced by our industry or human activity aided by the actual grace required for the exercise of the virtues, then that state is called passive. For example, when the wind blows with such force that a boat advances without the necessity of rowing, its progress does not depend on the activity of the oarsman. There is, therefore, more than a difference of degree between the human mode of the virtues and of the corresponding actual grace and the divine mode of the gifts of the Holy Ghost; there is a specific difference. This specific difference would not exist if the divine motion were only more intense. The difference arises from the fact that the objective regulation of the act is formally different, according as it proceeds from reason, which, enlightened by faith, deliberates in a human manner; or from the inspiration of the Holy Ghost, superior to all human deliberations and to every discursive process, whether it is intrinsic to prudence, or whether it disposes the soul to make at a desired moment acts of faith, hope, or charity.[52]

---

that we receive with docility and that makes us accomplish acts which we would not succeed in producing by our personal efforts aided by grace. St. Teresa says, in speaking of the prayer of union (fifth mansion, chap. 1): "Here God does not leave us any other share than that of a fully submissive will." Likewise St. Felicitas remarked to one of her jailers when she was suffering the pains of childbirth: "Today it is I who suffer; but then (during martyrdom) there will be another in me who will suffer for me, because I also will suffer for Him." This is the difference between the virtue and the gift.

[52] *Summa*, Ia IIae, q.68, a.1: "Human virtues perfect man according as it is natural for him to be moved by his reason in his interior and exterior actions. Consequently, man needs yet higher perfection, whereby to be moved by God. . . . Even the Philosopher says in the chapter on Good Fortune (*Ethic. Eudem., loc. cit.*) that for those who are moved by divine instinct there is no need to take counsel according to human reason, but only to follow their inner conscience, since they are moved by a principle higher than human reason. This then is what some say, viz., that the gifts perfect man for acts which

This difference appears in infused contemplation especially at its beginning and in its progress. It is helpful to recall the ascent described by St. Teresa and St. John of the Cross. In the aridity of the night of the senses, the gift of knowledge dominates by acquainting us especially with the vanity of created things; [53] in the night of the soul, the gift of understanding [54] shows us not so much the goodness of God as His infinite majesty, and by contrast our wretchedness. Between the two nights and especially after the second, the superhuman mode of the gift of wisdom is not only latent, but becomes more and more manifest to an experienced spiritual director. The soul, under the illumination of the Holy Ghost, thus possesses this quasi-experimental knowledge by connaturality with divine things. This knowledge can certainly not be had at will; while one can at will, with an actual grace, make an act of faith even when in the state of mortal sin.

In some perfect souls, this predominance of the superhuman mode of the gift of wisdom is striking (and at times even accompanied by graces *gratis datae,* by prophetic light); in others it is diffuse, but nevertheless very real. In these souls the practical gifts of counsel, fortitude, and fear, or those of piety and knowledge, are more manifest. But they are truly under the direction of the spirit of wisdom, and its light, like that diffused in the air, without attracting one's gaze, penetrates everything and gives to all life a superior tone, as appreciable as the difference between day and night.

This grace of infused contemplation, even in the diffuse

---

are higher than acts of virtue." Cf. John of St. Thomas on this article. It is clear that every actual grace does not dispense us from deliberating.

St. Thomas speaks thus (*In Rom.* 8: 14) on the text: "For whosoever are led by the Spirit of God, they are the sons of God": "Homo spiritualis, non quasi ex motu proprie voluntatis principaliter, sed ex instinctu Spiritus Sancti inclinatur ad aliquid." Cf. Froget, O.P., *De l'habitation du Saint-Esprit dans les âmes justes,* Part IV, chap. 6, p. 407.

[53] *Summa,* IIa IIae, q.9, a.4.
[54] *Ibid.,* q.8, a.7.

state, certainly differs from the sensible consolations which sometimes accompany vocal prayer or the meditation of beginners. St. Teresa clearly marks this difference [55] by showing what distinguishes "spiritual tastes from the consolations acquired in meditation." "We secure the latter," she says, "by our reflections, by means of considerations on created things, and by a painful labor of the understanding. And as, after all, they are the fruit of our efforts, they noisily fill the basin of our soul with some spiritual profit." The saint also compares these acquired consolations to water which comes through pipes from a distance. On the contrary, when speaking symbolically of the consolations of God, which she has called elsewhere the prayer of quiet, she writes: "In the other fountain, the water proceeds from the same source, which is God. Moreover, when it pleases His Majesty to grant us a spiritual favor, this water flows from the most intimate depths of our being with extreme peace, tranquillity, and sweetness. But whence it springs and in what manner, that I do not know."

It is possible to have a certain affective knowledge of God by the simple exercise of faith united to charity. This is the case with the consolations acquired in meditation, in which emotion may have a large part.[56] Infused contemplation, moreover, requires a special illumination or inspiration of the Holy Ghost to which precisely, as we have seen, the gift of wisdom renders us docile.

This gift, like the other six gifts and the infused virtues, is related to charity and most certainly grows with it. In a truly docile soul, infused contemplation ought thus normally to appear and then to develop. Consequently there should

[55] *The Interior Castle,* fourth mansion, chap. 2.

[56] See what St. Thomas says about the passions or emotions resultant by redundance (Ia IIae, q.24, a.3 ad 1um); of sensible joy, the effect of the devotion of the will (IIa IIae, q.82, a.4); and of the effects of communion (IIIa, q.79, a.1 ad 2um).

normally be a progressive predominance, either striking or diffuse, of the divine mode of the gift of wisdom over the human mode of meditation or of acquired prayer. In this way appears the supernatural prayer of which St. Teresa speaks. This prayer, which ought always to unite the soul more closely to God, is sometimes accompanied by ecstasy, by interior words, or even by visions. Yet these things are only accidental and transitory phenomena which pass, while infused contemplation continues. If the light of prophecy (*lumen propheticum*) co-operates at times in this contemplation, it is in a concomitant manner. Graces *gratis datae* belong to an order inferior to that of the virtues and gifts.[57] With this in mind, we can easily harmonize four recently proposed opinions as to the nature of the mystical state.[58] The first holds that it consists in an infused knowledge of God and of divine things; the second, in an infused love; the third, in a special passivity of the soul more acted upon than acting; and the fourth, in a simple and loving attention to God. The last cannot, in fact, be prolonged without a rather manifest intervention of the gifts.[59]

[57] *Summa*, Ia IIae, q.111, a.5. In this article St. Thomas states that sanctifying grace is "nobler than gratuitous grace." It is helpful to reread the office for the feast of St. Teresa, particularly the Little Chapter in which only the gift of wisdom is mentioned: "Wherefore I wished, and understanding was given me: and I called upon God, and the spirit of wisdom came upon me" (Wis. 7: 7).

[58] *Revue d'ascétique et de mystique*, October, 1920. On the question of mystical contemplation, cf. pp. 333–336.

[59] The first two opinions can be reconciled by the principle of the mutual causality of knowledge and love, "causae ad invicem sunt causae in diverso genere." From different points of view, there exists here priority either of knowledge or of love, as there is, for example, at the end of the deliberation when the free will determines upon the last practical judgment which directs its choice. The third opinion mentions the special passivity which is proper, at one and the same time, to infused knowledge and to infused love, which are united in the simple and loving attention of which the fourth opinion speaks. It is not, therefore, very difficult to reach an understanding on this point; the divergencies in this case may be only verbal.

IV. WHETHER CONTEMPLATION PROCEEDS EXCLUSIVELY FROM
THE GIFT OF WISDOM, OR ALSO FROM FAITH UNITED TO CHARITY

It would be an error, as we have seen, to declare that the intervention of the gifts of the Holy Ghost is reserved to the mystical state. It would assuredly be another mistake to exclude the exercise of the theological virtues from the mystical state. On the contrary, the mystical state, according to the great masters, consists in the most perfect exercise of these virtues, which are the highest of all. How can this assertion be reconciled with what we have just said about the predominance of the divine mode of the gifts in this state?

Some writers seem to hold that contemplation is not an act of faith, but that it presupposes an act of faith, at once distinct from it and simultaneous with it, as the deduction of a theological conclusion presupposes the knowledge of the principles of faith. This conception seems to conform but slightly to the perfect simplicity of the contemplative act, which is in no way discursive, and which dwells immediately on the mysteries of faith, penetrating and tasting them. Besides, the greatest mystics, such as St. John of the Cross, always declare that infused contemplation is an eminent act of living faith. Evidently they mean faith united to the gift of wisdom, and to a superior degree of this gift.[60] Therefore, together with Cajetan,[61] Joseph of the Holy Ghost,[62] and a number of other commentators of St. Thomas,[63] we think that there are not two simultaneous acts, but that infused contemplation is an act which proceeds, in so far as its sub-

[60] *The Ascent of Mount Carmel*, Bk. II, chaps. 2, 5, 8: Faith is the only proximate and proportionate means which enables the soul to attain to the divine union; chap. 9; Bk. III, chaps. 4, 6.

[61] On IIa IIae, q.45, a.1.

[62] *Cursus theol. scol.-mysticae*, Vol. II, dist. 13, p. 395, where Suarez is also quoted as admitting this conclusion.

[63] This seems to be the thought of John of St. Thomas, *De donis*, d.18, a.4; a.2, no. 25: "Dona ad excellentius perficiendum et exercendum virtutes theologicas deserviunt." Cf. T. Vallgornera, O.P., *Theol. myst. S. Thomae*, I, 471; II, 446.

stance is concerned, from infused faith, and with respect to its superhuman mode, from the gift of wisdom. The perfect contemplative is he who lives by faith and who, while believing supernatural mysteries, penetrates them, sounds their depths, tastes them, and assimilates them, or rather allows himself to be assimilated by them. It is he who is not content with believing, but who fully lives his faith (*justus ex fide vivit*), and who judges everything according to it, that is, according to the very thought of God, as if he saw with the eye of God. Charity also co-operates in contemplation, since charity is what moves us to contemplate God that we may love Him better.[64]

This would seem to be the meaning of St. Thomas' statement that: "The gifts perfect the virtues by raising them above the human mode; as the gift of understanding perfects the virtue of faith." [65] "The theological virtues (uniting us to the Holy Ghost) are superior to the gifts which they regulate," [66] and nevertheless receive a new perfection from them. "The operation which proceeds from the virtue perfected by the gift is called a beatitude." [67]

V. THE FRUITS OF THE HOLY GHOST AND THE BEATITUDES

By the gifts of the Holy Ghost the just soul becomes, as it were, a musical instrument from which the interior Master may draw marvelous harmonies: "Instrumentum musicum a Spiritu pulsatum divinamque gloriam et potentiam canens." [68] The soul thus sings the glory of God, a fact demonstrated by every page of the lives of the saints.

[64] *Summa*, IIa IIae, q.180, a.1.

[65] *Quaest. disp. de caritate*, a.2 ad 17um; III, d.34, q.1, a.1.

[66] "Sicut virtutes intellectuales praeferuntur virtutibus moralibus et regulant eas; ita virtutes theologicae (per quas unimur Spiritui Sancto moventi), praeferuntur donis Spiritus Sancti et regulant ea." Thus faith is the remote rule of the intellectual gifts, which can be exercised only on the truths of faith. Their proximate, immediate rule is the illumination of the Holy Ghost, which constitutes the formal motive of penetrating or sweet, infused contemplation.

[67] St. Thomas, *Super Isaiam*, chap. 11.

[68] St. Gregory Nazianzen, *Orat. ad popul.*, XLIII, no. 67.

Scripture compares a just man to a tree planted near running water, and giving its fruit in due season.[69] "The fruit of the Spirit is charity, joy, peace, patience, benignity, goodness, longanimity, mildness, faith, modesty, continency, and chastity." [70]

In what do these fruits differ from the virtues and the gifts? As St. Thomas explains,[71] they are not habits, but acts which proceed in us from the influence of the Holy Ghost and which man delights in. They are thus opposed to what may be called the fruits of reason.

The beatitudes are still higher. By this term we designate certain acts of the present life which, by reason of their very special perfection, are the pledge, the meritorious cause and, as it were, the first fruits of perfect beatitude.[72] "By reason of their perfection, they are assigned to the gifts rather than to the virtues." [73]

"Blessed are the poor in spirit: for theirs is the kingdom of heaven." [74] The virtue of poverty may inspire the detachment that makes us use the goods of earth with moderation; but it is the gift of fear that inspires scorn of them in comparison with superior goods.

"Blessed are they that mourn: for they shall be comforted." It is the gift of knowledge which shows us the vanity of transitory good, the gravity of sin as a spiritual evil, as an offense against God. Happy is he who sheds the tears of a holy contrition.

"Blessed are the meek: for they shall possess the land." The virtue of meekness makes us completely overcome the impetuosity of anger; but it is especially the gift of piety that

[69] Ps. 1: 3.
[70] Gal. 5: 22 f.
[71] *Summa*, Ia IIae, q.70, a.1, 2.
[72] St. Thomas, Ia IIae, q.69, a.1; q.70, a.2.
[73] *Ibid.*, q.70, a.2.
[74] Matt. 5: 3.

bestows calmness, serenity, perfect self-possession, and entire submission to the will of God.

These three are the beatitudes of flight from and deliverance from sin. The next two, as St. Thomas says, are the beatitudes of the active life of a Christian who, freed from evil, engages in the pursuit of good with all the ardor of his heart.

"Blessed are they that hunger and thirst after justice: for they shall have their fill." To desire justice, perfect order, is the effect of the virtues; but to hunger and thirst after it, to be tormented by this hunger, is the fruit of a loftier inspiration.

This thirst for justice should not become a bitter zeal with regard to the guilty; consequently our Lord says: "Blessed are the merciful: for they shall obtain mercy." Attentive to the sufferings of others, the merciful are able to give that counsel which reanimates and encourages. Accordingly the spirit of counsel corresponds to this beatitude.

This union of justice and mercy is one of the most striking signs of the presence of God in the soul; for He alone can intimately harmonize virtues that are apparently so contrary.

Lastly we have the beatitudes of the contemplative life. "Blessed are the clean of heart: for they shall see God." A truly pure heart is like a limpid fountain where God is reflected even in this life. The gift of understanding enables us to catch a glimpse of the divine beauty, in proportion to the growing purity of our intention.

"Blessed are the peacemakers: for they shall be called the children of God." According to St. Augustine and St. Thomas, this beatitude corresponds to the gift of wisdom which makes us see, as it were experimentally, all things in God; for every good thing comes from Him, and evil occurs only when it is permitted in view of a greater good. The gift of wisdom thus reveals the admirable order of the providential plan. Now, peace is the tranquillity of order. A contemplative soul not only possesses peace; it can communicate it to others. A contemplative soul does not allow itself to be troubled in its higher part by painful, unexpected events; it receives all from the hand of God as a means or an occasion of approaching closer to Him. Wisdom bestows a radiant peace, leading us to love our enemies. It is the mark of the true children of God who never for an instant, so to speak, lose the thought of their heavenly Father. At the beginning of its life, a soul that was stained with egoism, was often preoccupied with self, and perhaps referred everything to self; now it is the thought of God which possesses it, and it refers everything to Him. This peace, which is the fruit of the gift of wisdom and which the world cannot give, is found fully on earth only in the mystical life, which is characterized precisely by this gift, united to perfect charity and very lively faith. This is what makes St. Paul say to the Philippians: [75] "Rejoice in the Lord always; again, I say, rejoice. Let your modesty be known to all men. The Lord is nigh. Be nothing solicitous; but in everything, by prayer and supplication, with thanksgiving, let your petitions be made known to God. And the peace of God, which surpasseth all understanding, keep your hearts and minds in Christ Jesus."

Such is the fruit of that wisdom which Scripture praises in these words: "And I preferred her before kingdoms and thrones, and esteemed riches nothing in comparison of her. . . . For all gold in comparison of her, is as a little sand, and silver in respect to her shall be counted as clay. I loved her above health and beauty, and chose to have her instead of light: for her light cannot be put out. Now all good things came to me together with her, and innumerable riches through her hands. And I rejoiced in all these: for this wisdom went before me, and I knew not that she was

[75] Phil. 4: 4–9.

the mother of them all. Which I have learned without guile, and communicate without envy, and her riches I hide not. For she is an infinite treasure to men, which they that use, become the friends of God." [76] "And if a man desire much knowledge: she knoweth things past, and judgeth of things to come: she knoweth the subtilties of speeches, and the solutions of arguments. . . . I purpose therefore to take her to me to live with me." [77] . . . "Lord of mercy, . . . give me wisdom that sitteth by Thy throne, and cast me not off from among Thy children. . . . Send her out of Thy holy heaven, and from the throne of Thy majesty, that she may be with me, and may labor with me, that I may know what is acceptable with Thee. . . . For who among men is he that can know the counsel of God? or who can think what the will of God is? . . . And who shall know Thy thought except Thou give wisdom, and send Thy holy Spirit from above." [78] What more beautiful prayer could be found by which to ask God with humility and confidence for the spirit of wisdom, which is the principle of contemplation and the source of peace?

To the beatitude of the peacemakers is added the last, which is the confirmation and manifestation of the others: "Blessed are they that suffer persecution for justice' sake: for theirs is the kingdom of heaven." When man is confirmed in spiritual poverty, meekness, love of justice, and the other beatitudes, persecution is powerless to detach him from these goods and to deprive him of interior peace and joy. Thus the soul is stamped with the likeness of Christ crucified by the last trials it undergoes to reach sanctity. Then it comprehends in a practical way our Lord's words: "Blessed are ye when they shall revile you, and persecute you, and speak all that is evil against you, untruly, for My sake. Be glad and rejoice, for your reward is very great in heaven." [79] Are not

[76] Wis. 7: 8–14.
[77] *Ibid.*, 8: 8 f.
[78] Wis., chap. 9.
[79] Matt. 5: 11.

these the words that gave birth in the hearts of the saints to their thirst for suffering and martyrdom?

In this way the gifts of the Holy Ghost which are in every just soul and which develop normally, as infused habits, with charity, prepare us progressively for the loftiest and most heroic acts of the spiritual life. The word "mystical" is rightly applied to the spiritual life that has reached this degree of intimacy with God. In some perfect souls, the gifts of contemplation especially are manifest; in others, those of action. But even among the latter, the spirit of wisdom is what directs their lives and illumines all with its diffuse light.

# CHAPTER VI

## THE CALL TO CONTEMPLATION OR TO THE MYSTICAL LIFE

### ARTICLE I

### *The Different Meanings of the Word "Call"*

WE will consider the general and remote call, the individual and proximate call, the sufficient call, and the efficacious call.

When the call to mystical contemplation, properly so named, is discussed, and the question is raised as to whether this call is general or particular, we need a clear definition of the word "call" or "vocation," which may have very different acceptations.

First of all, "called to the mystical life" does not mean raised, conducted, chosen, or predestined to the mystical life. "For many are called, but few chosen," are the words used in the parable of the wedding guests.[1]

Theologians observe [2] that the vocation may be either ex-

---

[1] This is the meaning of the words "called" and "chosen," that is, chosen for glory, in Matt. 20: 16; 22: 14; 24: 24; Mark 13: 20, 22, 27; Luke 18: 7. This is also the current meaning in theology. However, in the writings of St. Paul (I Cor. 1: 26 f.) "called" has the same meaning as "chosen," because he speaks of the efficacious vocation to faith and to the Christian life, and of election to grace, not to glory. Cf. Vosté, O.P., *Comment. in Ep. 1 ad Thessal.*, 1: 4. St. Thomas observes on this subject that the efficacious vocation to the Christian life and election to the same life are identical; but the word "vocation" is used in relation to the new life, and "election" in relation to the world whence one has drawn and chosen.

[2] Cf. St. Thomas, I a, d.41, q.1, a.2 ad 3um, and *In Epist. ad Rom.*, chap. 8, lect. 6; and the Salamanca theologians, *De praedestinatione*, Disp. IV, dub. 3: "Quaenam vocationes electorum sunt effectus praedestinationis eorum?" According to these theologians and many other Thomists, even inefficacious vocations, which the elect resist, are an effect of predestination. Cf. Billuart, *De Deo*, Diss. IX, a.6, 1.

terior, that is, it may come through the Gospel, preaching, direction, reading; or interior, by reason of a grace of light and attraction.[3] The exterior call is general when it is addressed to all without distinction; it becomes individual when it reaches such or such a one in particular. Thus all pagans are in a general way called to the Christian life by the Gospel, before such or such a one is called in an individual manner.

The vocation may, on the contrary, be special when it is addressed only to a group of men, such as the vocation to the priesthood. It may even be very special and unique, as the vocation of Mary, Mother of God, or that of St. Joseph. It may be very particular, as that of a founder of a religious order, or indeed as that to enter a determined order, for example, the Carthusians.

The interior vocation may be, like sufficient grace, remote or proximate. Since "the habitual grace of the virtues and the gifts," which all the just possess, reaches the plenitude of its normal development only in the mystical life, properly so called, all the just are called to this life in a remote manner. This is our opinion, as well as that of the authors who admit the general call to the mystical life. St. Teresa found this teaching expressed in several passages in Scripture, two of which she quotes [4] in *The Way of Perfection*.[5]

Even in the opinion of these authors, all souls do not individually receive the proximate vocation to the mystical life. This vocation exists only when the three signs mentioned by St. John of the Cross, and before him by Tauler, can be proved to exist in the soul: (1) meditation becomes

[3] Generally the exterior vocation and the interior vocation are united, as the objective motion (*quoad specificationem*) and the subjective motion (*quoad exercitium*); as preaching and the grace which inclines the soul to adhere to it. These two constitute a single vocation.

[4] Matt. 11: 28: "Come to Me all you . . ." John 7: 37 f.: "Jesus stood and cried, saying: If any man thirst, let him come to Me, and drink. . . . Out of his belly shall flow rivers of living water."

[5] Chaps. 19, 20.

impracticable; (2) the soul has no desire to fix its imagination on any particular interior or exterior object; (3) the soul takes delight in being alone with God and fixing its loving attention upon Him.[6] We will explain these signs farther on (pp. 372 f.).

This proximate vocation to the mystical life may itself be either sufficient or efficacious, as we find in the parable of the wedding feast. Each of the guests was called individually. "The kingdom of heaven is likened to a king, who made a marriage for his son. And he sent his servants to call them that were invited to the marriage; and they would not come. . . . But they neglected, and went their ways, one to his farm, and another to his merchandise. . . . Then he saith to his servants: The marriage indeed is ready; but they that were invited were not worthy. Go ye therefore into the highways; and as many as you shall find, call to the marriage." [7]

"Efficacious" may, in this case, be understood either in the Thomistic sense, which is ours, or in the Molinistic sense. The Thomists find a greater gratuity in the gift of God because, according to St. Thomas, grace is efficacious of itself, and leads us sweetly and firmly to the salutary consent which it produces in us and with us. In Molina's opinion, grace is rendered efficacious by our good consent, the free determination of which, as determination, would come exclusively from us and not from God.[8]

---

[6] Cf. St. John of the Cross, *The Ascent of Mount Carmel*, Bk. II chaps. 11–13, and *The Dark Night of the Soul*, Bk. I, chap. 9. Cf. also the work which may be considered a summary of Tauler's teaching, *The Institutions*, chap. 35.

[7] Matt. 22: 2–10.

[8] Cf. St. Thomas, *De malo*, q.6, a.1 ad 3um: "Deus movet quidem voluntatem immutabiliter propter efficaciam virtutis moventis, quae deficere non potest; sed propter naturam voluntatis motae, quae indifferenter se habet ad diversa, non inducitur necessitas, sed manet libertas." It is thus St. Thomas understands St. Paul's expression: "For it is God who worketh in you, both to will and to accomplish, according to His good will" (Phil. 2: 13). Cf. also Ia IIae, q.112, a.3: "If God intends, while moving, that the one whose heart He moves should attain to grace, he will infallibly attain to it, according to John 6: 45: 'Everyone that hath heard of the Father and hath learned cometh

Although the Thomists commonly say that the remote call to the mystical life is general, they in no way diminish the gratuity of the individual, proximate call. They always presuppose the mystery of predestination, as St. Augustine and St. Thomas understand it.[9]

Moreover, the proximate vocation to the mystical life may be delayed, like that of the laborers of the eleventh hour, who received as much as those who had been called earlier. At the end of this parable [10] and that of the wedding feast, our Lord says: "For many are called, but few are chosen." [11]

A proximate, efficacious vocation to the mystical life is not necessarily an efficacious vocation to the highest degrees of the mystical life or to a high perfection; that depends on predestination in the order of the divine intentions, and on the fidelity of the soul in the order of execution. "It is true," says St. John of the Cross, "that souls, whatever their capacity, may have attained union, but all do not possess it in the same degree. God disposes freely of this degree of union, as He disposes freely of the degree of the beatific vision." [12] St. Thomas expresses the same opinion when he discusses predestination.[13]

---

to Me.'" Likewise Ia, q.105, a.4; Ia IIae, q.10, a.4, c and ad 3um; q.111, a.2 ad 2um; q.113; *De veritate*, q.22, a.8, 9. Contrary to what Molina said later, St. Thomas wrote (*In Matth.*, 25:15): "Qui plus conatur, plus habet de gratia; sed quod plus conetur, indiget altiori causa." Likewise *In Ep. ad Ephes.*, 4: 7, and Ia IIae, q.112, a.4.

9 See Ia, q.23, a.5. Modern authors who deny this general call, as if they fear to impair the gratuity of the proximate, individual call, are mostly Molinists. They are inspired by principles other than those of St. Thomas. They assume that ordinarily it is we who render divine grace efficacious. Then they regard as essentially extraordinary the passive states, in which grace seems efficacious of itself, in which our free determination comes from God who produces it in us and with us, and in which the soul needs only to commit itself into the hands of God and to use its own activity merely to make itself more dependent on Him. Cf. Molina, *Concordia* (1876 ed.), pp. 230, 459, 565.

10 Matt. 20: 1–16.

11 Cf. *infra*, p. 379, and also St. Teresa, *The Interior Castle*, fifth mansion, chap. 1.

12 *The Ascent of Mount Carmel*, Bk. II, chap. 5.

13 St. Thomas, Ia, q.23, a.5 ad 3um.

Such are the different meanings of the word "call." They can be seen at a glance in the following synopsis, which should be read from the bottom up so as to follow the ascending progress. In it we do not mention the special vocation, such as that to the priesthood, since we are speaking here only of the call to the mystical life, which, in our opinion, is first of all general, then individual; first remote, then proximate.

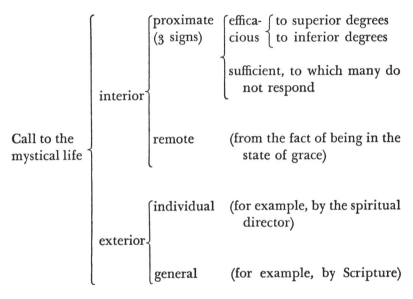

| | | proximate (3 signs) | effica-cious | to superior degrees |
| | | | | to inferior degrees |
| | interior | | sufficient, to which many do not respond | |
| Call to the mystical life | | remote | (from the fact of being in the state of grace) | |
| | exterior | individual | (for example, by the spiritual director) | |
| | | general | (for example, by Scripture) | |

This division should solve several other questions.[14]

If, therefore, a writer who is accepted as an authority denies the call of all souls to contemplation, meaning by this the proximate call, as one can see from the principles of his teaching and from the context, we need not for this reason conclude that he denies the remote call.

With the different meanings of the word "vocation" thus

14 It is thus the sacerdotal vocation is not only exterior (by the bishop), but also interior (by grace). Canon 1353 of the Code of Canon Law states that pastors should train in piety and in studies children in whom they find "signs of an ecclesiastical vocation" in order "to cultivate this germ of vocation in them."

precisely determined, the teaching on the general and remote call of souls to the mystical life is more easily understood. To have a clear grasp of this doctrine, we must distinguish, as is always done in ethics, what belongs to the nature of things (*per se*) from what is an accidental exception (*per accidens*). Theologians, seeking to establish a law, speak formally of the nature of things, and not of the accidental circumstances that cause variations in the application of the law. For example, a certain act is morally good by its very nature, because of itself it produces a certain effect willed by God; and it remains morally good even if accidentally it no longer produces that effect.[15] Or again, what is entirely legitimate and salutary in itself, such as daily communion, may accidentally cease to be so, if the subject does not fulfil the required conditions. Nothing is more sanctifying in itself than Eucharistic communion, but accidentally it may become a sacrilege. *Corruptio optimi pessima.* Nothing is better than true mysticism, nothing worse than false mysticism.

Even in the order of vegetable and animal life, for lack of certain conditions, many laws are applied only in the majority of cases, *ut in pluribus* as the Scholastics say; these are approximative laws, to use the terminology of present-day scholars. Because many acorns do not produce oaks, we cannot deny the law that the acorn is naturally made to produce an oak. Even if it is planted with this end in view, favorable external conditions, required for the development of the seed that it contains, may be lacking.

Likewise, because the majority of men follow their pas-

[15] Cf. Cajetan, on IIa, IIae, q.153, a.3: "Praecepta moralia attendunt ad id quod secundum naturam est, et non ad id quod per accidens in hac vel complexione, vel aetate invenitur." Cajetan makes this remark frequently against those who forget that St. Thomas speaks formally of the nature of things, prescinding from accidental circumstances. "Auctoris sermo et doctrina est formalis et nihil detrimenti patitur ex his quae sunt per accidens." Thus St. Thomas himself answers his own question as to whether an oath is licit: It is in itself, but it may become illicit if bad use is made of it; that is, if one takes an oath without necessity and the desired precautions; just as Eucharistic communion may become a sacrilege (IIa IIae, q.89, a.2).

sions instead of controlling them, as St. Thomas observes,[16] must we reject the law that man, by his nature as a rational being, is called to live in a reasonable manner? Because many men are lost, must we deny that the entire human race was ordained by God for a supernatural end, the beatific vision? Because many Christians sin mortally, is it necessary to deny that the grace received in baptism is by its very nature made to endure forever and to grow unceasingly until death? Is it not eternal life begun?

Normally a little child, who from the age of seven receives communion several times a week, should not cease receiving the bread of life, and each day he ought to approach the holy table with better dispositions. If he perseveres in this way and is generally faithful to the graces he receives, will he not normally, at least at the end of his life, reach the mystical life, properly so called? Is this something different from the plenitude of the life of faith and of the love of God, different from perfect docility to the Holy Ghost?

After having determined the various meanings of the word "call," general or individual, remote or proximate, sufficient or efficacious, we will examine whether it is true that all souls in the state of grace are called in a general, remote, and sufficient manner to the mystical life, and how the individual, proximate call, whether sufficient or efficacious, is manifested.

These distinctions are necessary if we are to solve this problem of spirituality, which is so much studied in our day. It is practical, however, to recall that more attention must be paid to the perfect practice of the virtues—humility, self-denial, obedience, patience in trial, the spirit of faith and confidence in God in prayer despite interior aridities and obscurities, and fraternal charity—than to the more or less

---

16 See Ia, q.49, a.3 ad 5um: "In man alone does evil appear as in the greater number; because the good of man as regards the senses is not the good of man as man—that is, in regard to reason; and more men seek good in regard to the senses than good according to reason." On this point see the general index to the works of St. Thomas, *Tabula aurea*, under the word "Malum," no. 37.

mystical form of prayers which may lead thereto. This is so much the more true because the degree of prayer is not easily known, especially in those periods called the dark night where the soul is contemplative without knowing it. This is the explanation of the fact that in the process of beatification the heroic degree of the virtues is examined much more closely than the form of prayer. The latter is learned only with difficulty from documents; it suffices, however, to become acquainted with the heroic practice of the theological virtues in order to know that a soul was very intimately united to God.[17] Moreover, certain souls reach mystical prayer with greater rapidity than others, which are much more advanced. Souls are also found which draw greater profit from these prayers, others less. Some souls are more virtuous than mystical, and vice versa.

All of this is very important in fact, and should not be forgotten when insistence is laid, as is done in this article, on the general law, and on the extremely varied applications of which we seek the formula and the doctrinal basis according to traditional teaching. But conformably to this law, it is also very useful and practical to know whether or not souls have passed through the night of the senses and that of the soul; for without this double passive purification, souls cannot attain the full perfection of the Christian life. The way leading to it in the midst of trials is that indicated by St. Teresa in her well-known *Bookmark:*

> "Let nothing disturb thee;
> Nothing affright thee;
> All things are passing;
> God never changes;
> Patient endurance
> Attaineth to all things;

[17] We could easily point out in the lives of almost all the saints the interior trials which correspond to the mystical state, called by St. John of the Cross the passive night of the senses and of the spirit.

Who God possesseth
In nothing is wanting;
Alone God sufficeth." [18]

Anyone who is imbued with these dispositions, who has taken this step and willingly allows himself to be conducted in his prayer and in all phases of his life by Mary Mediatrix, who leads us to the intimacy of Christ, and by Christ, who brings us to the Father, will attain to true humility, which will draw upon him the grace of contemplation and of divine union. This happy result will be attained in spite of unfavorable conditions, by reason of the profound, strong, and gentle influence of these two mediators, who have been given us in our weakness.[19]

## ARTICLE II

### The General and Remote Call to Mystical Contemplation

The question we are studying may be formulated exactly either by considering the life of grace in an abstract manner, or concretely by studying the souls which have received this light. In the first case, the intimate law of the superior development of the divine seed, *semen gloriae,* is considered; in the second case, as in the parable of the sower, the variable conditions of the soil are considered. Likewise the two following questions are distinct: (1) Is grace by its very essence the seed of eternal life? (2) Does God give, not only to all men in general, but to each person individually, sufficient grace to obtain salvation?

We will, therefore, consider first the general and remote call of souls in the state of grace to the mystical life; and

[18] Translation by Longfellow.
[19] Cf. Blessed Grignion de Montfort, *Traité de la vraie devotion à Marie,* chap. 4, art. 5. St. Teresa, *The Interior Castle,* epilogue.

secondly, the individual and proximate call. In another article, we will examine the objections that may be raised against this doctrine.

THE THREE PRINCIPAL REASONS WHICH ESTABLISH
THE GENERAL AND REMOTE CALL

The question confronting us is whether the life of grace can have its full, normal development without the mystical life, properly so called. This latter, as we have seen, is characterized by the predominance of the gifts of the Holy Ghost and of their divine mode, specifically distinct from the human mode of the virtues which characterizes the ascetical life.[1] According to what we have said in the preceding article, it appears certain to us that the mystical life thus defined is the adult age of the Christian life. For a clear grasp of this doctrine, the division of the supernatural should be recalled (cf. *supra*, p. 59).

It is evident from this division that the supernatural nature of a miracle, of prophecy, of the gift of tongues, etc., is inferior to that of sanctifying grace, of the infused virtues, and of the gifts of the Holy Ghost. As a help in discerning among these forms of the supernatural, those which are ordinary, although eminent, and those which are extraordinary, the classic division of the divine power directed by wisdom should also be recalled.

Our problem in this question is to examine whether the essential foundation of the mystical state belongs to the first

[1] Cf. St. Thomas, Ia IIae, q.68. The mystical state is identified with the passive way. It is, consequently, entirely distinct not only from graces *gratis datae*, like prophecy, but also from certain special and extraordinary favors, such as interior words, which may be ordained especially to the sanctification of the soul receiving them, and sometimes accompany infused contemplation and the mystical union, without constituting its essence. They are concomitant, accessory, and passing phenomena which may be declared essentially extraordinary, without impairing the doctrine according to which mystical contemplation itself is not essentially or intrinsically extraordinary, but only extrinsically so.

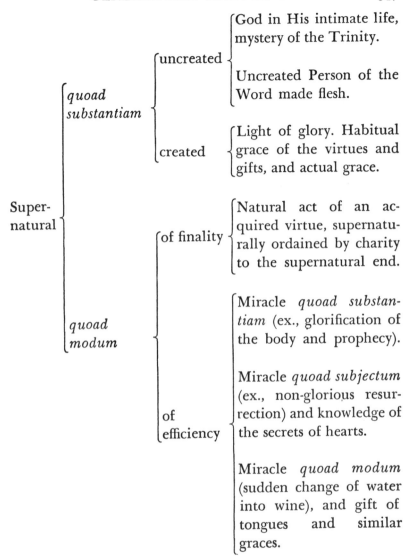

Supernatural
- quoad substantiam
  - uncreated
    - God in His intimate life, mystery of the Trinity.
    - Uncreated Person of the Word made flesh.
  - created
    - Light of glory. Habitual grace of the virtues and gifts, and actual grace.
- quoad modum
  - of finality
    - Natural act of an acquired virtue, supernaturally ordained by charity to the supernatural end.
  - of efficiency
    - Miracle quoad substantiam (ex., glorification of the body and prophecy).
    - Miracle quoad subjectum (ex., non-glorious resurrection) and knowledge of the secrets of hearts.
    - Miracle quoad modum (sudden change of water into wine), and gift of tongues and similar graces.

category or to the third; the third, while extraordinary, is inferior to the first, which alone contains eternal life begun. Is the mystical life the full normal development of the life of grace? We are concerned here not only with the collective sanctity of the Church, which requires even graces *gratis*

| Divine power ordained or directed by wisdom | ordinary (according to laws) | super-natural | 1: life of grace, sanctity, eternal life. |
| | | natural | 2: ex., natural life of the intellect. |
| | extraordinary (outside of ordinary laws) | super-natural | 3: ex., extraordinary visions, private revelations. |
| | | natural | 4: ex., miracle in the physical order. |

*datae,* such as that of the discernment of spirits, but with what is normally necessary in the majority of cases for a soul to reach sanctity.[2]

The reasons for the affirmative answer must be based on the life of grace considered in its essence, and not only on exterior signs or statistical material. As a matter of fact, it is not sufficient to say that this call is general because there are mystical souls in every human condition; among the ignorant and the learned, priests and laity, religious and seculars, in the contemplative orders and also in the active orders. This reason is probable, but is insufficient; for we can just as well say that artists are to be found among all classes of people, and yet the artistic vocation in the natural order is not general but special. It is a particular gift not granted or promised to all.

Likewise, to establish that God wishes to save all men, we must do more than show that He wishes to save men from every condition of life; Jews and pagans, learned and illiterate, rich and poor.

To prove that all souls in the state of grace are in a general

[2] Cf. *supra,* pp. 235–38, for the meaning of the words "ordinary" and "extraordinary."

and remote manner called to the mystical life, as they are to that of heaven, the reasons for this call must be based on the very nature of the life of sanctifying grace, or "grace of the virtues and the gifts." This life may be considered chiefly in three ways: in its principle, grace itself; in its progress, perfect purification from sin and imperfection; in its end, the life of heaven. These three considerations are not accidental, exterior, or material, but essential and formal. In other words, to show that the interior life has its full, normal development here only in the mystical life, properly so called, we must demonstrate: (1) that their principle is the same; (2) that the progress of one is complete only in the other; (3) that their end is the same, and that only the mystical life prepares immediately and perfectly for this end. These are, as we shall see, the principal reasons proving the normal though eminent character of the mystical life.

### A. THE BASIC PRINCIPLE OF THE MYSTICAL LIFE IS THE SAME AS THAT OF THE COMMON INTERIOR LIFE

The basic principle of the mystical life is sanctifying grace, or "the grace of the virtues and the gifts." It manifests itself in the interior ascetical life according to the human mode of the virtues; in the mystical life, according to the superhuman mode of the gifts which predominates in it. These gifts, as habitual dispositions rendering us docile to the inspirations of the Holy Ghost, grow, as do the infused virtues, with charity, which in this life ought always to develop, through our merits and holy communion, according to the requirements of the first precept of love which has no limit.[3] Therefore the soul cannot possess charity in a high degree without having the gifts, as habitual dispositions, in a corresponding degree.[4] It follows that a truly generous and faithful soul

---

[3] *Summa,* IIa, IIae, q.184, a.3.

[4] Cf. Ia IIae, q.66, a.2: All the virtues, as *habitus,* by reason of their relation (and the same must be said for the gifts which are also connected with

will come more and more under the immediate direction of the Holy Ghost, and the human mode of its activity will be gradually subordinated to the divine mode of the inspirations of the interior Master. This mode should end by dominating, a condition which characterizes the mystical life.

The objection has been raised that if progress is normal, the virtues and gifts should be perfected *pari passu*, without the mode of the gifts eventually prevailing over the mode of the virtues. This objection fails to reckon with what St. Thomas has proved [5] and with what we have explained in accordance with his teaching,[6] namely, that the human mode of the infused virtues is essentially imperfect in relation to our supernatural end, for it is that of the human faculty in which these virtues are received. The purpose of the gifts is precisely to remedy this imperfection by joining with the virtues, as occurs especially in infused contemplation.[7]

Hence the imperfection of the human mode of the virtues should be corrected in proportion as the soul approaches perfection, so much the more so, as it is a question here not only of believing the mysteries, but of penetrating them, tasting them, judging all by them, living by them and that, not in a transitory, but in an habitual manner. The influence of the gifts should be exercised more in proportion as the soul needs to be purified in its inmost depths, where God penetrates, so as to root out the seeds of death, the existence of which we ourselves do not suspect. God alone can eradicate them by

---

them in charity, Ia IIae, q.68, a.2, 5) grow together, while keeping their difference of perfection like the fingers of one's hands. A man may, however, have a greater natural inclination to practice one virtue than another, or he may be more inclined by the grace of God to make acts of that virtue. Likewise St. Thomas, when speaking of the connection of the gifts, says: "One cannot be perfect without the others" (Ia IIae, q.68, a.5 ad 3um). Yet one soul has greater excellence in the acts of one than of another.

[5] *Summa*, Ia IIae, q.68, a.1, 2.

[6] Cf. *supra*, pp. 281 ff.

[7] In fact, it proceeds as to its substance from faith, and as to its mode from the gift of wisdom.

applying iron and fire to them. This explains why, in the normal progress of the life of grace, the superhuman mode of the gifts should end by dominating and prevailing over the human mode of the virtues. Habitual facility thus supernaturalizes us more and more, and eventually the virtues are no longer exercised without the co-operation of the gifts, without an almost constant direction on the part of the interior Master, who unites us more and more closely to His life and His action. This is the prelude of eternal life. "A thing is perfect so far as it attains to its principle" [8] and is united to it. Each of our acts is perfect in proportion as God imprints His manner, His inimitable mark, more deeply upon it. The sovereign efficacy of His action in us does not destroy our liberty; it is His action which causes our liberty, by producing in us and with us even the free mode of our acts.[9] He alone can thus penetrate our souls, since He is closer to us than we are to ourselves. The mystical state with its constant docility is none other than the perfect fruit of efficacious grace, as conceived by St. Paul, St. Augustine, and St. Thomas. Only in this way does the soul attain to the living and profound knowledge of God's infinite grandeur and of its own wretchedness, of the value of grace and the gravity of sin.

"But, someone will say," declares St. Teresa in the objection she raises to her own doctrine,[10] "if for long days and years I considered what a frightful thing it is to offend God, and how those who are lost are His children and my brethren; and if I were to weigh the perils to which we are exposed in this world, and how advantageous it would be for us to leave this wretched life, would that not suffice? No, my daughters, the pain to which these reflections give rise in us would be quite different from the torture of which I speak. With the grace of God and by many considerations we can experience

---

[8] St. Thomas Ia, q. 12, a. 1.
[9] *Ibid.*, q. 19, a. 8.
[10] *The Interior Castle*, fifth mansion, chap. 2.

this grief; but it does not penetrate the very depths of our being like the other which seems to rend and grind the soul without its co-operation, and at times even without its wish. What is this sorrow, then, and whence does it come? I will tell you. You remember those words of the Bride, which I quoted to you, but with another meaning: 'He brought me into the cellar of wine, He set in order charity in me.' [11] In this quotation you have the explanation of what you asked me. This soul has so completely abandoned itself into the hands of God and loves Him so greatly that, as a result, it is so submissive that it knows and wishes nothing, but that God should dispose of it according to His good pleasure. In my opinion, this is a grace which God bestows only on a soul which He considers entirely His. His will is that, without knowing how, the soul should issue forth stamped with His seal. . . . O God of goodness! It is Thou alone who dost all! Thou dost demand but one thing, that we abandon our wills to Thee, in other words, that the wax offer no resistance."

Attentive reading of this quotation, which expresses the mystical suffering of the soul at the sight of the greatest evil, sin, will reveal the full development of the grace of the virtues and the gifts which we received in baptism—perfect abandonment, most pure charity, equally lively faith, and complete docility to the Holy Ghost who impresses His seal on the faithful soul. This demonstrates that the principle of the common interior life contains the seed of the mystical life. It is, therefore, called to develop under this superior form which is on earth the flower of the supernatural life.[12]

[11] Cant. 2: 4.

[12] Some theologians have taught that the Holy Ghost moves souls in two ways: (1) according to the common mode which accommodates itself in everything to the human mode and does not exceed the ordinary laws of grace; (2) according to an extraordinary and preternatural mode of which mystical authors speak. Cf. Billot, *De virt. infusis*, pp. 173, 188.

These expressions seem to show that for these theologians mystical contemplation is essentially extraordinary and not eminent only. If they hold this

In some perfect souls the gifts of action will be especially prominent; but the gift of wisdom will have a diffuse, though very real, influence.

In virtue of the fact that this principle is common both to the ordinary interior life and to the mystical life, we must add that by the progress of charity [13] we can come to merit, in the strict sense of the word (*de condigno,* condignly), the superior degrees of the gifts of the Holy Ghost, considered as habitual dispositions, connected with charity. Thereby we merit, at least in the broad sense (*saltem de congruo,* congruously), the actual inspirations corresponding to these superior degrees of the gifts; for, as a rule (and the propriety of this is evident), the Holy Ghost enlightens and inspires souls according to the degree of their habitual docility, humility, and love of God.[14]

---

opinion, we no longer see how they remain faithful to the teaching of St. Thomas on the gifts. It is clear that each of the gifts cannot have two distinct modes, a distinction not only of degree but of nature. There would then be two *habitus* specifically distinct; the first would develop in vain, for it would never attain the second. Moreover, it would be incomprehensible why, above the acquired virtues and the infused virtues with a human mode, there would still be necessary an exercise of the gifts according to a human mode, distinct from their exercise according to their divine mode. The human mode of the gifts would be identical with that of the infused virtues. The opinions mentioned above might, however, be explained in a way not opposed to the teaching we have set forth according to the principles of St. Thomas. As a matter of fact, we recognize that the inspirations of the gifts of the Holy Ghost are exercised at first in a latent manner which is suited to the human mode, and that later their superhuman mode becomes manifest and frequent. The latter may even be called extraordinary when it is accompanied by graces *gratis datae,* destined for the benefit of one's neighbor, such as the grace called *sermo sapientiae.* This is what St. Thomas means in IIa IIae, q.45, a.5, as Cajetan explains, *ibid.;* John of St. Thomas, *De donis,* d.18, a.2, 9; and Joseph of the Holy Ghost, *Cursus theol. myst.,* II, 236 ff. Compare this text (IIa IIae, q.45, a.5) with Ia IIae, q.111, a.4 ad 4um.

[13] Cf. Ia IIae, q.114, a.8. St. Thomas shows that we can merit condignly the increase of grace and glory, by quoting this text from the Book of Proverbs, 4: 18: "But the path of the just as a shining light, goeth forward and increaseth even to perfect day." But what we cannot merit is the very principle of merit, the grace of justification, and the efficacious grace which preserves us *in statu gratiae,* particularly that of final perseverance. Cf. *ibid.,* a.5, 9.

[14] Condign merit is based on divine justice; it is a right to a reward. Congruous merit is based on divine friendship, *in jure amicabili,* or at least on

This is the teaching concerning the merit *saltem de congruo* of Thomistic mystical theologians who follow St. Thomas, St. John of the Cross, and St. Teresa. Among these theologians are Philip of the Blessed Trinity, O.C.,[15] Vallgornera, O.P.,[16] and Meynard, O.P.[17] From this teaching on merit, it is evident that the actual grace of contemplation can be merited more than that of a happy death, which is, nevertheless, necessary to salvation.[18]

The first reason for the remote and general call of souls in the state of grace to the mystical life rests, therefore, on the

---

the liberality of God. The first renders us worthy of reward; the second, as the name indicates, implies only propriety.

[15] *Summa theologiae mysticae* (1874), II, 311.

[16] *Mystica theologia D. Thomae* (1911), I, 445.

[17] *Traité de la vie intérieure* (1885), II, 128.

[18] The grace of a happy death or of final perseverance cannot be merited condignly in the strict sense of the word, nor even strictly congruously. It is, however, necessary for salvation and we ought certainly to desire it, to dispose ourselves for it, and to ask for it incessantly, because persevering prayer will obtain it for us. The same may be said for the grace of conversion or justification for a sinner. It cannot be merited, since it is the principle of merit; yet anyone in the state of mortal sin ought, with the actual grace offered him, to desire it and ask for it. These are profound mysteries of the efficacy of grace and of predestination. Cf. Ia IIae, q. 114, a. 5, 9.

The grace of justification and that of final perseverance are necessary for salvation, but they cannot be merited condignly. The same is true of efficacious graces which keep us in the state of grace.

The grace of infused contemplation is not gratuitous, since one can progressively merit condignly a very high degree of the gift of wisdom, considered as a *habitus*, and since the Holy Ghost generally inspires souls according to the degree of their habitual docility.

Moreover, we must add to merit the impetrative power of prayer. Since we ought to ask for the grace of a happy death, which we are unable to merit, a fervent soul may indeed ask also, with as much confidence as humility, for the grace of contemplation in order to live the mysteries of salvation more fully, to know its own wretchedness better, to humble itself on this account, and to be less indifferent to the glory of God and the salvation of souls. Reduced to common terms, this is what the soul requests when it recites the *Veni Creator* with sincerity. The grace of contemplation is thereby less gratuitous than graces *gratis datae*, such as the grace of a miracle or prophecy, which are in no way necessary to our personal sanctification. After all, the fact remains that the Holy Ghost breathes where He wills, and when He wills; for we do not exercise at will the acts which proceed from the gifts of the Holy Ghost. Cf. *infra*, pp. 409 ff., "An examination of some theoretical difficulties," in particular as to merit.

basic principle of this life, that is, the grace of the virtues and the gifts. This fundamental reason may also be more concretely expressed and even confirmed thereby in the following terms: there is no sanctity without the heroism of the infused virtues, connected with charity; that is, without a high degree of these virtues, described by St. Thomas when he speaks of the perfecting virtues and especially of the perfect virtues.[19]

The gifts of the Holy Ghost, as habitual dispositions connected with charity, grow with it. The Holy Ghost ordinarily moves us according to the degree of our habitual docility, and with greater frequency as we become more docile. Consequently, as a rule,[20] there is no sanctity unless the soul is often moved by the Holy Ghost according to the superior degrees of the gifts. This constitutes the mystical life in the broad sense and also in the strict sense, the passive state in which the human mode of our activity no longer dominates, but rather the activity of the Holy Ghost, and our completely docile passivity.[21]

In relation to this subject, the statement of Benedict XIV in regard to the heroicity of virtues and their connection should be read. It is this connection, he says, which was lacking in the heroes of paganism and also in the false martyrs, who died obstinately persisting in their errors; they did not pray for their executioners.[22] For the proof of heroic virtue, he lays down four necessary conditions: (1) the matter must be difficult, above the common strength of man; (2) the acts must be accomplished promptly, easily; (3) they must be accomplished joyously; (4) they must be performed not only once or rarely but often, when the occasion presents itself.

---

[19] *Summa*, Ia IIae, q.61, a.5; q.68, a.1 ad 1um; *In Matth.*, 5.
[20] We do not speak here of any case in particular, but of a general law.
[21] *Summa*, Ia IIae, q.68, a.3 ad 2um. St. John of the Cross held that the virtues of the purified soul of which St. Thomas speaks belong to the mystical life. Cf. *Œuvres* (2d ed.), II, 42.
[22] *De Servorum Dei beatificatione*, Bk. III, chap. 21, "de virtute heroica."

This supposes a high degree of charity and a proportionate degree of the gifts of the Holy Ghost.

This teaching clarifies the meaning and the compass of the first reason that we invoked: namely, that the basic principle of the mystical life is identical with that of the common interior life. Farther on we shall see the objections that may be raised against this first reason.[23] We will now consider the second, which considers what the progress of the interior life demands.

## B. IN THE PROGRESS OF THE INTERIOR LIFE THE PURIFICATION OF THE SOUL IS NOT COMPLETE WITHOUT THE PASSIVE PURIFICATIONS, WHICH BELONG TO THE MYSTICAL ORDER

This progress should, in fact, be brought about by the purification from sin, from its results, and from imperfections. It is twofold: an active purification or mortification which we impose on ourselves; and a passive purification which has its origin in the divine action within us.[24] Although exterior trials supernaturally borne contribute greatly to our purification, yet, according to the great masters, especially St. John of the Cross, this work is normally completed only by the passive purifications of the senses and of the soul.

According to these same masters, these painful purifications, which are a sort of anticipated purgatory, belong to the mystical order, properly so called. Wholly generous souls are purified by the Holy Ghost while they are on earth, to such an extent that they do not, through their own fault, have to undergo after death the meritless purification of purgatory. Ordinarily we must pass through this crucible in one way or

---

[23] Cf. *infra*, chap. 5, art. 4; chap. 6, art. 1.

[24] It proceeds especially from the gift of understanding. Cf. St. Thomas, IIa IIae, q.8, a.7. Ia IIae, q.69, a.2 ad 3um: "In this life . . . the (mind's) eye being cleansed by the gift of understanding, we can, so to speak, see God."

another; either in this life while meriting, or in the life to come without meriting.[25]

This reason appears decisive to one acquainted with the reasons given by St. John of the Cross to explain the necessity of the double, passive purification of the senses and of the soul.[26] We have already (chap. 4, art. 1) given a brief exposition of these purifications, and (chap. 5, art. 3) we have shown how St. Teresa describes the night of the soul at the beginning of the sixth mansion

According to St. John of the Cross, God almost immediately bestows the grace of the passive purification of the senses on persons who are habitually recollected.[27] The entrance into this purification is indicated by inactivity of the imagination,[28] the human or discursive mode of prayer disappears; the soul must content itself with a loving and peaceful attention to God.[29] His grace, which is then given to it, is no longer sensibly manifest; it is entirely spiritual, which explains why the sensible part is cowardly in regard to action, but the spirit is generous and strong.[30] In the light of the gift

25 We say that ordinarily the soul must pass through this crucible. There are, in fact, exceptions, to mention only that of children who die immediately after their baptism. They will not, however, have as high a degree of glory as if they had merited in trial. As for martyrs who before their torture did not pass through the crucible of which we speak, they did pass through it in their last sufferings. This explains why St. John of the Cross says of souls which have undergone the very painful night of the soul: "As a result of their perfect purification by love, they will not pass through purgatory" (*The Dark Night of the Soul*, Bk. II, chap. 20).

Likewise Tauler states (Sermon 55) on the subject of beginners, who remain faithful to the commandments: "It is rather an exception for them to live in sufficient purity to avoid purgatory, although that may occasionally happen." It may occur, for example, in the case of a young religious who dies immediately after profession. If he had lived longer, he would probably have fallen again into faults which would exact the purification of which we are speaking either before or after death. In any case, no one goes to purgatory after death except through his own fault. If he had been more faithful to grace, he could have avoided it.

26 *The Dark Night of the Soul*, Bk. I, chap. 3; Bk. II, chap. 1.

27 *Ibid.*, Bk. I, chap. 8.

28 *Ibid.*, chap. 9.

29 *Ibid.*, chap. 10.

30 *Ibid.*, chap. 9.

of knowledge, the soul sees in itself wretchedness and unworthiness which it was ignorant of in the time of its prosperity; at times it believes itself abandoned by God. But in
suffering, it is purified of numerous imperfections and exercised in the virtues that perfectly subject the flesh to the
spirit.[31] Thus, interior liberty grows through the twelve
fruits of the Holy Ghost, and the love of God through an
ardent desire to serve Him. St. John of the Cross offers a
good summary of his doctrine when he says: "The night of
sense is common, and the lot of many among beginners. . . .
As the manner in which they behave when they first start out
on the way to God is not noble, and since they become en-
tangled in sensible tastes and self-love, God intervenes to
make them progress by freeing them from their vulgar conception of love. He wishes to lift them up to Himself, to
make them abandon the inferior exercise of sense and reasoning, by which they seek God in a petty manner in the midst
of the obstacles which we have pointed out, and to introduce
them into the more profitable exercise of the spirit, which
will permit them to communicate less imperfectly with
God." [32]

This passive night of the senses, which seems to consist
especially in the disappearance of the so-called sensible graces,
marks rather the appearance of spiritual graces; the human
mode of prayer ceases only because the superhuman mode of
the contemplative gifts begins to become frequent and manifest. *Corruptio unius, generatio alterius:* the grain of wheat,
cast into the earth, dies that the seed which it bears may
develop; just so, the soul must die to its too human manner
of thinking of God and loving Him that it may live in the
divine manner which the Lord wishes to see in it. It is thus
that the soul enters upon the illuminative way.[33]

[31] *Ibid.*, chaps. 11–13.
[32] *The Dark Night of the Soul,* Bk. I, chap. 8.
[33] *Ibid.*, Bk. I, chap. 14: "The soul has gone forth: it has begun to penetrate
the way of the spirit, which the proficient and the advanced follow, and which

Since the object of the passive purification of the senses is the perfect subjection of the passions to the intellect and will, the object of the purification of the soul—proceeding especially from the illumination of the gift of understanding —is the full subjection of the spirit to God and the purification from all alloy not only of the moral virtues, but also of the theological virtues, which unite us immediately to God. This purification, granted to souls that have already made progress, is intended to remove habitual imperfections of which we are so often unaware, and which are an obstacle to divine union.[34] It marks the entrance into the unitive way, according to St. John of the Cross. He expresses himself in the following terms: [35] "The dark night (of the soul) is a certain inflowing of God into the soul, which cleanses it of its ignorances and imperfections, habitual, natural, and spiritual. Contemplatives call it infused contemplation. . . . But it may be asked: 'Why does the soul call the divine light, which enlightens the soul and purges it of its ignorances, the dark night?' . . . The first reason is that the divine wisdom is so high that it transcends the capacity of the soul, and is, therefore, in that respect, darkness. The second reason is based on the meanness and impurity of the soul and, in that respect, the divine wisdom is painful to it, afflictive and dark also. . . . We take for granted a principle of the Philosopher, namely, the more intelligible and evident divine things are, the darker and more hidden they are to the soul naturally. Thus the clearer the light, the more it blinds the eyes of the owl. So the divine light of contemplation, when it beats on the soul not yet perfectly enlightened, causes spiritual darkness, because it not only surpasses its strength,

---

is also called the illuminative way, or the way of infused contemplation." This traditional conception of the illuminative way is far superior, as is evident, to that which has been set forth by several non-mystical writers since the seventeenth century.

[34] *Ibid.*, Bk. II, chap. 2.
[35] *Ibid.*, chap. 5.

but because it blinds it and deprives it of its natural perceptions. It is for this reason that St. Dionysius and other mystical theologians call infused contemplation a ray of darkness, that is, for the unenlightened and unpurified soul . . . 'clouds and darkness are round and about him.' [36] . . . God is surrounded by a cloud and darkness. He dwells in 'light inaccessible.'

"The soul seeing its own impurity distinctly though dimly in this bright pure light, acknowledges its own unworthiness before God and all creatures. What pains it still more is a fear that it never will be worthy and that all its goodness is gone." [37] The suffering is such that the soul believes itself crushed under an immense weight; it is broken and overwhelmed at the sight of its miseries and feels itself wrapped in a mortal cloud. "So great are the weakness and impurity of the soul that the hand of God, which is so soft and so gentle, is felt to be so heavy and oppressive, though neither pressing nor resting on it, but merely touching it and that, too, most mercifully; for He touches the soul not to chastise it, but to load it with His graces." [38]

The soul cannot, as before, raise its mind and heart to God; it feels that God has interposed a cloud which cuts off the way of prayer.[39] The light of this purification permits the soul to see only its sins and miseries.[40] In this darkness it distinguishes, however, better than before between what is more and what is less perfect.[41] To enjoy the fruits of this purification, the soul must suffer from the impression that it will never possess God.[42] It must pass through this crucible for "one single, actual, or habitual particular affection is

[36] Ps. 96: 2.
[37] *The Dark Night of the Soul*, Bk. II, chap. 5.
[38] *Ibid.*
[39] *Ibid.*, chap. 5.
[40] *Ibid.*, chap. 13.
[41] *Ibid.*, chap. 8.
[42] *Ibid.*, chap. 9.

sufficient to prevent the perception, taste, and communication of the subtle sweetness of the spirit of love which contains all sweetness within itself in an eminent degree." [43] This night of purification is also a safe road, "for it holds the appetites, affections, and passions, lulled, asleep, and mortified. Were they awake and active, they would not fail to oppose the departure" of the soul toward these higher regions. [44]

This passive purification, this refinement of the spirit, is "indispensable for union with God in glory. After death, impure souls pass through the fires of purgatory; in this life, the soul attains to union only by undergoing the fire of trials, which are more violent for some than for others, and proportionate in length to the degree of union to which God intends to raise them and to their need of purification." [45] From these trials we can judge the sufferings of purgatory. Its fire has no effect on those who have no faults to expiate; [46] it is dark and material; that of this life is spiritual and obscure. [47] In this life, the soul is purified while meriting; after death, without meriting.

These purifications are the most efficacious means leading to divine union, because they alone free humility and the three theological virtues from all alloy. They alone bring into powerful relief the entirely supernatural formal motive of these highest virtues. They oblige us to make extremely meritorious acts, which thus increase the gifts tenfold by immediately obtaining for us a great increase of faith, hope, and charity. They oblige us to believe for the sole motive that God has said it. Moreover, they make us adhere firmly to the first revealing Truth, in an order infinitely superior

43 *Ibid.*
44 *Ibid.*, chap. 15.
45 *The Living Flame of Love*, st. II, 5.
46 *The Dark Night of the Soul*, Bk. II, chap. 10.
47 *Ibid.*, chap. 12.

to a sensible miracle and to the human reasoning that discerns it.[48] They oblige us to hope against all human hope for the pure motive that God, who is all powerful and good, is infinitely helpful, *Deus auxilians,* and will not abandon us first. They lead us to love Him, not for the sensible or spiritual consolations He grants us, but for Himself, because He is infinite goodness; to love Him above all things and more than ourselves, because He is infinitely better than we are.

Happy are those who pass through these painful purifications, which alone can fully supernaturalize them and conduct them to the summit of faith, hope, and charity. Since these passive purifications belong to the mystical order, we must conclude that the mystical life is not extraordinary in its very essence, but is on the normal way of sanctity. Now that we have studied the means, we will consider the end of the interior life.

C. THE END OF THE INTERIOR LIFE IS THE SAME AS THAT
OF THE MYSTICAL LIFE, BUT THE LATTER PREPARES
THE SOUL MORE IMMEDIATELY FOR IT

Heaven is the end of the interior life. Although in fact quite rare, the normal summit of the development of the life of grace on this earth should be a very perfect disposition to receive the light of glory immediately after death,

---

[48] When a soul passing through this night of the spirit is suffering from temptations against faith, and is at the same time blinded, so to speak, by the divine light which illumines the depths of mysteries, it would be singularly strange to advise as a remedy the reading of a good, well-reasoned study on apologetics. The divine work, which the soul is undergoing, has precisely for its object to raise the soul above reasoning and to make it adhere in an entirely supernatural manner to the first uncreated and revealing Truth ("Veritas prima in dicendo, auctoritas Dei revelantis"). At such a time the soul should ask the Lord for the grace of faith, the inspiration and illumination of the Holy Ghost which elevates our will and intellect even to the uncreated and eternal Word of God, the Author of grace, in order to make them adhere to it in spite of the darkness, with a certitude superior to that of the most evident rational principles. IIa IIae, q.1, a.1; q.4, a.8. See *supra,* pp. 63–77.

without passing through purgatory. As a matter of fact, no one goes to that place of suffering, where there is no merit, except through his own fault, because he has neglected graces received or offered. It is in the radical order to see God immediately after death; that is why the souls in purgatory suffer so greatly at not seeing Him.

The perfect disposition to receive the beatific vision immediately after death can be only the intense charity of a fully purified soul, coupled with the earnest desire to see God, such as we find them in the mystical union, and more especially in the transforming union. This last is, therefore, the summit of the development of the life of grace on earth; in it alone do we find the full development of the supernatural life.

It would be easy to show that this third reason, like the two preceding reasons, has been more or less explicitly formulated by all the great masters of mysticism. Let us merely recall what St. Thomas says about the superiority of the contemplative life over the active life.

The contemplation of God is not a means to the moral virtues and the works of the active life; on the contrary, it is the end to which they are subordinated as means and dispositions.[49] The moral virtues dispose to the contemplative life by producing peace, quiet in the passions, and purity.[50] Prudence serves wisdom, as a guard serves the king.

God is the end and object of the theological virtues and the corresponding gifts, whereas He is merely the end of the moral virtues, which have a created object.

The contemplative life, with its beginning and end in love, is the eminent exercise of the theological virtues. In it the soul burns to see the beauty of God.[51] Contemplation itself is not perfection; perfection is found essentially in

---

49 *Summa*, IIa IIae, q.180, a.2, c and ad 2um.
50 *Summa*, Ia IIae, q.58, a.5.
51 See IIa IIae, q.180, a.1, 7.

charity. But contemplation is the most excellent means united to the end, since it joins us to God,[52] for "the contemplative life is directed to the love of God, not of any degree, but to that which is perfect." [53] By it man "offers his soul in sacrifice to God," [54] and it is, so to speak, a beginning of perfect beatitude "for it bestows on us a certain inchoate beatitude, which begins now and will be continued in the life to come." [55]

Thus the contemplative life is better than the active life.[56] It is proper to man according to his soul's noblest faculty. It can be more continuous than the active life. For example, Mary remains at our Lord's feet to listen to His words, while Martha busies herself. Although it contains great trials, the contemplative life is more delightful and more meritorious, because the love of God is in itself more meritorious than love of our neighbor.[57] It is sufficient to itself, moreover, and is not busy about many things. It is loved for itself, while the active life is ordained to something other than itself. This is why the psalmist says: "One thing I have asked of the Lord, this will I seek after; that I may dwell in the house

[52] "The contemplative life pertains directly and immediately to the love of God" (ibid., q.182, a.2).

[53] Ibid., a.4 ad 1um.

[54] "A sacrifice is rendered to God spiritually when something is offered to Him; and of all of man's goods, God especially accepts that of the human soul when it is offered to Him in sacrifice. Now a man ought to offer to God, in the first place his soul; . . . in the second place, the souls of others. . . . And the more closely a man unites his own or another's soul to God, the more acceptable is his sacrifice to God; wherefore, it is more acceptable to God that one apply one's own soul and the souls of others to contemplation than to action. Consequently, the statement that no sacrifice is more acceptable to God than zeal for souls, does not mean that the merit of the active life is preferable to the merit of the contemplative life, but that it is more meritorious to offer to God one's own soul and the souls of others, than any other external gifts" (ibid., a.2 ad 3um).

[55] Ibid., q.180, a.4.

[56] Ibid., q.182, a.1.

[57] "Wherefore, that which pertains more directly to the love of God is generically more meritorious than that which pertains directly to the love of our neighbor" (ibid., a.2).

of the Lord all the days of my life." [58] The contemplative life is a sort of holy repose in God (*otium sanctum*): "Be still and see that I am God." [59] It is occupied with divine things; the active life, with human affairs: "In the beginning was the Word; behold Him to whom Mary listened," says St. Augustine. "And the Word was made flesh; behold Him whom Martha served." [60] Moreover, Christ Himself said: "Mary hath chosen the best part, which shall not be taken away from her." [61] St. Augustine observes: "It is not that your part, O Martha, is bad, but that Mary's is better. Why is it better? Because it will not be taken from her. A day will come when the burden which necessity imposes on you will be withdrawn; but the sweetness of truth is eternal." [62]

This contemplative life exists fully only in the mystical life, which is the true prelude to that of heaven. All, even those who are engaged in the active life, should strive for it in virtue of the first precept; prayer is no less necessary to them. If the conditions of their life render the highest forms of contemplation less accessible, its substance is not refused them; on the contrary, our Lord invites us all. "Those who are more adapted to the active life can prepare themselves for the contemplative by the practice of the active life," [63] by fulfilling its duties for the love of God. It would be an error to think that a person should pray well for the purpose of accomplishing well the duties of his state: for example, in order to take good care of the sick or to teach well, as if prayer and union with God were ordained and subordinated to these acts which are inferior to them. Rather, the active soul should accomplish the duties of its state out of love for God, to be more closely united to our Lord and to make Him loved

[58] Ps. 26: 4.
[59] Ps. 45: 11.
[60] *De verbis Domini*, serm. 27.
[61] Luke 10: 42.
[62] *De verbis Domini*, serm. 27.
[63] St. Thomas, IIa IIae, q.182, a.4 ad 3um.

more, so that its activity should become as it were the exterior radiation of its prayer, of its union with God, which is the most important part of activity. Thus the mystical life, far from harming action, is its living source.

St. Augustine says: "Holy leisure is longed for by the love of truth; but it is the necessity of love to undertake requisite business. If no one imposes this burden upon us, we are free to sift and contemplate truth; but if it be laid upon us, we are necessitated for love's sake to undertake it. And yet not even in this case are we obliged wholly to relinquish the sweets of contemplation; for were these to be withdrawn, the burden might prove more than we could bear." [64] St. Thomas says that, when a person is called from the contemplative to the active life, it should not be by way of subtraction from the first, but by addition of the second.[65] This is why the apostolate should flow, as he says elsewhere, from "the plenitude of contemplation." [66] The faithful, the interior souls who come to listen to the word of God, expect it to be given to them in a divine manner, which is but the radiation of contemplation.

The contemplative life, which by its intimacy with the interior Master and its perfect docility to His inspirations merits the name of mystical life, or life hidden with Christ in God, is therefore truly the normal prelude to that of heaven.

In the preceding pages we have discussed the three principal reasons for the remote and general call of just souls to the mystical life. They are fundamental since they rest: (1) on the common principle of the interior life and of the mystical life, and on the law of the progress of the gifts as *habitus*, or habitual dispositions, connected with charity; (2) on the necessity of the passive purifications, which belong

---

[64] *City of God*, Bk. XIX, chap. 19.
[65] *Summa*, IIa IIae, q.182, a.1 ad 3um.
[66] *Ibid.*, q.188, a.6.

to the mystical life and are the most efficacious means to lead the soul to divine union on earth; (3) on the common end of the interior and of the mystical life, and on the perfection normally required to receive the beatific vision immediately after death, and that not in its lowest degree. These three considerations of the principle of the supernatural life, of its most efficacious means, and of its end are not accidental or material; they are essential and formal, and thus permit us to establish the law of the superior development of the divine seed, of the life of grace, *semen gloriae*.

Therefore it seems certain that the mystical life, characterized by the predominance of the gifts of the Holy Ghost, is required for the full perfection of the Christian life. Is this likewise true of mystical contemplation, properly so called? After granting what precedes, certain writers, who hestitate to answer this question, explain their attitude by saying that in some souls the dominant gifts of the Holy Ghost are those relating especially to action; in their prayers and in the psalmody the dominant gift is piety; yet their prayer is not properly passive, nor is there any frequent and manifest intervention of the contemplative gifts of understanding and wisdom. Consequently these souls would be in the mystical life, which is superior to the ascetical, but without having mystical contemplation, properly so called, the prayer of passive recollection or of quiet.

As we have already stated, the gifts of contemplation may as yet intervene in these souls only in a diffuse manner; the mystical life is still imperfect in them. It may be accompanied by a great generosity, which merits the name of perfection without, however, being the full perfection of the Christian life.[67] This last, to be truly a plenitude, requires a

---

[67] As St. Teresa frequently observes, the delights of contemplation are not required for perfection, and not even for very high perfection. As a matter of fact, mystical contemplation is often arid and painful. Cf. Saudreau, *La*

complete development of the entire spiritual organism, including the superior gifts of understanding and wisdom.[68] It is the prelude to the life of heaven, the perfect, immediate preparation for the beatific vision, which is given only to entirely purified souls when they desire it keenly.

This seems to us, in conformity with tradition, to be St. Thomas' doctrine on the relations of the gifts of the Holy Ghost with the progress of charity.[69] In the different religious orders, it is also the teaching of St. Bonaventure, Tauler, Ruysbroeck Louis de Blois, Dionysius the Carthusian, St. Teresa, St. John of the Cross, Father Lallemant, S.J., and his disciples, Father Surin, S.J., and others as Canon Saudreau proves at length in the third edition of his work on *The Life of Union with God according to the Great Masters of Spirituality*.[70] Father Lamballe holds the same opinion in his book entitled *Contemplation*. We agree with these authors and with Father Arintero, O.P., that the supernatural life has its full development in this life only in the transforming union, such as it is described by St. John of the Cross and by St. Teresa in the seventh mansion. It will

---

*vie d'union à Dieu, d'après les grands maîtres de la spiritualité* (3d ed.), p. 263, where he quotes several texts from St. Teresa's writings.

[68] In other words, the mystical contemplation of the mystery of God present in us is required for the full perfection of the life of grace, if we take this word "perfection" not only in the broad sense and from the moral point of view, but in the strict and metaphysical sense, which in this case expresses the full development of the supernatural organism.

[69] See particularly Ia IIae, q.69, a.2: "Whether the rewards assigned to the beatitudes refer to this life?" They are, he says, granted to the perfect (not only to some of them) as a prelude to the life of heaven, "by a kind of imperfect inchoation of future happiness." See also IIa IIae, q.45. "Every Christian," says St. Thomas, "should participate in the contemplation of God, for the precept (Ps. 45: 11) applies to all: 'Be still and see that I am God'" (IIIa, d.36, q.1, a.3 ad 5um). If this is true of every Christian, what must be said of the Christian who has reached the full perfection of the interior life?

[70] The third edition is more complete than the former editions and contains (notably p. 290) the result of the research done by Father Colunga, O.P., on the struggle between the spirituals and the intellectuals at the time of Cano.

be sufficient to recall here some characteristic texts and also those which seem opposed to them.

Speaking of the passive purification of the senses, which belongs to the mystical order, St. John of the Cross says, as we have seen: "The soul must pass through this dark night in order to become perfect." [71] "The soul has set out and begun to penetrate the way of the spirit, the way of the proficient and the advanced, which is also called the illuminative way, or the way of infused contemplation." [72] "It is God alone who must raise the soul to this supernatural state. What is required of the soul is that, so far as it can, it should prepare itself for it. This is possible naturally, especially when we consider the divine help which ordinarily accompanies effort. As the soul makes progress in rejecting forms and emptying itself of them, God gives it union. In this operation the soul is passive." [73] "In the case of religious, this change often takes place after a relatively short time, for having renounced the world they more easily fashion their senses and spirit according to the will of God." [74] "As soon as the soul succeeds in carefully purifying itself of forms and sensible images, it will bathe in that pure and simple light which will become for it the state of perfection. As a matter of fact, this light is always ready to penetrate the soul; forms and veils of creatures create an obstacle to its infusion." [75]

Farther on, after showing the necessity of the passive purification of the soul in order to reach full perfection,[76] St. John of the Cross tells us that such perfection is found only in the transforming union where "the soul is no longer

[71] *The Dark Night of the Soul*, Bk. I, chap. 1.
[72] *Ibid.*, Bk. I, chap. 14.
[73] *The Ascent of Mount Carmel*, Bk. III, chap. 1.
[74] *The Living Flame of Love*, st. III, verse 3.
[75] *The Ascent of Mount Carmel*, Bk. II, chap. 15.
[76] *The Dark Night of the Soul*, Bk. II, chap. 1.

troubled by the devil, or the flesh, or the world, or the appetites. It can now say: 'Winter is now past, the rain is over and gone. The flowers have appeared in our land.' " [77]

St. Teresa expresses the same idea in the beginning of the fifth mansion: "Thus all we who wear the holy habit of Carmel are called to prayer and contemplation. This is our first object . . . and yet I declare to you that very few of us prepare themselves so that our Lord may reveal to them the precious pearl of which we are speaking. I admit we are outwardly virtuous. But how many things we lack, and what need we have to banish all negligence in order to acquire the virtues necessary to attain to contemplation!" [78]

In *The Way of Perfection*, speaking of infused contemplation and the living waters of prayer, St. Teresa enunciates this general principle, which she later develops (chaps. 20, 21, 23, 25, 29, 33). We have already quoted some of these texts. "Remember, our Lord invited 'Any man': He is truth itself; His word cannot be doubted. If all had not been included He would not have addressed everybody, nor would He have said: 'I will give you to drink.' He might have said: 'Let all men come, for they will lose nothing by it, and I will give to drink to those I think fit for it.' But as He said, unconditionally: 'If any man thirst let him come to Me,' I feel sure that, unless they stop halfway, none will fail to drink of this living water." [79] The saint says in chapter 21: "I maintain that this is the chief point; in fact, that everything depends on their having a great and a most resolute determination never to halt until they reach their journey's end, happen what may, whatever the consequences are, cost what it will, let who will blame them . . . whether the earth itself goes to pieces beneath their feet." The general call of

[77] *The Spiritual Canticle*, Part III, st. 22.
[78] *The Interior Castle*, fifth mansion, chap. 1.
[79] Chap. 19.

souls to the mystical life could not be more clearly affirmed. And yet, St. Teresa, Tauler, and St. John of the Cross occasionally make reservations. We read, for example, in *The Way of Perfection:* [80] "It does not follow, because all the nuns in this convent practise prayer, that they must all be contemplatives. Such an idea would greatly discourage those who do not understand the truth that contemplation is a gift of God.[81] . . . Sometimes our Lord comes very late, and pays as much all at once as He has given to others during many years."

Why does St. Teresa make these reservations, which seem at first glance to contradict the principle of the general call of souls to infused contemplation? She herself says: [82] "The last chapter seems to contradict what I said, when in order to console those who were not contemplatives I told them that God had made many ways of reaching Him, just as He has made 'many mansions.' I repeat that His Majesty, being God, knows our weakness and has provided for us. He did not say: 'Let some men come to Me by drinking this water, but let others come by some other means.' His mercy is so great that He hinders no one from drinking of the fountain of life. . . . Indeed, He calls us loudly and publicly to do so. He is so good that He will not force us to drink of it, but He gives it in many ways to those who try to follow Him, so that none may go away disconsolate or die of thirst. From this overflowing river spring many rivulets, some large, others small, while there are little pools for children—by children, I mean beginners, unformed in virtue. You see, sisters, there

[80] Chap. 17.

[81] Even if all souls, and more particularly all Carmelites, are called to contemplation, it evidently does not follow that all must be contemplatives from the start. As St. Teresa says in the text which we quote, God often delays greatly in bestowing this gift. It may even happen that a very generous soul, which is naturally much inclined to the active life, would attain to infused contemplation only after a longer period than the ordinary span of life.

[82] *The Way of Perfection*, chap. 20.

is no fear you will die of drought on the way of prayer. . . . Then take my advice; do not loiter on the road, but struggle manfully, until you perish in the attempt." [83]

The restrictions made above by St. Teresa do not, therefore, concern the remote general call, but the proximate individual call, which we shall now consider.

## ARTICLE III

*The Individual and Proximate Call to Contemplation*

The aforementioned reservations made by St. Teresa, St. John of the Cross, and Tauler, are not, we maintain, directed toward the general law of the full development of the life of grace, considered in itself, but toward the ground in which the divine seed is received, as we read in the parable of the sower. "And whilst he soweth some fell by the wayside, and the birds of the air came and ate them up. And other some fell upon stony ground, where they had not much earth: and they sprung up immediately, because they had no deepness of earth. And when the sun was up they were scorched: and because they had no root, they withered away. And others fell among thorns: and the thorns grew up and choked them. And others fell upon good ground: and they brought forth fruit, some an hundredfold, some sixtyfold, and some thirtyfold. He that hath ears to hear, let him hear." [1] Again, among trees, the cedar or the palm normally reaches a great height when the soil and climate are favorable; but it is quite otherwise in an unfavorable climate. Just so, the question of the call to the mystical life is complicated and in a way materialized as soon as the life of grace is no longer considered in itself, but in the souls that receive it.

Because souls are in the state of grace, are they thereby

[83] *Ibid.*
[1] Matt. 13: 4–9.

called one and all to the essentially mystical life? First of all, clearly they are not all predestined to it; for predestination infallibly produces its effect, without, however, doing violence to liberty. It is a fact that all souls in the state of grace do not reach the mystical life. It is also evident that they are not all individually called to it in a proximate manner; for the three signs of this call, enumerated by Tauler,[2] later on by St. John of the Cross, and commonly accepted, are certainly not found in all of them.

## 1. THE THREE PRINCIPAL SIGNS OF THE PROXIMATE CALL

1) Meditation becomes difficult or even impracticable. "The imagination remains inert; the taste for this exercise has disappeared; and the sweetness formerly produced by the object on which the imagination dwelt, has changed into dryness. As long as sweetness persists and the soul can in meditating pass from one thought to another, meditation must not be abandoned, except when the soul is in peace and in quiet, of which I shall speak in describing the third sign." [3] St. Teresa teaches the same doctrine in the fourth mansion,[4] where she says that if the soul has not yet received the grace of "supernatural recollection," we must "take care not to stop the movement of our thoughts . . . and remain there like dolts." From these quotations it is evident that these two great saints are speaking of the passage from meditation to infused contemplation, and not to an acquired contemplation, which would be an intermediate state.[5]

2) A second sign is necessary, for the difficulty or impossibility of meditating might come from physical illness, from a distraction, from lack of recollection, or from some other

---

[2] Tauler's teaching on this subject is summarized by his disciples in the *Institutions*, chap. 35.

[3] *The Ascent of Mount Carmel*, Bk. II, chap. 13.

[4] Chap. 3.

[5] Cf. *supra*, pp. 221-35.

similar cause, as happens even to those who preserve a taste for this exercise. Exactly stated, the second sign is that "the soul no longer has any inclination to fix the imagination or the senses on any particular interior or exterior object. I do not say that the imagination will no longer manifest itself by the coming and going which is characteristic of it—and which takes place even in profound recollection—but that the soul will have no desire to fix it deliberately on these objects." [6] For example, when reading, one feels the need of closing the book; if praying vocally, one is inclined to interrupt this prayer in order to give oneself up to the contemplation of God. This is due to an interior inspiration. "It is not, therefore, surprising that such a soul should experience pain and distaste when, once it has begun to enjoy this peace, it is forced to resume meditation and to begin again the work of particular considerations. Its condition is like that of an infant torn away from its mother's breast while it was nursing. . . . Or picture to yourself one who, after having removed the rind from a fruit, is, when tasting it, commanded to peel the rind which has already been removed. He can find no rind and ceases to taste the fruit which he already had. He is like one who lets go the prize in order to grasp a shadow." These explanations from the writings of St. John of the Cross show clearly that [7] in his opinion the passage from meditation to infused contemplation is normal, even though we cannot produce contemplation by our own effort. After peeling the fruit, we taste the substance.

3) A third sign is necessary because the first two are not decisive. Melancholy or some other indisposition might produce in us a suspension of our faculties, as it were, during which the soul would take pleasure in doing nothing and in remaining inactive. "The third and most decisive sign is this: The soul delights to be alone with God, fixing its attention

[6] *The Ascent of Mount Carmel*, Bk. II, chap. 13.
[7] *Ibid.*, chap. 14.

lovingly on Him. It does not make any particular considerations, and enjoys interior peace and an impression of repose
and quiet. The powers, memory, understanding, and will,
do not manifest themselves by acts and exercises. I mean that
the soul does not give itself up to discursive acts, which consist in going from one subject to another, but is absorbed in
the knowledge of and attention to God. This knowledge is confused, general, and loving, and does not tarry on any particular perception." [8] Just so, a child looks lovingly at its
mother without thinking of anything distinct, but only of
the fact that she is its mother. At the outset this loving gaze of
the soul is so subtle and delicate that it passes almost un-
perceived.[9] Here, there is no longer, as there was in meditation, clearly perceptible co-operation on the part of the
imagination. Moreover, at the beginning the soul does not
let itself be satisfied with this love which is given to it; it
seeks love under a more sensible form. "Once the soul,
however, lets itself be introduced into peace, it will not fail
to penetrate farther and farther into it. As the loving thought
of God becomes clear, the soul finds it more attractive than
anything in the world because of the peace, rest, sweetness,
and delight which it draws from it without effort." [10] The
last words of this sentence help to prove that St. John of the
Cross is really discussing infused contemplation, even in this
first work, *The Ascent of Mount Carmel.* Chapter 15 makes
the matter clear.[11] In *The Ascent of Mount Carmel,* St. John
describes chiefly the part we can have in this contemplation,
not indeed in producing it, but in preparing ourselves for
it or in favoring its exercise.[12] In the following work, *The*

[8] *Ibid.,* chap. 13.
[9] *Ibid.*
[10] *Ibid.*
[11] *Ibid.,* chap. 15: "In this state God communicates Himself to the soul
which remains passive . . . and the soul, when it thus receives the supernaturally infused light, understands all, while remaining passive."
[12] *Ibid.,* chap. 14. St. John shows here that God sometimes favors souls by
granting His contemplative love without the intermediate preparation. This

*Dark Night of the Soul,* he describes particularly God's action and our passivity. These phases do not follow each other chronologically; instead, they are two subordinate aspects of the interior life; in this case, the soul is "more passive than active," [13] but preserves the liberty of consenting to the superior inspiration which the Holy Ghost gives it to make it act divinely.

The three signs given in *The Ascent of Mount Carmel* are repeated in *The Dark Night of the Soul;* [14] there they are more markedly formulated as indications of God's purifying work in us, or of purifying aridity: (1) The soul no longer finds savor or consolation in divine things (known by way of the senses) or in any created thing—these last words indicate that this state does not come from tepidity or attachment to creatures; (2) The soul preserves ordinarily in its remembrance of God the fear of not serving Him and of going backwards, because it no longer experiences sweetness in divine things—this fear is another sign that this powerlessness does not come from tepidity; (3) The soul finds difficulty in meditating, as it did in the past, by having recourse to the imagination. "The reason for this is that God is beginning to give Himself no longer by means of reasoning, but by the simple act of contemplation which He inspires in us."

Other indications may confirm these three necessary and classic signs. St. Teresa delights in adding the complete gift of oneself to God, scorn of all earthly things, a great humility, and the desire for heaven. Infused contemplation may, however, be granted to souls that do not as yet possess such high virtues; often it is contemplation which gives them: "All good things came to me with her," [15] as the Book of Wisdom

---

recalls what St. Teresa says of the water wheel apropos of the supernatural prayer of quiet, for which the soul usually prepares itself by certain work of the mind. (Cf. *Life,* chap. 14.)

[13] St. Thomas, Ia IIae, q.68, a.1, 3; IIa IIae, q.52, a.2 ad 1um.

[14] Bk. I, chap. 9.

[15] Wis. 7: 11.

says. It is especially the infused knowledge of the goodness of God which makes us love Him and practice virtue for love of Him. These three signs, then, suffice to prove the proximate call of a soul to infused contemplation.

## II. OBSTACLES TO THIS PROXIMATE CALL; ITS VARIETIES

True, the three signs, which we have just explained, are not found in all souls in the state of grace. But we believe that each and every one is called to the mystical life in a remote and sufficient manner, since the grace of the virtues and gifts, which they have received, contains, by reason of the intimate law of its development, the seed of the mystical life, which is the normal prelude to that of heaven.[16]

What is meant by a remote and sufficient call? It means that, if all souls were faithful in avoiding, as they ought, not only mortal but venial sin, if they were, each according to his condition, generally docile to the Holy Ghost, and if they lived long enough, a day would come when they would receive the proximate and efficacious vocation to a high perfection and to the mystical life, properly so called. They have, in fact, received its radical principle. Until that day comes, however, we may simply say that they are not as yet called to it; just as we say that infidels, who have never heard the Gospel preached, are not as yet individually called to the Christian life, even though all pagans have a general vocation

16 The expression "remote sufficient grace" is current in theology in another question, which resembles this one and which concerns not only all souls in the state of grace, but all men; i. e., is it possible for each and every one to be saved? God has not only prepared in general, but offers and gives to all men, and each one in particular, in view of his salvation, sufficient help, sufficient at least in a remote manner, according to the conditions of each one. It is thus that the proximate sufficient grace to pray is a remote sufficient grace to perform the salutary work in view of which one prays. If the soul does not resist this remote sufficient grace, it will receive the proximate sufficient grace to act well. If this last grace is not resisted, efficacious grace will be received, which will make us accomplish the salutary work. Cf. Billuart, *De Deo*, diss. 7, a.8. This doctrine applies even to infidels and hardened sinners.

to the Christian life, as the sole way of salvation willed by God for all men.[17]

Many souls will not develop enough spiritually to be suitably prepared for the mystical life. This is due especially to a lack of humility, purity of heart, simplicity of gaze, recollection, and generosity; or also because they are naturally too much inclined to be outward-minded; or because, being too much absorbed in study or the cares of administration, they do not sufficiently love the silent and profound prayer which leads to union. How easy it is to tarry on the way and to live a superficial life! Lastly these souls often lack good spiritual direction or a suitable environment. They will not be called to the mystical life in a proximate manner. Perhaps, for lack of certain conditions which do not depend on their will, some of them, although generous, would reach the mystical life only after a longer period than the ordinary span of human existence.[18]

Others, who as a rule are more advanced, will be called to the mystical life in a proximate and sufficient manner, but all will not respond to this call. Many will become discouraged after their first steps in the dark night. This last group is numerous, and according to St. John of the Cross, in this difficult passage they are often badly directed by their spiritual guide.[19]

[17] St. Thomas, *I Sent.*, q.41, a.2 ad 3um. "Vocatio semper est temporalis, quia ponit adductionem quamdam ad aliquid. . . . Est quaedam vocatio temporalis ad gratiam, cui respondet et electio temporalis et aeterna; haec autem vocatio est vel interior per infusionem gratiae, vel exterior per vocem praedicatoris."

[18] This explains several reservations made by Tauler, St. Teresa, and St. John of the Cross, on the principle of the general call. They have in mind individual cases which arise from particular obstacles.

[19] *The Living Flame of Love*, st. III, v. 3: "Being ignorant of spiritual ways and what characterizes them, these directors turn souls away from the delicate unctions by which the Holy Ghost prepares them for divine union. They content themselves with prescribing contemptible recipes which they have invented or found by chance in their reading, and which are hardly suitable for beginners. . . . They persist in not allowing souls to advance—even if God's desire manifests itself formally—beyond their principles and methods

Others will be called in a proximate and efficacious manner to the mystical life, but they will not advance beyond its lower degrees because of lack of generosity or direction. As the parable of the sower tells us, there are good souls which yield thirtyfold; this does not represent the summit of the normal development; others give sixtyfold; and some yield a hundredfold. These last will be called in a proximate and efficacious manner to the higher degrees of the mystical life, to the transforming union. From this fact, we shall see that they were predestined to it.

"Many are called, but few are chosen," St. Teresa remarks apropos of the fifth mansion.[20] We should humbly aspire to be among this élite. As it is of faith, in contradiction to Jansenistic teaching, that he who does not save his soul, can do so by means of the sufficient grace given him; we must also say that an adult who, after neglecting many graces, reaches only a lower degree of glory, could without being predestined thereto reach a much higher degree, and he would have attained it if he had been more faithful.[21] Only the saints, after generously using the time of trial, reach the plenitude of the perfect age, though not all, however, attain to great sanctity. In the transforming union, which is in this life the age of sanctity, there are, to be sure, many degrees lower than that attained by St. Paul or St. John. Likewise in a forest, many oaks reach their full normal height and tower above many others less developed, without reaching the height of certain giant oaks, which are truly exceptional.

This explains a much controverted text from *The Dark Night of the Soul*.[22] In this passage, St. John of the Cross

---

which are limited to discursive acts and those of the imagination. Forbid souls to pass beyond the limits of their natural capacity, and what poor fruit they will gather!"

[20] *The Interior Castle*, fifth mansion, chap. 1.

[21] On this point, cf. St. Francis de Sales, *Treatise on the Love of God*, Bk. II, chap. 11.

[22] Bk. I, chap. 9.

states first the general principle: "Once the soul has entered the purification (i. e., the passive purification of the senses), inability to discourse only increases. . . . The soul will end by abandoning (in prayer) all sensible operations, if it is truly to advance (*si es que han de ir adelante*)." Then he adds: "For those who do not go by the way of contemplation (*porque los que no van por camino de contemplación*), it is otherwise; in their case, the night of the senses is often interrupted. In turn, it makes itself felt and then disappears; at one time discursive meditation is impossible, and at another, it becomes easy. God keeps them in this way, then, only in order to try them and humble them; to refine their appetites in order to turn them away from a vicious gluttony in spiritual matters; and not to lead them to the way of the spirit, which is that of contemplation, properly so called. God does not, in fact, raise [23] to contemplation all who desire to attain it by following the way of the spirit; He does not even take half of them. Why? He alone knows. These last (whom God does not raise to contemplation, properly so called) [24] never finish weaning the senses so that they completely abandon considerations and reasoning. They have this grace only intermittently, as we have just said."

This text does not deny the remote general call of souls in the state of grace to the mystical life; it only denies the proximate and efficacious individual call of many to the perfection of this life. The good souls mentioned in this text are those which, in the parable of the sower, yield a thirty-fold harvest. This does not represent the normal summit of the life of grace; others will yield sixtyfold and even a hundredfold, as the parable tells us.

St. John of the Cross does not say that the souls of which

[23] St. John of the Cross says clearly: "God does not raise" (*lleva*), and not: "God does not call." "Many are called, but few are chosen."

[24] The original text says: "These last"—that is, those whom God does not raise.

we are speaking are called to a high perfection without being called in a proximate manner to the superior degrees of the mystical life. He even teaches the contrary. In his opinion, a soul cannot obtain lofty perfection without passing through the night of the senses and even that of the spirit.[25]

And if St. John of the Cross is asked why God does not raise to contemplation, properly so called, all those who desire to attain it by following the way of the spirit and why He takes only half of them, he will not answer, as certain commentators would have him do, that contemplation, properly so called, is essentially extraordinary and that it reaches beyond the summit of the normal life. On the contrary, he answers: "God alone knows." In like manner, St. Augustine says apropos of the text, "Many are called, but few are chosen": "Why God draws one and not another, seek not to judge, if thou dost not wish to fall into error." [26] This is the mystery of predestination,[27] of which St. John of the Cross himself says: "It is true that souls, whatever their capacity, may have attained union, but all do not possess it in the same degree. God disposes freely of this degree of union, as He disposes freely of the degree of the beatific vision." [28] In this opinion, St. John of the Cross agrees with Tauler, Louis de Blois, Ruysbroeck, and the other great mystics.

Finally, St. John of the Cross speaks more clearly on this subject in *The Living Flame of Love:* [29] "We must explain here why there are so few who reach this high state of perfection and union with God. It is certainly not because God wishes to limit this grace to a small number of superior souls; His desire is rather that this high perfection should be com-

---

[25] *The Dark Night of the Soul,* Bk. I, chaps. 3, 14; Bk. II, chap. 1.

[26] St. Thomas quotes this text and expresses the same opinion in Ia, q.23, a.5 ad 3um.

[27] Father Lamballe, in his *La contemplation,* pp. 70, 72, gives this explanation of this text from St. John of the Cross.

[28] *The Ascent of Mount Carmel,* Bk. II, chap. 5.

[29] St. II, v. 5.

mon to all. It is only too often that He seeks in vain for vessels capable of containing such perfection. He sends light trials to a soul, and it shows itself weak and immediately flees all suffering . . . which is intended to refine and to polish it. Consequently, God does not continue to purify such souls and to draw them from earthly dust by mortifying them. . . . O souls who dream of walking in tranquillity and consolation in the spiritual way, if you but knew how necessary it is for you to be tried in order to attain this security and consolation!" After the description of the transforming union,[30] he says: "O souls created for such glories, . . . of what are you thinking? What are you doing? How sad your blindness is! You close your eyes to the most dazzling light and do not listen to the powerful voices which solicit you!"

Even in the natural order, the greater number of men do not succeed in disciplining their passions, although they are all called to do so by their very nature as rational beings. Likewise, among those who spend many years in the study of some science (such as mathematics, law, or medicine), only a small number acquire a profound knowledge of it. Inventors and extraordinary geniuses are rare. Similarly in the order of the life of grace, not even half the number of interior souls are raised to the summit of the normal development of the supernatural life. "Many are called, but few are chosen," as St. Teresa so often remarks. We should, however, humbly desire to be numbered in this élite, as we should desire to grow in charity without placing any limit on its progress.

The doctrine that all souls in the state of grace have the remote and sufficient helps to reach the mystical life offers no greater difficulties than that other doctrine, which is certain, namely, that all men, including unfaithful souls and hardened sinners, have both in general and in particular the necessary helps to save their souls.

[30] *The Spiritual Canticle*, IV, st. 39, v. 1.

## ARTICLE IV

*The Conditions Ordinarily Required for Infused Contemplation*

### AN EXAMINATION OF THE PRINCIPAL DIFFICULTIES RELATING TO THE GENERAL CALL

We have given the reasons for our aceptance of a general and remote call to the mystical life of all souls in the state of grace, although this call becomes individual and proximate only when it can be proved that the three classic signs of the beginning of the mystical life, explained by St. John of the Cross, exist in the soul. This individual proximate call remains sufficient and inefficacious in those who resist it. In others it is efficacious in one of two ways: either it leads only to the inferior degrees of the mystical life, or it leads higher and even to the transforming union, the summit of the normal development of the interior life.

The three principal reasons we adduced for affirming the general and remote call are : (1) The radical principle of the mystical life is the same as that of the common interior life, the grace of the virtues and the gifts; (2) In the progress of the interior life, the purification of the soul cannot be complete without the passive purifications, which belong to the mystical order; (3) The mystical life is the normal prelude to the beatific vision, the goal of the life of grace.

This teaching presupposes what we have set forth [1] on sufficient and on efficacious grace. We summed it up in the masterly words of Bossuet: "Let us learn to bow our intellects before the divine obscurity of this great mystery and confess two graces, one of which (sufficient grace) leaves the intellect without any excuse before God, and the other (efficacious grace) does not let it glory in itself." [2]

---

[1] Cf. chap. 3, arts. 3, 4.
[2] Bossuet, *Œuvres complètes* (1845), I, 643.

It is not surprising that the traditional teaching about the general and remote call of all just souls to the mystical life should encounter obscurity or difficulty. These difficulties are not any greater than those raised against the doctrine commonly taught in the Church as to the salvation which is offered and is possible to all men who have the use of reason, even to those who have not been able to hear the Gospel preached. All receive sufficient grace (at least remote) to reach eternal life.

Since this is so and since the mystical life is the prelude to eternal life, why not admit the general and remote call which we maintain? The principal difficulties are three: (1) It is objected that, even while admitting the principles of St. Thomas in relation to the increase of the grace of the virtues and gifts, if things are considered in the concrete rather than in the abstract, it becomes evident that Christian souls generally lack the conditions of the mystical life, and that through no fault of theirs; (2) It must not be forgotten that some souls have received only one or two talents, and not five; (3) The doctrine of the general, even though remote, call seems by its nature to lead some to presumption and illusion, and others to discouragement. We will examine these different points.

## I. DO GENEROUS INTERIOR SOULS GENERALLY LACK THE PRINCIPAL CONDITIONS ORDINARILY REQUIRED FOR THE MYSTICAL LIFE?

Some writers tell us that the attainment of mystical contemplation requires conditions that are impossible of realization for the majority of souls, no matter how generous they may be. According to this opinion, a special environment is necessary, such as a Carthusian or a Carmelite monastery, where silence, solitude, and long hours of prayer are the common rule. Without this atmosphere, a special temperament inclined to recollection and prolonged prayer is needed. Lastly, we are told that a soul must have appropriate spiritual guidance, directing it more and more toward the contemplative life. These conditions are usually wanting in the lives of the majority of generous interior souls that remain in the world or that enter active or even mixed religious orders. The cares of administration which occupy superiors and the demands which intellectual work makes on a priest whose principal activity is teaching, also hinder the development of the mystical life, properly so called, even in interior souls much attached to their duties.

We now offer our reply to this objection. Even if the above mentioned conditions, difficult of realization for many, were required, we should not, as a result, necessarily conclude that the mystical life is not the normal summit of the development of the life of grace. We should simply have to say that, for the attainment of this summit, conditions are demanded which are difficult of realization in the world, or even in a religious life that is not very fervent. In this case the soul is like a cedar, which attains the summit of its normal development only in certain conditions of soil and climate.

Moreover, the conditions enumerated, though very useful, are not the chief ones. We recognize the fact that environment has its importance; also that a calm temperament is much better disposed to the contemplative life than a restless and agitated spirit.[3] It may indeed be that among these

---

[3] St. Thomas, IIa IIae, q.182, a.4 ad 3um: "He that is prone to yield to his passions on account of his impulse to action is simply more apt for the active life by reason of his restless spirit. . . . Others, on the contrary, have the mind naturally pure and restful, so that they are apt for contemplation. . . . Those who are more adapted to the active life can prepare themselves for the contemplative by the practice of the active life; while, none the less, those who are more adapted to the contemplative life can take upon themselves the works of the active life so as to become yet more apt for contemplation." Thus all ought to tend toward contemplation as the normal prelude to the life of heaven.

last, some, even though quite generous, would reach the mystical life only after a period longer than the ordinary span of life. And it is certain that bad spiritual direction often allows souls to vegetate or turns them away from infused contemplation, whereas another type of direction would definitely turn them toward contemplation.

However important these conditions may be, they remain superficial compared to others which are the chief ones. Here again the same rule holds true as in the matter of salvation, which is possible to all who possess a developed conscience, even to those not born in a Christian environment, who are strongly inclined to evil, and who have not had an opportunity to hear the Gospel preached. If they ordinarily follow the dictates of their conscience, they will be mysteriously led from grace to grace, from fidelity to fidelity, to eternal life.

Anyone who wishes to advance in the spiritual life and to prepare himself for the grace of contemplation must, to the best of his ability, use the great means which the Church gives us all. The assiduous reception of the sacraments, daily hearing of mass, frequent communion, love of the Eucharist, devotion to the Holy Ghost, filial and incessant recourse to the Sacred Heart of Jesus [4] and to the Blessed Virgin, mediatrix of all graces, are evidently necessary.

Contemplation is a fruit of true devotion to the Blessed Virgin, as explained by Blessed Grignion de Montfort.[5] He says that, without a great love for her, a soul will attain union with God only with extreme difficulty. "It is necessary to pass through dark nights, combats, strange agonies, sharp thorns, and frightful deserts. By the way of Mary, the soul advances with greater sweetness and tranquillity. Along this way it encounters many crosses and great difficulties to

---

[4] It is fitting to unite ever more closely devotion to the Blessed Sacrament and that to the Sacred Heart of Jesus in devotion to the Eucharistic Heart of Jesus, in order to thank our Lord for the act of supreme love by which He gave us the Holy Eucharist.

[5] *Traité de la vraie devotion à Marie,* chap. 4, art. 5 (1909 ed., p. 119).

overcome, but our good Mother keeps so close to her faithful servants . . . that, in truth, this virginal road is a path of roses in spite of the thorns." It thus leads more easily and surely to divine union. Mary, wonderful to relate, makes the cross easier and, at the same time, more meritorious: easier, because she sustains us with her gentle hand; more meritorious, because she obtains for us a greater charity, which is the principle of merit, and because, by offering our acts to our Lord, she increases their value. By reason of her pre-eminent charity, Mary merited more while performing the easiest acts than all the martyrs in their tortures.

Another great means to prepare for the grace of contemplation, a means within the reach of all interior souls, is found in the liturgy, in an ever more intimate union with the great prayer of the Church. "The graces of prayer and of the mystical state have their type and source in the hieratic life of the Church; they reflect in the members the likeness of Christ which is perfect in the body." [6] Liturgical prayer recited with recollection, in union with our Lord and His mystical body, obtains for us holy lights and inspirations which illumine and inflame our hearts. Consequently it is advisable to make mental prayer after the psalmody which prepares us for it; just as after mass and holy communion, it is well to prolong our thanksgiving, and if possible devote an hour to it.

Lastly, the frequent reading of Scripture and the study of sacred doctrine, undertaken in a truly supernatural manner, are other excellent means to prepare the soul for contemplation. Thus the ancients [7] used to say that divine reading (*lectio divina*) by pious study (*studium*) leads to meditation (*meditatio*), then to prayer (*oratio*), and finally to contemplation (*contemplatio*).[8]

---

6 Father Clérissac, O.P., *Le mystère de l'Église*, p. 102.
7 *The Rule of St. Benedict*, chap. 48.
8 See IIa IIae, q. 180, a. 3.

Of course certain interior dispositions are necessary if we are to make good use of the great means which the Church proposes to all. These dispositions constitute the chief conditions ordinarily required for the mystical life.[9] As a rule they accompany the proximate individual call to contemplation; in very generous souls they may supply for exterior conditions if these cannot be had.

Spiritual authors group these dispositions as follows: (1) purity of heart; (2) simplicity of spirit; (3) profound humility; (4) love of recollection and perseverance in prayer; (5) fervent charity.[10]

Who can say that these interior dispositions are beyond the strength and the graces offered him? St. Jerome writes: "One man may tell me that he cannot fast; but can he declare that he cannot love? Another may affirm that he cannot preserve virginity, or sell all his goods in order to give the price to the poor; but can he tell me that he cannot love his enemies? All that is necessary is to look into one's own heart . . . , for what God asks of us is not found at a great distance."[11] On the other hand, if we become even a little negligent, how easy it is to fail in the interior conditions we have just enumerated!

The *purity of heart* mentioned in the beatitude, "Blessed are the clean of heart: for they shall see God," is the fruit of exterior and interior mortification, which is not practiced without suffering. We must not be attached to sin, must not condone our faults or make peace with them. The soul must enter upon the narrow way that leads to true life; better than ever before, it will understand our Lord's words, "Many are called, but few are chosen." It must also be ready to pass through the fire of sufferings, for purity of heart should grow with contemplation through the purifying trials

[9] They are not, however, always required, for mystical contemplation is sometimes granted to souls that are still very imperfect.

[10] Philip of the Blessed Trinity, O.C.D., *Summa theologiae mysticae*, II, 305.

[11] St. Jerome, *Comm. in Matth.*, chap. 5.

which God sends to those humbly and ardently desiring His divine intimacy. As Scripture tell us, He is jealous; He removes the persons and the things to which the soul might become attached and makes it pass through a crucible to cleanse it of all its blemishes. When inordinate inclinations and the disorders of sensuality, egoism, self-love, and intellectual and spiritual pride have disappeared, and purified heart is like a spotless mirror reflecting the beauty of God. Who can say that he is unable to have a clean heart?

*Simplicity of spirit* is born of this cleanness of heart and, like it, should be keenly desired by everyone. Holy Scripture often mentions it: "His communication is with the simple." [12] "If thy eye be single, thy whole body shall be lightsome." [13] "Be ye therefore wise as serpents and simple as doves." [14] Without simplicity it is impossible to have a high degree of wisdom, which is learned from God without guile.[15] Simplicity of spirit evidently does not consist in unceremoniously telling our every thought and feeling, at the risk of contradicting ourselves from day to day when circumstances and impressions are changed. In spite of appearances, such conduct is quite the contrary of simplicity; it leads to confusion, disturbance, incoherence, and rambling. The simplicity of which we are speaking shares in that of God and consists in seeing in God all things, all events, whether happy or unhappy, all persons, friends or enemies, and all we have to do, whether agreeable or painful. It produces unity of spirit, for he who possesses it sees that everything is willed, or at least permitted, by God for His glory and that of His elect. Consequently, that all ought to aspire to this superior unity and simplicity of spirit, is evident. The presence of simplicity in the soul indicates that the gift of wisdom is already well developed, and that the soul possessing it habit-

12 Prov. 3: 32.
13 Matt. 6: 22.
14 Matt. 10: 16.
15 Wis. 7: 13.

ually is very close to mystical contemplation, if it does not already have it.

This simplicity is manifested by a great rectitude of life; from this point of view, St. Thomas speaks of it when he is discussing the virtue of truth or veracity as opposed to falsehood. "Simplicity," he says, "is contrary to duplicity, by which a man makes himself out to be something other than what he is interiorly." It is a perfect uprightness and even a certain candor, in the good sense of the word, which leads us to acknowledge our defects easily because we do not cease to see the one thing necessary above all others. To have ordinarily in our relations with our neighbor the undiminished simplicity of the dove together with the prudence of the serpent evidences a high degree of the light of divine wisdom. It is a proximate disposition for mystical contemplation. Who can say that this superior simplicity is not, upon the whole, within the reach of generous souls?

*Humility of heart* is no less attainable than the preceding dispositions. In fact, it is born of them at the realization of the distance separating the infinite perfection of God from the nothingness of creatures, which of themselves are incapable of existing, acting, and directing themselves as they should. Anyone who already possesses this virtue in a high degree, who is happy to recognize his nothingness and abjection before God, who loves to be nothing so that God may be all, to humble himself before what is divine in every other soul, is prepared for the grace of contemplation. Our Lord Himself says: "I confess to Thee, O Father, Lord of heaven and earth, because Thou hast hid these things from the wise and prudent, and hast revealed them to little ones." [16] "Unless you be converted, and become as little children, you shall not enter into the kingdom of heaven." [17] If you become

[16] Matt. 11: 25.
[17] Matt. 18: 3.

as little children, you shall enter heaven; and by contemplation the soul enters it in a quasi-experimental manner even
in this life. "Take up My yoke upon you, and learn of Me,
because I am meek, and humble of heart: and you shall find
rest to your souls." [18]

This rest for the soul is to be found especially in loving
contemplation. "God resisteth the proud and giveth grace
to the humble." [19] He makes them humble in order to load
them with His gifts. Humility prepares the soul for contemplation, for it already sings the praise of God's glory. *The
Imitation* says that contemplatives are few in number because there are few souls profoundly humble. To receive the
grace of contemplation, ordinarily the soul must have made
a profound act of true humility which colors its whole life.
When a soul has often and practically recognized the fact
that its entire existence depends absolutely on God, that it
continues to exist only by Him, that it acts well only by
reason of His grace, which works in us both to will and to
accomplish, that it directs its energies only by His light, that
it has sinned frequently, and that it is an unprofitable
servant deserving of scorn; then the soul generally obtains
the grace we are speaking of.

*Love of recollection,* fidelity to the grace of the present
moment, and perseverance in prayer are also dispositions
which should not be lacking in generous souls. These dispositions necessitate a reaction against the agitation of what
today is called strenuous life. As a matter of fact, it is not
life, but a fever, a deadly illness; it is materialism in action.
After turning away from God and from the true life of the
soul, it seeks its equivalent in multiplied and increasingly
intense activity, which is often a complete loss; for the finite
can never equal or become the Infinite. To a true contem-

[18] Matt. 11: 29.
[19] Jas. 4: 6.

plative, people who are devoted to an exaggerated intensity of life must seem like walking corpses; dead men running, as an old ballad says.

"Is the decay of faith astonishing," asks a recent translator of the works of Tauler, "since no one any longer has time to think of faith? Materialism has snuffed out spirituality. Yet the desire for God, who is man's end, still persists in human hearts, with the result that more than ever before there is an indefinable uneasiness in the world. Souls are suffering and dying of this unconscious desire for the Infinite." [20] The reaction from this uneasiness should raise up many contemplative vocations. This is an important argument for the doctrine we are defending here, namely, that an unfavorable environment provokes a salutary reaction in good souls.

Materialism in action extends unfortunately to the things of the spirit and prevents many souls from believing they are called to contemplation. It turns them away from recollection and perseverance in prayer. Even spiritual subjects have been developed along the lines of a material science which, instead of giving us a doctrinal judgment founded on principle, presents us with a jumble of material information which is often useless and impossible to classify. Apparently the more there is, the more science grows. In reality, this entirely material multiplicity puts a great distance between us and the unification of learning, that higher view of the whole which deserves to be called wisdom, and to be called contemplation when it is accompanied by the love of God.

If the present problem of the general call of souls to the mystical life were studied according to the methods of this material science, a doctrinal solution would never be reached; on the contrary, it would seem that no conclusions can be reached, a skeptical attitude which is no evidence of superi-

[20] Cf. *Œuvres de Tauler*, translated into French by Father Noël, O.P., IV. 215–16, translator's note.

ority. Were this problem studied in the light of theological wisdom, in the works of the great masters, and also in the light of the gift of wisdom, which is particularly important here, the result would be quite different.

We can scarcely exaggerate the importance of Tauler's teaching on the dangers of a completely material study for a religious who should aspire to contemplation. Speaking even of religious, the great mystic observes that some of them are like cisterns receiving water only from drains and not from the fountain of living water. Without an interior life, they spend themselves on outward things, and pride is the result. He says these intellectuals, infatuated with themselves and their intellect, which is nourished solely by creatures, are cisterns. Their mental attainments cannot support them in trials and will be confounded at death.[21]

In his explanation of the parable of those who refused the invitation to the feast, Tauler says: "Who could count today the number of men who act in the same way. . . . Everyone, I speak not only of lay people, but also of ecclesiastics and religious, is busy about his affairs. What negotiations and innumerable occupations continually distract and absorb the world! The very thought of it all is enough to set one reeling. We surround ourselves with so many things, whereas a tenth of them would suffice; for, after all, time on earth is short and uncertain. We ought to remember that this world is merely a passage to eternity, and then we would use temporal things with moderation and be satisfied with the necessities of life. It would be better to die of hunger on the way than to let ourselves be encumbered and crucified by so many occupations." [22]

Tauler is not speaking here of apostolic work which is the radiation of the interior life, but of countless useless, or at

---

21 Cf. Tauler, *First Sermon on the Ascension* (Noël ed.), II, 401.
22 Tauler, *Second Sermon for the Twentieth Sunday after Trinity* (Noël ed.), IV, 215.

least unsanctified, occupations. If his words were true of his time, what must be said of ours? With such conditions it is not astonishing that only a small number of souls attain to contemplation. These conditions, however, represent essential disorder, which turns souls away from the recollection and prayer necessary to any interior life. Keeping this in mind, we easily understand why our Lord said at the end of the parable of the wedding feast: "Many are called, but few are chosen."

This is not true in a normal Christian life, even in the world. Without excessive difficulty, generous souls attain by meditation to a simple and spontaneous affective prayer, which is an excellent disposition to mystical or infused contemplation.[23]

*Fervent charity* toward God and our neighbor is the last of the dispositions that we listed as requisite for contemplation. The love of God for man unites us to Him; and the gifts of the Holy Ghost, which are the principles of infused contemplation, being connected with charity, develop with it. "Wisdom as a gift of the Holy Ghost judges aright about them (divine things) on account of connaturality with them. . . . This sympathy or connaturality for divine things is the result of charity, which unites us to God." [24] Hence it is inconceivable that a soul should reach a high degree of charity without having a proportionate degree of the gift of wisdom as an habitual disposition, because the Holy Ghost inspires and illumines souls, as a general rule, according to the degree of their habitual docility. These souls not only earnestly desire and humbly ask for the grace of contemplation, which will increase their love and adoration, but they cannot re-

---

[23] Theologians who follow St. Thomas and St. John of the Cross have never admitted that so-called acquired contemplation is the end of spiritual progress in this life; rather, they see in it a proximate preparation for infused contemplation. With Philip of the Blessed Trinity (*Summa theol. myst.*, II, 309), they agree in saying: "Contemplatio acquisita cum auxilio gratiae comparata, est optima dispositio ad contemplationem supernaturalem."

[24] St. Thomas, IIa IIae, q.45, a.2.

strain themselves from exclaiming: "God is so beautiful; everything in Him deserves admiration even to the forgetfulness of all else. He should indeed be the sole object of our love. It is painful to see how little He is known and how few souls admire His infinite grandeur. How many Christians would love Him if they knew by experience His goodness and tenderness, which are so different from what these words usually connote! They would love Him, even to the complete forgetfulness of self and the world, that they might find again all souls in Him, since these souls are loved by Him."

This explains why the gift of infused contemplation is ordinarily granted to the perfect, as many theologians teach.[25] The perfect have, in fact, merited in the strict sense of the word (condignly) a high degree of the gift of wisdom, considered as an habitual disposition; and they have thus merited, at least in the broad sense of the word (congruously),[26] the actual superior inspirations commensurate with this degree of the gift.[27]

Evidently the principal conditions ordinarily required for the mystical life are not, as a rule, lacking in generous interior souls, even if they are detained in the world and are unable to enjoy the silence and solitude of the cloister. Like St. Catherine of Siena, they can build an interior cell in their hearts and find God there.

## 2. PARTICULAR OBSTACLES TO CONTEMPLATION

After reading the preceding section, souls that have not received the grace of contemplation may question whether

[25] Cf. Philip of the Blessed Trinity, C.D., *Summa theol. myst.*, II, 310, and Anthony of the Holy Ghost, C.D., and Vallgornera, O.P., who express the same opinion in the same section of their mystical theologies which follow the division used in that of Philip.

[26] This is the very expression of the theologians we have just quoted. Cf. Philip, *ibid.*, p. 311.

[27] This is the principal reason why we cannot accept the thesis recently upheld by Farges and Pourrat, who consider mystical contemplation as essentially extraordinary.

they themselves are setting up some obstacle to contemplation.

The obstacle always comes from an inordinate attachment, from selfishness. In many souls it is in the will; they choose their own way; in other words, they wish to go to God by using means of their own selection, and they demand, as it were, that God should come to them according to their way. They count not a little on their own activity instead of allowing God to act in them, and they desire to build up their perfection without His help. No slight obstacle is interposed when a soul wishes to direct itself in matters that should not be under its direction; it runs the risk of more or less consciously opposing the superior direction of the Holy Ghost. To want to be a center, to wish that good be done by us, or at least by our religious family or convent, and in our way, is an ineffectual preparation for contemplation, which is characterized precisely by being God's way. "I confess to Thee, O Father, Lord of heaven and earth, because Thou hast hid these things from the wise and prudent, and hast revealed them to little ones." Occasionally, it is in the poorest little convents, which seem to have no influence, that the most contemplative and holiest souls are to be found.

In other souls, the obstacle to contemplation is found in the mind. They try to analyze everything psychologically, and to record it in order to evaluate their slight progress. Consequently they turn their gaze upon themselves instead of on God. True, self-knowledge is always necessary even in the highest states,[28] but this self-scrutiny should not be separated from the soul's attention to God. Is not the best examination of conscience that which questions sincerely what rec-

[28] St. Teresa, *The Interior Castle*, first mansion, chap. 2: "This knowledge of self is so necessary, even to souls admitted by God to His own dwelling, that they should never depart from it no matter how high they may be raised. Moreover, even though they should wish to do so, they could not do it."

ord the day has left in the Book of Life? If this is done, the light of the Holy Ghost will effect what St. Augustine asked in his prayer: "That I may know Thee, O Lord, and that I may know myself." "In my opinion," says St. Teresa, "we will never succeed in knowing ourselves well unless we try to know God; by contemplating His greatness, we will discover our baseness. . . . If, on the contrary, we never rise above our own miseries, we will reap distinct harm. . . . Self-knowledge becomes warped if we never take our thoughts off ourselves, and I am not a bit astonished at that. That is why I maintain, my daughters, that we should fix our eyes on Jesus Christ, our treasure, and on the saints; there we shall learn true humility. By this way, I repeat, our intellect will be ennobled, and self-knowledge will cease to make us fearful and cowardly." [29]

Among those who analyze themselves too much, some leave off their prayer to find out whether it conforms to the descriptions given by mystical authors, and also to ascertain what degree they have reached. Others imagine that, in order to live by these things, it is sufficient to know them exteriorly, and they try of themselves "to eliminate images and to empty their minds." By so doing they expose themselves to every kind of illusion; they confound a simple intellectual speculation about the Deity, which is superior to the divine perfections that it contains in its eminence, a speculation within the reach of every philosopher, even though he is in the state of mortal sin, with the infused contemplation described by Dionysius when he speaks of the great darkness. [30] They forget that the principle which leads to Christian contemplation is to love God for Himself. They lose themselves in abstract speculations and do not comprehend the love of

[29] *Ibid.*
[30] This error fails to take cognizance of the fact that infused knowledge is infused, that it presupposes a special inspiration of the Holy Ghost, and that it proceeds, not from love of the joys of knowledge, but from love of God.

Christ. With a great amount of unconscious pride, they might thus go completely astray and end in a theosophical or Buddhistic contemplation.

Lastly, certain souls appear better prepared in some respects, since they would willingly allow God to operate in them, and do not pride themselves on knowing everything; but their heart seeks in God enjoyment rather than God Himself. In this they are deceived, for it is a crucified God whom we must love, and intimacy with Him is often found in suffering. Undoubtedly joy and unequaled happiness come later, but this is not what the soul should seek.

Some souls that have opposed all these obstacles to the grace of God have had the happiness of seeing Him overthrow them all in order to prove once more that He came to seek sinners and to save that which was lost. Perhaps the intimacy of prayer was necessary for their salvation; if they had not obtained it, they might have wished to enjoy their faculties for themselves and to find in a forbidden love or in the satisfactions of pride what exists in divine love alone. Priceless treasures are often wasted by shutting oneself up in self. We should invoke God's help in the following prayer: "O Lord, take me from myself, and give me strength to give myself completely to Thee."

### 3. WHAT SHOULD BE THOUGHT OF SOULS THAT HAVE RECEIVED ONLY ONE OR TWO TALENTS?

Is it morally possible for souls that have received only one or two talents to reach the divine intimacy we are now discussing? Even though they could do so only with great difficulty, it would not follow that this divine intimacy is essentially extraordinary. Not all the oaks in a forest attain the height of their normal growth; some are stunted. We find an analogy in the spiritual order. God casts more or less beautiful divine seed into souls according to His good pleasure; and sometimes this seed encounters such obstacles that it is very difficult for it to attain its complete normal development.

But we must remember what St. Thomas says: "The very least grace is sufficient to resist any degree of concupiscence"; [31] that is, the very least sufficient grace gives this power, and the very least efficacious grace makes it become an act. As Cajetan,[32] Gonet,[33] and several other Thomists remark, this is true of the slightest sufficient grace considered in itself, but perhaps not of this grace when it is in a soul that is both very weak and much tempted. Thus the heat of boiling water drives away the cold; but, since water is not the natural subject of heat, the heat in turn is driven out by the cold if the fire is not kept up.

It should be remembered, however, that the privilege of frequent communion is offered to these less favored souls. If they receive the Holy Eucharist frequently with growing fervor of will, why should they not, at the end of a long life, by daily fidelity reach at least the lower degrees of the mystical life? Perhaps, as the parable of the sower relates, they will yield a thirtyfold harvest, while others will yield sixtyfold or a hundredfold.[34] We must keep in mind the parable of the laborers of the eleventh hour, who, out of gratitude, worked so well that they earned the same reward as those who had worked since morning. Let us also recall the good thief and the graces he must have received when he heard the words of the dying Christ: "Amen, I say to thee, this day thou shalt be with Me in paradise." Finally, it must be remembered that the majority of the elect pass through purgatory after death by reason of their own fault, that is, because of negligences that prevented the perfect

---

[31] *Summa,* IIIa, q.62, a.6 ad 3um.
[32] Cajetan, on Ia IIae, q.109, a.9, no. 4.
[33] Gonet, *Clypeus theol. thom., de gratia,* disp. I, a.6, par. 2, no. 305.
[34] Cf. *supra,* p. 345.

purification they could have reached in this life [35] with the help of grace.

[35] Cf. *infra*, p. 409. We offer the following explanation of this particular point. According to Christian tradition, absolute purity is necessary for entrance into heaven; all the dust and rust which have encrusted the soul must be removed before it can be raised to the beatific vision, in other words, before it can see God as He sees Himself. This purification must therefore affect not only the sensual part, but also the spiritual part, of the soul. Consequently it is perfect, as St. John of the Cross shows (*The Dark Night of the Soul,* Bk. I, chap. 3; Bk. II, chap. 1), only when the soul has passed through what he calls the double passive night of the senses and of the soul. It is not a subject of wonder, then, that he writes apropos of souls that have passed through the dark night of the spirit: "Because of their perfect purification by love, they will not have to pass through purgatory" (*op. cit.,* Bk. II, chap. 20). In note 25 on p. 357, we quoted an almost similar expression of Tauler; and St. Thomas says (*Contra Gentiles,* Bk. IV, chap. 91): "Ad visionem Dei creatura rationalis elevari non potest, nisi totaliter fuerit depurata . . . unde dicitur de Sapientia quod nihil inquinatum in ea incurrit." St. Thomas also believes that the pains of purgatory are much greater than the pains of this life. Cf. St. Catherine of Genoa, *Treatise on Purgatory.*

Moreover, we stated that to avoid purgatory, where the soul no longer merits, ordinarily or in principle it must before death, while meriting, pass through the passive purifications of the senses and of the soul, which alone assure the perfect and stable purity of the soul in its higher as well as in its lower part.

Someone may ask what is to be thought of so many Christians for whom the world of the spiritual life is only an illusion, or for whom the life of prayer is a snare. What is to be thought of people who have not leisure to study these things, or minds able to understand them; or of those who are better endowed, but who lack time and favorable circumstances? After all, God does not give everyone a temperament that inclines to the heroism necessary for undergoing the passive purifications of the soul.

The answer to these objections must be:

1) That we affirm, as ordinarily or in principle true, what we said following the teaching of St. John of the Cross; that is, that there are exceptions, and exceptions which prove the rule. We have already listed them; for example, children who die immediately after baptism, or a religious who dies immediately after making perpetual profession with great fervor. If these children or this religious, however, continued to live, they would probably have fallen into faults and imperfections which would have required the perfect purification of which we spoke. In a sense, they die accidentally at a good moment, before reaching a stable perfection, and they will not have as high a degree of glory in heaven as if they had continued to live and merit.

2) There are equivalents of the passive purifications, for example, martyrdom, or a very intense contrition like that which the good thief, who was so near the dying Jesus, must have had.

3) Moreover, the pains of purgatory may be either very intense and short, or longer and less violent, like the passive purifications in this life.

4) Some souls that are naturally rather good, but without fervor of will or

## 4. IS THIS DOCTRINE OF A NATURE TO LEAD SOME SOULS TO PRESUMPTION AND OTHERS TO DISCOURAGEMENT?

The objection may be raised that, if the doctrine of the general and remote call of all just souls to the mystical life is accepted, some souls may be inclined to anticipate God's time and simulate passive prayer, which would lead them to quietism or semi-quietism. Others, it may be objected, may become discouraged if, in spite of their generosity, they do not have the signs of passive prayer, and they may be led to think they will never be able to reach the full perfection of the Christian life.

This objection fails to appreciate the true meaning of the doctrine we have just set forth, or it considers only the harmful application which an imprudent director might make of it.

This is evident from the way St. Thomas answers a similar objection to the expediency of vows. The objection is phrased thus: He who makes a vow exposes himself to sin against this vow; therefore it is not expedient for him to make it. St. Thomas answers: [36] "When danger arises from the deed itself, this deed is not expedient—for instance, that one cross a river by a tottering bridge. But if the danger arise through man's failure in the deed, the latter does not cease to be expedient: thus it is expedient to mount on horseback, though there be danger of a fall from the horse: else it would

---

interest in spiritual things, have many defects, to which they do not give much heed. If they die in this condition, after having merely sufficient contrition, they will certainly have much to suffer in order to reach the perfect purity necessary to enter heaven.

5) Finally, for many persons the passive purifications on earth may be less painful than those borne by the great saints; for in the case of the latter these sufferings are in proportion not only to the imperfections that have to be eradicated, but also to the very high degree of charity, of apostolic and reparatory life, to which God wishes to lead them.

[36] *Summa,* IIa, IIae, q.88, a.4 ad 2um.

behove one to desist from all good things, since they may become dangerous accidentally. Wherefore it is written (Eccles. 11: 4): 'He that observeth the wind shall not sow, and he that considereth the clouds shall never reap.' " Should people quit using knives because now and then a man cuts himself? Are the vows an obstacle to perfection, because by making them a person indirectly exposes himself to transgress them occasionally? And should we fear to lead fervent souls humbly to desire the true mystical life, simply because there is a false one? Must a very great good be renounced through fear of something unbecoming which might accidently arise?

What does St. Teresa say about those who think it dangerous to follow the way of prayer and to desire to drink from the fountain of living water? In *The Way of Perfection* she says: "A want of humility, of the virtues, may endanger you, but prayer—prayer! Never would God permit this. The devil must have originated these fears and so brought about, by crafty tricks, the fall of certain souls that practised prayer. . . . Therefore, sisters, banish these misgivings: take no notice of public opinion. . . . Cast aside these causeless fears. . . . Beware, daughters, of a certain kind of humility suggested by the devil, which is accompanied by great anxiety about the gravity of our past sins. He disturbs souls in many ways by this means, until at last he stops them from receiving holy communion by doubts as to whether they are in a fit state for it." [37] Elsewhere, speaking of those who inspire such vain fears in souls, she says: "I, also, am acquainted with these semi-doctors who are always suspicious. They have cost me quite dear." [38]

The doctrine which we have explained is not at all dangerous in itself, or when applied by prudent directors. Joseph of the Holy Ghost, a Carmelite well known for his

[37] *The Way of Perfection*, chaps. 21, 39.
[38] *The Interior Castle*, fifth mansion, chap. 1.

work on mystical theology, sums up this doctrine in two propositions, which he gives exactly as the expression of traditional teaching: "If it is a question of infused contemplation, taken in the sense of rapture, ecstasy, and similar favors, we can neither apply ourselves to it nor ask it of God nor desire it. But if it is a question of infused contemplation itself, as an act of contemplation, although we can certainly not have it through our own activity aided by grace, we can aspire to it, by desiring it ardently and humbly asking God for it." [39] The union of these two words "ardently" and "humbly" recalls the *fortiter et suaviter* of Scripture; it solves the problem by the conciliation of humility and magnanimity. St. Thomas has beautifully explained the harmony between these two virtues which are apparently so contrary. Humility, he says, by inclining us profoundly before God, reminds us of our wretchedness; while magnanimity makes us aspire to great things, even to the divine intimacy which God offers us.[40] A Christian should keenly aspire to these great things, and by increasingly perfect fidelity prepare him-

[39] Joseph of the Holy Ghost, *Cursus theologiae mystico-scolasticae,* Vol. II, Praed. II, disp. XI, q.2, concl. 2, 3. He says (no. 23) that this last conclusion (that we can aspire to contemplation, etc.) is admitted by Alvarez de Paz, Philip of the Blessed Trinity, Anthony of the Holy Ghost, Vallgornera, and commonly by the mystics, *communiter mystici;* and that he cannot understand why Anthony of the Annunciation, another Carmelite, in his *Disceptatio mystica,* places infused contemplation among the graces *gratis datae.* Joseph of the Holy Ghost (*ibid.,* p. 236) says that this is a great mistake, *magnam aequivocationem passus est,* and a false interpretation of the passage from St. Thomas, IIa IIae, q.45, a.5 Cf. Ia IIae, q.111, a.4 ad 4um; and *In I Cor.* 12: 8.

[40] On the reconciliation of the most profound humility and the loftiest magnanimity, such as it is found in the souls of the saints, cf. St. Thomas, IIa IIae, q.129, a.3 ad 4um: "Magnanimity makes a man deem himself worthy of great things in consideration of the gifts of God. . . . Humility makes a man think little of himself in consideration of his own deficiency, and magnanimity makes him despise others in so far as they fall away from God's gifts; since he does not think so much of others as to do anything wrong for their sake. Yet humility makes us honor others and esteem them better than ourselves in so far as we see some of God's gifts in them," which are always very superior to what we have of ourselves, that is, our indigence and personal defects. These two virtues are, therefore, contrary only in appearance, and not in reality like vice and virtue.

self for them, and humbly wait for the divine mercy to bestow them. In the present article, we have insisted particularly on humility, which corrects presumption, and on the desire of hope and charity, which, united to forgetfulness of self, corrects discouragement. It is well to keep in mind that, by reason of the connection of the virtues, profound humility is impossible without great magnanimity, as the lives of the saints show. As St. Paul says, we bear an exceedingly precious treasure, grace and the Blessed Trinity, in a fragile vase; the greater our knowledge of the fragility of the vase, the greater also will be our appreciation of the value of the treasure, and the keener our aspiration to live intimately by it. This is taught by the passive purifications, a mystical state which, far from making the soul proud, humbles it profoundly. Without these purifications, it is scarcely possible to love to be nothing in order that God may be all; *amare nesciri et pro nihilo reputari.*

The doctrine leading to presumption is the teaching that all interior souls are called to the mystical life, not only in a general and remote manner, but in a proximate and individual way. Were this mistake made, the director should advise souls to practice the repose of passive prayer even before he had been able to prove the existence in them of the three signs enumerated by St. John of the Cross, and discussed in the course of these pages.[41] The soul would thus end in quietism.

The doctrine leading to discouragement is that which would maintain that interior souls are not generally called, even in a remote manner, to the divine intimacy of the mystical life. Many souls would thus be retained in the lower forms of the spiritual life and many, in spite of their generosity, would despair of reaching intimate union with God in this life.

Others, before undergoing the passive purifications of the

41 Cf. *supra*, p. 373.

senses and of the soul, might decide, and not without
presumption, that they had reached the ordinary unitive
life, and that it would be enough for them to remain in it,
since the higher degrees are extraordinary, and humility does
not permit one to aspire to them.

To combat the excess of quietism or semi-quietism, care
should be taken not to fall into the opposite extreme, a
sort of practical naturalism which breaks the progress of the
interior life. As usual in these great problems, truth is found
in a happy mean above two extreme errors, which are opposed to each other; truth, like a summit, dominates the
ramblings and contradictions of error. Moreover, it rises
above an inconsistent eclecticism which always goes only
halfway, which cannot affirm anything precisely, and which
oscillates from right to left because it fails to see the superior
principles that alone reconcile the most varied aspects of
reality. The apparent antagonisms are resolved by the equi-
librium of their terms carried to the highest degree; on this
summit harmony is reached, for example, between humility
and magnanimity. Every interior soul ought to strive humbly
and ardently for great things. Humility in itself should not
be inferior to magnanimity, for these virtues, in appearance
so contrary, grow together and mutually strengthen each
other; at one and the same time, they preserve the soul from
pride and discouragement. The apparent contradiction between them is solved by what St. Paul says: "For God . . .
has shined in our hearts . . . but we have this treasure in
earthen vessels." If we consider the fragility of the vessel,
we can never humble ourselves too greatly; if we consider
the value of the treasure, we can never too greatly desire the
intimate reign of God in our souls and the more and more
perfect fulfilment of the first precept which knows no limit.
"Thou shalt love the Lord thy God with thy whole heart,
and with thy whole soul, and with all thy strength, and with
all thy mind," in order to become truly "an adorer in spirit

and in truth." We can never too greatly desire to grow in charity and in divine wisdom which, like all the gifts, grows with it.

This doctrine does not, therefore, lead good souls either to discouragement or to presumption, but, like the dogma of predestination, it makes them aspire to divine union by instilling in them a holy fear of not being sufficiently generous and docile to the Holy Ghost. It does not lead to discouragement any more than do the passive purifications, which are intended to refine the virtue of hope by the struggle against temptations to despair. These temptations arise when God Himself reveals more clearly to the soul the height of the goal to be attained. In this light the soul sees more and more its own wretchedness, and must then, in spite of the devil's suggestions, hope against all hope. This purification is necessary that the soul may be completely and forever cured of vain self-complacency, and that the roots of pride and presumption may be completely extirpated. Instead of leading to pride, mystical contemplation destroys it and teaches humility, as God alone can. "Where humility is, there also is wisdom"; [42] and where profound humility is, there is also lofty wisdom, that which comes from the Father of light. As the author of *The Imitation* says, there are so few contemplatives because the number of profoundly humble souls is so small.

This doctrine, therefore, makes it possible to reply to the difficulties proposed against it; it is thereby newly confirmed and appears more and more as the true expression of traditional teaching. To live it, however, we need what many authors have called "the second conversion." What this should be may be determined from what we have just said about the interior conditions ordinarily required for mystical contemplation or for the virtues which prepare for it. If there are few perfect souls, this is because there are few

[42] Prov. 11: 2.

that follow the direction of the Holy Ghost. His seven gifts often have little effect in many souls because they are, as it were, fettered by contrary habits and affections. More or less deliberate and frequent venial sins exclude the graces necessary to produce the acts of the gifts.[43] But we cannot doubt their existence, because Scripture, tradition, and the liturgy speak of them, and, if the obstacles were removed, we should ordinarily see the gradual realization of what the Church makes us implore in the *Veni Creator:*

> Creator, Spirit, all divine,
> Come visit every soul of Thine,
> And fill with Thy celestial flame
> The bosoms Thou Thyself didst frame.
>
> The sevenfold mystic gifts are Thine,
> Finger of God's right hand divine;
> His gracious promise sent to teach
> The tongue a rich and heavenly speech.
>
> Kindle with fire brought from above
> Each sense, and fill our hearts with love
> And grant our flesh so weak and poor
> That strength which lasts forevermore.

This prayer, which should be said by the faithful soul with an ever increasing fervor of will, reminds us that the life of grace is eternal life begun; and it ends by asking for the normal fruit of this "grace of the virtues and of the gifts," the infused contemplation of the Blessed Trinity dwelling in us:

> To us, through Thee, the grace be shown
> To know the Father and the Son:
> And Spirit of Them both, may we
> Forever hold firm trust in Thee.

[43] Father Lallemant, S.J., *Doctrine spirituelle*, pp. 113, 187 ff., 203.

Consequently the mystical life is the plenitude of faith, hope, charity, and the gifts which accompany them; in other words, the normal prelude to the life of heaven.

We must have confidence in the divine promises. Aridity is not the result of tepidity, when, instead of love of the world, interest in our spiritual advancement predominates. We must trust in the Holy Ghost who dwells in us and who increases His work in us in proportion to our growing fidelity to the first commandment: "Thou shalt love the Lord thy God with thy whole heart, and with thy whole soul, and with all thy strength, and with all thy mind" in order to become "adorers in spirit and in truth." Our Lord said: "I will not now call you servants . . . but I have called you friends." We should believe in the wholly divine strength of the grace received in baptism, of the Holy Ghost who was given to us. We do not see this strength any more than we see the life hidden in an acorn from which a vigorous oak grows. If the oak is encircled by a band of iron, the bark will soon grow over it. Who can measure the supernatural energy contained in the grace of the virtues and the gifts, which is none other than eternal life begun? Who can set a limit to the work of sanctification which the Holy Ghost has begun in us, and prevent souls from reaching even the inner sanctuary where the Blessed Trinity dwells? "Wherefore I wished, and understanding was given me: and I called upon God, and the spirit of wisdom came upon me." [44] "I confess to Thee, O Father, Lord of heaven and earth, because Thou hast hid these things from the wise and prudent, and hast revealed them to little ones." [45]

[44] Wis. 7: 7.
[45] Matt. 11: 25.

## SOME THEORETICAL DIFFICULTIES
### CAN THE GRACE OF CONTEMPLATION BE MERITED?
### ARE THE REQUIRED CONDITIONS NORMAL?

Some objections in the speculative order may be raised against the doctrine we have expounded. Particularly deserving of examination is the objection which bears on the question as to whether the grace of contemplation can be merited at least congruously.

The first objection: "The law of the development of grace in man ought not to be understood only for grace abstractly considered, but for grace as capable of being shared by human nature. It is thus St. Thomas (*qu. disp. de caritate,* a. 10) distinguishes between: (1) the absolutely perfect charity which God alone can have; (2) the perfect charity which man can have only in heaven; and (3) the perfect charity which he can have in this life. St. Thomas expresses the same opinion in IIa IIae, q. 24, a. 8, and IIIa, q. 7, a. 10."

It is easy to answer that, in the question of the general and remote call,[46] we considered the grace of the virtues and the gifts, not in a purely abstract manner, independent of the mode according to which it exists in angels or in man, but as it exists in the human soul even in this life. This quasi-ideal soul was itself considered as a beginner, a proficient, and finally as perfect. And we insisted particularly on one point, namely, that infused contemplation does not require infused ideas like those of the angels, but that acquired ideas suffice, as they do for the act of faith. The question is, therefore, concerned with grace in so far as it can be shared by man in this life, and not in purgatory or in heaven.

Moreover, in the question of the individual call [47] we considered the life of grace as capable of being shared in and as participated in by an individual soul, according as it pos-

---

46 Cf. *supra,* pp. 337 f., 340, 345 f.
47 Cf. *supra,* p. 372.

sesses or does not possess the three signs mentioned by Tauler and later by St. John of the Cross, signs which have become the classic indications of the beginning of infused contemplation. Furthermore, in this second question the distinction between the merely sufficient call and the efficacious call (efficacious in the Thomistic sense, whether it be to the lower degrees of the mystical life or to the higher degrees) safeguards the gratuity of God's gift, just as in the case of the grace of conversion or that of final perseverance.

Therefore it is in entire conformity with the doctrine taught by St. Thomas (*qu. disp. de. caritate*, a. 10), since even the transforming union [48] is included in what St. Thomas calls *caritas perfecta secundum tempus, scilicet quae potest haberi in hac vita*.[49]

Every soul should be sufficiently purified at the moment of death to go straight to heaven without passing through purgatory, where it will be detained only through its own fault in neglecting graces that were granted or offered it. It will suffer so greatly in purgatory from the deprivation of the sight of God only because it is radical to the order established by God to see Him immediately after death. The fact that there are a great many retarded souls should not make us forget the normal way of sanctity, to which every Christian should aspire in order to be in the radical order willed by God.

Those who object to our teaching on this subject insist further. "It seems," they say, "that a law of grace (of its growth and perfection) cannot be as rigorously formulated as a law of nature. Grace, which is a participation in the divine nature and an absolutely gratuitous gift, has not by reason of this double title and, as it were, form, any measure that can regulate its perfection and mode of growth other than the free love of God for each man in particular."

[48] Cf. *The Interior Castle*, seventh mansion.
[49] Cf. IIa IIae, q.24, a.8; q.184, a.2, which were explained at length *supra*, pp. 156–98.

This interesting objection leads us to state definitely an important point. Certainly, according to the teaching of St. Thomas [50]—and St. John of the Cross expresses the same opinion [51]—the degree of glory of each predestined soul and the corresponding degree of charity at the hour of death depend on God's good pleasure. In addition, neither the first grace nor that of final perseverance can be merited; [52] and we shall see that not even any efficacious help which keeps us in the state of grace can be merited condignly, or according to the strict meaning of the word "merit." [53]

Nevertheless, if God gratuitously places a soul in the order of grace, and maintains it therein, then the laws of this order apply to that soul. Among these laws of the order of grace, some are absolutely rigorous and without exception; for example, there are truths of faith which must, not only of precept but of necessity, be believed by adults as an indispensable means of salvation. Likewise, it is impossible to have a supernatural love of God without faith; besides, the infused virtues are connected with charity, just as the gifts are.[54] This connection presupposes numerous mutual relations between the infused virtues and the gifts, relations which are the laws of the supernatural organism. As a result, in Ia IIae and IIa IIae of the *Summa*, almost every article dealing with the relations of the virtues to each other, or of the gifts to each other, or of the gifts with the virtues, contains a law belonging to the order of grace.

[50] *Summa*, Ia, q.23, a.5.

[51] *The Ascent of Mount Carmel*, Bk. II, chap. 5.

[52] St. Thomas, Ia IIae, q.114, a.5, 9.

[53] Condign merit is a supernatural and free act, the value of which constitutes a right to a supernatural reward, to the increase of grace, and to eternal life. It is, therefore, founded on justice. Congruous merit is not merit in the strict sense but rather in the broad sense of the term. It is not founded on justice but on friendship, *vel in jure amicabili, vel solum in liberalitate et benignitate praemiantis.*

[54] Cf. Ia IIae, q.65; q.68, a.5. Faith and hope can subsist in a soul in the state of mortal sin; but then they do not, properly speaking, deserve the name of virtues. Cf. Ia IIae, q.65, a.4 ad 1um: "Faith and hope . . . can be without charity, although they are not virtues without charity."

This is the way we can merit condignly (or in the strict sense, a rigorous law) the increase of charity which is accompanied by that of the infused virtues and of the gifts.[55] This is so true that a soul cannot have charity in a heroic degree without having the other infused virtues and the gifts (as *habitus*) in a proportionate degree.[56] This law is more rigorous than the law in virtue of which the five fingers of the hand develop at the same time. In the sensible order, there are exceptions, inasmuch as matter sometimes escapes the domination of the directing form or idea which organizes it. The infused virtues, which are mutually connected, considered formally, grow simultaneously without exception: "Their growth in man is equal, as the fingers . . . grow in proportion to one another." [57] The same is true of the gifts that are connected with them in charity.[58]

A further objection is offered: "If this point of view were entirely exact, there would be no need of hesitation in saying that the mystical state can, at a given moment, be merited condignly."

We answer this objection [59] in our frequently reiterated statement that a distinction must be made between the gifts themselves, considered as habitual dispositions, and the acts that proceed from them.

It is true that we can merit condignly the increase of charity, of the virtues, and of the gifts as *habitus,* and that in this life no limit can be placed on this augmentation.[60]

[55] See Ia IIae, q. 114, a. 8.

[56] *Ibid.,* q. 66, a. 2.

[57] *Ibid.,* and the *Commentary of the Theologians of Salamanca,* no. 2.

[58] *Ibid.,* q. 68, a. 5. The spiritual organism should develop proportionately in all its parts so that their harmony may subsist, just as our corporal organism does. But as in the body a part may hypertrophy to the detriment of the other parts, so in the spiritual life the harmony of the virtues may be compromised as a result of certain defects. In some souls, for example, faith is not developed in proportion to other virtues and to scientific or philosophical culture. This disorder may reach such a degree that he who suffers from it becomes a spiritual dwarf.

[59] Cf. *supra,* p. 353.

[60] *Summa,* IIa IIae, q 24, a.7.

The Holy Ghost moves souls as a rule according to the degree of their infused *habitus,* of their habitual docility (provided there is no obstacle, venial sin or imperfection; in case there is, the meritorious act is weak, *remissus,* inferior to the degree of charity). Consequently Thomists [61] usually say that the just man, who perseveres in fervor, can merit *saltem de congruo* (at least in the broad sense of the word "merit") the grace of infused contemplation. Why do they say *saltem,* at least congruously? Because in the grace of infused contemplation there is something merited strictly or condignly, that is, a high degree of the gifts of understanding and wisdom, considered as *habitus;* it is an act, and the mystical state is this act which lasts a certain time. But this act supposes an efficacious, actual grace. According to Thomists, we cannot strictly or condignly merit the efficacious help which keeps us in the state of grace. Why is this? Because the principle of merit does not fall under merit: that is why neither the first grace nor the efficacious help which maintains us in the state of grace nor the gift of final perseverance, though so necessary to salvation, can be merited condignly.[62]

Moreover, if a just man could strictly merit efficacious grace A, by it he would likewise merit efficacious grace B, and so on to the grace of final perseverance, which would

---

[61] Vallgornera, *Theol. myst. D. Thomae,* q.3, disp. 3, a.6, no. 5; Meynard, *Traité de la vie intérieure* (1885), II, 128; Philip of the Blessed Trinity, *Theol. myst.* (1874), II, 311, and Anthony of the Holy Ghost, *Directorium mysticum,* tr. III, sec. 6, no. 240.

[62] See Ia IIae, q.114, a.9. On this article, cf. John of St. Thomas, no. 1: "Principium meriti non potest cadere sub meritum: sed auxilium et motio divina, qua aliquis movetur a Deo, ut non succumbat tentationibus, nec gratiam interrumpat per peccatum, tenet se ex parte principii meriti, quia auxilium et motio est principium operandi, et in hoc solum consistit quod moveat ad opus; igitur non potest cadere sub meritum." No. 4: "Conservatio est continuatio primae productionis . . . , unde qui mereretur auxilia continuativa gratiae, seu perseverantiam, consequenter mereretur ipsam continuationem principii meriti, quod est gratia secundum quod se tenet ex parte Dei moventis ad conservandum. . . . Quod probat non posse sub meritum cadere motionem divinam, non quamcumque, sed quatenus est conservativa gratiae, quae est principium meriti." Cf. Salmanticences, *ibid.,* nos. 89-109.

thus be merited condignly. Whence it follows that many graces necessary to salvation cannot be the object of strict merit. It should not surprise us then that the actual efficacious grace of infused contemplation cannot be merited condignly, even though it is in the normal way of sanctity. It can be merited more than the grace of final perseverance, for it would be an exaggeration to say that this last can be merited at least congruously.[63] But in one sense the actual grace of infused contemplation is more gratuitous than that necessary to the obligatory exercise of the infused virtues, for we use infused virtues when we wish to do so. The same is not true of the gifts, although by our fidelity we can prepare ourselves to receive the inspiration of the Holy Ghost. Indeed, we ought to prepare ourselves for it; and if we do this generously, a day will come when the grace of contemplation will be given to us quite frequently. God ordinarily gives it to the perfect, provided there are no accidental obstacles; but He gives it either in aridity and night, or in light and consolation.[64]

The following objection is offered: "What you consider accidental and what you are a bit inclined to scorn theoretically because it is material, is perhaps part of that material causality, which is as indispensable to the essence of the composite (nature and grace) as formal causality, although in an inferior rank."

We must answer this objection by stating that souls receive grace according to the obediential power which is the same

[63] Cf. Ia IIae, q.114, a.9; also the Commentary of Billuart. He shows that according to the principles of St. Thomas it seems that final perseverance cannot be merited by a congruous merit properly so called, but only by a congruous merit improperly so called. While condign merit is founded on justice (*jus ad praemium*) and congruous merit, properly so called, on *jure amicabili, secundum leges amicitiae,* congruous merit improperly so called is founded *in liberalitate et benignitate Dei.*

[64] Moreover, by prayer we can obtain the grace of a happy death, which cannot be merited; in like manner the interior soul ought to ask humbly for the grace of contemplation. Cf. *supra,* p. 354 note 18.

in all.[65] As for the material causality, which prepares for the reception and increase of grace, it is itself the effect of an actual grace of supernatural order. According to St. Thomas, this is the meaning of the axiom: "If man does what is in him to do, God will not deny him grace."[66] The infusion and increase of grace certainly require an aptness, for no form or perfection is produced in a subject unless the subject is disposed for it; but it is God Himself who thus disposes our souls, or who moves them supernaturally to prepare themselves.[67] Grace and charity are not given to us in proportion to our natural capacities or dispositions, for they surpass them infinitely.[68] Consequently Thomists teach that it is our super-

[65] What is more, the obediential power or capacity to receive grace is no greater in angels than in men. It is according to this capacity that the soul is the subject of grace.

[66] Cf. Ia IIae, q.109, a.6. This article concludes as follows: "Hence it is clear that man cannot prepare himself to receive the light of grace except by the gratuitous help of God moving him inwardly." The reason for this is that the order of the agents must correspond to the order of the ends, and that only a supernatural agent can move to a supernatural end. *Ibid.*, ad 2um. "Hence when a man is said to do what is in him to do, this is said to be in his power according as he is moved by God." Therefore, to a man doing what is in him to do (with the help of actual grace), God does not deny (habitual) grace.

[67] See Ia IIae, q.112, a.2: Taking grace in the first sense (habitual) a certain preparation of grace is required for it, since a form can only be in disposed matter. *Ibid.*, ad 3um. "So likewise, when God infuses grace into a soul, no preparation is required which He Himself does not bring about." The same is true for the increase of charity, IIa IIae, q.24, a.2, and the following articles.

[68] See IIa IIae, q.24, a.3: "Since charity surpasses the proportion of human nature . . . it depends, not on any natural virtue, but on the sole grace of the Holy Ghost who infuses charity. Wherefore the quantity of charity depends neither on the condition of nature nor on the capacity of natural virtue, but only on the will of the Holy Ghost who divides His gifts according as He will." *Ibid.*, ad 2um: "The form does not surpass the proportion of the matter; they are both of the same genus. In like manner, grace and glory are referred to the same genus, for grace is nothing else than a beginning of glory in us. But charity and nature do not belong to the same genus, so that the comparison fails." It is not, therefore, only the mystical graces which are gratuitous, in this sense that the Holy Ghost gives them when He wills, but it is also the degree of charity given at the moment of justification to an adult who is converted with greater fervor than another, under the impulse of a stronger actual grace. St. Thomas, *ibid.*, ad 1um.

natural acts which not only merit, but physically prepare for the augmentation of charity.[69]

We considered these supernatural dispositions for infused contemplation at considerable length in the preceding chapters.[70] That teaching on the subject is classical, and it would be an unpardonable fault to neglect it. These dispositions, as we have seen, are chiefly: (1) great purity of heart, "Blessed are the clean of heart"; (2) great simplicity of mind which seeks only the truth; (3) profound humility; (4) habitual recollection; (5) perseverance in prayer; (6) fervent charity. This last disposition is the most important together with a profound humility. In the order of material preparation, humility is fundamental, according to St. Thomas, *ut removens prohibens,* inasmuch as it removes the principal obstacle which is pride, intellectual pride so frequent in a certain type of learning, or spiritual pride.[71] This is why St. Teresa insisted so strongly on this fundamental disposition in all her works, particularly in the Epilogue to *The Interior Castle.* Our Lord Himself taught this to us when He exclaimed: "I confess to Thee, O Father, Lord of heaven and earth because Thou hast hid these things from the wise and prudent, and hast revealed them to little ones." Often, by reason of humility, the inequality of supernatural conditions or of graces balances marvelously the inequality of natural conditions or dispositions. In the exposition of traditional teaching, too much insistence cannot, therefore, be placed on the supernatural dispositions to contemplation. And who can answer that he is unable to have this purity

---

[69] Cf. Billuart, *De caritate,* diss. II, a.2.

[70] Cf. *supra,* pp. 388–95.

[71] See IIa IIae, q.161, a.5: "Humility makes a man a good subject to ordinance of all kinds and in all matters." *Ibid.,* ad 2um: "First, by way of removing obstacles: and thus humility holds the first place, inasmuch as it expels pride, which God resisteth, and makes man open to receive the influx of divine grace. Hence it is written (Jas. 4: 6): God resisteth the proud, and giveth grace to the humble. In this sense humility is said to be the foundation of the spiritual edifice."

of heart, simplicity of mind, profound humility, spirit of prayer, and charity? We ought to beg God to give us these dispositions.

We have, moreover, considered the external conditions that favor contemplation and union with God. They are: a certain solitude, silence, sufficient time given to prayer, no overburdening, no useless reading, no preoccupations foreign to our vocation. To these external conditions must be added natural aptitude and also enlightened direction. If many of these exterior conditions are lacking, it is difficult to reach contemplation, which no longer has its normal environment, Profound humility and ardent charity, however, may supply this lack, especially if joined with great devotion to the Blessed Virgin and to the Eucharistic Heart of Jesus.[72] He who habitually begins his prayer with these two mediators, will be led by them to intimate union with God, since the object of the Blessed Virgin's influence is to lead us to her Son, and that of Christ to lead us to the Father.

When suitable external conditions are lacking, it may happen that generous souls will reach contemplation only after a period of time longer than the usual span of life; but they tend to it as to the normal prelude of the beatific vision. And the active life itself, according to St. Thomas, is thus ordained to the contemplative life, for which it should prepare us.[73]

To revert to the proposed objection, we have shown in the preceding chapter [74] that we understand "accidental" or *per accidens* in the same sense as St. Thomas does. Since sanctifying grace is, in fact, a beginning of eternal life

---

[72] Cf. Blessed Grignion de Montfort, *Le traité de la vraie dévotion à Marie,* chap. 4, art. 5, and the summary of this treatise, *Le secret de Marie,* made by Blessed Grignion. With a view to mental prayer, it is also well to meditate often on the office and mass of the Sacred Heart, and also on the office and mass of the Eucharistic Heart which have been recently approved by the Church.

[73] *Summa,* IIa IIae, q.181, a.1 ad 3um; q.182, a.4.

[74] Cf. *supra,* pp. 341–43.

(*inchoatio vitae aeternae, semen gloriae*), it is of itself *(ratione sui)* inamissible and should continually increase, especially through daily communion. But we hold this treasure in a fragile vessel and, because of the subject or of the defectibility of our free will, grace can be lost or may increase very little. Now this loss or even this check in its development is opposed to the intrinsic law of the divine seed, which was created to develop continually until eternal life is reached. This opposition characterizes sin in its various degrees. Whoever does not advance in the spiritual life, retrogresses.[75]

In view of the three fundamental reasons quoted in the preceding chapter,[76] we know that in principle (*per se loquendo*), infused contemplation is in the normal way of sanctity, given the above mentioned interior dispositions and good direction in a favorable environment. But if accidentally good direction, which should be normal in the Church, is lacking, and with it silence and recollection, and if the environment opposes contemplation instead of favoring it, then even generous souls may possibly not attain to infused contemplation in this life. This is similar to the case of a good intellect in a milieu that is strongly prejudiced against the teaching of St. Thomas. In such a situation, a good intellect will find great difficulty in reaching a clear grasp of St. Thomas' doctrine. This also represents something accidental.[77]

To know what is the normal way of sanctity and the full development of the grace of the virtues and the gifts, we must consider how this grace grows in principle (*per se*) in suitable and not contrary interior and exterior conditions. The same rule holds good in the spiritual order as in the natural order. When we wish to discover what a certain seed will produce, for example, the seed of a cedar, we plant it in

[75] Cf. *supra*, pp. 188 f.
[76] Cf. *supra*, pp. 345–67.
[77] Cf. *supra*, pp. 341–43.

suitable soil; otherwise it will not reach the summit of its normal development. We are speaking, therefore, of souls in a Christian environment which corresponds to the designs God has on them.

Another difficulty may be stated as follows: "From the sole concept of grace formally considered, we cannot deduce a priori that the mystical state is normal, even in the sense which has just been expressed. The proof should be supplemented at least by the observation of facts, or by having recourse to theological authority, tradition for example."

This objection is easily answered. The three fundamental proofs proposed in the preceding chapter [78] are individually, as well for the major as for the minor and the conclusion, founded not only on the concept of the grace of the virtues and the gifts, but on tradition and the experience of the perfect life, as it has been described especially by St. Teresa and St. John of the Cross. Moreover, ten to fifteen years' experience in ministering to contemplative communities, and even to those of fervent mixed life, suffices to show that the experience of the perfect life conforms even today with what the saints have told us about it.

Therefore infused contemplation is in the normal way of sanctity for the following reasons: (1) It proceeds from the grace of the virtues and the gifts accorded to every baptized person, and it appears when the superhuman mode of the gifts begins to prevail, as is proper for perfection, over the human and imperfect mode of the virtues.[79] This takes place in the illuminative and especially in the unitive way. (2) In this life the soul is perfectly purified in the depths of its faculties only by the passive purifications of the senses and of the soul, which belong to the mystical order and are accompanied by infused contemplation, at least by initial or arid contemplation. (3) Infused contemplation and the very ar-

[78] Cf. *supra,* pp. 245–67.
[79] Cf. *supra,* pp. 299, 324–26.

dent desire to see God are, according to tradition and the experience of the perfect life, the normal prelude to the beatific vision. Therefore, since heaven is accessible to all, as much must be said of what is its ordinary prelude in the perfect.[80]

Although eminent, the grace of infused contemplation is in the normal way of sanctity, even of the sanctity which every Christian should have before death in order to avoid purgatory and, immediately after the separation of the soul from the body, to be in the radical order willed by God, and not to be painfully deprived of the beatific vision for a longer or shorter time.

There is a further objection: "No one can question the fact that the spiritual progress expressed under these three aspects is in the normal line of the formal development of grace. But does not human nature in this life (*in via*) present in its normal state such resistance to this growth that this development should be considered an extraordinary favor? The beatific vision is, indeed, in the order of the formal development of grace, but it would be essentially extraordinary to receive it here below. Now, between the normal conditions of human life and the exterior and interior conditions required for the mystical life, almost as great a distance exists as between life and death."

Here again we reply with St. Thomas,[81] that the beatific vision cannot take place in this life without rapture, and that it excludes the co-operation of the imagination. The case is quite otherwise with infused contemplation, which we are here considering. It is, therefore, conformable to the

[80] The Teresian Congress of Madrid (see *El Monte Carmelo* of Burgos, May, 1923) approved the following conclusion: "Since the virtues find their ultimate perfection in the gifts, and the gifts reach their perfect actuation in contemplation, it results that contemplation is the *ordinary 'way'* of sanctity and of habitually heroic virtue." Theologians are more and more agreed in accepting this teaching. On this subject, see our "Chronique de théologie mystique" in *La vie spirituelle*, June, 1923.

[81] See IIa IIae, q.175, a.4; q.180, a.5.

normal state of man in this life.[82] In addition, we should not forget that there is less distance between a just man on this earth, even though he is not a mystic, and a saint in heaven, than between this just man and a sinner deprived of grace; for nature is not the seed of grace, whereas grace is the seed of glory, or eternal life begun, *inchoatio vitae aeternae*. No great distance separates the normal conditions of a perseveringly fervent Christian life from the conditions required for the mystical life.[83]

The conditions required for the mystical life are found both in contemplative orders and in fervent communities devoted both to contemplation and to action, and even in Christian marriage when it is truly what it ought to be.[84] Many experienced directors have found in all these walks of life, among generous souls habitually faithful to the Holy Ghost, many that have reached the mystical state. Recently one of these directors wrote as follows: "Many believe themselves to be on the mystical way and qualified to write and speak about it, who have no true experience of it. . . . On the other hand, many lead the mystical life unawares and sometimes are very far advanced in it without suspecting that God is doing very great things in them, or realizing that theirs is the mystical life. I have found such in all walks of life, notably among the poor and little children and among

---

82 See IIa IIae, q. 180, a.5 ad 2um: "In the present state of life, human contemplation is impossible without phantasms, because it is connatural to man to see the intelligible species in the phantasms, as the Philosopher states (*De anima*, iii). Yet intellectual knowledge does not consist in the phantasms themselves, but in our contemplating in them the purity of the intelligible truth: and this is not only in natural knowledge, but also in that which we obtain by revelation. For Dionysius says (*Coel. hier.*, ii) that the divine glory shows us the angelic hierarchies under certain symbolic figures, and by its power we are brought back to a single ray of light, i. e., to the simple knowledge of the intelligible truth. It is in this sense that we must understand the statement of Gregory that contemplatives do not carry along with them the shadows of things corporeal, since their contemplation is not fixed on them, but on the consideration of the intelligible truth."

83 Cf. *supra*, pp. 393 f.

84 Cf. *supra*, p. 384.

illiterate persons, and even among savage tribes of North America." [85] The author of these lines goes so far as to maintain that ordinarily a soul does not persevere in fervor, humility, self-forgetfulness, and generosity, without attaining to the life of intimate union with God; in other words, to the essence of the mystical life. This does not prevent him from writing: "An amazing fact is that a comparatively enormous number of persons remain beginners all their lives. Very few, even among religious and clerics and secular persons making a profession of piety, very few indeed are those who really go beyond the threshold of the mystical life and who answer the loving, pressing invitation of God: 'Friend, go up higher' (Luke 14: 10)." [86] As we said in the preceding chapter,[87] this explains the fact that conditions necessary for the mystical life are not generally lacking in the case of generous interior souls. If we are inclined to hold a contrary opinion, we should take care not to seek in an unfounded theory the justification of a certain spiritual mediocrity. We should not assert that the mystical life is extraordinary, simply to avoid the obligation of aspiring to it by that despoiling of self which prepares for it.

We might add that unfavorable surroundings often provoke a salutary reaction in good souls, especially in very good ones; and the Lord helps them in proportion to the difficulties to be overcome. For example, the suffering caused by injustice reveals to us the worth of justice; self-sufficiency and pride, which become unendurable, demonstrate the worth of humility. Love of truth, relish for the word of God, solid piety, all of which are not content with appearances, react by common accord and quite spontaneously against empty and pretentious learning, which alters everything by its false spirit. The lack of simplicity in life empha-

---

[85] Dom Louismet, *The Mystical Life,* p. 8.
[86] *Ibid.,* p. 23.
[87] Cf. *supra,* p. 384.

sizes the desirability of that frank cordiality without which there is no true union of hearts and minds in God. A discordant note, which violates the order of charity by placing the love of neighbor above the love of God, startles us and by contrast recalls the grandeur of the first precept. Falsehood under its various forms shows us the worth of truth; the absence of truth in varying degrees is one of the greatest obstacles to the life of prayer. A soul becomes contemplative only if it is established in the truth, because infused contemplation is simply the immediate effect of the direct operation of God's truth on the soul to bring it to a greater love.

Finally, the chief obstacle comes from certain subtleties of intellectual or spiritual pride which, especially when found in those who direct souls, can have irremediable consequences, at least for a time. In this case, mystical grandiloquence is no less to be feared than a certain sterile intellectualism. This explains by contrast why more real contemplation and sanctity are sometimes found in poor convents that are very little known, but are exceedingly dear to our Lord Jesus Christ. The divine mercy often compensates for the inequality of natural conditions by great graces. "Blessed are the poor in spirit." Deep humility supplies for other conditions in the life of union with God. The two great mediators, Jesus and Mary, stoop to the humble in order to lead them to the intimacy of the Father. We have only one life, and on it our eternity depends. As Tauler says, if we have not entered the divine intimacy before we are advanced in years, we run the risk of not entering it in this life, even though it is the normal prelude to heaven.

Lastly, this objection is offered: "The conditions generally required for the mystical life, although normal to grace, are abnormal to human nature, which is not made normally for these conditions of life. In the habitual mode of acting which characterizes the mystical state, and in the terrible passive purifications, there is an annihilation of nature to which nature is not essentially ordained. This annihilation is not required for simple justification or for the life of grace according to the human mode of the virtues. . . . Finally, in this life the normal prelude of the beatific vision is charity, strictly speaking, and not infused contemplation proceeding from the gift of wisdom."

This objection, which devotes more attention to the exigencies of nature than to those of grace, is reminiscent of the spirit of certain Christian humanists rather than of the spirit of wisdom mentioned here. It fails to recognize several essential points that we have expounded at length.

1) It loses sight of the scope of our Lord's teaching on the mystery of the cross. In St. Luke's Gospel (9: 23) we read: "And He said to all: If any man will come after Me, let him deny himself, and take up his cross daily, and follow Me. For whosoever will save his life shall lose it; for he that shall lose his life for My sake, shall save it." From this point of view, the conditions of the mystical life which seem abnormal to nature are not so to nature regenerated by grace; they are not abnormal to Christian life, considered especially in its full perfection attainable on this earth. A Christian should imitate Christ crucified. The passive purifications are not opposed to the harmony of nature and grace. These purifications, more or less painful according to the faults to be expiated and to the degree of supernatural life to which God wishes to conduct the soul,[88] are, like the cross, necessary, according to the saints, in order to reach this perfect harmony, which on earth finds its complete realization only in the fully developed unitive life, that is, in the mystical life and its superhuman mode.[89] In it alone the virtues apparently

[88] Cf. *supra*, p. 357.

[89] St. Thomas even says of the theological virtues, independently of the gifts: "The theological virtues are above man as stated above (q.58, a.3 ad 3um). Hence they should properly be called not human but superhuman or Godlike" (Ia IIae, q.61, a.1 ad 2um). Consequently it is only among the virtues which are properly human that the four cardinal virtues are called

so contrary harmonize completely: the loftiest wisdom with prudence, attentive to the slighest detail; strength with meekness; mercy with justice. In the unitive life alone the supernatural life becomes truly connatural without losing any of its elevation. It is like a second nature whose acts are spontaneous and very simple because the purified soul refers all to God [90] instead of referring all instinctively to self.

We should not forget, however, that fallen nature rises again to its natural normal state only by the grace which heals *(gratia sanans),* and that without this grace we cannot observe all the natural laws or love God, the Author of our nature, above all else, even in a natural way. St. Thomas is explicit in his teaching on this point. He says: "In the state of perfect nature, man referred the love of himself and of all other things to the love of God as to its end; and thus he loved God more than himself and above all things. But in the state of corrupt nature, man falls short of this in the appetite of his rational will, which, unless it is cured by God's grace, follows its private good, on account of the corruption of nature." [91]

2) The objection would, in addition, lead one to maintain,

---

principal virtues, in spite of the incomparable superiority of the theological virtues, which are directed toward the last end. Cf. *ibid.*

[90] Cf. *supra,* pp. 37, 40 f., 152 ff.

[91] *Summa,* Ia IIae, q. 109, a. 3, 4. In the works of St. Thomas, see the references to the *fomes peccati* and the wounds; cf. *Tabula aurea* under these words.

That Thomists are faithful to St. Thomas is shown when they teach generally that man in the state of fallen nature, not as yet regenerated, is weaker in regard to good than he would have been in the state of pure nature. On the article quoted, see the Commentaries of Lemos, Alvarez, Billuart, John of St. Thomas, and especially Salmanticenses, *De gratia,* tr. XIV, q. 109, disp. 2, dub. 2–5, nos. 99, 102, 116, 129, 135. Among modern theologians, this is the opinion of St. Alphonsus; it is generally the doctrine of spiritual authors, who echo the writing of the saints. Cf. *The Imitation of Christ,* Bk. III, chaps. 54, 55. Such seems to be also the natural meaning of the texts of the ecclesiastical magisterium where it speaks of the wounds of fallen nature and of free will not destroyed but attenuated, weakened, and of the *fomes peccati;* cf. Denzinger (10th ed.), nos. 174, 181, 198, 788, 793, 1275, 1616, 1627, 1634 ff., 1643.

in opposition to what we have set forth about the sublimity of the first commandment,[92] that the majority of just souls could not by progressive fidelity reach Christian perfection, that is, the third degree of charity. As we have seen,[93] this degree is normally accompanied by the third degree of the gifts, which belongs to the mystical order. God is prompt in giving the grace of contemplation to those who are prepared for it, but man is slow in preparing suitably by perfect humility and abnegation.

3) It would also follow that for the majority of the elect purgatory would be inevitable, since they could not be perfectly purified in this life. This error fails to take into account the fact that, in the order willed by God, purification should be undergone in this life with the resulting merit, instead of after death without merit.[94]

4) It is not only charity which in perfect souls is the normal prelude to the beatific vision, but charity accompanied by the virtues of the purified soul *(purgati animi)*,[95] by the gifts in the third degree, and by the beatitudes, the reward of which belongs in a sense to this life.[96]

The solution of these objections confirms the doctrine we taught in the preceding chapter on the general and remote call of just souls to the mystical life, which is in the normal way of sanctity, on the normal way to heaven, to which all the just are most certainly called. This explains our summary of this doctrine in the following outline. Its meaning and scope can now be better understood. By reading from the bottom up, the ascending movement of grace in our souls is followed.

---

[92] Cf. *supra*, pp. 191–98, 399.

[93] Cf. *supra*, pp. 299–310.

[94] Cf. *supra*, pp. 356 f., 400 ff.

[95] *Summa*, Ia IIae, q.61, a.5.

[96] *Ibid.*, q.69, a.2, and ad 3um, commentary on "Blessed are the clean of heart: for they shall see God."

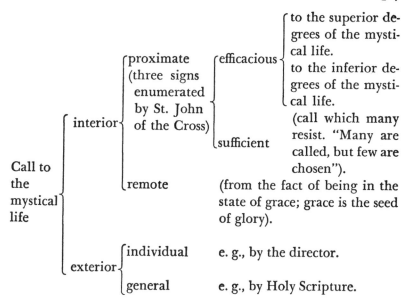

Call to the mystical life
- interior
  - proximate (three signs enumerated by St. John of the Cross)
    - efficacious
      - to the superior degrees of the mystical life.
      - to the inferior degrees of the mystical life.
    - sufficient (call which many resist. "Many are called, but few are chosen").
  - remote (from the fact of being in the state of grace; grace is the seed of glory).
- exterior
  - individual — e. g., by the director.
  - general — e. g., by Holy Scripture.

### VENIAL SIN AND IMPERFECTION, OBSTACLES TO DIVINE UNION

Too much insistence cannot be placed on the divers obstacles hindering the exercise of the gifts of the Holy Ghost in our souls. Father Lallemant, S.J., gives a clear exposition of these hindrances in his beautiful book, *The Spiritual Doctrine*.[97] He says: "It has been asked why the majority of religious and devout persons who lead a lukewarm spiritual life make so few acts of the gifts of the Holy Ghost, since, being in the state of grace, they possess them. . . . It is surprising to see so many religious who, after living in the state of grace for forty or fifty years, saying mass daily, and performing all the holy exercises of the religious life, and consequently possessing the gifts of the Holy Ghost in a very high physical degree, corresponding to that sort of perfection in grace which theologians call gradual or a physical increase

[97] Part IV, chap. 3, art. 3.

—it is surprising, I repeat, to see that these religious give no evidence of the gifts of the Holy Ghost in their actions and conduct. Their life is entirely natural, for when blamed or disobliged they show their resentment; they are very eager for praise, esteem, and the applause of the world, and take great pleasure in these things. They love and seek their ease and all that flatters self-love.

"This should not be a subject of amazement, for the venial sins which they commit continually hold the gifts of the Holy Ghost, as it were, bound [98] in such a way that it is not at all surprising that they do not show their effect. It is true that the gifts grow, like charity, habitually and in their physical being; but not actually, and in that perfection which corresponds to the fervor of charity and which increases our merit, because venial sins are opposed to the fervor of charity and consequently hinder the operation of the gifts of the Holy Ghost. . . . It is past all conception, says St. Lawrence Justinian, how many sins fill our hearts if we do not take care to purify them constantly. . . . Few people give themselves wholly to God, and abandon themselves so completely to the conduct of the Holy Ghost that He alone lives in them and is the principle of all their actions."

Moreover, people often neglect to correct a multitude of imperfections which are not, at least essentially, venial sins. St. John of the Cross [99] names many of them, when he speaks of the imperfections of beginners and of proficients.[100]

[98] In the same chapter, Father Lallemant says: "Venial sins, which they commit in great number, exclude the graces necessary to produce acts of the gifts of the Holy Ghost. God refuses them the help of His graces, because He foresees that if He gave them these graces in their present disposition, they would be of no use to them, since their will is bound by a thousand fetters which would prevent them from consenting." These bonds are contrary habits and affections.

[99] *The Dark Night of the Soul*, Bk. I, chap. 3; Bk. II, chap. 2.

[100] He makes a distinction between habitual imperfections and actual imperfections. Among the habitual imperfections in beginners, he lists the inclination to spiritual sensuality and to spiritual pride. Venial sins are often

In this matter, it is important to see how, according to the opinion of the best Thomists, imperfection differs from venial sin. At first glance, this distinction seems contrary to two principles enunciated by St. Thomas. He teaches [101] that there are no deliberate individual or concrete acts which are indifferent, that is, which are neither morally good nor morally bad. If they are indifferent by reason of their object, as, for example, taking a walk, they are either good or bad by reason of the end which the person intends; because man, when acting deliberately, ought always to do so for a right end. If he does this, the act is morally good; otherwise, it is bad. Hence it does not seem that between virtuous acts and venial sins there can be any place for what is called an imperfection.

Elsewhere St. Thomas teaches [102] that the perfection of charity falls under the precept of the love of God, if not as matter, or something to be accomplished, at least as the end toward which every Christian, each according to his condition, should tend. Consequently it seems that when he does not accomplish all that he can at a given moment, he commits a venial sin, slight perhaps, but real. Therefore imperfection does not seem distinct from venial sin.

St. Thomas, nevertheless, often speaks of good acts which are imperfect. This is the case with acts of charity that are notably inferior to our degree of charity (*actus remissi*): for example, when, having five talents, we act as though we had

---

the result. There are also first movements of impatience, sensuality, and pride which precede all actual advertence, and sometimes even the advertence possible in beginners, especially when they are fatigued or drowsy. Cf. St. Thomas, Ia IIae, q.74, a.3 ad 2um: "This corruption of the *fomes* does not hinder man from using his rational will to check individual, inordinate movements, if he be presentient of them, for instance, by turning his thoughts to other things." Cf. *ibid.*, Salmanticences; also Ia IIae, q.17, a.7; q.80, a.3 ad 3um; IIa IIae, q.154, a.5; *De malo*, q.7, a.6 ad 6um.

[101] See Ia IIae, q.18, a.9.
[102] See IIa IIae, q.184, a.3.

only two.[103] Besides, when St. Thomas [104] defines initial fear, which is intermediate between servile fear (the fear of suffering) and filial fear (the fear of sin), he says that initial fear does not differ essentially from filial fear (it is, therefore, not a venial sin); but that it is something imperfect, for it is accompanied by a certain amount of servile fear. A man who as yet possesses only initial fear, says St. Thomas, "is inclined toward good, not only through love of justice, but also for fear of punishment; for this fear ceases in a soul that possesses perfect charity." As a matter of fact, servile fear diminishes with the progress of charity, while filial fear increases.

The reason which serves as a basis for the distinction between venial sin and imperfection has been clearly expounded in the Thomistic school by the Carmelites of Salamanca.[105] Their doctrine is as follows: Venial sin cannot be ordained to the end of charity *(est irreferibile ad finem caritatis)* for it is a disordered act, in the order of means, as mortal sin is disordered in relation to the last end from which it turns us aside.[106]

On the contrary, what is called "an imperfection" is a morally good act which can be ordained to the end of charity, but which lacks a certain perfection suitable to spiritual progress.

For a clear understanding of this distinction we must, as the Carmelites of Salamanca say, observe that an imperfect act (often called an imperfection) is not absolutely identified with the absence of perfection (or formal imperfection) which is found in it. This absence of perfection is certainly

---

103 *Summa,* IIa IIae, q.24, a.6 ad 1um (and the Thomistic commentators); also Ia IIae, q.114, a.8 ad 3um. Cf. *supra,* pp. 188–98. The progress of the soul should be uniformly accelerated, and each communion more fervent and fruitful than the preceding, since each ought to increase charity in us and thus dispose us for a better reception of the Holy Eucharist the next day.

104 See IIa IIae, q.19, a.8.

105 *Cursus theol., De peccatis,* tr. XIII, disp. 19, dub. 1, nos. 8 and 9, and *De incarnatione* (in St. Thomas, IIIa, q.15, a.1, *De impeccabilitate Christi*), where it is shown that no venial sin or imperfection was possible in Christ.

106 *Summa,* Ia IIae, q.88, a.2.

not good. But the imperfect act we are speaking of is morally good, though it does not possess the degree of perfection suitable to spiritual progress. It can, therefore, be ordained to the end of charity.

It is not an indifferent act *in individuo,* since it is good. Properly speaking, neither is it opposed to the precept of the love of God, for the perfection of charity does not fall under this precept as *materia,* something to be done *sub gravi* or *sub levi,* but only as the end. Sin is committed only when there is a transgression of a precept with respect to the matter of this precept, whether obligatory *sub gravi* or *sub levi.* An imperfect act is opposed only to a counsel, which in itself does not oblige. As a matter of fact, we must preserve the distinction between the precepts and the counsels, whether the latter are contained in the Gospel, or are directly inspired by God in a certain soul. The Holy Ghost often makes a soul comprehend that a certain act is better for it, but that it is not obliged to that act, unless it has made the vow of doing what is most perfect.

The division of imperfections, analogous to that of venial sins, has its origin in this definition. Thus, there are imperfections: (1) *ex genere suo;* (2) *ex parvitate materiae;* (3) *ex indeliberatione.*

1) An imperfection *ex genere suo,* or by its very nature, is of such a kind that even when deliberate it does not become a venial sin. To this class belong supernatural and meritorious acts that are imperfect *(remissi)* relative to our degree of charity: for example, when a proficient makes an act of charity proportionate to the virtue of beginners. Likewise initial fear is imperfect because of servile fear which accompanies it and which should diminish with the progress of charity. To this category may also be linked natural acts that are not forbidden, but that are not in accord with spiritual progress, and that would surprise us in a mortified person and especially in the saints, unless a special reason

motivated them: for example, the use of certain needless things, such as tobacco; certain ways of amusing oneself or of taking pleasure in scientific or artistic things; in study, an activity that has been branded as "natural" because it is not sufficiently supernaturalized by the motive prompting it. We may place in this class the omission of something which we think is better for us, and to which at the time, from a lawful but less perfect motive, we prefer something less good: for example, when, although we could make a visit to the Blessed Sacrament, we prefer to spend our time at a useful philosophical study which could be postponed. This act in itself is not evil, nor is it so for us unless by a special vow we are obliged to do what is most perfect. Therefore it is good, since concretely no deliberate act is indifferent; but it is less good than the other. We should not stigmatize as evil what is only less good. But we should keep in mind this imperfection in the order of good, remembering that, as venial sin disposes to mortal sin, imperfection disposes to venial sin. If we desire to keep to what is strictly obligatory with God, He, who often gives us much more than what is strictly necessary, will on His part diminish His graces.

Moreover, in the cases quoted there will, as a matter of fact, accidentally be venial sin, since the motive for our not doing what is best for us here and now is frequently negligence or laziness.[107]

2) There are imperfections *ex levissima materia,* because the matter or object involved is extremely slight, and man is not obliged to deliberate on these extremely slight things: [108] for example, some little negligence in one's bearing.

3) Finally, there are imperfections *ex imperfectione actus,*

---

107 It is unlawful to omit something which is better for us for the sole motive that we are *not obliged* to it, and that we wish to use our liberty. Several Thomists rightly remark that this is a will without just motive, *volitio otiosa carens pia utilitate aut justa necessitate.* Cf. Billuart, *De actibus humanis,* diss. IV, a.6, solv. obj. 3.

108 See Ia IIae, q. 14, a. 4.

that is, through lack of attention or deliberation. In this category are ranged acts that are good by reason of their object, but that are accomplished in a mechanical fashion as a result of involuntary distraction. These acts are not sins, although they lack the perfection which comes from attention.[109] To this class belong also the very first disordered movements of sensuality, which are produced before we can be aware of them and repress them. They are an imperfection destined to disappear chiefly as a result of the passive purifications of the senses and of the soul; and they become rare in a perfect soul. As much must be said of the defective way in which a perfect soul accomplishes a good act; for example, in the necessary repression of evil, even the saints sometimes —and that quite contrary to their intention—mingle some movement of anger which slightly exceeds the just measure. [110] Lastly, to this class belongs the purely material transgression of a precept through invincible ignorance.

There are certainly many imperfections which, though not essentially venial sins, take from our lives the harmony, peace, and vigor suitable to spiritual progress. They appear particularly in the common life, especially in acts requiring a greater perfection: for example, chanting the office too slowly or too rapidly may annoy our neighbor without our being aware of it; playing the organ in a certain way may become a hindrance to prayer rather than an aid. It may be these acts contain no venial sin, properly so called, but an imperfection springing from our temperament, from fatigue, from a defect in our training, or from a certain cast of char-

---

[109] But, as a matter of fact, in these there is often negligence and, as a result, venial sin, when one could and should consider and deliberate.

[110] St. Thomas observes (IIIa, q.15, a.9 ad 3um), apropos of anger, that when Christ drove the buyers from the Temple His anger was perfectly holy and proportioned to the motive which inspired it; while in us anger, even when commanded and moderated by right reason, slightly disturbs the gaze of contemplation; for when the operation of one of our faculties is intense, it often hinders the act of another faculty. "This is the reason why any movement whatsoever of anger, even if it be tempered by reason, dims the mind's eye of him who contemplates." This disappears gradually in the saints.

acter inclined either to neglect details or, on the contrary, to become absorbed in them. A more perfect charity, characterized by a greater delicacy toward God and our neighbor, accompanied by the gifts of the Holy Ghost in a proportionate degree, would cause these imperfections to disappear gradually.

We have already listed [111] several imperfections that constitute obstacles to contemplation. Especially important are those indicated by St. John of the Cross in *The Dark Night of the Soul:* [112] the inclination to seek enjoyment in God rather than God Himself; the first movements of spiritual pride; the stains of the old man which persist in the spirit even after the passive purification of the senses; a certain dullness of the mind; natural rudeness, the result of sin. "Proficients themselves are subject to distractions and to dissipation of mind. . . . Some use their spiritual goods in a manner that is not very interior. . . . They thus expose themselves to delusion by the suggestions of the devil or their own fancy. . . . This matter is inexhaustible. . . . In order to show the necessity of the night of the soul, we must add that there is not one among the proficients, however great may be his efforts, who is exempt from many natural affections and imperfect habits, which must be purified before divine union is attained." [113]

This is another argument in favor of the doctrine that these passive purifications and infused and obscure contemplation, which is the principle of the purifications, are truly in the normal way of sanctity. "This dark night is an inflowing of God into the soul to purify it of its habitual ignorances and imperfections, both natural and spiritual. Contemplatives call it infused contemplation and mystical theology, in which God instructs the soul secretly in the perfection of

[111] Cf. *supra*, pp. 395 ff.
[112] Bk. I, chap. 3; Bk. II, chap. 2.
[113] *Ibid.*

love, without any intervention on its part, and without its understanding in what this infused contemplation consists. . . . How does it happen that the soul calls the divine light a dark night? . . . There are two reasons for this. The first is that the divine wisdom transcends by reason of its elevation the capacity of the soul, and for that very reason is darkness for it. The second reason lies in the baseness and impurity of the soul which makes the light painful, afflictive, and at the same time dark for it. . . . Although still in darkness, the soul sees none the less clearly its own impurity by means of this light. It is persuaded that it is unworthy of God or of any creature. . . . The divine and obscure light places clearly before it all its infidelities." [114] Thereby it learns true humility, which prepares it to receive an abundance of divine grace, for "God gives His grace to the humble," and He makes them humble in order to load them with His gifts.

Such is the way of true life, the only sure road to eternal beatitude. "Blessed are the undefiled in the way, who walk in the law of the Lord. Blessed are they that search His testimonies: that seek Him with their whole heart. . . . I have run the way of Thy commandments, when Thou didst enlarge my heart," [115] by divine charity, in the light of life, which reveals Thy grandeur and omnipotence, and Thy infinite mercy toward us. The voice of the psalms is that of contemplation, animating the great prayer of the Church. To live truly by faith, every believing soul should aspire to this contemplation. In this aspiration humility and magnanimity, by reason of the connection of the virtues, ought to be united; and only when they are united, are they genuine. [116] Only a profoundly humble soul can in a fitting manner aspire to the great things promised by Christ to those who wish to follow Him; from the very fact that a soul is humble,

---

[114] *The Dark Night of the Soul*, Bk. II, chap. 5.
[115] Ps. 118: 1–2, 32.
[116] *Summa*, IIa IIae, q. 129, a. 3 ad 4um.

it will be filled to overflowing: *Deposuit potentes de sede, et exaltavit humiles.*

## ARTICLE V

### *Extraordinary Graces that Sometimes Accompany Infused Contemplation*

The doctrine we have expounded receives additional confirmation from the comparison of infused contemplation with the extraordinary graces that sometimes accompany it, and yet are distinct from it. These extraordinary graces generally belong to the charisms, or graces freely bestowed *(gratis datae),* enumerated by St. Paul: "Now there are diversities of graces, but the same Spirit. . . . And the manifestation of the Spirit is given to every man unto profit. To one indeed, by the Spirit, is given the *word of wisdom;* and to another, the *word of knowledge,* according to the same Spirit; to another, *faith* in the same Spirit; [1] to another, the *grace of healing* in one Spirit: to another, the *working of miracles;* to another, *prophecy;* to another, the *discerning of spirits;* to another, *diverse kinds of tongues;* to another, *interpretation of speeches.* But all these things one and the same Spirit worketh, dividing to everyone according as He will." [2] St. Paul places charity far above these gifts: "And if I . . . have not charity, it profiteth me nothing." [3]

As St. Thomas shows, sanctifying grace and charity are much more excellent than these charisms; the former unite us immediately to God, our last end, whereas the charisms are ordained chiefly for the benefit of our neighbor and

[1] This does not mean the theological virtue of faith, since the latter is common to all Christians; rather St. Paul means a special certitude and security which God grants especially to theologians or to preachers so that they may transmit His divine word with a conviction which nothing can shake. Cf. *infra,* p. 441 note 29.

[2] See I Cor. 12: 4, 7–11; cf. Rom. 12: 6.

[3] See I Cor. 13: 3.

only prepare him to be converted, without giving him divine life.[4] As a rule, they are not essentially supernatural like sanctifying grace, but only preternatural like a miracle and prophecy.[5]

St. Thomas shows clearly the nature of these charisms by his division of them.[6] This classification is set forth in the following table:

| Graces gratuitously given to instruct one's neighbor concerning divine things | 1. Graces that give full knowledge of divine things | *faith* or special certitude as to principles.<br>*word of wisdom,* on the principal conclusions known through the first cause.<br>*word of knowledge,* on the examples and effects which manifest the causes. |
| | 2. Graces that confirm divine revelation | by works { *gift of healing.* / *gift of miracles.* }<br>by knowledge { *discerning of spirits.* / *prophecy.* } |
| | 3. Graces that aid in preaching the word of God | *gift of tongues.*<br>*gift of interpretation of speeches.* |

[4] *Summa,* Ia IIae, q. 111, a. 5: "Now the end is always greater than the means. But sanctifying grace ordains a man immediately to a union with his last end, whereas gratuitous grace ordains a man to what is preparatory to the end; i. e., by prophecy and miracles, etc., men are induced to unite themselves to their last end. And hence sanctifying grace is nobler than gratuitous grace." Ia IIae, q. 111, a. 1 ad 3um: "Sanctifying grace adds to the notion of gratuitous grace something pertaining to the nature of grace, since it makes man pleasing to God. And hence gratuitous grace which does not do this keeps the common name, as happens in many other cases." As the animal devoid of reason is simply called "animal," so these graces of inferior order, which in themselves do not render man agreeable to God, are called "graces gratuitously given."

[5] See *supra,* p. 59, for the distinction between the supernatural *quoad substantiam* and the supernatural *quoad modum.*

[6] See Ia IIae, q. 111, a. 4.

To these charisms may generally be attached the extraor-dinary favors that sometimes accompany infused contem-plation; that is, private revelations, visions, and supernatural words, which St. John of the Cross discusses at length in *The Ascent of Mount Carmel.*[7] He takes great pains to distinguish them from infused contemplation, which is attached to the grace of the virtues and of the gifts, or sanctifying grace. This teaching of St. John of the Cross rests theologically on St. Thomas' treatise on prophecy,[8] where six articles [9] are devoted to the rapture which sometimes accompanies pro-phetic revelation, as it may also accompany infused contem-plation.

According to St. Thomas, prophetic revelation may be made in three ways: by a sensible vision; an imaginary vision; or an intellectual vision; and the prophet may be awake, asleep, or in ecstasy. Occasionally in fact, a sensible, out-ward sign appears to the eyes or an exterior voice is heard.[10] At other times, to express His thought to us, God co-ordin-ates certain images that pre-exist in our imagination, or He imprints new ones on it.[11] More rarely He acts directly on the intellect by co-ordinating our acquired ideas or by im-printing new ideas, called infused.[12] There is always infused prophetic light, and indeed it alone suffices, for example, to interpret certain signs, as Joseph interpreted the dreams of Pharao.[13]

If the prophet is awake, the vision is more perfect than if given to him during sleep, because he has the full use of his faculties.[14] Occasionally the so-called imaginary vision or the intellectual vision is accompanied by ecstasy, or aliena-

7 Bk. II, chaps. 10–31.
8 *Summa*, IIa IIae, q.171–75.
9 *Ibid.*, q.175.
10 *Ibid.*, q.174, a.1 ad 3um.
11 *Ibid.*, q.173, a.2 ad 1um.
12 *Ibid.*, ad 2um.
13 *Ibid.*, q.173, a.2.
14 *Ibid.*, q.174, a.3.

tion of the senses.[15] A partial or total ecstasy may be a natural effect of the absorption of the superior faculties in the object manifested; the soul may no longer be attentive to exterior things.[16] If, on the contrary, ecstasy, so to speak, precedes the vision or contemplation and prepares for it, it is extraordinary like rapture, properly so called, which carries with it the idea of a certain violence, by lifting the soul above inferior things in order to fix it in God.[17] Christ and the Blessed Virgin had all these charisms in an eminent degree, but without losing the use of their senses; from the very beginning of their lives, they were superior to ecstasy and rapture.[18]

Following these principles, St. John of the Cross draws a clear distinction between general and obscure infused contemplation [19] and different modes of particular and distinct supernatural knowledge: (1) *visions,* sensible, imaginary, or intellectual; [20] (2) *revelations;* [21] (3) *interior words.*[22] After enumerating these modes of knowledge, St. John of the Cross adds: "In regard to obscure and general knowledge, there is no division; it is contemplation received in faith. This contemplation is the end to which we should lead the soul; all other knowledge should be directed toward this, beginning with the first; and the soul should progress by detaching itself from all of them." [23]

---

[15] *Ibid.,* a.1 ad 3um.

[16] Cf. St. Thomas, *De veritate,* q.13, a.3: "Cum totaliter anima intendat ad actum unius potentiae, abstrahitur homo ab actu alterius potentiae." Cf. IIa IIae, q.173, a.3, on partial or total ecstasy. Neither is necessary to prophecy or contemplation. Cf. *ibid.*

[17] See IIa IIae, q.175, a.1 and a.2 ad 1um: "Rapture adds something to ecstasy . . . a certain violence in addition."

[18] Cf. IIIa, q.10, 11.

[19] *The Ascent of Mount Carmel,* Bk. II, chaps. 1–9.

[20] *Ibid.,* chaps. 10–24.

[21] *Ibid.,* chaps. 25–27.

[22] *Ibid.,* chaps. 28–31. St. John of the Cross links with distinct supernatural knowledge (chaps. 10 and 32) the divine touches received in the will, which produce spiritual sentiments in it and "react on the intellect." We will discuss them at the end of this article.

[23] *Ibid.,* Bk. II, chap. 10.

To bring out clearly what is explicit in the traditional teaching on this point, we will proceed from the general to the particular. Consequently, following the example of St. Thomas,[24] we will first discuss revelations, to see the special modes of their manifestation, that is, either by vision, or by words. But we should note that visions and locutions are particular modes of revelation only when they disclose hidden things of the future, the present, or the past.

We will also proceed from the lower to the higher by considering in each of these categories the sensible, imaginary, and intellectual manifestations, according as they progressively reveal the works of God and God Himself.

Finally, it is also fitting to go from the exterior to the interior by considering first among these favors those that are manifestly directed toward the benefit of our neighbor and are more directly connected with charisms or graces *gratis datae,* particularly with prophecy; this is the case especially with private revelations. Others among these favors approach the order of sanctifying grace, because they are directly ordained to the sanctification of the person who receives them. They prepare the soul for divine union according as they make God better known and lead the soul to love Him, often amid great trials. This is particularly the case with various interior words and also with divine touches received in the will, which St. John discusses last.[25]

### DIVINE REVELATIONS

Divine revelations are the supernatural manifestation of a hidden truth by means of a vision, a word, or a prophetic instinct; they presuppose the gift of prophecy. They are called public if they have been made by the prophets, Christ, or the Apostles, and are proposed to all by the Church, which preserves them in Scripture and tradition. They are called

24 See IIa IIae, q. 171, 173, 174.
25 *The Ascent of Mount Carmel,* Bk. II, chap. 32.

private when they are ordained only for the particular benefit of those who are favored with them. Private revelations, no matter what their importance, do not belong to the deposit of Catholic faith.

Those who receive divine revelations, recognized as such, should after prudent judgment most certainly incline respectfully before this supernatural manifestation.[26] According to some theologians, they ought even to believe in them with divine and theological faith, for, in their opinion, these revelations contain the formal motive of faith, the authority of God revealing.[27] According to other theologians,[28] anyone who receives a certain private revelation should adhere to it immediately, not through divine faith but by prophetic light; [29] and the supernatural certitude should last or, on the contrary, give way to a moral certitude if the prophetic illumination disappears.

In approving the revelations made to the saints, the Church declares simply that they contain nothing contrary to Scripture and to Catholic teaching, and that they may be proposed as probable to the pious belief of the faithful.[30] Private revelations may not be published without the appro-

[26] Benedict XIV, De serv. Dei beat., Bk. III, last chap., no. 12. C. de Lugo, S.J., De fide, disp. I, sec. 11.

[27] Card. Gotti, O.P., Theol. schol. dogm., Vol. I, tract. 9, q. 1, dub. 3, no. 2: "Verius existimo, revelationem privatam, etiam ex parte rei revelatae, esse credendam ab eo, cui fit, fide divina theologica. . . . Quia ubicumque est eadem ratio formalis objecti, ibi est idem specie habitus." When attempts were made to obtain a denial of her divine mission from St. Joan of Arc, she answered that she had to believe in it as in the mystery of the redemption; and several times she appealed to the pope in this matter, as supreme judge of these things.

[28] Salmanticenses, De fide, disp. I, dub. IV, 104 and 111: In favor of this opinion, they quote St. Thomas and his principal commentators. They observe in particular that a number of these revelations bearing on temporal things have not a sufficient bond with the first object of theological faith.

[29] It may also proceed from faith, which is mentioned among the gratituous graces (I Cor. 12: 4–10). According to the Salmanticenses, loc. cit., no. 113, "Praedicta fides confertur ut in plurimum doctoribus Ecclesiae circa articulos fidei catholicae."

[30] Benedict XIV, op. cit., Bk. II, chap. 32, no. 11.

bation of ecclesiastical authority.[31] Even in those approved as probable by the Church, some error may slip in; for the saints themselves may attribute to the Spirit of God what proceeds from the depths of their own soul, or may falsely interpret the meaning of a truly divine revelation. This is explained by the fact that there are many degrees in prophetic light, from the simple, supernatural instinct to perfect revelation. When there is only a prophetic instinct, the meaning of things revealed and even the divine origin of the revelation [32] may remain unknown. It was in this way that Caiphas prophesied, without being aware of it, when he said, "that it was expedient that one man should die for the people." [33]

The soul receiving a truly divine revelation should with humility and simplicity communicate it in a few words to its spiritual director, but should not become attached to it and should perfectly obey the minister of Jesus Christ.[34] The gift of prophecy may, it is true, be found in those who do not possess these qualities, but such an exception is rare.

Before regulating its conduct by private revelation, a soul that is truly enlightened by God will always consult its director or some other learned and discreet person. St. Teresa insists particularly on this point.[35] This is especially necessary since the soul may easily go astray in the interpretation of revelations, either because it considers them too literally, or because they are sometimes conditional.[36] A learned, prudent, and virtuous confessor, however, has graces of state which make him avoid error, especially when he fervently prays for these graces.

St. John of the Cross, who so often invites us to desire

[31] Cf. the decree of Urban VIII, March 13, 1625, confirmed by Clement IX, May 23, 1668.
[32] St. Thomas, IIa IIae, q.173, a.4.
[33] John 18: 14.
[34] Cf. Bona, *De discretione spirituum,* chap. 20.
[35] *The Interior Castle,* sixth mansion, chap. 3.
[36] *The Ascent of Mount Carmel,* Bk. II, chaps. 19, 20.

ardently and humbly the infused contemplation of the mysteries of faith and also divine union, reproves the desire for revelations in terms even more forcible than those employed by the other saints. On this point he is in complete accord with St. Vincent Ferrer,[37] and shows that by this curiosity the soul desiring revelations gives the devil an opportunity to lead it astray; [38] that this inclination takes away the purity of faith; [39] produces a hindrance for the spirit; [40] certainly denotes a lack of humility; [41] and exposes it to many errors.[42] To ask for revelations shows also a lack of respect toward Christ, because the fulness of revelation has been given in the Gospel.[43] God sometimes grants these extraordinary favors to weak souls; [44] but to desire them is at least a venial sin, even when the soul has a good end in view.[45] They are of value only because of the humility and love of God which they awaken in the soul.[46] This statement in regard to revelations shows clearly the error of imprudent directors who, impelled by curiosity, are excessively concerned with souls favored by visions and revelations.[47] This attention is likely to cast the soul into trouble and illusion, and turn it away from the road of humility through a vain complacency in extraordinary ways.

Furthermore, the desire for revelations turns the soul from infused contemplation. St. John of the Cross makes this clear when he says: "The soul imagines that something great has taken place, that God Himself has spoken, when in reality

---

[37] St. Vincent Ferrer, *Traité de la vie spirituelle,* chap. 13.
[38] *The Ascent of Mount Carmel,* Bk. II, chap. 11.
[39] *Ibid.*
[40] *Ibid.,* chap. 16.
[41] *Ibid.,* chaps. 16, 17.
[42] *Ibid.,* chaps. 21, 27.
[43] *Ibid.,* chaps. 19, 22. Under the Old Law it was licit to ask for revelations; it is not so under the law of the Gospel, for all revelation is found in Christ.
[44] *Ibid.,* chap. 21.
[45] *Ibid.*
[46] *Ibid.,* Bk. III, chaps. 9, 12.
[47] *Ibid.,* Bk. II, chap. 22.

there is very little, or nothing, or less than nothing. In truth, of what use is that which is void of humility, charity, mortification, holy simplicity, silence, etc.? This is why I affirm that these illusions offer a great obstacle to divine union, for if the soul makes much of them, this fact alone drives it very far from the abyss of faith. . . . The Holy Ghost enlightens the recollected intellect according to the measure of its recollection. The most perfect recollection is that which takes place in faith. . . . Infused charity is in proportion to the purity of the soul in a perfect faith: the more intense such charity is, the more the Holy Ghost enlightens the soul and communicates His gifts to it." [48] No words could more strongly condemn the longing for revelations and make the soul desire that perfect spirit of faith, which is found in infused contemplation and which leads to divine union.

Therefore it is a serious and frequent error to confound the desire for revelations with a desire for infused contemplation; the former is blameworthy and also turns the soul away from infused contemplation, which is highly desirable. St. John of the Cross thus gives us the best commentary on St. Thomas' words: "Sanctifying grace is nobler than gratuitous grace." [49] In other words, sanctifying grace (with charity and the gifts connected with it) is far superior to the charisms, and even to prophecy, the hightest of all. We thus return to the teaching of St. Paul on the eminence of charity.[50]

We must distinguish two kinds of private revelations: (1) revelations properly so called, disclosing secrets about God or His works; (2) revelations improperly so called, giving a greater understanding of supernatural truths already known by faith.[51]

1) Revelations manifesting secrets to us are much more subject to illusions. God sometimes reveals to the living the

---

[48] *Ibid.*, Bk. II, chap. 29.
[49] See Ia IIae, q.111, a.4.
[50] See I Cor., chap. 13.
[51] *The Ascent of Mount Carmel*, Bk. II, chap. 25.

time which remains to them on this earth, the trials which they will undergo, what will happen to a nation, to a certain person.[52] The devil is clever in counterfeiting these things and, to gain credit for his lies, he begins by nourishing the spirit with truths and likely things.[53] St. John of the Cross says: "It is almost impossible to escape his wiles if the soul does not immediately get rid of them, because the spirit of evil knows well how to assume the appearance of truth and give this appearance credit." [54] "In order to be perfect there is, therefore, no reason to desire these extraordinary supernatural things. . . . The soul must prudently guard itself against all these communications if it wishes, in purity and without illusions, to reach divine union by the night of faith." [55] No words could make a clearer distinction between these extraordinary supernatural things and infused contemplation, and more effectively show that infused contemplation is normal in the perfect.

2) Revelations improperly so called, which give us a greater understanding of revealed truths, are associated with infused contemplation, especially if they concern God Himself and do not stop at particular things, but profoundly penetrate His omnipotence, wisdom, or infinite goodness. "This profound loving knowledge is, moreover, accessible only to a soul in union with God; they are this union itself, for they have their origin precisely in a certain contact of the soul with the Divinity. Consequently it is God Himself who is felt and tasted, though He is not perceived manifestly in full light, as He is in glory; but the touch is so strong and so profound, by reason of the knowledge and attraction, that it penetrates the substance of the soul. It is impossible for the devil to interfere in this and to deceive by imitation, for nothing is comparable to it, or approaches it in enjoyment

52 *Ibid.*, chap. 27.
53 *Ibid.*
54 *Ibid.*
55 *Ibid.*

and delights. These touches savor the divine essence, eternal life, and the devil cannot counterfeit such lofty things." [56] We will treat this subject again at the end of this article when we speak of divine touches. "In regard to the other perceptions," St. John of the Cross adds, "we said that the soul should abstract itself from them, but this duty ceases before these, since they are the manifestations of that union to which we are trying to conduct the soul. All that we have taught previously on the subject of despoliation and of complete detachment was directed toward this union; and the divine favors which result from it are the fruit of humility, of the desire to suffer for the love of God, with resignation and disinterestedness as to all reward." [57]

### VISIONS

Visions are revelations when they disclose hidden things; otherwise, they are distinguished from revelations. They are, as we have said, either sensible, imaginary, or intellectual.

*Sensible or corporal visions* generally represent our Lord, the Blessed Virgin, or the saints. They are not signs of great virtue, for they are sometimes granted beginners to detach them from worldly things. They are subject to the illusions of the imagination and of the devil. If the vision is common to a great number of persons, it is a sign that the apparition is exterior, without its thereby being certain that it is of divine origin.[58] If it is individual, the dispositions of the witness who declares that he has had it must be attentively examined and great circumspection must be exercised.

Those who are favored with these apparitions of our Lord, the Blessed Virgin, and the saints should render to the persons represented the honors due them, even though the apparition should be the result of an illusion of the imagina-

---

[56] *The Ascent of Mount Carmel,* Bk. II, chap. 26.
[57] *Ibid.*
[58] Cf. St. Thomas, Ia, q.51, a.2.

tion or of the devil, for as St. Teresa says: "Although a painter may be a wicked man, honor should none the less be paid to a portrait of Christ done by him." [59] In this case also, the director should be consulted, for he will be able to recognize whether these apparitions are graces of God, by their conformity to the teaching of the Church and by the good dispositions toward the practice of virtue which they leave in the soul. The soul itself should be faithful in reaping the fruits of sanctity which God proposes by granting it these favors.[60] These apparitions must never be desired or asked of God.[61]

*Imaginary visions,* so called because they are produced in the imagination by God or by the angels, are granted when a person is either awake or asleep. According to the Gospel, St. Joseph was on several occasions supernaturally instructed in a dream; and the lives of the saints contain many similar instances. That a dream may be supernatural, it should not be explicable by the laws of memory and imagination; to be divine, it should not contain anything contrary to revealed doctrine or to good morals.[62] Although this divine origin may be hard to discern, ordinarily when the soul seeks God sincerely, He makes Himself felt either by a profound feeling of peace, or by events that confirm the vision; thus in a dream a sinner may be warned of the urgent necessity of conversion, or a just man may be advised of a grave decision to be made.

Imaginary visions are subject to the illusions of the imagination and of the devil.[63] We have three signs by which to discern whether they are of divine origin: (1) when they cannot be produced or dismissed at will, but come suddenly and

---

[59] *The Interior Castle,* sixth mansion, chap. 9. Signs of respect should be given only conditionally if the soul thinks that perhaps the devil wished in this way to make himself adored under the figure of Christ. Cf. St. Thomas, IIIa, d.9, q.1, a.2; q.6 ad 3um.

[60] Cf. Vallgornera, *Theol. myst. D. Thomae,* q.3, disp.5, a.1, no.13.

[61] *The Ascent of Mount Carmel,* Bk. II, chap. 11.

[62] St. Thomas, IIa IIae, q.95, a.6; q.173, a.2.

[63] *The Ascent of Mount Carmel,* Bk. II, chap. 16.

last but a short time; (2) when they leave the soul in great peace; (3) when they produce fruits of virtue, a very great humility and perseverance in good.[64]

A divine imaginary vision, granted while a person is awake, is almost always accompanied by at least partial ecstasy so that the soul may distinguish the interior apparition from external impressions; [65] there is ecstasy also because a soul enraptured and united to its God loses contact with external things.[66] There is no perfect imaginary vision without an intellectual vision, which makes the soul see and penetrate its mystical meaning.[67] For example, the former may concern the sacred humanity of Christ; the second, His divinity.[68]

Imaginary visions should not be desired or asked of God any more than sensible visions; they are in no way necessary to holiness.[69] The perfect spirit of faith and obscure contemplation are of superior order and prepare the soul more immediately for divine union.[70]

*An intellectual vision* is the certain manifestation of an object to the intellect without any actual dependence on sensible images. It is brought about either by acquired ideas supernaturally co-ordinated or modified, or by infused ideas, which are sometimes of angelic order.[71] It requires an infused light, that of the gift of wisdom or of prophecy. It may refer to God, spirits, or material things, like the purely intellectual knowledge of the angels. The intellectual vision is at times obscure and indistinct, that is, it manifests with certitude the presence of the object without any detail as to its intimate nature. Thus St. Teresa often felt our Lord near her for

---

[64] Vallgornera, *loc. cit.,* no. 11; St. Teresa, *The Interior Castle,* sixth mansion, chap. 9.

[65] *Summa,* IIa IIae, q.173, a.3.

[66] *The Interior Castle, loc. cit.*

[67] St. Thomas, *De veritate,* q.12, a.12.

[68] St. Teresa, *Life,* chap. 29.

[69] *The Ascent of Mount Carmel,* Bk. II, chaps. 16, 17; *The Interior Castle, loc. cit.* Cf. *supra,* p. 256.

[70] *The Ascent of Mount Carmel,* Bk. II, chap. 8.

[71] *Summa,* IIa IIae, q.173, a.2 ad 2um; *De veritate,* q.12, a.12.

several days.[72] At other times the intellectual vision is clear and distinct; it is then more rapid and is a sort of intuition of divine truths or of created things in God.[73] It cannot be translated into human language.[74]

Intellectual visions, especially those caused by infused ideas, are free from the illusions of the imagination and of the devil; but at times what is only an over-excitement of the imagination or a suggestion of the devil[75] may be taken for an intellectual vision. The divine origin of these favors may be recognized from the effects they produce: deep peace, holy joy, profound humility, unshakable attachment to virtue.[76]

"By the very fact that this knowledge is communicated suddenly, independently of the will, it is useless for the soul to desire it . . . ; it ought simply to allow God to act when and how He wills. . . . These favors are not given to a soul which is attached to any good; they are the effect of a special love, which God bears toward the soul which strives for Him in detachment and disinterested love."[77]

The loftiest intellectual visions, since they are inferior to the beatific vision, cannot attain the divine essence *sicuti est,* but only by a certain manner of representation due to infused ideas, "por cierta manera de representación."[78] In the opinion of a number of authors, the intellectual visions which frequently accompany the transforming union[79] are the equivalent of a special revelation which gives the soul the certitude of being in the state of grace and of predestination. St. John of the Cross even says: "In my opinion, the soul can never be placed in possession of this state (the transforming

---

[72] St. Teresa, *Life,* chap. 27.
[73] *The Interior Castle,* sixth mansion, chap. 10; *The Ascent of Mount Carmel,* Bk. II, chaps. 22, 24.
[74] *The Interior Castle, loc. cit.*
[75] *The Ascent of Mount Carmel,* Bk. II, chap. 24.
[76] *Ibid.*
[77] *The Ascent of Mount Carmel, loc. cit.*
[78] *The Interior Castle,* seventh mansion, chap. 1.
[79] Cf. *supra,* pp. 256–58.

union) without at the same time being confirmed in grace." [80]

*Supernatural words* are manifestations of God's thought which are heard either by the exterior senses or by the interior senses or directly by the intellect. Hence there is an analogy between them and visions, which they sometimes accompany.

An auricular supernatural word is a vibration formed in the air by the ministry of angels. For example, St. Luke tells us [81] that Zachary heard the angel Gabriel speak to him. The same angel Gabriel said to Mary: "Hail, full of grace." [82] Like corporal visions, these locutions are subject to illusions; the same rule should be applied to them for discerning those of divine origin.

Imaginary supernatural words are heard by the imagination, when the person is either awake or asleep. They sometimes seem to come from heaven; at other times from the depths of one's heart. They are perfectly distinct, although not heard with bodily ears.[83] They are not easily forgotten; those especially which contain a prophecy remain graven on the memory.[84] They can be distinguished from those of our

[80] *The Spiritual Canticle*, st. 22. Philip of the Blessed Trinity (*Theol. myst. Prooem.*, a.8), Scaramelli (*Dir. myst.*, tr. II, chap. 22 no. 258) and several other authors hold that so sublime a state demands that God reveal to the soul, His spouse, the indissoluble friendship that exists between them. On this point, see Meynard, O.P., *La vie intérieure*, Vol. II, no. 270. In this way certain passages from the writings of the great orthodox mystics are made to harmonize with the decree of the Council of Trent, namely, that without a special revelation no one on earth can have absolute certitude that he is in the state of grace, and with even greater reason that he will persevere in it until death. Cf. *Concilium Tridentinum*, Sess. VI, chaps. 9 and 13; canons 13, 14, 16.

Cf. Salmanticenses, *De gratia*, q.110, disp. 3, dub. 11, no. 259, on the question of confirmation in grace and its difference from the gift of final perseverance. This gift of confirmation in grace is, they say, a certain participation in the impeccability of the blessed, and needs to be completed by a special protection on the part of God; for this reason it is superior to the gift of final perseverance, which all the predestined receive.

[81] Luke 1: 19.
[82] Luke 1: 28.
[83] St. Teresa, *Life*, chap. 25.
[84] *Ibid.*

spirit by the fact that they are not heard at will, and that they are words and works at one and the same time. For example, when they reprove us for our faults, they suddenly change our interior dispositions and render us capable of undertaking everything for the service of God.[85] Consequently it is often easy to discern them.[86] When it is the devil who makes these imaginary words heard, they not only do not produce good effects, but, on the contrary, produce evil effects. The soul is disturbed troubled, frightened, disgusted; and if it experiences any sensible pleasure, it is very different from divine peace.[87]

Intellectual words are heard directly by the intellect without the intermediary of the senses or imagination, in the way the angels communicate their thoughts to one another. They suppose a divine light and the co-ordination of pre-existent acquired ideas, and at times of infused ideas.[88] "It is a wordless language, which is the tongue of the fatherland." [89]

St. John of the Cross teaches that intellectual words may be either successive, formal, or substantial.[90] Successive intellectual words are produced only in the state of recollection; they come from our spirit which is enlightened by the Holy Ghost, and with such facility and new views that the understanding cannot imagine that they spring from its own depths.[91] These successive words are subject to illusion, for the spirit, which at the beginning followed only the truth, may deviate, go astray, and fall into a thousand extravagances, inasmuch as the devil often insinuates himself into these successive words, especially when people are attached to them. He acts with even greater reason in this way toward

[85] *Ibid.*
[86] *Ibid.*
[87] *Ibid.* Cf. also St. Thomas, Ia, q.111, a.1, 3; q.114; Ia IIae, q.80, a.1-3.
[88] Cf. St. Thomas, Ia, q.107, a.1; also Cajetan's commentary.
[89] St. Teresa, *Life*, chap. 27.
[90] *The Ascent of Mount Carmel*, Bk. II, chaps. 28-31.
[91] *Ibid.*, chap. 29.

those who are bound to him by a tacit or formal act, with heretics, and especially with heresiarchs.[92]

Successive words come from God when they simultaneously produce in the soul an increase of charity and humility. But it is often difficult to discern clearly supernatural love from a certain natural love, and true humility from pusillanimity. Hence it is difficult to recognize the divine origin of successive words.[93] They should not be desired, for obscure faith is far superior to them.[94]

Formal intellectual words are so called "because the soul knows formally that they are uttered by another, without any contribution on its part . . . and it can hear them when not recollected, and even when far from thinking of what is said." [95] They are, therefore, very different from those we have discussed, and are at times very precise; for example, Daniel says that an angel spoke to him.[96] These locutions ordinarily explain some teaching, clear up some point; this effect is always produced, even though the soul may experience repugnance in fulfilling the divine order.[97] God allows this repugnance to subsist that He may preserve the soul from natural eagerness with regard to great things; if, on the contrary, the Lord inspires humiliating things, He gives greater facility to accomplish them.[98]

These formal intellectual words are in themselves free from illusions, since the understanding cannot contribute anything to them, and the devil cannot act directly on the in-

---

[92] Ibid.

[93] Ibid., Bk. II, chap. 29. Likewise circumspection and reserve must be ·exercised in regard to what St. Thomas calls instinctus propheticus (IIa IIae, q.171, a.5; q.173, a.4). This instinct or supernatural attraction is an interior illumination which does not give certitude as to its divine origin. These interior movements must not be scorned, but, before giving them too much attention and following them, they must be rightly discerned.

[94] The Ascent of Mount Carmel, Bk. II, chap. 29.

[95] Ibid., chap. 30.

[96] Dan. 9: 22.

[97] Ex. 3: 11.

[98] The Ascent of Mount Carmel, Bk. II, chap. 30.

tellect.[99] "The soul ought not, however," says St. John of the Cross,[100] "to esteem formal words much more than successive words. If it pays attention to them, it swerves from faith, which is the proper and immediate means of divine union. This exposes it to easy deception by the devil, the more so as in many cases good communications are with difficulty distinguished from evil communications.[101] What they say should not be immediately translated into action, nor should they be held in esteem no matter what their origin. It is indispensable to make them known to an experienced confessor or to a discreet and learned person. . . . If an experienced person is not to be found, the soul should keep whatever is substantial and sure in these words; disregard the rest; and speak of it to no one, lest a counselor be found who would do the soul more harm than good. The soul should not place itself at the mercy of anyone at all, for it is of prime importance whether one acts judiciously or is deceived in such matters."

Substantial intellectual words are formal locutions which effect immediately what they announce. We read in *The Ascent of Mount Carmel:* "For example, God says formally to a soul: Be good! and instantly the soul becomes good. Or He says: Love Me!, and at once the soul possesses and experiences in itself true love of God. Or again He may say: Fear nothing, and at that very instant, strength and peace come upon that soul. . . . Thus, God said to Abraham: 'Walk before Me, and be perfect.' (Gen. 17: 1), and instantly perfection was given to him, and thenceforth he walked reverently before God. . . . A single one of these words instantly operates more good than

99 Cf. St. Thomas, Ia, q.111, a.1, 3; q.114, a.1–4; Ia IIae, q.80, a.1–3; also Cajetan, Curiel, and Suarez; cf. Cardinal Bona, *De discretione spirituum*, chap. 17; and Nicholas of Jesus Mary, C.D., *Elucidatio phrasium myst. operum Joannis a Cruce*, chap. 5, no. 4.

100 *The Ascent of Mount Carmel, loc. cit.*

101 Although the devil cannot act directly on man's intellect and will, his artifices may frequently be taken for words of God, by our confounding what immediately touches the intellect with what takes place in the imagination.

the efforts of a lifetime. When the soul receives such locutions, it has only to abandon itself; it is useless to desire or not to desire them, for there is nothing to repulse, nothing to fear. The soul ought not even to seek to effect what is said, for God never utters substantial words in order that we should translate them into acts; He Himself brings about their effect. This is what distinguishes them from successive and formal locutions. . . . Illusion is not to be feared here, for neither the understanding nor the devil can interfere in this matter . . . unless the soul has given itself to the devil by a voluntary pact; but then the effect is quite different. . . . Every word of his is as pure nothingness in the presence of God. . . . Substantial words are, therefore, a powerful means of union with God. . . . Happy the soul to which God addresses them." [102] God's words are living flames in purified souls.[103]

There is a fourth kind of favor which frequently [104] accompanies infused contemplation, that is, divine touches, which are imprinted in the will and which "react on the intellect. . . . They give, thus, a very lofty and sweet intellectual penetration of God." [105] These touches are thereby attached to "particular and distinct contemplation." [106] They do not depend on the activity of the soul, or on its meditations, although these prepare the soul for them.

These divine touches are occasionally so profound and intense that they seem imprinted "in the very substance of the soul." God, in fact, who preserves the very substance of the soul in existence by a virtual contact, which is creation continued,[107] produces, preserves, and increases sanctifying grace therein, whence the virtues infused into the faculties [108] spring. He also moves these faculties, either by proposing an

[102] *The Ascent of Mount Carmel*, Bk. II, chap. 31.
[103] *The Living Flame of Love*, st. 1, 1.
[104] *The Ascent of Mount Carmel*, Bk. II, chap. 32.
[105] *Ibid.*
[106] *Ibid.*
[107] Cf. St. Thomas, Ia, q.8, a.1–3; q.43, a.3; q.104, a.1, 2; q.105, a.3, 4.
[108] St. Thomas, Ia IIae, q.110, a.3, 4.

object to them, or by applying them to the exercise of their acts, and that from within.[109] The divine touch of which we are speaking is a supernatural motion of this type, but one of the most profound. It is exercised on the very depths of the will and of the intellect, where these faculties take root in the substance of the soul whence they arise.[110] In truth, our will is, in a way, infinite in its profundity; for this reason created things cannot exercise an invincible attraction on it. It is free to love them or not to; only God seen face to face infallibly attracts it and captivates it, even to the very well-spring of its energies.[111] So-called substantial divine touches [112] affect this basis of the will and of the intellect. The very substance of the soul experiences things only through these faculties.[113] But God, who is closer to the soul than it is to itself, inasmuch as He preserves it in existence, can from within touch and move the very foundation of the faculty by a spiritual contact which reveals itself as divine. This depth is also

[109] *Ibid.*, q.9, a.4; q.10, a.1, 2, 4.

[110] *Ibid.*, q.113, a.8, and *De veritate*, q.28, a.3: "Ipse Deus, qui justificat impium, tangit animam, gratiam in ea causando. . . . Mens autem humana aliquo modo tangit Deum, eum cognoscendo et amando." At the moment of justification, there is a divine action causing the very essence of the soul to pass from spiritual death to life by producing in it sanctifying grace, which is eternal life begun. The mystical favor of which we are speaking makes us, in a way, take cognizance of this divine influx into the very depths of our being. It is often preceded by the passive purification of the spirit, which notably deepens the work done in us by God at the moment of our conversion (Ia IIae, q.113, a.8, "De ordine eorum quae ad justificationem concurrunt"). It is as if the Author of grace deepened anew, but much more profoundly, the furrow in which the divine seed is to grow.

[111] See Ia IIae, q.10, a.2.

[112] Cf. Vallgornera, *Theol. myst. D. Thomae*, q.3, disp.5, a.9, nos. 1, 3, 4.

[113] In the opinion of St. Thomas, no created substance can operate, feel, perceive, or love of itself, but only through its faculties; it has received them for that purpose. Cf. Ia, q.54, a.1: "Whether an angel's act of understanding is his substance?" A.2: "Whether in the angel to understand is to exist?" A.3: "Whether an angel's power of intelligence is his essence?" Q.77, a.1: "Whether the essence of the soul is its power?" A.2: "Whether there are several powers of the soul?" It is in the light of these articles that, to avoid all error, we should understand what Tauler, Louis de Blois, and St. John of the Cross say of the depths of the soul. Cf. Louis de Blois, *Institutio spiritualis*, chap. 12, where it is said that the depth of the soul is the origin of the higher faculties, *virium illarum est origo*. Cf. *infra*, p. 458.

called the summit of the spirit in relation to sensible things, according as they are considered either as exterior or as inferior to it. With this in mind, we understand what St. John of the Cross says on this subject: "Nothing is more calculated to dissipate this delicate knowledge than the intervention of the natural spirit. Since it is a question of a sweet supernatural communication, it is useless to try to comprehend it accurately, for that is impossible; the understanding has only to accept it. If, on the contrary, the soul seeks to provoke it or desires it, it may happen that what it conceives comes from itself, and thereby gives the devil the opportunity of presenting counterfeit knowledge. . . . Passive acceptance in humility is, therefore, incumbent on the soul. God grants these favors according to His good pleasure, and it is the humble and thoroughly detached soul that receives God's preference. By acting in this way, the progress of the soul suffers no interruption, and such knowledge serves efficaciously to advance it. These touches are touches of union serving to unite the soul passively to God." [114]

St. John of the Cross has described these favors at greater length in *The Dark Night of the Soul* [115] and in *The Living Flame.* [116] In his opinion, they are obtained only by the practice of despoilment and detachment from all creatures. By one of these touches of love, the soul is rewarded for all its works and sufferings. The substance of God, which is identical with His creative, preserving, and sanctifying action, touches the substance of the soul and makes itself felt as divine and sovereign. This teaching clarifies the doctrine that the mystical state is the normal completion of Christian perfection, provided it is distinguished from certain accessory facts which sometimes accompany it. But, to establish the truth of this doctrine, we must guard against several confu-

[114] *The Ascent of Mount Carmel,* Bk. II, chap. 32.
[115] Bk. II, chap. 23.
[116] St. 2, v. 3.

sions which contemporary writers, in their desire to return to traditional teaching, apparently have not always sufficiently avoided.

## II. CONFUSIONS TO BE AVOIDED IN EXPOUNDING THE TRADITIONAL DOCTRINE

1) In order to show that infused contemplation is not an extraordinary grace like revelations and visions and that it ought to be desired and asked for by generous interior souls, we need not lessen the mystical state or link it too closely with what it really is not. Affective prayer, or the acquired prayer of recollection, described by St. Teresa,[117] should not be confounded with the supernatural recollection which she speaks of.[118]

2) A chasm should not be interposed between the initial mystical state (fourth mansion) and what essentially constitutes simple union, complete union, and the transforming union, described in the fifth, sixth, and seventh mansions. The summit of the normal development of the grace of the virtues and of the gifts is, in this life, found only in the transforming union, which is the normal termination of the initial mystical state.[119]

3) The essence of these supernatural mystical states should not be confounded with the extraordinary facts which sometimes accompany them. These accessory facts, described by St. Teresa especially in the fifth and sixth mansions, often disappear in the seventh.[120] In fact, these phenomena accompany chiefly the influence of the Holy Ghost "on the faculties" rather than what "touches the substance of the soul," as the mystics say. This wholly intimate action of God on the depths of the soul is found principally in the trans-

---

117 *The Way of Perfection*, chap. 28.
118 *The Interior Castle*, fourth mansion, chap. 3.
119 Cf. *supra*, pp. 256 ff.
120 Cf. *supra*, pp. 251–58.

forming union, a state in which, as a rule, ecstasies have disappeared.[121]

It is in the depths of the soul that everything ends, and in a sense it is there that everything began, without our having been aware of it. This influence of the Holy Ghost "on the depths of the soul" in fact precedes, without our knowing it, the influence which the Holy Ghost exercises more manifestly "on the faculties." The completely purified soul experiences this action in its very depths, when it has at length entered the sanctuary where God dwells and operates from the moment of justification or of conversion.[122] In the opinion of Tauler, Louis de Blois,[123] St. John of the Cross,[124] and

[121] Cf. *supra*, p. 258.

[122] Cf. St. Thomas: "Illabi menti convenit soli Deo." IIIa, q.8, a.8 ad 1um; q.64, a.1; Ia IIae, q.112, a.1; *In Joan.*, 13, lect. 4; *In I Cor.*, 2, lect. 2. In *De veritate* (q.10, a.1) we read: "Mens in anima nostra dicit illud quod est altissimum in virtute ipsius; unde cum secundum id quod est altissimum in nobis divina imago inveniatur in nobis, imago non pertinebit ad essentiam animae nisi secundum mentem prout nominat altissimam potentiam ejus; et sic mens, prout in ea est imago, nominat potentiam animae et non essentiam, vel si nominat essentiam, hoc non est nisi in quantum ab ea fluit talis potentia." The thirteen articles of this question *De mente* in the treatise *De veritate* should be read in connection with this point of doctrine.

[123] *Institutio spiritualis*, chap. 12, 2: "The soul becomes fit to contemplate with calm, simplicity, and delights, without gross images, and without any intellectual illusions, the abyss of the divinity. It is then that, turned entirely toward God by pure love, and an incomprehensible light illuminating, so to speak, the depths of its essence, the eye of the reason and the intellect is, as it were, dazzled by it. . . . The soul knows then by experience that God is infinitely superior to every image, . . . and to all that the intellect can comprehend. . . . It loses itself in the solitary and obscure immensity of the divinity; but to lose itself in this way is to find itself again." All this admirable chapter is, as it were, a summary of the teaching of Tauler, which Louis de Blois defended.

[124] Cf. *The Living Flame of Love*, st. 1, v. 3: The most profound center of the soul: "It is in the substance of the soul, inaccessible to the senses and the devil, that this joy of the Holy Ghost develops. He alone is capable, in the center of the soul and in its intimate depths, of making it act and operate without the intervention of the senses." The activity of the soul tends toward this center, as a stone toward the center of the earth; and it more closely approaches it in proportion as its charity is more intense.

Cf. *The Spiritual Canticle*, Part I, st. 1, v. 1: "The Word, the Son of God, together with the Father and the Holy Ghost, is essentially hidden in the intimate being of the soul. Whence it must be concluded that if the soul wishes to find the Spouse, it must live detached by affection and will from all creatures,

St. Teresa,[125] who have spoken so frequently of this "depth of the soul," at the end of the passive purifications of the spirit the soul experiences, without seeing it, this "substantial" action of God in which everything has its beginning, at which everything terminates, and beyond which it seems that there is nothing. This is why what is called the depths of the soul, in relation to sensible things considered as exterior, is called the summit of the spirit in relation to these same things considered as inferior.[126]

4) The three traditional ways should, moreover, not be confused with what is only an imperfect form of them. From what precedes, it is clear why, according to the tradition preserved by St. John of the Cross, the perfect purgative way requires the passive purifications of mystical order; why he calls the illuminative way the way of infused contemplation; [127] and why the unitive way is normally completed only in the transforming union, the prelude to heaven. These three ways are often lessened because writers describe them merely from the outside. St. John of the Cross gazed upon them from above, and this is why he penetrated to their depths. He must have received the gift of wisdom in a very high degree in order to have discussed with so great mastery such deep supernatural things, for the light of life illumines all the pages of his work.

5) Divine touches must not be likened to revelations and visions, which are, properly speaking, extraordinary and, as it were, exterior facts. It is true that St. John of the Cross distinguishes general and obscure infused contemplation from distinct supernatural knowledge,[128] and that he links with the latter the divine touches impressed on the will, which

---

enter into profound recollection, and act toward the world as if it did not exist."

125 Cf. *The Interior Castle*, especially the seventh mansion, chap. 2.
126 Cf. *supra*, pp. 258, 455.
127 *The Dark Night of the Soul*, Bk. I, chap. 14.
128 *The Ascent of Mount Carmel*, Bk. II, chap. 10.

have their reaction on the intellect. But these divine touches, without being essential to infused contemplation, by their influence on the will help to constitute union with God [129] and are not to be feared.[130] Thereby they differ notably from events which are properly extraordinary and in a way exterior, like revelations and visions, which the saint declares are often dangerous.[131]

It would also be a gross error to confound these divine touches, this contact which has been called substantial, with the emotions of the sensitive part; and likewise it would be a mistake to confuse "the tastes," which St. Teresa mentions,[132] with the consolations acquired by meditation.

6) Since analysis is necessary because of our weakness, it has, especially in these matters, a drawback that must be corrected by synthesis. The desire to be too precise in this matter leads to division, and as a result to the materialization of what is a unit in the reality of the spiritual life. Therefore in these questions we can keep to the truth only by considering them in the light of higher principles, as did St. Thomas and great mystics like St. John of the Cross. Consequently a material and mechanical exactness, which they do not share, has been applied to these spiritual matters. Hence many commentaries on the spiritual works of the great doctors resemble these works in the same way as a polygon inscribed within a circle resembles the circle; the complexity of the former is in proportion to the simplicity of the latter. This brings about the loss of the strong security with which these great speculative and mystical teachers dealt with these lofty questions. By applying the highest principles to them, they gave in controversies over secondary points only due importance to them. This attitude alone, which is notably different from that of many modern writers, placed them on the way of

[129] *Ibid.*, chap. 30.
[130] *Ibid.*
[131] *Ibid.*, chaps. 10, 11, 16, 17, 18, 25, 27.
[132] *The Interior Castle*, fourth mansion, chap. 2.

truth and enabled them to formulate it with a perfection that has never since been attained. No one will be able truly to perfect their work, unless he has received the same grace as they received. We should, therefore, become their disciples without pretending to complete their work immediately. We would accomplish much if we could even succeed in understanding them clearly. In order even to comprehend them fully, it would be necessary to equal them.

Some recent critics have claimed that the mystical life properly so called cannot be explained by the principles formulated by St. Thomas. In their opinion, probably he did not have this special form of the interior life in view when he formulated them. To this we answer with Dom Louismet: "If such a universal writer as St. Thomas Aquinas does not speak of mystics as a peculiar class, is it not because for him, as for the Areopogite, all Christians are *de jure* mystics? . . . And if he never mentions a separate body of mystical doctrine, is it not because for him there is no mystical doctrine distinct from the common deposit of faith?" [133] As a matter of fact, it is faith fully lived in persevering generosity in the love of God. "By Catholic traditional mysticism I mean the mysticism with which the Epistles of St. Paul and St. John, and the other canonical epistles, and all the other Scriptures, are overflowing. It is the mysticism of the everlasting sacrifice of the Lamb on the cross and on our altars, and of the whole sacred liturgy around it: the mysticism of the Missal, of the Ritual, of the Pontifical, of the Ceremonial of Bishops, of the Breviary, and of the Martyrology." [134] We do not believe that this assertion would be contradicted by true mystics who experience the higher life to which every Christian should aspire.

[133] *The Mystical Life*, pp. xiii f.

[134] *Ibid.*, pp. xi f. We should like, however, to find in the writings of Dom Louismet a sharper distinction between the mystical life, properly so called, and fervent Christian life, and to see him accentuate and develop what he has said on this subject. *Ibid.*, pp. 8, 23.

# INDEX

*If you have enjoyed this book, consider making your next selection from among the following . . .*

Prices subject to change.

St. Vincent Ferrer. *Fr. Pradel, O.P.* . . . . . . . . . . . . . . . . . . . . . . . 9.00
The Life of Father De Smet. *Fr. Laveille, S.J.* . . . . . . . . . . . . . . . . 18.00
Glories of Divine Grace. *Fr. Matthias Scheeben* . . . . . . . . . . . . . . . 18.00
Holy Eucharist—Our All. *Fr. Lukas Etlin* . . . . . . . . . . . . . . . . . . . . 3.00
Hail Holy Queen (from *Glories of Mary*). *St. Alphonsus* . . . . . . . . . . 9.00
Novena of Holy Communions. *Lovasik.* . . . . . . . . . . . . . . . . . . . . . 2.50
Brief Catechism for Adults. *Cogan* . . . . . . . . . . . . . . . . . . . . . . . . 12.50
The Cath. Religion—Illus./Expl. for Child, Adult, Convert. *Burbach* . . . 12.50
Eucharistic Miracles. *Joan Carroll Cruz* . . . . . . . . . . . . . . . . . . . . . 16.50
The Incorruptibles. *Joan Carroll Cruz* . . . . . . . . . . . . . . . . . . . . . . 16.50
Secular Saints: 250 Lay Men, Women & Children. PB. *Cruz.* . . . . . . . 35.00
Pope St. Pius X. *F. A. Forbes* . . . . . . . . . . . . . . . . . . . . . . . . . . . . 11.00
St. Alphonsus Liguori. *Frs. Miller and Aubin* . . . . . . . . . . . . . . . . . 18.00
Self-Abandonment to Divine Providence. *Fr. de Caussade, S.J.* . . . . . . . 22.50
The Song of Songs—A Mystical Exposition. *Fr. Arintero, O.P.* . . . . . . . 21.50
Prophecy for Today. *Edward Connor* . . . . . . . . . . . . . . . . . . . . . . . 7.50
Saint Michael and the Angels. *Approved Sources* . . . . . . . . . . . . . . . 9.00
Dolorous Passion of Our Lord. *Anne C. Emmerich* . . . . . . . . . . . . . . 18.00
Modern Saints—Their Lives & Faces, Book I. *Ann Ball* . . . . . . . . . . . 21.00
Modern Saints—Their Lives & Faces, Book II. *Ann Ball.* . . . . . . . . . . 23.00
Our Lady of Fatima's Peace Plan from Heaven. *Booklet* . . . . . . . . . . . 1.00
Divine Favors Granted to St. Joseph. *Père Binet* . . . . . . . . . . . . . . . 7.50
St. Joseph Cafasso—Priest of the Gallows. *St. John Bosco.* . . . . . . . . . 6.00
Catechism of the Council of Trent. *McHugh/Callan* . . . . . . . . . . . . . . 27.50
The Foot of the Cross. *Fr. Faber.* . . . . . . . . . . . . . . . . . . . . . . . . . . 18.00
The Rosary in Action. *John Johnson* . . . . . . . . . . . . . . . . . . . . . . . . 12.00
Padre Pio—The Stigmatist. *Fr. Charles Carty* . . . . . . . . . . . . . . . . . 16.50
Why Squander Illness? *Frs. Rumble & Carty.* . . . . . . . . . . . . . . . . . 4.00
The Sacred Heart and the Priesthood. *de la Touche* . . . . . . . . . . . . . . 10.00
Fatima—The Great Sign. *Francis Johnston* . . . . . . . . . . . . . . . . . . . 12.00
Heliotropium—Conformity of Human Will to Divine. *Drexelius* . . . . . . 15.00
Charity for the Suffering Souls. *Fr. John Nageleisen* . . . . . . . . . . . . . 18.00
Devotion to the Sacred Heart of Jesus. *Verheylezoon.* . . . . . . . . . . . . 16.50
Who Is Padre Pio? *Radio Replies Press* . . . . . . . . . . . . . . . . . . . . . 3.00
The Stigmata and Modern Science. *Fr. Charles Carty* . . . . . . . . . . . . 2.50
St. Anthony—The Wonder Worker of Padua. *Stoddard* . . . . . . . . . . . 7.00
The Precious Blood. *Fr. Faber* . . . . . . . . . . . . . . . . . . . . . . . . . . . . 16.50
The Holy Shroud & Four Visions. *Fr. O'Connell* . . . . . . . . . . . . . . . 3.50
Clean Love in Courtship. *Fr. Lawrence Lovasik* . . . . . . . . . . . . . . . . 4.50
The Secret of the Rosary. *St. Louis De Montfort* . . . . . . . . . . . . . . . . 5.00
The History of Antichrist. *Rev. P. Huchede* . . . . . . . . . . . . . . . . . . . 4.00
St. Catherine of Siena. *Alice Curtayne* . . . . . . . . . . . . . . . . . . . . . . 16.50
Where We Got the Bible. *Fr. Henry Graham.* . . . . . . . . . . . . . . . . . . 8.00
Hidden Treasure—Holy Mass. *St. Leonard* . . . . . . . . . . . . . . . . . . . 7.50
Imitation of the Sacred Heart of Jesus. *Fr. Arnoudt* . . . . . . . . . . . . . 18.50
The Life & Glories of St. Joseph. *Edward Thompson* . . . . . . . . . . . . . 16.50
Père Lamy. *Biver.* . . . . . . . . . . . . . . . . . . . . . . . . . . . . . . . . . . . . 15.00
Humility of Heart. *Fr. Cajetan da Bergamo.* . . . . . . . . . . . . . . . . . . 9.00
The Curé D'Ars. *Abbé Francis Trochu* . . . . . . . . . . . . . . . . . . . . . . 24.00
Love, Peace and Joy. (St. Gertrude). *Prévot* . . . . . . . . . . . . . . . . . . 8.00

*At your Bookdealer or direct from the Publisher.*
**1-800-437-5876        www.tanbooks.com        Fax 815-226-7770**
Prices subject to change.

**Fr. Garrigou-Lagrange, O.P.**
**1877-1964**

FATHER Reginald Marie Garrigou-Lagrange, O.P. (1877-1964) was probably the greatest Catholic theologian of the 20th century. (He is not to be confused with his uncle, Père Lagrange, the biblical scholar.) Fr. Garrigou-Lagrange initially attracted attention in the early 20th century, when he wrote against Modernism. Recognizing that Modernism—which denied the objective truth of divine revelation and affirmed an heretical conception of the evolution of dogma—struck at the very root of Catholic faith, Fr. Garrigou-Lagrange wrote classic works on apologetics, defending the Catholic Faith by way of both philosophy and theology. Fr. Garrigou-Lagrange taught at the Angelicum in Rome from 1909 to 1960, and he served for many years as a consultor to the Holy Office and other Roman Congregations. He is most famous, however, for his writings, having produced over 500 books and articles. In these he showed himself to be a thoroughgoing Thomist in the classic Dominican tradition.

Fr. Garrigou-Lagrange was best known for his spiritual theology, particularly for insisting that all are called to holiness and for zealously propounding the thesis that infused contemplation and the resulting mystical life are in the normal way of holiness or Christian perfection. His classic work in this field is *The Three Ages of the Interior Life*, in which the Catholic Faith stands out in all its splendor as a divine work of incomparable integrity, structure and beauty, ordered to raise man to the divine life of grace and bring to flower in him the "supernatural organism" of Sanctifying Grace and the Seven Gifts of the Holy Ghost—the wellsprings of all true mysticism. Among his other famous theological works are *The Love of God and the Cross of Jesus, The Mother of the Saviour and our Interior Life, Providence, Predestination, Life Everlasting* and *Christ the Saviour*. His most important philosophical work was *God, His Existence and Nature: A Thomistic Solution of Certain Agnostic Antinomies*.

The works of Fr. Garrigou-Lagrange are unlikely to be equalled for many decades to come.